THE YALE EDITION OF THE

WORKS OF SAMUEL JOHNSON

VOLUME I

Diaries, Prayers, and Annals

SAMUEL JOHNSON

Diaries, Prayers, and Annals

EDITED BY E. L. M^CADAM, JR.

WITH DONALD AND MARY HYDE

NEW HAVEN: YALE UNIVERSITY PRESS

LONDON: OXFORD UNIVERSITY PRESS

CONTENTS

ILLUSTRATIONS

PREFACE

In printing Johnson's prayers, meditations, diaries, and auto-biographical fragments we were faced with the fact that most of these exist in numerous scattered manuscripts which were not written as units—a complete year in a single manuscript, for example. On the contrary, Johnson sometimes made unrelated entries at the end of such real units as his Welsh diary. Instead of printing manuscripts intact, therefore, we have divided them as needed to make a chronological account, and have included a chronological list to show when we change from one manuscript to another; in the list we also give the present owner of the manuscript, if known.

We have followed Johnson's spelling except for slips of the pen, which we correct, giving his spelling in a note. His erratic spelling of proper names is corrected in the commentary. His accentuation of Greek words we have not corrected. We have supplied punctuation silently, but have added a note when there are two possible interpretations of meaning. We have capitalized the beginning of sentences except in "Aegri Ephemeris," where it seemed unnecessary. Where Johnson's manuscript is not known, we have followed the printed text cited.

Since many of the prayers are rough drafts, we have shown deleted and inserted passages in the notes, deletions by pointed brackets (⟨ ⟩) enclosing the passage deleted, and insertions by carets (ʌ ʌ) enclosing such passages. Nearly all of these changes are stylistic. Deletions involving content can, almost without exception, be identified as Strahan's. These we have restored to the text, using the same brackets and carets in the notes.

We began our work many years ago and had conceived of it as an independent book. But when Yale University planned a complete edition of Johnson, we were glad to accept the committee's invitation to include this work in the edition. By its nature, this volume differs from those which will follow. We have therefore used a somewhat different textual method from that of the other editors.

We wish to record our thanks to these libraries, which have made their manuscripts available to us: the Bodleian; the British Museum; the Henry E. Huntington Library; Johnson House, London; the Pierpont Morgan Library; Pembroke College, Oxford; and Yale; and to Mr. Arthur Pennant and Mr. Cecil Tildesley for a like kindness.

For reading our manuscript or proofs in whole or in part, and for many suggestions, we are indebted to Mr. G. W. Bond, Fellow and Librarian of Pembroke College, Oxford, and, for the Editorial Committee, Dr. R. W. Chapman, Professor James L. Clifford, Professor Robert Halsband, Professor Allen T. Hazen, Professor Frederick W. Hilles, Professor William R. Keast, Mr. Herman W. Liebert, Dr. Robert F. Metzdorf, Dr. L. F. Powell, and Sir Sydney C. Roberts.

Particular acknowledgement for many suggestions as to treatment, aid in research, and proofreading is due to Mr. George Milne, who has also compiled the index.

For corrections for the second printing, we are indebted to Professor H. W. Garrod of Oxford and Mr. F. L. Lucas of Cambridge.

INTRODUCTION

Johnson's diaries contain examples of his earliest writing—earlier than any known letters—and, taken as a whole, form an important body of work, giving information on the events of his life, his fluctuating and often tormented states of mind, his health, and his voluminous reading. With the autobiographical fragments and notes, as well as his prayers, which are often closely bound up with the day's activity or the crises of his life, they present an intimate picture of Johnson which is only equalled or surpassed by Johnson's letters and Boswell's *Life*. But these materials have never been available together—much has not previously been printed and the rest has been scattered—and we have therefore decided to include them within one cover. Some of the diaries have been printed many times, notably those written in France and Wales; some of the fragments have appeared in the editions of *Prayers and Meditations* and in Hawkins's and Boswell's biographies; other diaries and fragments have come to light only in the last generation of discoveries and are here published for the first time. Even those well known deserve fuller annotation than they have had in view of new manuscript material and the steadily increasing activity of scholars.

Johnson gave a terse definition of a diary in his *Dictionary*: "an account of the transactions, accidents, and observations of every day; a journal." This is a fair description of his own practice, except that "every day" is more often "now and then," and his observations are frequently so abbreviated that detective work is needed to explain what he is thinking.

In advising many of his friends to keep journals, particularly Mrs. Thrale, Boswell (who hardly needed such advice), and Bennet Langton, he enlarged on his definition: "the great thing to be recorded is the state of your own mind," "a man loves to review his own mind," and more at length:

> I know not any thing more pleasant, or more instructive, than to compare experience with expectation, or to register from

time to time the difference between idea and reality. It is
by this kind of observation that we grow daily less liable to
be disappointed. . . . Let me know what you expected, and
what you have found. At least record it to yourself before
custom has reconciled you to the scenes before you, and the
disparity of your discoveries to your hopes has vanished from
your mind.

(*Boswell Papers*, VI.105; *Life*, II.217, III.228, I.337.)

In these elaborations of his definition we begin to understand
why the journal had such an appeal to Johnson: it was a way to
place in permanent form one's daily mental processes, to review
them, and to compare them. Nothing could be more welcome to
the moral philosopher.

The form and nature of Johnson's diaries vary widely. Most
are made up of short jottings: notes of his activities, of his reading, of his work, of the letters he wrote. One, his last medical
journal, is almost wholly in Latin, and bits of Latin and Greek are
scattered in others. One, the "Welsh Diary," is in places written
with such fullness of description that one is tempted to think that
Johnson felt that it might make the basis of a book, like his *Journey to the Western Islands*. On two occasions he leaned towards
autobiography, in the "Annales," when he was about to court Mrs.
Porter, and in the "Annals," begun in the year he met Mrs.
Thrale. It may not be fanciful to suggest that meeting these two
women, the most important in his life, caused him to make an
extensive review of his life. The *Prayers and Meditations* were
often occasioned by his self-examination at New Year's, at Easter,
and on his birthday, examinations which were not only religious
but moral, and frequently concerned with his work or lack of it,
his unwillingness to rise in the morning, his failure to read as
much as he thought he should. In other words, these prayers and
meditations are directly connected with his daily life as reflected
in his diaries and are inseparable from the diaries themselves.

One other feature of the diaries is the frequency of gaps, large
and small. Johnson lapsed from regular journalizing only too
often, and his burning of two large quarto diaries just before his
death leaves further gaps which can be only partly filled by Bos-

well's surreptitious transcripts. The piecemeal dispersal of manuscripts after Johnson's death, some of which have never been recovered, and some of which have been cut into small bits as souvenirs for many people, provides the last complication.

We have therefore decided that a conventional printing of the diaries with footnotes does not meet our problem. Since several of the manuscripts overlap even for a period of years, we have printed each entry chronologically, regardless of its source. Furthermore, we have in a running commentary included all the usual footnote information except textual variants and have bridged gaps with a brief story of Johnson's activities garnered from his letters and the various biographies. Translations or paraphrases of his Latin or Greek are also included in the commentary.

THE SOURCES

1. *An Account of the Life of Dr. Samuel Johnson, from his birth to his eleventh year, written by himself* Johnson evidently called "Annals," since that is the title Wright printed on the first page of text. It is one of two known fragments of autobiography, and was probably written for Johnson's own satisfaction, since some of his interjections, like "dear Mother," are so personal that it is unlikely that he intended the work for publication or even the perusal of friends. He may have thought of showing it to Mrs. Thrale, but she does not refer to it. It *is* certain, and somewhat ironic, that his two principal biographers, Hawkins and Boswell, did not know of its existence.

The *Account* was first published in London in May 1805 by Richard Wright with this preface:

> It will be expected, that the Editor of the following curious and interesting pages should give an account of the manner in which the original MSS. came into his possession.
>
> Mr. Boswell, in his admirable Life of Dr. Johnson, thus observes:
>
> "The consideration of the numerous papers of which he was possessed seems to have struck Johnson's mind with a sudden anxiety; and, as they were in great confusion, it is much to

be lamented that he had not intrusted some faithful and discreet person with the care and selection of them; instead of which, he, in a precipitate manner, burnt masses of them, as I should apprehend, with little regard to discrimination. . . . Two very valuable articles, I am sure, we have lost; which were two quarto volumes, containing a full, fair, and most particular account of his own life, from his earliest recollection."

It does not appear, that the MS. from which the following short account of Dr. Johnson's early life is copied, was one of the two volumes to which Boswell alludes; although it is evident, from his enumeration of particular dates in the blank pages of the book, that he intended to have finished these Annals, according to this plan, with the same minuteness of description, in every circumstance and event.

This Volume was among that mass of papers which were ordered to be committed to the flames a few days before his death, thirty-two pages of which were torn out by himself, and destroyed; the contents of those which remain are here given with fidelity and exactness. Francis Barber, his black servant, unwilling that all the MSS. of his illustrious master should be utterly lost, preserved these relicks from the flames. By purchase from Barber's widow they came into the possession of the Editor. . . .

The original MSS. are deposited in the Museum of Antiquities and Natural Curiosities, belonging to the Editor; which is open to the inspection of the publick.

Mrs. Barber was disposing of Johnson's manuscripts as late as 1804, when she gave away a fragment now owned by Mr. McAdam. Unless she had a cache separate from her husband's, this may indicate that she sold Wright's manuscript to him not very long before he printed it. The Museum ceased to exist and its contents were dispersed a few years after the publication of the *Account*. The manuscript was sold to a Mr. Huybens as part of a lot at Sotheby's on 19 March 1819, and this is the last record of its location. We therefore print from Wright's text. His accuracy is in some doubt, for he states in his preface that Johnson tore out thirty-two pages from the volume and later gives the gap as thirty-eight pages; one misreading of Johnson's difficult hand, "knew" for "know," can be discovered in the first section describing the years 1710–11.

It is not easy to date the manuscript. Wright notes, without direct quotation, that the first paragraph was written in 1765. In a later entry ("In . . . 67, when I was in Lichfield") Johnson left a blank to be supplied. Since he was in Lichfield from May to about 18 October 1767, any one of six months would fit. That he did not remember at the time of writing suggests a rather long interval since his visit. The only other indication of date is puzzling: "It was not till about 1768, that I thought to calculate the returns of my father's trade, and by that estimate his probable profits." "About 1768" is sufficiently vague and suggests that this entry was made four or five years later. It is not clear that Johnson did make a written calculation even in 1768, for, unless he had in the meantime forgotten, he says in the "Welsh Diary," about 18 August 1774, that he has not yet done this: "To note down my Father's stock, expences, and profit." The year 1772 is therefore perhaps not too late to date some parts of the "Annals." A possible corroboration of this date may lie in his meditation for 18 April 1772: "I have of late turned my thoughts with a very useless earnestness upon past incidents."

2. The "1729–1734 Diary," written in Latin, consists of three leaves with numbered pages, all used except page four. The leaves, measuring ten by seven and a half centimetres, were probably cut from a memorandum book, since Johnson twice in the text describes the diary as "libellus," which may mean diary or memorandum book as well as little book. Moreover, when he says that he takes it with him as a companion, he cannot be referring to separate sheets. Boswell described the diary as "a parcel of loose leaves" (*Life*, 1.74).

"Annales" consists of three loose, unnumbered leaves measuring twelve by nine centimetres, probably cut as well from a memorandum book. The title and entries, also in Latin, are in block letters unlike Johnson's cursive hand in the diaries. Beneath the

title, Johnson's date, 10 November 1734, shows that the record was
made at one time, not a diary but rather an attempt, at twenty-
five, to set down the principal events of his life for permanent remembrance.

   Hawkins obtained the diary and "Annales" as an executor of
Johnson's will. After using them, for they were important sources
of information on Johnson's early years, he returned them to
Frank Barber, Johnson's residuary legatee. Later Frank delivered
them to Boswell, who, after making use of both, wrapped them
together in a folded sheet of paper, writing on it the inclusive
title "Johnson's Annales." This packet remained until recently
among Boswell's papers at Malahide Castle in Ireland. Both the
diary and "Annales" are now printed for the first time in full.
They are important in the clarification they give of certain events
in Johnson's youth not previously made clear by the partial quotations of Hawkins and Boswell.

3. Shortly before his death Johnson gave the manuscripts of
Prayers and Meditations to his young clergyman friend George
Strahan to edit and publish, and Strahan fulfilled both his obligations, later depositing the manuscripts in the library of Pembroke
College, Oxford, where they remain. They consist of fourteen pa-
perbound volumes of various sizes, some with loose leaves slipped
in. Book I seems to have been put together late, probably after
Johnson's death. It contains material dated from 7 September 1738
to 18 September 1760, each leaf endorsed by Johnson on the verso,
usually with just a date but sometimes with the occasion, as "Introductory Prayer" and "Mother" and once, the first prayer, with
the date it was transcribed, 1768. Book II, sewed perhaps by
Johnson, contains prayers for Easter 1761 and 1765 on the same
sheet and that for 28 March 1762 on another. Book III, endorsed by Johnson on the cover, has the Easter and birthday
prayers for 1764. Book IV was bound by Strahan or some later
person, since a note by Strahan on the last page is pasted down;
it contains matter from September 1765 to October 1766. Book V
Johnson endorsed "1767" on the cover. Book VI, 1768–71, consists
mostly of unbound leaves and contains many undated prayers,
the chronology of which we have had to determine from contents,

paper, and ink, as did Strahan and Hill before us, since they might have been slipped into the volume at any time. Book VII Johnson endorsed on the cover "1772"; Book VIII he endorsed "1773–1774." Book IX he endorsed "Easter 1775. 1776," but it includes the prayer for 25 July 1776; similarly Book X he endorsed "Easter 1777," but it includes his birthday prayer. The next two he endorsed respectively 1778 and 1779. Book XIII covers the next two years; a date "1781" on the cover may not be in Johnson's hand. Book XIV, without endorsements, contains prayers for 1782 and 1784.

The fact that eight or perhaps nine of the books were dated by Johnson and all the prayers in the first book endorsed by him not only suggests how important he considered them but also reveals more orderliness than one might have expected.

In addition to Johnson's endorsements, each prayer has a number in Strahan's hand, but except for the first, which he marked "No. 1" (the second he marked "No. 50"), the numbers have no meaning, unless Strahan at one time planned to group the prayers according to subject and later abandoned the notion. There are many other notes of his, usually merely repeating Johnson's titles or giving an indication of the contents, such as that for 6 October 1782, "On leaving Mr. Thrale's family." In no case have we found this material informative, and we have therefore not reproduced it.

Some of these manuscripts are fair copies, but many more are working drafts with interlineations or deletions by Johnson, mainly stylistic. Most of his deletions can be read without difficulty. Strahan's erasure, however, was very heavy. He blocked out words, lines, and paragraphs so completely that often relatively few traces of the words remain. In two cases we have been assisted by the survival of another manuscript with the same text, but for the most part we have depended on infra-red photographs or an infra-red converter to decipher some few passages where the surface of the paper has not been destroyed by the editing.

That this heavy editing was done by Strahan and not Johnson is proved in part by four places where Strahan has inserted a word above a heavy deletion, and in part by the innocent character of what deleted matter we have been able to read: references to his religious scruples, to a young minister who read the wrong lesson at church, to his diet, to his contrition for sin. On the other hand, Strahan printed many parts of Johnson's diaries which Johnson would certainly have omitted as having no relevance to the book of prayers which he had in mind. Strahan's deletions, where legible, we have restored to the text.

After Strahan's first edition of the *Prayers and Meditations* in 1785, he continued to add material. Two new prayers were added in the second edition and another in the third. The manuscripts of these are not at Pembroke and perhaps never were; they may have been lent. This may also be the explanation of the absence of six other manuscripts printed in the first edition. In a single case we know that Strahan had only a transcript by someone else; the original survives.

The careful rewriting which Johnson devoted to his prayers will show how important he thought them and will remind the reader that Johnson himself intended to publish a selection of them.

4. On 5 May 1776, probably while at Johnson's house, Boswell secretly transcribed several entries from the large diary which Johnson burned shortly before his death. These are written on a quarto sheet and range from 1753 to 1765, which gives us partial dating for the burned journal. Boswell used them in part in the *Life,* omitting all reference to Johnson's determination to remarry, bowdlerizing a meditation to make less severe Johnson's reflections on his neglect of public worship, and altering the date of one meditation so that it could be used for Easter Monday in place of one that he omitted for that day. All passages are here restored.

5. The diary for 1765–84, a bound volume, was discovered by Colonel Isham at Malahide Castle in 1937. It runs from 1 January 1765 to 1 January 1778, with large gaps, and resumes as "Aegri Ephemeris," Johnson's record of his last illness, on 6 July 1784, ending on 8 November, about five weeks before his death. Boswell both refers to the diary and quotes from it in the *Life,* but he may have been discouraged from using it more extensively by the fact

that parts of it are unusually difficult to decipher, even for Johnson's often difficult hand. Moreover, it is all contained within the
period when Boswell and Johnson were intimate, and hence Boswell could rely on his own journals. It is, however, the longest and
fullest of any of Johnson's diaries now known and is therefore of
major significance. It is here published for the first time.

6. The prayers and meditations from Good Friday through
Easter, 1766, with an isolated entry for 4 May, are in the Bodleian,
except for that part for 29 March beginning "I was yesterday very
heavy," which is in the Hyde collection. They were printed by
Hill, partly from a copy; our text shows a few new readings. In
contents they are very similar to other prayers and meditations;
one may guess that Barber withheld them from Strahan to dispose of later.

7. The Welsh diary was first edited by Duppa, who received some
help from Mrs. Thrale-Piozzi, and re-edited by Croker, Hill, and
Powell in their editions of the *Life*. A fresh collation has furnished some new readings, and we have added considerable annotation about the places the party visited and the books Johnson
read or looked at. Many side lights are furnished by Mrs. Thrale's
parallel journal, first published by Broadley and now in the Hyde
collection. In the Welsh diary Johnson recorded his activities in
the left column by date, and often added other notes in a second
column (see Plate facing p. 164). We have intercalated these notes
with the entries to which they refer. For some entries Mrs. Thrale's
diary corrects the chronology.

8. The diary of the French tour is a fragment running from 10
October to 5 November 1775. Since the volume is marked "France
II," Boswell plausibly conjectured that Johnson burned the first
volume in his well-known fire. There must have been also a third,
since the second breaks off in the middle of a sentence, but it was
probably short, as the party was home on 12 November. First published in the *Life*, the diary has recently been edited with Mrs.
Thrale's French journals by Moses Tyson and Henry Guppy. We
have been able to correct a few readings and have added materially
to the information about the books which Johnson saw or read.

9. The list of Johnson's receipts and expenditures between 22 September and 28 October (1776?), owned by Mr. Cecil Tildesley of Penkridge, Staffordshire, England, was first published by Powell in the *Life*, IV.511. It is very similar to other lists in the diaries, and may have been torn out of one. It is worth cherishing for Johnson's record of two shillings "Purloined by Mr. T."

10. Three small leaves formerly owned by Locker-Lampson are now in the Henry E. Huntington Library. They contain entries for 9 and 11 August 1781 and for July to September 1783, a mixture of meditation and diary, and were first printed by Hill.

11. The diary for 1782 is written in *The Gentleman's New Memorandum Book improv'd: or, The Merchant's and Tradesman's Daily Pocket Journal for the Year 1765*, when the days of weeks and months corresponded with those in 1782. Johnson recorded his daily activities in the first column of the printed Diary, under "Appointments" (see Plate facing p. 336). In the second column, under "Occasional Memorandums," he entered additional comments that commonly refer to the same day. Opposite these entries he kept his "Week's Account." To make the chronological sequence understandable, we have dispersed the weekly accounts and have intercalated all three columns by date as precisely as possible. We have silently added to Johnson's texts the printed dates and days of the week. Boswell had the book and quoted from it, but not extensively. It was purchased at the Auchinleck sale in 1917 by Miss E. H. Dowden, was used by Dr. Powell in his edition of the *Life*, and is now in the Bodleian. It is particularly interesting for its account of Johnson's last visit to Brighton with Mrs. Thrale.

12. A single leaf describing Johnson's visit to Heale in September 1783, perhaps once joined to the leaf in the Henry E. Huntington Library describing his return from that visit, is now lost. It was exhibited at Lichfield in 1909, when it was in an extra-illustrated set of Davies's *Garrick*. Broadley reproduced the verso of the leaf in his *Chats on Autographs*, 1910. Professor R. W. Rogers quoted from both sides of the leaf in his four-page pamphlet *A Leaf from the Private Note Book of Samuel Johnson*, Princeton, 1922, but

his quotations from the side reproduced by Broadley are most unreliable. We have been forced to use his quotations from the recto,
inasmuch as the leaf has disappeared.

13. The memoranda for 8 to 10 June 1784 listed by Hill in
Prayers and Meditations, are now printed for the first time.

14. "Repertorium" consists of eight leaves stitched together, of
which two pages, "Preces," dated 31 October 1784, were printed
by Hill. It is a mixture of cryptic but revealing notes on reading,
a list of early Church Fathers, and some jottings relative to the
book of prayers which Johnson was still thinking of compiling.
It is now in Professor Tinker's collection at Yale.

15. Miscellaneous manuscripts of prayers not needing separate
treatment are: that for 1 January 1751 (*Works*, 1787, XI, 191);
that for 5 September 1784 (*Works*, 1787, XI, 192); that for 18
September 1784 (Johnson House, London) ; that for 5 December
1784, in Professor Tinker's collection at Yale, and that for 1
August 1784, the present ownership of which we do not know.
Two prayers of 1782, written for Lucy Porter, are now printed
from the manuscripts she inserted in a book of prayers, now
owned by Mr. Arthur Pennant, of St. Asaph, North Wales. Johnson's transcripts of these two prayers are at Pembroke.

16. Lost manuscripts which survived Johnson, other than those
already mentioned, are more numerous. Hawkins quoted from a
diary entries for 27 August and 7 September 1736, and printed
one prayer for 1782 and three for 1783. Strahan printed thirteen
prayers or meditations now lost, six for 1752, two each for 1755,
1756, and 1768, and one for 1783. Croker added a prayer which we
have tentatively dated 1759 and a meditation for 1782, both from
the Rose MSS. The first has been dismembered: a slip bearing the
last five lines is in Professor Tinker's library. Boswell printed a
meditation conjecturally assigned to 1753 and also quoted from
diaries of 1755, 1768, 1773, 1774, 1775, 1779, and 1784. Finally,
Hill found in an auction catalogue a few words quoted from a
fragment of a diary of 1768.

SHORT TITLES

Anecdotes — H. L. Piozzi, *Anecdotes of the Late Samuel Johnson,* 1786.

"Annals" — *An Account of the Life of Dr. Samuel Johnson, from His Birth to His Eleventh Year,* ed. Richard Wright, 1805.

Boswell Papers — *Private Papers of James Boswell from Malahide Castle,* ed. Geoffrey Scott and F. A. Pottle, 18 vols. 1928–34.

Broadley — A. M. Broadley, *Dr. Johnson and Mrs. Thrale,* 1910.

Clifford — J. L. Clifford, *Hester Lynch Piozzi,* 1941.

Croker — Boswell's *Life of Johnson,* ed. J. W. Croker, 5 vols. 1831.

French Journals — *French Journals of Mrs. Thrale and Dr. Johnson,* ed. Moses Tyson and Henry Guppy, 1932.

Guppy — notes by Dr. Guppy in preceding item.

Hawkins — Sir John Hawkins, *The Life of Samuel Johnson,* 1787.

Letters — *The Letters of Samuel Johnson,* ed. R. W. Chapman, 3 vols. 1952; referred to by number.

Life — Boswell's *Life of Johnson,* ed. G. B. Hill, revised and enlarged by L. F. Powell, 6 vols. 1934–50.

Miscellanies — *Johnsonian Miscellanies,* ed. G. B. Hill, 2 vols. 1897.

Powell — notes by Dr. Powell in *Life.*

Reade — A. L. Reade, *Johnsonian Gleanings,* 11 vols. 1909–52.

Strahan — Johnson's *Prayers and Meditations,* ed. George Strahan, 1785; 2d ed. 1785, 3d ed. 1786; both add a few prayers.

Thraliana — *Thraliana, the Diary of Mrs. Hester Lynch Thrale,* ed. Katharine C. Balderston, 2 vols. 1942.

IN TEXTUAL NOTES, *carets* ($_\wedge$ $_\wedge$) *enclose material inserted by Johnson or Strahan, pointed brackets* (⟨ ⟩) *material deleted.*

DIARIES, PRAYERS,
AND ANNALS

ANNALS

1. 1709–10.

Sept. 7,* 1709, I was born at Lichfield. My mother had a very difficult and dangerous labour, and was assisted by George Hector, a man-midwife of great reputation. I was born almost dead, and could not cry for some time. When he had me in his arms, he said, "Here is a brave boy."

In a few weeks an inflammation was discovered on my buttock, which was at first, I think, taken for a burn; but soon appeared to be a natural disorder. It swelled, broke, and healed.

My Father being that year Sheriff of Lichfield, and to ride the circuit of the County next day, which was a ceremony then

* 18, of the present stile. Johnson

The title "Annals" is almost certainly Johnson's. (He had used the Latin form in 1734 for his first autobiographical notes.) The numbered divisions, which apparently are Johnson's, refer to the years of his life. When Wright's book, the *Account*, is referred to, we use his title.

Against the date of his birth Johnson noted, "18, of the present stile." This was the New Style, the Gregorian Calendar adopted in England in 1752, adding eleven days. Johnson began to use this style on 1 January 1753, as his diary in that year shows. That Mrs. Johnson was forty and bearing her first child probably explains her difficult labour, and baptizing the baby on the day of his birth shows that the parents feared that he might not live. The "man-midwife," George Hector, was a surgeon, the uncle of Edmund Hector, Johnson's schoolfellow and lifelong friend, who himself became a surgeon in Birmingham (*Life*, 1.526). After this paragraph Wright notes, "This was written in January, 1765," but gives no evidence for the dating.

The sheriff's ride round the boundaries of the city, which is also performed with great pomp; he was asked by my mother, "Whom he would invite to the Riding?" and answered, "All the town now." He feasted the citizens with uncommon magnificence, and was the last but one that maintained the splendour of the Riding.

I was, by my father's persuasion, put to one Marclew, commonly called Bellison, the servant, or wife of a servant of my father, to be nursed in George Lane, where I used to call when I was a bigger boy, and eat fruit in the garden, which was full of trees. Here it was discovered that my eyes were bad; and an issue was cut in my left arm, of which I took no great notice, as I think my mother has told me, having my little hand in a custard. How long this issue was continued I do not remember. I believe it was suffered to dry when I was about six years old.[1]

It is observable, that, having been told of this operation, I always imagined that I remembered it, but I laid the scene in the wrong house. Such confusions of memory I suspect to be common.

1. ∧How long . . . old.∧

---

legally a county, still takes place on 8 September. Stopping en route for refreshments was customary.

Johnson's foster mother, Joan Marklew (1675?–1746) was the second wife of John Marklew, a young brickmaker who worked for Michael Johnson (Reade, III.56–8). Before her marriage, as Joan Winckley, she had been a servant in the household of William Robinson in Sadler Street, and possibly in Michael Johnson's. The Marklews' unusual double name, says Wright, "is yet common in Lichfield, and is usually so distinguished." Their house in George Lane was four hundred yards from the Johnsons'. Hill suggests that Johnson may have had their garden in mind when he wrote in his *Swift*: "Almost every boy eats as much fruit as he can get, without any great inconvenience."

The incision in Johnson's arm, kept open with threads or horsehairs, was intended to drain the infection from his system.

My mother visited me every day, and used to go different ways, that her assiduity might not expose her to ridicule; and often left her fan or glove behind her, that she might have a pretence to come back unexpected; but she never discovered any token of neglect. Dr. Swinfen told me, that the scrofulous sores which afflicted me proceeded from the bad humours of the nurse, whose son had the same distemper, and was likewise short-sighted, but both in a less degree. My mother thought my diseases derived from her family.

In ten weeks I was taken home, a poor, diseased infant, almost blind.

I remember my aunt Nath. Ford told me, when I was about . . . years old, that she would not have picked such a poor creature up in the street.

In . . . 67, when I was at Lichfield, I went to look for my nurse's house; and, inquiring somewhat obscurely, was told "this is the house in which you were nursed." I saw my nurse's

---

Dr. Samuel Swinfen, or Swynfen, Johnson's godfather, a man of good family and a graduate of Pembroke College, Oxford, lodged with the Johnsons at this time. Whether Johnson was named after his maternal uncle Samuel Ford or after Swinfen is not clear and perhaps was not intended to be clear, as Reade suggests (III.55).

"Aunt Nath. Ford" was Jane (1682–1729), the wife of Johnson's uncle Nathaniel, after whom Johnson's younger brother Nathaniel was named. Her harsh realism about her nephew was offset by a lively disposition, as Reade says.

Johnson's visit to Lichfield in 1767 lasted from early May till about 18 October.

His foster brother, eighteen months his senior, was so nearly blind from infancy that as an adult he was unable to earn a living (Reade, x.22). He was therefore reading a large Bible: he could read no other.

son, to whose milk I succeeded, reading a large Bible, which my nurse had bought, as I was then told, some time before her death.

Dr. Swinfen used to say, that he never knew any child reared with so much difficulty.

2. 1710–11.

In the second year I know[2] not what happened to me. I believe it was then that my mother carried me to Trysul, to consult Dr. Atwood, an oculist of Worcester. My father and Mrs. Harriots, I think, never had much kindness for each other. She was my mother's relation; and he had none so high to whom he could send any of his family. He saw her seldom himself, and willingly disgusted her, by sending his horses from home on Sunday; which she considered, and with reason, as a breach of duty. My father had much vanity, which his adversity hindered from being fully exerted. I remember, that, mentioning her legacy in the humility of distress, he called her *our good Cousin Harriots*. My mother had no value for his relations; those indeed whom we knew of were much lower than hers. This contempt began, I know not on which side, very early: but, as my father was little at home, it had not much effect.

2. Wright: "knew"

————————————

Lichfield having no oculists, Johnson was taken to the house of Mrs. Johnson's first cousin, Mrs. Harriots, a childless widow in her late forties living at Trysul, the manor house, near Wolverhampton, where he could be examined by a well-known physician, Dr. Thomas Attwood of Worcester. The Johnsons' relative poverty was reason enough for Mr. Johnson's lack of "kindness" for Mrs. Harriots, and his offending her sabbatarianism by sending out his horses on Sunday was a human reaction. Johnson commented on 1 June 1770 in his diary on the "regularity" of Mrs. Harriots's

My father and mother had not much happiness from each other. They seldom conversed; for my father could not bear to talk of his affairs; and my mother, being unacquainted with books, cared not to talk of any thing else. Had my mother been more literate, they had been better companions. She might have sometimes introduced her unwelcome topick with more success, if she could have diversified her conversation. Of business she had no distinct conception; and therefore her discourse was composed only of complaint, fear, and suspicion. Neither of them ever tried to calculate the profits of trade, or the expenses of living. My mother concluded that we were poor, because we lost by some of our trades; but the truth was, that my father, having in the early part of his life contracted debts, never had trade sufficient to enable him to pay them, and maintain his family; he got something, but not enough.

---

household, implying, evidently, regularity of religious observances. Mr. Johnson's absences from home attending book auctions and his stalls in other cities perhaps prevented such slights to Mrs. Harriots from having serious consequences. At any rate, in 1728 she bequeathed to Mrs. Johnson "a pair of her best flaxen sheets and pillow cases, as well as a large pewter dish and a dozen pewter plates," and £40 (Reade, x.68). Mr. Johnson's "humility of distress" at that time may be imagined.

The financial background of the Johnsons' domestic unhappiness is complex and not altogether clear. Mr. Johnson may have borrowed to establish his bookshop as a young man, and even more probably did so in 1706 when he bought the library of the Earl of Derby, some 2900 volumes, though this could not be described as the early part of his life. In the next year he bought the property in Market Street for £80, tore down the existing building, and built a new one, in which Johnson was born. There were several publishing ventures which may have been unsuccessful. Mrs. Johnson had brought her husband a dowry of about £440, but he had been unable to carry out his part of the bargain in adding £100

It was not till about 1768, that I thought to calculate the
returns of my father's trade, and by that estimate his probable
profits. This, I believe, my parents never did.

3. 1 7 1 1 — 1 2 .

This year, in Lent —12, I was taken to London, to be touched
for the evil by Queen Anne. My mother was at Nicholson's, the
famous bookseller, in Little Britain. My mother, then with
child, concealed her pregnancy, that she might not be hindered from the journey.[3] I always retained some memory of
this journey, though I was then but thirty months old. I remembered a little dark room behind the kitchen, where the
jack-weight fell through a hole in the floor, into which I once
slipped my leg. I seem to remember, that I played with a string
and a bell, which my cousin Isaac Johnson gave me; and that

3. ∧My mother, then . . . journey.∧

---

to a trust fund. All this is quite enough to cause "complaint, fear,
and suspicion." No record exists of Johnson's calculation of the
returns on his father's trade. If he had written one out "about
1768," he had forgotten it in 1774, when he proposed, in his
Welsh Diary, "To note down my Father's stock, expences, and
profit."

Scrofula, or king's evil, was suspected of causing the loss of
vision in Johnson's left eye, and Sir John Floyer, the well-known
Lichfield physician, advised that the thirty-months-old child be
taken to London to be touched by the Queen, who was the last
British monarch to exercise this supposed power. Nicholson's
shop, where they stayed, was near Mrs. Johnson's cousin Cornelius
Jesson. Mrs. Johnson was pregnant with Nathaniel, her only other
child.

The jack weight in the room behind Nicholson's kitchen was
part of the mechanism that turned the spit. Of Johnson's cousin

there was a cat with a white collar, and a dog, called Chops, that leaped over a stick: but I know not whether I remember the thing, or the talk of it.[4]

I remember a boy crying at the palace when I went to be touched. Being asked "on which side of the shop was the counter?" I answered, "on the left from the entrance," many years after, and spoke, not by guess, but by memory. We went in the stage-coach, and returned in the waggon, as my mother said, because my cough was violent. The hope of saving a few shillings was no slight motive; for she, not having been accustomed to money, was afraid of such expenses as now seem very small. She sewed two guineas in her petticoat, lest she should be robbed.

We were troublesome to the passengers; but to suffer such inconveniences in the stage-coach was common in those[5] days to persons in much higher rank. I was sick; one woman fondled me, the other was disgusted.[6] She bought me a small silver cup and spoon, marked SAM. I. lest if they had been marked s. I. which was her name, they should, upon her death, have been taken from me. She bought me a speckled linen frock, which I knew afterwards by the name of my London frock. The cup was one of the last pieces of plate which dear Tetty sold in our

4. ⌄I seem ... of it.⌄   5. Wright: "these"   6. ⌄I was sick ... disgusted.⌄

---

who gave him the string and bell, nothing is known. Johnson's care in writing this passage is noteworthy, since these things he is not sure he remembers, whereas he is certain of his recollection of the position of the counter in the shop. It is curious that he here mentions nothing of his visit to the Queen, though he told Mrs. Thrale that "he thought he had some confused Remembrance of a Lady in a black Hood" (*Thraliana*, p. 160). He was presented with an amulet which he long wore, "an angel of gold, with the impress of St. Michael the archangel on the one side, and a ship under full sail on the other" (Hawkins, p. 4).

distress. I have now the spoon. She bought at the same time two teaspoons, and till my manhood she had no more.

My father considered tea as very expensive, and discouraged my mother from keeping company with the neighbours, and from paying visits or receiving them. She lived to say, many years after, that, if the time were to pass again, she would not comply with such unsocial injunctions.

I suppose that in this year I was first informed of a future state. I remember, that being in bed with my mother one morning, I was told by her of the two places to which the inhabitants of this world were received after death; one a fine place filled with happiness, called Heaven; the other a *sad* place, called Hell. That this account much affected my imagination, I do not remember. When I was risen, my mother bade me repeat what she had told me to Thomas Jackson. When I told this afterwards to my mother, she seemed to wonder that she should begin such talk so late as that the first time could be remembered.

The date at which Johnson's wife was forced to sell his cup cannot be determined, since the period of their distress was a long one. Hill guessed 1744, which is reasonable. The spoon was probably among Johnson's effects at his death, and went, by will, to Johnson's executors in trust for the use of his servant Frank.

The expensiveness of tea was not a matter of Mr. Johnson's narrowness: Hill notes that in 1731 various grades sold from 10s. to 35s. a pound; these figures should be multiplied by seven to approximate modern values. In this, as in the rest of the "Annals," there is nothing to bear out Boswell's statement that "Johnson's mother was a woman of distinguished understanding" (*Life*, I.38). Johnson himself told Mrs. Thrale, "I did not respect my own mother, though I loved her" (*Anecdotes*, p. 27). That she had some ingenuity in educating her son, however, is shown by her telling him to repeat to Jackson, their servant, what she had just told him about heaven and hell, thereby to fix it in his memory.

[*Here there is a chasm of thirty-eight pages in the manuscript.*]

examination. We always considered it as a day of ease; for we made no preparation, and indeed were asked commonly such questions as we had been asked often before, and could regularly answer. But I believe it was of use at first.

On Thursday night a small portion of Aesop was learned by heart, and on Friday morning the lessons in Aesop were repeated; I believe, not those in Helvicus. On Friday afternoon we learned *Quae Genus*; I suppose that other boys might say

---

The gap in the manuscript, which Wright gives as thirty-*two* pages in his preface, covers the years when Johnson learned to read, at home with his mother and at Mrs. Oliver's "dame's school" for small children, when he was four or a little later, his progressing to Thomas Browne's school, when he was about six, and his entering the Lichfield Grammar School about January 1717, when he was seven. Johnson is describing his studies there when the story resumes with the usual Thursday examination.

All of the schoolbooks mentioned were used in studying Latin. The Aesop, as appears later, was that edited by the Commonwealth schoolmaster Charles Hoole, with English and Latin on facing pages. Christopher Helwig, Latinized as Helvicus, was a German Greek scholar (1581–1617), whose *Familiaria Colloquia Auctoritate Superiorum Selecta et Adornata*, 1613, now very rare, went through at least eight German editions in the seventeenth century and reached an "editio novissima" at Nuremberg in 1715 (copy at University of Illinois). Soon after the first edition it was, according to the title page of the 1715 edition, "with the consent of the author turned into German," which was printed facing the Latin text. Of the fifty dialogues, thirty-three are from Erasmus's *Colloquies*, originally written for Erasmus's pupils at Paris in 1496, twelve from Juan Luis Vives, and five from Hermannus Schottenius, author of *Instructio Prima Puerum*, 1527. A London printing described as the eleventh edition appeared in 1673 (copy in the Bodleian). It is in Latin only and contains no vocabulary.

their repetition, but of this I have now no distinct remembrance. To learn *Quae Genus* was to me always pleasing; and *As in Praesenti* was, I know not why, always disgusting.

When we learned our Accidence we had no parts, but, I think, two lessons. The boys that came to school untaught read the Accidence twice through before they learned it by heart.

The grammar used was some form of William Lily's *Short Introduction of Grammar*, which had been used in most English schools since 1542, often in its original form and sometimes as adapted by progressive men like Charles Hoole. Known as the Royal Grammar, after the mid-eighteenth-century revision it lasted another century as the Eton Grammar. The introduction to the parts of speech, written in English, occupies the first fifth of the book, the construction of the parts of speech, "the concords of Latin speech," the next tenth, also in English, and an extended grammar and prosody in Latin the rest. The Latin phrases Johnson quotes are those with which prominent sections begin, all the rules being put into jingles to aid in memorizing. After an introductory section on spelling and nouns, nouns are dealt with fully in the part beginning "Propria quae maribus." "Quae genus" concludes nouns and pronouns. "As in praesenti," a longer section, treats the conjugation of verbs, and since it is much more difficult, it is easy to see why it was "disgusting" to Johnson.

"Accidence" Johnson defines as "the little book containing the first rudiments of grammar, and explaining the properties of the eight parts of speech." This sounds as though he had used a separate book, but the description is also that of the first, English part of Lily. "We had no parts" may refer to parts of speech, though that meaning had been obsolete for a century. Lily's preface, still printed as late as 1732, speaks of "examining of the parts and the rules," and the title of a book by John Brinsley gives a further hint: *The Posing of the Parts: or, A Most Plaine and Easie Way of Examining the Accidence and Grammar. By Questions and Answers, Arising Directly Out of the Words of the Rules*, 1628. Applying this to Johnson's discussion, we might say that while

When we learned *Propria quae Maribus,* our parts were in the Accidence; when we learned *As in Praesenti,* our parts were in the Accidence and *Propria quae Maribus;* when we learned *Syntaxis,* in the former three. *Propria quae Maribus* I could repeat without any effort of recollection. I used to repeat it to my mother and Tom Johnson; and remember, that I once went as far as the middle of the paragraph, "Mascula dicuntur monosyllaba," in a dream.

On Saturday, as on Thursday, we were examined. We were sometimes, on one of those days, asked our Catechism, but with no regularity or constancy. G. Hector never had been taught his Catechism.[7]

7. ₍G. Hector . . . Catechism.₎

---

the boys memorized the first section, they did not have a question and answer period; while they memorized the next section, they had a question and answer period on the first in the words they had memorized, and so on. "Syntaxis" is the last section of the grammar proper and corresponds to the earlier "construction of the eight parts of speech."

Johnson's memorizing the 141 lines of "Propria quae maribus" and probably the examples, together extending to sixteen pages, seems a considerable feat for a child of seven or eight and is perhaps a tribute to the patience of his mother and his fifteen-year-old cousin Tom, the youngest son of Johnson's uncle Andrew. Tom seems to have been living with the Michael Johnsons at this time, probably learning his trade at Michael's parchment factory. In later years he fell into want and Johnson befriended him and his children. The part of "Propria quae maribus" which Johnson repeated in his dream is sixty-four lines, spread over five pages, with the examples. That fifty years later Johnson should remember the opening words of the paragraph where he broke off is an extraordinary example of his tenacious recollection of these details of his early schooling.

The George Hector who had not been taught his catechism was the son of the doctor who had delivered Johnson. The entry im-

The progress of examination was this. When we learned *Propria quae Maribus*, we were examined in the Accidence; particularly we formed Verbs, that is, went through the same person in all the Moods and Tenses. This was very difficult to me; and I was once very anxious about the next day, when this exercise was to be performed, in which I had failed till I was discouraged. My mother encouraged me, and I proceeded better. When I told her of my good escape, "We often," said she, dear mother! "come off best, when we are most afraid." She told me, that, once when she asked me about forming verbs, I said, "I did not form them in an ugly shape." "You could not," said she, "speak plain; and I was proud that I had a boy who was forming verbs." These little memorials sooth my mind. Of the parts of Corderius or Aesop, which we learned to repeat, I have not the least recollection, except of a passage in one of the Morals, where it is said of some man, that, when he hated another, he made him rich; this I repeated emphatically in my mother's hearing, who could never conceive that riches could bring any evil. She remarked it, as I expected.

---

plies that Johnson had learned his; a similar implication lies in the remark above about the boys who had not learned the accidence before entering the school.

Johnson's trouble with the conjugation of verbs introduces the most personal passage in the "Annals." His interjection, "dear mother!" and his comment, "These little memorials sooth my mind," make it evident that the "Annals" was not written with a view to publication, if its lack of arrangement and coherence has not already suggested this.

The book by Mathurin Corderius or Cordier, friend of Calvin, was probably used in the form of Charles Hoole's *M. Corderius's School Colloquies, English and Latin,* 1657, which reached a twenty-ninth edition in 1808, winning out over two other English versions, one of which, Willymott's, reached a tenth edition in 1760. The 228 dialogues are in parallel columns of English and

I had the curiosity, two or three years ago, to look over Garretson's Exercises, Willymot's Particles, and Walker's Exercises; and found very few sentences that I should have recollected if I had found them in any other books. That which is

Latin, obviating the need of a vocabulary, and, simple at first, become increasingly more difficult. They were written for boys of just Johnson's age: one (1.29) says, "I am not as yet eight years old." They are frequently lively and amusing; for example, one is a discussion between two boys about a third who borrowed a book from a schoolmate and then pawned it.

In Hoole's Aesop the ninth fable is the City Mouse and the Country Mouse. Hoole's moral, which does not occur in other versions, is: "Riches indeed make shew of pleasure; but if you look into them, they contain danger and bitterness. There was one Eutrapelus, who, when he would do his enemies the greatest mischief, made them rich, using to say, He thus took revenge on them, for they were like to receive with their riches a great burden of cares."

Johnson's looking over schoolbooks "two or three years ago" may be connected with the series of letters he wrote to George Strahan in 1763 about learning Latin. John Garretson's *English Exercises for School-boys to Translate into Latin* reached a fourteenth edition in 1716. It was often used, as Johnson says later, with another book, by "W. H., teacher of a private school," *Hermes Romanus ... a Collection of Latin Words and Phrases for the Translating of Garretson's English Exercises into Latin*, 1711. William Willymott's *English Particles Exemplified in Sentences Designed for Latin Exercises*, 1703, is self-explanatory. William Walker's "Exercises" is apparently his *Treatise of English Particles ... with a Praxis upon the Same*, 1655, which treats prepositions and adverbs largely, under each giving a series of examples in English and Latin, and following with a number of similar examples in Latin only. At the end of the book are ten dialogues in parallel columns of English and Latin, with the particles keyed to the earlier section. In an appendix is a phrase book, with such

read without pleasure is not often recollected nor infixed by conversation, and therefore in a great measure drops from the memory. Thus it happens that those who are taken early from school, commonly lose all that they had learned.

When we learned *As in Praesenti*, we parsed *Propria quae Maribus* by Hool's Terminations; and, when we learned *Syntaxis*, we parsed *As in Praesenti*; and afterwards *Quae Genus*, by the same book; sometimes, as I remember, proceeding in order of the rules, and sometimes, particularly in *As in Praesenti*, taking words as they occurred in the Index.

The whole week before we broke up, and the part of the week in which we broke up, were spent wholly, I know not why, in examination; and were therefore easy to both us and

---

things useful to schoolboys as, "I will *break* your pate: Diminuam tibi cerebrum, Terence." Walker also edited Lily's *Grammar*. Johnson advised Strahan not to learn Walker's *Particles* "at all by heart, but look in it from time to time and observe his notes and remarks, and see how they are exemplified" (*Letters* 151). This was probably not the method of the Lichfield School, but Strahan was nineteen years old, not eight.

Johnson's comment on these three books is curious. One would expect him to say that he found little that he recollected, after more than fifty years. But he did recall sentences, probably many, in these books, which he would not have recalled in others. And one should distinguish between the books of exercises and the fables and dialogues, for it is evident that in Aesop, for example, he anticipated his mother's reaction to Eutrapelus, and was gratified that she responded as expected. Some of these things, therefore, were read with pleasure and "recollected and infixed by conversation." And that he remembered the school with pleasure was due not only to Hawkins's kind treatment, but also, inseparably with this, to the fact that he "really excelled the rest." The "multitude of novelties" which this period supplied shows that Johnson was greatly stimulated by this experience; it is not the

the master. The two nights before the vacation were free from exercise.

This was the course of the school, which I remember with pleasure; for I was indulged and caressed by my master, and, I think, really excelled the rest.

I was with Hawkins but two years, and perhaps four months. The time, till I had computed it, appeared much longer by the multitude of novelties which it supplied, and of incidents, then in my thoughts important, it produced. Perhaps it is not possible that any other period can make the same impression on the memory.

10. 1719.

In the Spring of 1719, our class consisting of eleven, the number was always fixed in my memory, but one of the names I have forgotten, was removed to the upper school, and put under Holbrook, a peevish and ill-tempered man. We were removed sooner than had been the custom; for the head-master, intent upon his boarders, left the town-boys long in the lower school. Our removal was caused by a reproof from the Town-

---

reaction of a boy bored by discipline and dull books. His later remark that "a man ought to read just as inclination leads him; for what he reads as a task will do him little good" (*Life*, 1.428), has more to do with men than children.

Humphrey Hawkins, as Reade discovered, was a man of about fifty when Johnson entered the school, where Hawkins had been undermaster for at least twenty-two years. That he was not a graduate of Oxford or Cambridge may have hindered his advancement, but it does not seem to have soured his disposition.

The Reverend Edward Holbrooke, usher in the school to whom Johnson was now assigned, was a recent Cambridge graduate, twenty-three years old. His peevishness may have been magnified in the boy's mind, since Johnson was disappointed at being taken from Hawkins. Dr. Taylor described him to Boswell as "one of

clerk; and Hawkins complained that he had lost half his profit. At this removal I cried. The rest were indifferent. My exercise in Garretson was somewhere about the Gerunds. Our places in Aesop and Helvicus I have totally forgotten.

At Whitsuntide Mrs. Longworth brought me a "Hermes Garretsoni," of which I do not remember that I ever could make much use. It was afterwards lost, or stolen at school. My exercise was then in the end of the Syntax. Hermes furnished me with the word *inliciturus*, which I did not understand, but used it.

This task was very troublesome to me; I made all the twenty-

---

the most ingenious men, best scholars, and best preachers of his age" (*Life*, 1.44). John Hunter, the headmaster, had been intent on the boarders, Reade suggests, partly because there was more income from them, and partly because they were of higher social status than the day students. The town clerk who reproved him was Johnson's godfather Richard Wakefield.

The Mrs. Longworth who gave Johnson a *Hermes Garretsoni* is unidentified. That she "brought" it sounds as though she was a visitor to Lichfield, perhaps a relative, who knew that Garretson was difficult enough without such a phrase book as *Hermes*. It is remarkable that Johnson remembered with such exactness his position in a book at two dates so near each other: "about the Gerunds" in the spring, and "in the end of the Syntax" at Whitsuntide, 28 May in that year; unless his "then" refers to the period when his *Hermes* disappeared. *Inliciturus* does not occur in the only edition of *Hermes* available to us, 1771 (British Museum). Hence it appears that Wright misread Johnson's hand. The most likely word is *indicaturus* in Dialogue XVII, to be used to translate "they will signify the teacher." It is not surprising that Johnson should not have understood this awkward expression. His using it anyway, is so characteristic of an average bright youngster that it must not pass unnoticed.

His doing more than the assigned number of exercises, trouble-

five exercises, others made but sixteen. I never shewed all mine; five lay long after in a drawer in the shop. I made an exercise in a little time, and shewed it my mother; but the task being long upon me, she said, "Though you could make an exercise in so short a time, I thought you would find it difficult to make them all as soon as you should."

This Whitsuntide, I and my brother were sent to pass some time at Birmingham; I believe, a fortnight. Why such boys were sent to trouble other houses, I cannot tell. My mother had some opinion that much improvement was to be had by changing the mode of life. My uncle Harrison was a widower; and his house was kept by Sally Ford, a young woman of such sweetness of temper, that I used to say she had no fault. We lived most at uncle Ford's, being much caressed by my aunt, a good-natured, coarse woman, easy of converse, but willing to find something to censure in the absent. My uncle Harrison did not much like us, nor did we like him. He was a very mean and vulgar man, drunk every night, but drunk with little drink, very peevish, very proud, very ostentatious, but, luckily,

———————————

some though they were, is also characteristic of such a youngster, but his not showing all of them indicates that he had already learned something about the etiquette of school life. And the ability to work with bursts of speed but not with steady progress was something which plagued Johnson much later in life. It is surprising to find it so early and to see that his mother thought it typical of him. Johnson's many unhappy complaints about his indolence in later years, complaints which are hard to sympathize with in view of the long shelf of books he produced, are in a sense only paraphrases of this remark. The tone of moral obligation in "should" was to grow into a heavy imperative later on.

Mrs. Johnson's opinion that visiting one's relatives made for improvement was doubtless conditioned partly by the fact that all these relatives were hers, and her family was of higher social status than her husband's. John Harrison's wife had been Mrs. Johnson's

not rich. At my aunt Ford's I eat so much of a boiled leg of mutton, that she used to talk of it. My mother, who had lived in a narrow sphere, and was then affected by little things, told me seriously that it would hardly ever be forgotten. Her mind, I think, was afterwards much enlarged, or greater evils wore out the care of less.

I staid after the vacation was over some days; and remember, when I wrote home, that I desired the horses to come on Thursday of the first school week; and then, and not till then, they should be welcome to go. I was much pleased with a rattle to my whip, and wrote of it to my mother.

When my father came to fetch us home, he told the ostler, that he had twelve miles home, and two boys under his care. This offended me. He had then a watch, which he returned when he was to pay for it.

In making, I think, the first exercise under Holbrook, I perceived the power of continuity of attention, of application not

---

sister Phoebe; Sarah Ford was the eldest daughter of her brother Cornelius and seventeen at this time; and uncle Ford was either Nathaniel, whose wife told Johnson that she would not have picked up such a puny infant as he in the street, or the elder uncle Samuel. Nathaniel lived at Sutton Coldfield, seven miles from Birmingham. The short vignettes of Mrs. Ford and Harrison are in Johnson's most brilliant manner.

The picture of Johnson writing to his family not to send the horses until after school had begun, and his offence at his father's implication that the two boys, aged nine and six, were too young to take care of themselves, show him again as happy, normal, and independent.

Mr. Johnson's temporary possession of a watch may have been in Johnson's mind because he himself did not own one till he was fifty-nine, according to Hawkins (p. 460).

The picture of Johnson sitting at the kitchen windows learning for the first time the power of concentration is a vivid one—Sally

suffered to wander or to pause. I was writing at the kitchen windows, as I thought, alone, and turning my head saw Sally dancing. I went on without notice, and had finished almost without perceiving that any time had elapsed. This close attention I have seldom in my whole life obtained.

In the upper-school, I first began to point my exercise, which we made noon's business. Of the method I have not so distinct a remembrance as of the foregoing system. On Thursday morning we had a lesson, as on other mornings. On Thursday afternoon, and on Saturday morning, we commonly made examples to the Syntax.

Ford dancing almost unnoticed in the background. There are not many such visual images in Johnson's writing. That he so concentrated on his first exercise for Holbrooke suggests that he found the matter interesting and that he was determined to please his new master, sorry as he was to leave Hawkins. And that he was seldom later to attain the same "continuity of attention" reminds one how much of his mature work was drudgery.

The incident apparently took place some little time before Whitsuntide, for Johnson has said above that the class began with Holbrooke "in the Spring"; since Johnson did not return from Birmingham till almost the middle of June, that seems late to be called spring. Perhaps Sally had come down from Birmingham for a visit and then took the two boys back with her. Johnson's arrangement appears associational rather than chronological. If Johnson began with Holbrooke after Whitsuntide and did his first exercise during his vacation, which seems unlikely, the incident may have taken place in Birmingham.

Punctuating his exercises probably did not much interest Johnson, judging from his later manuscripts, which are very lightly punctuated. This, like spelling, was unimportant to the average eighteenth-century writer, since spelling and pointing were determined by the individual printing house practice, unless one was a purist like Boswell. The rest of the routine of the upper school Johnson remembered less well than he did that of the lower school,

We were soon raised from Aesop to Phaedrus, and then said our repetition on Friday afternoon to Hunter. I remember the fable of the wolf and lamb, *to my draught—that I may drink*. At what time we began Phaedrus, I know not. It was the only book which we learned to the end. In the latter part thirty lines were expected for a lesson. What reconciles masters to long lessons is the pleasure of tasking.

Helvicus was very difficult: the dialogue *Vestitus*, Hawkins directed us to omit, as being one of the hardest in the book. As I remember, there was another upon food, and another upon fruits, which we began, and were ordered not to pursue. In the dialogue of Fruits, we perceived that Holbrook did not know the meaning of *Uvae Crispae*. That lesson gave us great trouble. I observed that we learned Helvicus a long time with

---

probably because such things were no longer novelties. The earlier Thursday examination, and that of Saturday morning, were replaced by lessons. Saturday afternoon examinations, he implies, remained.

Johnson had already read a simple version of the fable of the Wolf and the Lamb as the second in Aesop. In Phaedrus, as in Aesop, the wolf, who has been drinking up-stream from the lamb, accuses the lamb of muddying the water for him, and the lamb's protests that this is impossible are unavailing. The class is translating and probably parsing.

The dialogues collected by Helvicus are not simplified or graded as to difficulty, but reproduced directly from the original authors. A collation of No. 17, "Ludus Globorum missilium," with a modern edition of Erasmus shows only minor variants. Of two dialogues on "Clothing" (2 and 26), both by Vives, perhaps the first was omitted, since by the time the second was reached, the pupils would have been under Holbrooke, not Hawkins. There are dialogues on the three meals of the day, No. 10, "Jentaculum," by Schottennius, No. 11, "Prandium," by Vives, and No. 23, "Coena," by Erasmus. The dialogue on fruits, No. 12, "Fructus

very little progress. We learned it in the afternoon on Monday and Wednesday.

Gladiolus Scriptorius.—A little lapse, we quitted it. I got an English Erasmus.

In Phaedrus we tried to use the interpretation, but never attempted the notes. Nor do I remember that the interpretation helped us.

In Phaedrus we were sent up twice to the upper master to be punished. The second time we complained that we could not get the passage. Being told that we should ask, we informed him that we had asked, and that the assistant would not tell us.

Novelli" by Schottennius, presents an unusual vocabulary, and is certainly difficult. "Uvae crispae" is explained as "Medici Ribes," which a botanist would recognize as a species of gooseberry, but Holbrooke need not have known that.

"Gladiolus scriptorius," "a little sword for a writer," Johnson must have remembered with amusement because it is such a magnificent expression for a pen-knife. It occurs in "Scriptio," No. 8, the second half of Erasmus's "Euntes in ludum literarium": "Deest mihi gladiolus scriptorius," "I don't have a pen-knife." It will be noticed that all the dialogues Johnson mentions are from the first half of the book. After a little lapse, a holiday perhaps, they did not continue with it, no doubt to the mutual satisfaction of Holbrooke and his class. But as a precaution Johnson got an English Erasmus.

Holbrooke's sending the class up to Hunter for punishment recalls one of Johnson's many comments on Hunter's severity: he "was very severe, and wrong-headedly severe. He used . . . to beat us unmercifully; and he did not distinguish between ignorance and negligence; for he would beat a boy equally for not knowing a thing, as for neglecting to know it." (*Life*, 1.44.) One wonders what Hunter told the class when informed that his assistant would not help them, but the manuscript breaks off at this point.

ANNALES

NOVRIS. 10ᵐᵒ 1734

A.D. 1709 SEPTRIS. 7ᵐᵒ·

Samuel Johnson Lichfieldiae natus est.

1725 MENSIBUS AUTUMNAL.

S.J. ad se vocavit C.F. a quo, anno proxime insequenti, Pen-
tecostes feriis, Lichfieldiam rediit.

Of the next six years Johnson left no known records. He remained in school, read at home, and probably helped his father
in the shop as he grew into adolescence.

In "Annales," the autobiographical notes he wrote in 1734, he
entered the fact that in the autumn of 1725 his cousin, the Reverend Cornelius Ford, fifteen years his elder, invited him to Pedmore, near Stourbridge. He remained there till Whitsuntide the
following June, when he returned to Lichfield.

Ford had heard of his young relation's unusual intellectual
powers, and he soon found him of such interest that he "was
unwilling to let him return, and to make up for the loss he might
sustain by his absence from school, became his instructor in the
classics, and farther assisted him in his studies" (Hawkins, p. 8).
Ford, the learned but profligate parson (said to be the original of
Hogarth's parson in *Midnight Modern Conversation*) exerted a
profound influence over Johnson. The sixteen-year-old boy bene-
fited greatly from the good qualities of Ford, his wide knowledge,
his wit, and his philosophy of general culture: he advised Johnson
"to study the Principles of every thing, that a general Acquaintance with Life might be the Consequence of his Enquiries—
Learn said he the leading Precognita of all things—no need per-
[haps] to turn over leaf by leaf; but grasp the Trunk hard only,
and you will shake all the Branches" (*Thraliana*, p. 171). For

ANNALES

Nov.ᵗⁱᵉ 11ᵐᵒ 1734

A.D. 1709 *Sept.ʳⁱⁱ 7ᵐᵒ*

Samuel Johnson Lichfieldiæ natus est.

1725 *Mensibus Autumnal.*

S.J. ad se vocavit C.F. a quo, anno proxime insequente, Antecostes ferijs Lichfieldiam redijt.

1728

Nov.ᵗⁱᵉ 1ᵐᵒ

S.J. Oxonium se contulit.

Johnson's "Annales," 1734

1728

NOVRIS. 1mo.

S.J. Oxonium se contulit.

Ford's excesses Johnson held a melancholy and tender regret all his life.

When Johnson returned to Lichfield, Hunter refused to readmit him after such an extraordinary absence, and therefore, partly through the influence of Ford, Johnson entered the grammar school at Stourbridge, where the Reverend John Wentworth was headmaster. There, he later told Percy, he "learnt a great deal from the Master, but nothing in his school" (*Percy Correspondence*, 1.43).

Late in the autumn of 1726 he was at home again, ready for college, but without money. Again he resumed work in the shop, read much, and earned the friendship of the cultured Gilbert Walmesley, who continued the broadening influence Ford had begun.

"Annales" now records Johnson's entering Oxford, but writing six years after the event he has made it a day late: the Caution Book of Pembroke College shows the receipt of seven pounds from Samuel Johnson, commoner, on 31 October. How Johnson was able to afford college is not definitely known. Taylor told Boswell that a Shropshire friend, Andrew Corbet, had "spontaneously undertaken to support him at Oxford, in the character of his companion; though, in fact, he never received any assistance whatever from that gentleman" (*Life*, 1.58). In the previous February Mrs. Johnson's cousin Mrs. Harriots had died, leaving Mrs. Johnson forty pounds, and it was perhaps this money, which would cover about a year's expenses, which made college possible.

The next thirteen months Johnson apparently spent at Oxford without even returning home for vacations, not an unusual practice at this date. His schoolmate Hector spoke of Johnson's "long absence from Lichfield" (Hawkins, p. 8). And his erratic devouring of books, a habit begun in the Lichfield bookstore, continued, with or without the help of his tutor, William Jorden.

1729

OCT. Desidiae vale dixi syrenis istius Cantibus surdam posthac aurem obversurus.

E veteribus Latinis maxime mihi desiderantur Lucretius, Velleius Paterculus Justinus et Graeviana Tullii Epist: Editio.

In October 1729, in the first extant diary, Johnson set himself to serious effort. The date and first sentence are quoted by Boswell, who translates, "I bid farewell to Sloth, being resolved henceforth not to listen to her syren strains." This characteristic resolution, for such it is in effect, is notable as coming soon after Johnson's twentieth birthday and near the end of his first year of college, when stock-taking would be in order.

The rest of the page consists of Johnson's attempt to implement his resolve, beginning, "Of the ancient Latins I greatly wish Lucretius, Velleius Paterculus, Justinus, and Graevius's edition of Tully's Letters." Lucretius's *De rerum natura*, a classic of both poetry and philosophy, is an obvious selection. The choice of Paterculus, author of a history of Rome from the fall of Troy to A.D. 29, suggests that Johnson wished to concentrate on the Augustans, since Paterculus is particularly interesting for his treatment of his own period, the death of Caesar to that of Augustus. In 1735 Johnson recommended Paterculus to his cousin Samuel Ford (*Letters* 3.3). Junianus Justinus, writing after the Silver Age of Latin, a rather minor epitomist of the earlier historian Pompeius Trogus, is unexplained, unless Johnson had a passing interest in the Macedonian monarchy. A folio edition of Justinus (Paris, 1636) was in his library at his death. J. G. Graevius's edition of Cicero's *Letters*, perhaps the best then available, could be had in the editions published in 1676–77 and 1693 in Amsterdam. Graevius was a German scholar with an international reputation, honoured by Louis XIV and William III, who made him Historiographer Royal. Johnson at least bought Cicero's *Letters* and Lucretius before leaving Oxford (Reade, v.223, 217).

OCT. 22. M quod feci Sept. 9 et 12 et 17. et 19 et 22 et 28 et 26.

Die	Hebdom:	Mense	Anno	Nov 21
10	60	240	2880	
30	180	720	8640	
50	300	1200	14400	
60	360	1440	17280	
150	900	3600	N: singulis Hebdomadis 6 Dies	
300	1800	7200	singulis mensibus 4 Hebdomadae	
400	2400	9600	Singulis Annis 12 menses nume-	
600	3600	14400	rantur.	

DECEMB. 1729. S.J. Oxonio rediit.

The next entry, under 22 October, suggests that Johnson even at this age was a far less diligent diarist than Boswell was to become: "Remember what I did on September 9, 12, 17, 19, 22, 28, and 26." Had he made entries on the other days of September on leaves now lost?

On 21 November Johnson tried to prod himself to study by making a table of what he could accomplish if he read regularly ten lines a day (making 60 a week, 240 a month, and 2880 a year, his week consisting, as his note says, of six days, his month of four weeks, and a year of twelve months). Then, realizing that ten lines a day was an absurdly low aim, he calculated his progress with goals from thirty to six hundred lines a day, not bothering, in the last few estimates, to carry out the totals for the year, which would be astronomical. He was to remain at Oxford less than a fortnight longer: his funds had run out.

"Annales" next records Johnson's leaving Oxford in December, and does not mention Oxford again, though his leaving his books there shows that he hoped to return. Both Boswell and Hawkins believed that Johnson returned to Oxford at an unspecified later period to make his total residence there about three years, but Johnson's silence in "Annales" and the evidence of the Pembroke

1731

Mensibus Aestivis S.J. C.F. amisit.

DECEMB. Patre orbatus est.

1731/32

MART 9[no.] S.J. Bosvorthiam petivit.

———————

College Buttery Books make this impossible (Reade, v.153). The Books show normal charges against Johnson of seven to twelve shillings a week from 1 November 1728 to 5 December 1729. The next week there is a smaller charge, and eight later small charges at infrequent intervals prove by their infrequency that he did not return after that date. Names were often carried on the books after men went out of residence, and these scattered charges represent small fines for absence from certain festivals, and quarterly charges.

Almost nothing is known of the next two years of Johnson's life. He returned home, worked in the bookstore, and attempted unsuccessfully to get a position as usher at the Stourbridge School. On 30 October 1731 in his first surviving letter he describes himself as "yet unemploy'd."

"Annales" records the loss by death of two of the important persons in his life: in the summer months his cousin and mentor Cornelius Ford, and in December his father. The burial register of St. Michael's, Lichfield, gives a closer date: "1731, Dec. 7. Buried Mr. Michael Jonson, a Magistrate of the City."

Four months later Johnson finally secured a post as usher at the grammar school of Market Bosworth in Leicestershire. There has long been confusion as to the dates of his stay, but "Annales" settles the matter, showing that he went there on 9 March 1732 (1731 Old Style) and left in July. Hawkins used "Annales," and his dates, therefore, are substantially correct. Boswell saw "Annales" but preferred to use instead an entry from the diary which

1732

JULIO 1732 Bosvorthiam reliquit.

JUL. 18. Libellum hunc in Manus resumsi, comitem cir-
cumlaturus. Totam hanc pagellam scripsi.—

JULII 15. Undecim Aureos deposui quo die quicquid ante
Matris funus (quod serum sit precor) de paternis bonis sperare
licet, 19⁸ scilicet Libras, accepi. Usque adeo mihi mea Fortuna
fingenda est. Interea ne paupertate Vires animi languescant,
ne in flagitia Egestas adigat, cavendum. N: de Viginti Libras⁹
unum prius detraxeram.

8. ∧19∧ ⟨Viginti⟩ ∧⟨octodecem⟩∧   9. MS: Libris

---

has since puzzled scholars, "Julii 16 Bosvortiam pedes petii," not
realizing that this was a second journey and that Johnson had
altered the date.

The diary entries are on the verso of the leaf written at Oxford
in 1729. Perhaps Johnson had made no entries in the meantime
because of discouragement. But in July he writes, "I took up this
little book again, intending to carry it about as a companion. I
wrote all this little page." And at the bottom he wrote, "On this
page I have put July for June." Hawkins saw this and when he
transcribed the passage for 15 July, through *cavendum*, he silently
altered the date to June, though he calls his transcription ver-
batim (p. 21). Boswell missed the point and made it July, which
alters the date of Johnson's visit to Lichfield to receive his share
of his father's estate. It is clear that Johnson wrote the whole
page on 18 July, when a momentary error for June occurred, and
his correction was not meant for the first entry. Neither Hawkins
nor Boswell mentions that Johnson scored through *Viginti* and
wrote "19" before it, for they did not reproduce, since they did
not understand, the last sentence of that day's entry, where Johnson made another slip, writing *Libris* for *Libras*. Two minor
variants in Boswell are unimportant. Hawkins's translation, cor-

JULII 16. Bosvortiam pedes petii.

JULII 17. J. Corbettum, apud B: Dixiam, ad prandium voca-
tus, vidi. Juvenem mihi quondam delectissimum nec quia me
quondam (ni fallor) plurimum amavit. (hac. pag: Jul: pro
Jun: hab:

---

recting his "twenty" to "nineteen" is: "June 15, I laid by eleven
guineas; on which day I received all of my father's effects which
I can hope for till the death of my mother, (which I pray may
be late), that is to say, nineteen pounds; so that I have my fortune
to make, and care must be taken, that in the mean time, the powers
of my mind may not grow languid through poverty, nor want
drive me into wickedness." Boswell's translation is more florid;
he elevates Johnson's simple remark about his mother's death into
"an event which I pray GOD may be very remote" (*Life*, 1.80). The
passage omitted by both biographers is: "Note: of twenty pounds I
had taken out one before." And at this point he must have deleted
Viginti and *octodecim* above that, and inserted "19." He had
perhaps borrowed a pound from his father which he now remembered as a charge on his bequest.

The next day, then, he "went to Bosworth on foot," a distance
of twenty-five miles, and resumed his irksome post as usher. On
the seventeenth, "on being called to dinner at B. Dixie's, I saw
J. Corbet, a youth once very delightful to me, and not because,
if I am right, he then loved me very much." John Corbet was a
younger brother of the Andrew Corbet who had not helped Johnson at Oxford. Their sister had married the Reverend Beaumont
Dixie, rector of Market Bosworth and the brother of Sir Wolstan
Dixie, the patron of the school. Johnson was staying with Sir Wolstan, in whose house, Boswell says, "he officiated as a kind of
domestick chaplain, so far, at least, as to say grace at table, but was
treated with what he represented as intolerable harshness; and,
after suffering for a few months such complicated misery, he relin-
quished a situation which all his life afterwards he recollected with
the strongest aversion" (*Life*, 1.84).

1 7 3 2

JULII

1 7 3 3

JUNII[10] 1mo apud F. Jervis Birminghamiae habitare incepi.
10. ⟨Julii⟩

––––––––––––

The date July 1732 heads a blank space on the next page of
the diary. There was nothing cheerful to record. By the twenty-
seventh he had given up his job and was back in Lichfield writing
to his college friend John Taylor of Ashbourne, at that time an
attorney, that it was like coming out of prison. He had heard
from Corbet, perhaps John, that there was a vacancy at the Ashbourne Grammar School, but he did not obtain the place.

Towards the end of 1732 Johnson accepted an invitation to visit
his old school friend Edmund Hector, now practising as a surgeon
in Birmingham. Hector lodged with Thomas Warren, the book-
seller-publisher of the *Birmingham Journal*, to which Johnson
soon contributed his first series of periodical essays, his first appearance in print except for his Latin translation of Pope's
Messiah made at Oxford. It is impossible to escape the conclusion
that Hector invited him with some such hope in mind, when one
remembers that Hector preserved some of Johnson's boyhood
compositions for about sixty years, when he gave them to Boswell.
No file of the *Journal* is known, and Johnson's first printed essays
therefore are lost.

"Annales" next records Johnson's taking up residence, on 1
June 1733, at the house of F. Jervis in Birmingham, and is the
source of Hawkins's mention of "Jarvis," a name which Boswell
omitted, saying merely that Johnson "hired lodgings in another
part of the town" (*Life*, 1.86). Johnson's future bride, Elizabeth
Jervis Porter, was then living in Birmingham with her first hus-

Mensibus hibernis Iter ad Abisiniam Anglicè reddidi.

1733/34

FEBRUARIO Lichfieldiam me recepi.

AUGUSTI 5to 1734. Conditiones edendi Politiani Poemata emisi.

---

band, Harry Porter, and there is the interesting possibility, which Hawkins suggests, that "F. Jervis" was a relation of hers.

The final entry for 1733 is interesting for its indication of the direction that Johnson's talents were to take: in the winter months he undertook his first book, a translation of Father Lobo's *Voyage historique d'Abissinie*. But indolence plagued him then as later. Hector tried to rouse him from it and urged him to go forward with the translation, saying that the printer depended on the work. Johnson could never resist a humanitarian appeal. He lay in bed, holding Lobo's book in his hand, and dictated to Hector, who later carried the sheets to the press and read almost all of the proof unaided by Johnson.

Johnson returned to Lichfield in February, and the last entry in "Annales" gives further indication of his growing interest in writing. On 5 August 1734 he sent out *Proposals* for publishing an edition of Politian's *Poems*. No copy of the *Proposals* has been traced; Hawkins and Boswell state that the project met with insufficient encouragement and was abandoned. Johnson retained, however, one benefit from the enterprise, a copy of Politian's *Works* which a friend of his, Robert Boyse, borrowed for his use on 15 June 1734 from the library of Pembroke College. This "very old and curious edition" was noted by Hawkins (p. 445) as being among Johnson's books at the time of his death, having been "used as his own for upwards of fifty years."

At about the time that Johnson issued his *Proposals* for Politian, Harry Porter died. Anna Seward, most unreliable of anecdotists, says that Johnson attended his sickbed with great assiduity. Be

1 7 3 4

Libellum hunc iterum in Manus resumsi.

Res[11] pauperi inter alienos agenti utiles inveni; fila serica et fibulas eiusdem cum vestibus coloris, fila[1] qualibus αἱ κνημίδες tran[a]ntur cum acubus.

---

that as it may, Johnson's courtship ensued, and he married the widow on 9 July following. It is tempting to imagine that the "Annales," which Johnson carefully drew up on 10 November 1734, was a review of his life induced by the possibility of this forthcoming marriage. He was twenty-five, he had received five guineas for his first book, he had published a series of periodical essays, and authorship must have seemed a possibility of livelihood. A fortnight later he wrote from Birmingham to Cave, publisher of the *Gentleman's Magazine* in London, offering "sometimes to fill a column" with "poems, inscriptions, &c. never printed before . . . likewise short literary dissertations in Latin or English, critical remarks on authours ancient or modern, forgotten poems that deserve revival, or loose pieces . . . worth preserving" (*Life*, 1.91). Cave's reply is not known; in any case, Johnson's association with the magazine did not begin till March 1738.

Sometime in 1734 Johnson "took this diary in hand again," only to note down a revealing remark about a poor man self-consciously coming among well-to-do strangers, which anticipates his famous line, "Slow rises worth, by poverty depress'd": "For a poor man going among strangers, I have found useful things to be silk thread and pins of the same colour as one's clothes (silk thread, that is, of the kind used for knitting stockings.)" The young bachelor is recording ways of disguising torn clothes. Why he should have used Greek for "stockings" is doubtful, unless momentarily he had forgotten the Latin word.

Euripidis Medea continet versus	1419
Phoenissae . . .	1754
Georgicorum Lib. 1.	514
Lib. 2.	542
Lib. 3	566
Lib. 4	566
Aeneidos Liber 1	760
2	804
3	718
4	705
5	871
6	901
Horatii Ars Poetica	476
Ovidii Met. 1	779
2	876
15	879
Theocriti Idyllium 1	152
Hiero	109
Theocriti Laus Ptolemaei . . .	137
Helenae Epithal. . .	58
Juvenalis Sat. 10	366

After a blank page, the next entries follow without a date. Boswell joined them with those of 1729, but it is hardly likely that these refer to that year. Johnson is again trying to introduce some orderliness into his reading and shows his usual fascination with arithmetic. He who later could laugh at those who read books through is now trying to do just that, probably to fill in some gaps in his education, though it is not to be inferred that he is reading Virgil, Ovid, and Juvenal for the first time.

A modern reader will find, like Johnson, that Euripides's *Medea* contains 1419 verses, but *The Phoenician Maidens* in a modern edition has 1766 or 1779, not 1754 (the line-division of the choruses varies). This may be a clue to the edition Johnson used, as

1736

FRIDAY, AUGUST 27TH. 10 AT NIGHT. This day I have trifled
away, except that I have attended the school in the morning.
I read to night in Rogers's sermons. To night I began the breakfast law anew.

———————————————— —

with the *Aeneid*, where, as compared with 756 lines in modern
texts, Johnson's volume had 760 in Book I. This shows that it contained the introductory lines written by Virgil but removed by
his literary executor:

> Ille ego, qui quondam gracili modulatus avena
> carmen, et egressus silvis vicina coegi
> ut quamvis avido parerent arva colono,
> gratum opus agricolis; at nunc horrentia Martis

"I am he who once tuned my song on a slender reed, then, leaving
the woodland, constrained the neighbouring fields to serve the hus-
bandmen, however grasping—a work welcome to farmers: but now
of Mars' bristling" (Fairclough). One finds another discrepancy
in Book II of Ovid's *Metamorphoses*, where the Loeb edition has
875 lines, listing no variants.

The list is particularly interesting as showing Johnson trying
to add to his rather limited acquaintance with the Greek poets,
though he had read in Homer and Euripides at Oxford (*Life*,
1.70). And remembering his later antipathy to pastorals, particularly of the eighteenth-century sort, one wonders what his reaction
was to one of the Greek fathers of the pastoral, in one of his most
typical idyls, "Thyrsis." The second listed is *Idyllium XVI*,
"The Charites," in which the author "bewails the indifference
of a money-loving age, and asks for the patronage of Hiero, then
general-in-chief, afterwards king, of Syracuse" (J. M. Edmonds).

The first diary ends with these entries: "The Panegyric of
Ptolemy," that is, of Ptolemy II, Philadelphus, who reigned 285–
247 B.C.; "The Epithalamy of Helen" on her marriage to Mene-
laus; and the satire which Johnson imitated in 1749 for *The
Vanity of Human Wishes*.

In May 1735 Johnson sent for his library of one hundred and

SEPT. 7TH, 1736. I have this day entered upon my 28th year. Mayest thou, O God, enable me for Jesus Christ's sake, to spend this in such a manner that I may receive comfort from it at the hour of death, and in the day of judgment. Amen.

I intend to-morrow to review the rules I have at any time laid down, in order to practice them.

---

fifteen books from Oxford, where he had left them for over five years, and began to formulate plans for an academy of his own, which would be possible with part of the £600 which his bride-to-be possessed. Towards the end of the month he took a temporary job preparing a boy for Oxford, and on 9 July he was married. Plans for the academy were put aside while he tried to obtain the headmastership of the school at Solihull, near Birmingham, but that failed. Then he rented a large house at Edial, near Lichfield, and towards the end of the year or early in 1736 opened his school there, with David and George Garrick and a few others as pupils. Advertisements in the *Gentleman's Magazine* for June and July 1736 brought little result.

The next diary entry was printed by Hawkins (p. 163) as "selected from the 'Annales,'" but as it is part of an English diary and does not have the autobiographical character of the Latin manuscript called "Annales" by Johnson, it must not have been part of that manuscript. It is now lost. Hawkins gave it a bracketed year, 1734, which is certainly wrong, since in that month Johnson was confidently going ahead with his Politian and is not known to have had even a temporary teaching position. We have therefore transferred it conjecturally to 1736 (when 27 August fell on Friday), when the school at Edial was operating, and immediately before the next entry printed by Hawkins, dated by Johnson in that year. Hill suggests that Rogers's sermons were *Sermons at Boyle's Lectures*, 1727, by the Reverend John Rogers, D.D. The "breakfast law" has not been explained.

The birthday prayer and comment are known only as printed by Hawkins. It was to become Johnson's custom on that day to

1 7 3 8

A PRAYER ON MY BIRTH-DAY.

SEPT. 7TH 1738. O God the Creatour and preserver of all Mankind, Father of all mercies, I thine unworthy servant do give thee most humble thanks, for all thy goodness and lovingkindness to me. I bless Thee for my Creation, Preservation

---

review his life and form new resolutions (usually to rise early and avoid sloth) or renew old ones. None had permanent effect.

During these months at Edial, Johnson began his tragedy *Irene*, and saw the school decline until about February 1737, when it closed. On 2 March Johnson and David Garrick started for London, "riding and tying," making one horse do and leaving it tied to a post while the walker caught up. Mrs. Johnson stayed in Lichfield till something permanent should develop. Nothing did. Johnson retired to Greenwich after a time to try to finish *Irene*, and in July wrote Cave again, this time proposing to translate Father Paul Sarpi's *History of the Council of Trent* from the Italian. Towards the end of the summer he returned to Lichfield, finished *Irene*, and with it in his pocket and his wife by his side, went back to London. Fleetwood of Drury Lane rejected *Irene*, and Johnson approached Cave again, with a Latin epigram in his praise. Cave printed this in the *Gentleman's Magazine*, and when soon thereafter Johnson showed him the manuscript of *London*, Cave printed this in separate form. Dodsley published the poem on 13 May 1738. Finally the translation of Sarpi was agreed on and in August Johnson had started it. At the same time he was editing Guthrie's *Parliamentary Debates* for the *Gentleman's Magazine*; soon he was subeditor of the magazine itself.

For the next fifteen years there are no extant diaries except for some fragments mingled with prayers and meditations in the Pembroke manuscripts and printed, for the most part, by Strahan.

Johnson begins the prayer on his twenty-ninth birthday with the address from the Prayer for all Conditions of Men, and continues by paraphrasing the first two sentences of the General

and Redemption, for the Knowledge of thy Son Jesus Christ,
for the means of Grace, and the Hope of Glory. In the days
of Childhood and Youth, in the midst of weakness, blindness,
and danger, Thou hast protected me; amidst Afflictions of
Mind, Body, and Estate thou hast supported me; and amidst
vanity and Wickedness thou hast spared me. Grant, O merciful Father, that I may have a lively sense of thy mercies. Create
in me a contrite Heart, that I may worthily lament my Sins,[2]
acknowledge my wickedness, and obtain Remission and forgiveness through the Satisfaction of Jesus Christ, And O
Lord, enable me by thy Grace to use all diligence in redeem-
ing the time which I have spent in Sloth, Vanity, and wickedness; to make use of thy Gifts to the honour of thy Name; to
lead a new life in thy Faith, Fear, and Love; and finally to
obtain everlasting Life. Grant this, Almighty Lord, for the
merits and through the mediation of our most holy and blessed
Saviour, Jesus Christ, to whom with Thee and the Holy
Ghost, three Persons and one God be all honour and Glory
World without end. Amen.

This is the first solemn prayer of which I have a copy.
Whether I composed any before this, I question.

2. ⟨and⟩ acknowledge

———————————

Thanksgiving, from the *Book of Common Prayer*. He endorsed
the manuscript: "Prayer on Birth-day 1738 tr. Jul [June?] 26.
1768." To this Strahan added, probably from the missing parchment book into which Johnson transcribed several prayers in
June 1768: "This is the first solemn prayer of which I have a copy.
Whether I composed any before this, I question." Since Johnson's
only earlier surviving prayer consists of a single sentence, one may
guess that in 1768 he had forgotten it, or perhaps it was too short
to qualify as "solemn."

In the next six years Johnson slowly established himself as a
writer. He made one last attempt to procure the headmastership
of a school, Appleby, near Market Bosworth, in the summer of

1 7 4 3 ?

Norris the staymaker—fair Esther—w. the cat—Children
—Inspection of the hand—stays returned—Lodging—guinea
at the stairs—Esther died—orderd to want nothing—house
broken up—advertisement—Eldest son—quarrel.
Herne 7. shillings—Haysman—arrested.

1739, but failed from the lack of a degree. He had left Tetty in
London, and took advantage of his being near his old home to
visit his mother, his stepdaughter Lucy Porter, and other friends
in Lichfield, and then went on to Ashbourne, where his school-
friend John Taylor was about to give up practice as an attorney to
enter the church. Here or nearby he met many people who in time
became good friends, notably Miss Hill Boothby, a woman a year
his senior blessed with both brains and charm as is shown in her
letters to him in the ensuing years. On his return to Lichfield he
arranged a mortgage on his mother's house, and in February 1740
sent his share, twenty pounds, to his ailing wife in London. By
April or earlier he was back with her, and did not return to
Lichfield for twenty-two years.

He resumed work with Cave on the *Gentleman's Magazine*,
contributing in quick succession his "little lives" of Admiral
Blake, Drake, and Barretier in the same year, and in 1741 beginning to write the *Parliamentary Debates*, which he had formerly
merely edited. In the next year the *Debates* continued, and he
issued the *Proposals* for the Harleian Catalogue, which itself appeared in five volumes during the next two years. More miscellaneous contributions to the *Gentleman's Magazine*, the *Harleian
Miscellany*, the *Life of Savage*, and extensive contributions to Dr.
James's *Medicinal Dictionary* kept him busy through 1744. His
private life is obscure during this period, quite probably because
his poverty and his aging wife's querulous disposition did not lead
him to invite friends to his house.

Richard Norris, a staymaker in Exeter Street, was Johnson's first
landlord in London, in 1737. His wife Esther died in October

1744/45

PRAYER ON NEWYEAR'S DAY.

JAN. 1. 1744/5. Almighty and everlasting God, in whose hands are life and death, by whose will all things were created, and by whose providence they are sustained, I return thee thanks that Thou hast given me life, and that thou hast continued it to this time, that thou hast hitherto forborn to snatch me away in the midst of Sin and Folly, and[3] hast permitted me still to enjoy the means of Grace, and vouchsafed[4] to call me yet again to Repentance. Grant, O merciful Lord,[4] that thy Call may not[4] be vain, that my Life may not be continued to encrease my Guilt, and that thy gracious Forbearance may not harden my heart in wickedness. Let me remember, O my

3. ⟨but⟩ hast: ∧and∧ hast   4. and ∧vouchsafed∧ . . . merciful ∧Lord∧ . . . may ∧not∧ be

---

1743, and this memorandum, apparently written some years later, includes Johnson's reminiscences of that period. The cryptic entries about the cat and the children may refer to Esther's playing with them. "Inspection of the hand" probably refers to palmistry, which Johnson defines as "the cheat of foretelling fortune by the lines of the palm," perhaps also part of the children's play. "Stays returned" sounds like a customer's complaint of poor workmanship. A guinea at the stairs may refer to payment in advance for lodgings. And we may expand the next entries thus: at Esther's death her funeral was elaborate, the household was broken up, and the furnishings advertised for sale, which caused a quarrel between Norris and his eldest son.

Mrs. Phoebe Herne (1709–81) was a cousin of Johnson's. He was supporting her lunatic daughter in 1777, which may be a clue to the date of these jottings. Nothing is known of Haysman or the arrest.

Johnson's first extant New Year's Day prayer is that of 1745.

In the spring of this year appeared Johnson's *Observations on*

God that as Days and Years pass over me, I approach nearer to the Grave where there is no repentance, and grant that by the assistance of thy Holy Spirit, I may so pass through this Life, that I may obtain Life everlasting for the sake of our Lord Jesus Christ. Amen.

1747/48

JAN. 1. 1747/8. Almighty and most merciful Father, who hast not yet suffered me to fall into the Grave, grant that I may so remember my past Life, as to repent of the days and years which I have spent in forgetfulness of thy mercy and neglect of my own Salvation, and so use the time which thou shalt yet allow me, as that I may become every day more diligent in the[5] duties which in thy Providence shall be assigned me, and that when at last I shall be called to Judgement I may be received as a good and faithful servant into everlasting happiness, for the sake of Jesus Christ our Lord. Amen.

5. MS: thy ... which ∧in∧ ... ∧and∧ that

Macbeth and his *Proposals* for a new edition of Shakespeare; the *Observations* were well received but the edition of Shakespeare was stopped by an objection by the publisher Tonson, who claimed perpetual copyright. Johnson had virtually ceased work on the *Magazine* and perhaps was beginning to plan the *Dictionary*. No publication of his for 1746 is known, but by June of that year negotiations with the publishers of the *Dictionary* were well advanced. In the next year the *Plan* of the *Dictionary*, addressed to Lord Chesterfield, appeared, and Johnson also furnished a *Prologue* for the opening of the Drury Lane Theatre under Garrick's management.

The next New Year's prayer, for 1748, is marked by Strahan, "Transcribed in the Parchment Book," but as before exists only in the Pembroke original. This year, with work on the *Dictionary*

1749/50

JAN. 1. 1749/50 AFTER 3 IN THE MORNING. Almighty
GOD, by whose will I was created, and by whose Providence
I have been sustained, by whose mercy I have been called
to the knowledge of my Redeemer, and by whose Grace whatever I have thought or acted acceptable to thee has been
inspired and directed, grant, O LORD, that in reviewing my
past life, I may[6] recollect thy mercies to my preservation[7] in
whatever state[8] thou preparest for me, that in affliction I may
remember how often I have been succoured, and in Prosperity
may know and confess from whose hand the blessing is received. Let me O LORD so remember my sins, that I may abolish
them by true repentance, and so improve the Year to which
thou hast graciously extended my life and all the Years which
thou shalt yet allow me, that I may hourly become purer in

6. may ⟨improve⟩   7. my ⟨support and comfort⟩ ∧preservation∧   8. whatever
∧state∧

---

continuing, Johnson prepared for Dodsley's two-volume work on
education, *The Preceptor*, a preface and his "Vision of Theodore,
the Hermit of Teneriffe," which Percy heard Johnson say was the
best thing he ever wrote. *The Vanity of Human Wishes* followed
in 1749, and also after years of delay the production and publication of his tragedy *Irene*, which brought him a substantial sum
of money but ended his career as a playwright. This year saw as
well Johnson's founding of the Ivy Lane Club, first of several
such in his life, where, Tuesday evenings at the King's Head, "a
famous beef-steak house . . . he constantly resorted, and, with a
disposition to please and be pleased, would pass those hours in
a free and unrestrained interchange of sentiments, which otherwise had been spent at home in painful reflection" (Hawkins,
p. 219).
    The New Year's prayer for 1750, written "after 3 in the morn-
ing," shows Johnson's nocturnal habit, so well known to his friends
in later days.

thy sight[9] so that I may live in thy fear, and dye in thy favour, and find mercy at the last day for the sake of JESUS CHRIST. Amen.

PRAYER ON THE RAMBLER.

Almighty God, the giver of all good things, without whose help all Labour is[1] ineffectual, and without whose grace all wisdom is folly, grant, I beseech Thee, that in this my undertaking thy Holy Spirit may not be witheld from me, but that I may promote thy glory, and the Salvation both of myself and others,—Grant this O Lord for the sake of Jesus Christ. Amen.[2] Lord bless me. So be it.

1750/51

JAN. 1. 1750/51. O Eternal God, who regardest all thy works with mercy, look upon my wants,[3] my miseries, and my

9. sight ⟨and find⟩   1. is ⟨without⟩   2. Amen. ‸Lord bless me   so be it‸
3. wants ⟨and⟩

The prayer on the *Rambler* must have been written shortly before 20 March 1750, when the first number of the periodical appeared. It is typical of the seriousness of Johnson's approach to a major new project and is paralleled later by a prayer before the study of law (26 September 1765) and one on engaging in politics with Hamilton (November 1765). Two years later, in the last number issued, Johnson was able to look back on the *Rambler* with satisfaction: "The essays professedly serious, if I have been able to execute my own intentions, will be found exactly conformable to the precepts of Christianity, without any accommodation to the licentiousness and levity of the present age. I therefore look back on this part of my work with pleasure, which no blame or praise of man shall diminish or augment."

During 1750, while the *Rambler* was under way, Johnson also wrote the *Prologue* for Milton's *Comus* and engaged in the Lauder controversy about the alleged plagiarisms in Milton.

The New Year's prayer for 1751, one of his shortest and simplest,

sins, grant that I may amend my life, and may find mercy both in this world and in the world to come by the help of thy Holy Spirit, for the sake of Jesus Christ. Amen.

1752

PRAYERS COMPOSED BY ME ON THE DEATH OF MY
WIFE, AND REPOSITED AMONG HER MEMORIALS,
MAY 8, 1752. Deus exaudi.—Heu!

APRIL 24, 1752. Almighty and most merciful Father, who lovest those whom Thou punishest, and turnest away thy anger from the penitent, look down with pity upon my sorrows, and grant that the affliction which it has pleased Thee

---

sounds more gloomy than that of the previous year. During the next months, while continuing with the *Rambler* and the *Dictionary*, Johnson wrote the life of Cheynel and contributed a dedication to his friend Charlotte Lennox's novel, *The Female Quixote*.

Three days after the last number of the *Rambler*, Mrs. Johnson died, on 17 March 1752, O.S. This was a bitter blow. There is ample evidence that their life together was not always smooth, but of Johnson's devotion to her there is no doubt. And after Tetty's death something like remorse repeatedly appears in the annual prayers with which he remembered the day of her death. It is perhaps only a feeling that with more effort, more forbearance, more patience with her infirmities, of which drink was one and opium another, he might have made their marriage more serene.

None of the prayers for this year are at Pembroke and those for April and May are not in Strahan's first edition. That for 26 April he obtained from Frank Barber for the third edition in 1796, and the others were first printed in the second edition, perhaps from the same source. Now Frank was not in the habit

to bring upon me, may awaken my conscience, enforce my
resolutions of a better life, and impress upon me such conviction of thy power and goodness, that I may place in Thee my
only felicity, and endeavour to please Thee in all my thoughts,
words, and actions. Grant, O Lord, that I may not languish in
fruitless and unavailing sorrow, but that I may consider from
whose hand all good and evil is received, and may remember
that I am punished for my sins, and hope for comfort only by
repentance. Grant, O merciful God, that by the assistance of
thy Holy Spirit I may repent, and be comforted, obtain that
peace which the world cannot give, pass the residue of my life
in humble resignation and cheerful obedience; and when it
shall please Thee to call me from this mortal state, resign myself into thy hands with faith and confidence, and finally obtain mercy and everlasting happiness, for the sake of Jesus
Christ our Lord. Amen.

APRIL 25, 1752. O Lord, our heavenly Father, almighty and
most merciful God, in whose hands are life and death, who
givest and takest away, castest down and raisest up, look with
mercy on the affliction of thy unworthy servant, turn away
thine anger from me, and speak peace to my troubled soul.
Grant me the assistance and comfort of thy Holy Spirit, that

---

of giving away such properties, and may have retained possession
of the manuscripts, merely allowing Strahan to copy them. In that
case the manuscripts may still exist, since Frank destroyed nothing, as far as is known.

"Hear, O Lord—Alas!" On 24 April, over five weeks after Tetty's
death, Johnson was still in anguish, but after the outcry which
heads this prayer, he tries, characteristically, to turn from "unavailing sorrow" to "resolutions of a better life."

Next day, in the second prayer, he is more specific about these
resolutions, made "when she lay dead before me," and eight years

I may remember with thankfulness the blessings so long enjoyed by me in the society of my departed wife; make me so
to think on her precepts and example, that I may imitate whatever was in her life acceptable in thy sight, and avoid all by
which she offended Thee. Forgive me, O merciful Lord, all
my sins, and enable me to begin and perfect that reformation
which I promised her, and to persevere in that resolution,
which she implored Thee to continue, in the purposes which
I recorded in thy sight, when she lay dead before me, in obedience to thy laws, and faith in thy word. And now, O Lord,
release me from my sorrow, fill me with just hopes, true faith,
and holy consolations, and enable me to do my duty in that
state of life to which Thou hast been pleased to call me, without disturbance from fruitless grief, or tumultuous imaginations; that in all my thoughts, words, and actions, I may glorify
thy Holy Name, and finally obtain, what I hope Thou hast
granted to thy departed servant, everlasting joy and felicity,
through our Lord Jesus Christ. Amen.

APRIL 2 6, 1 7 5 2, BEING AFTER 1 2 AT NIGHT OF THE 2 5 TH.
O Lord, Governor of Heaven and Earth, in whose hands are
embodied and departed spirits, if thou hast ordained the souls
of the dead to minister to the living, and appointed my departed wife to have care of me, grant that I may enjoy the
good effects of her attention and ministration, whether exer-
cised by appearance, impulses, dreams, or in any other manner
agreeable to thy government; forgive my presumption, enlighten my ignorance, and however meaner agents are em-

---

later (18 September 1760), he shows that he kept a copy of them:
"To consult the resolves on Tetty's coffin."

The third prayer is interesting for Johnson's tentative belief
in the appearance of spirits. Although many in his age considered
this to be superstition, he maintained that spirits had appeared

ployed, grant me the blessed influences of thy Holy Spirit, through Jesus Christ our Lord. Amen.

MAY 6, 1752. O Lord, our heavenly Father, without whom all purposes are frustrate, all efforts are vain, grant me the assistance of thy Holy Spirit, that I may not sorrow as one without hope, but may now return to the duties of my present state with humble confidence in thy protection, and so govern my thoughts and actions, that neither business may withdraw my mind from Thee, nor idleness lay me open to vain imaginations; that neither praise may fill me with pride, nor censure with discontent; but that in the changes of this life, I may fix my heart upon the reward which Thou hast promised to them that serve Thee, and that whatever things are true, whatever things are honest, whatever things are just, whatever are pure, whatever are lovely, whatever are of good report, wherein there is virtue, wherein there is praise, I may think upon and do, and obtain mercy and everlasting happiness. Grant this, O Lord, for the sake of Jesus Christ. Amen.

Our Father, &c.—The grace, &c.

MAY 6. I used this service, written April 24, 25, May 6, as preparatory to my return to life to-morrow.

Μακάριοι οἱ νεκροὶ οἱ ἐν κυρίῳ ἀποθνῄσκοντες ἀπάρτι

Apoc. xiv. 13.

_____

in the past, as in the Bible, and might again. He was nevertheless careful of possible impiety, as in this prayer, and of fraud, as with the Cock Lane ghost later.

On 6 May he was ready to give up his period of heavy mourning and "return to life to-morrow." The last part of the prayer proper is a paraphrase of the famous sentence in Philippians iv. 8: "Finally brethren, whatsoever things are true, whatsoever things are honest, whatsoever things are just, whatsoever things are pure, whatsoever things are lovely, whatsoever things are of good report; if there be any virtue and if there be any praise, think on these

BEFORE ANY NEW STUDY.

NOVEMBER. Almighty God, in whose hands are all the powers of man; who givest understanding, and takest it away; who, as it seemeth good unto Thee, enlightenest the thoughts of the simple, and darkenest the meditations of the wise, be present with me in my studies and enquiries.

Grant, O Lord, that I may not lavish away the life which Thou hast given me on useless trifles, nor waste it in vain searches after things which thou hast hidden from me.

Enable me, by thy Holy Spirit, so to shun sloth and negligence, that every day may discharge part of the task which Thou hast allotted me; and so further with thy help that labour which, without thy help, must be ineffectual, that I may obtain, in all my undertakings, such success as will most promote thy glory, and the salvation of my own soul, for the sake of Jesus Christ. Amen.

---

things." "Our Father, &c." and "The grace, &c." are Johnson's shorthand for the Lord's Prayer and the last prayer of Morning and Evening Prayer ("The grace of our Lord Jesus Christ, and the love of God, and the fellowship of the Holy Ghost, be with us all evermore"). And the Greek line from Revelation is: "Blessed are the dead which die in the Lord from henceforth."

In the next six months no publications of Johnson are known. It may be assumed that he continued with the *Dictionary*. In November Hawkesworth's *Adventurer*, modelled on the *Rambler*, began to appear. After the following March Johnson contributed to it often, but his prayer "Before any new Study," can hardly refer to the *Adventurer*, for which study was not required.

On 19 November Johnson repeats a theme already becoming familiar: to avoid idleness. One must emphasize over and over that Johnson's publications were many and important, even at this period of his career. Moreover, he was adding to his learning as always, erratically but solidly. He is thinking not of these things,

AFTER TIME NEGLIGENTLY AND
UNPROFITABLY SPENT.

NOVEMBER 19. O Lord, in whose hands are life and death,
by whose power I am sustained, and by whose mercy I am
spared, look down upon me with pity. Forgive me, that I have
this day neglected the duty which thou hast assigned to it,
and suffered the hours, of which I must give account, to pass
away without any endeavour to accomplish thy will, or to promote my own salvation. Make me to remember, O God, that
every day is thy gift, and ought to be used according to thy
command. Grant me, therefore, so to repent of my negligence,
that I may obtain mercy from Thee, and pass the time which
Thou shalt yet allow me, in diligent performance of thy commands, through Jesus Christ. Amen.

1753

JAN. 1, 1753, N.S. which I shall use for the future.
    Almighty God who hast continued my life to this day grant
that by the assistance of thy holy spirit I may improve the time
which thou shalt grant me to my eternal salvation. Make me
to remember to thy glory thy judgements & thy mercies. Make
[me] so to consider the loss of my wife whom thou hast taken
from me that it may dispose me by thy grace to lead the residue

----

but of the hours or days in which he does nothing significant.
Partly this is religious: he must account to God for talents not
employed to their full. But partly also it is obsessive.
    The New Year's prayer for 1753 was copied by Boswell at John-
son's house in Bolt Court, Fleet Street, on 5 May 1776, from the
extensive journal which Johnson burned a few days before his
death. These entries are now printed in full for the first time.
Boswell printed this prayer in the *Life*, 1.251, as far as "for Jesus
Christ's sake. Amen," omitting the rest. But the rest is particularly

of my life in thy fear. Grant this O Lord for Jesus Christ's sake.
Amen.

Our Father &c.
I hope from this day to keep the resolutions made at my
Wife's death
To rise early
To lose no time
To keep a Journal.

MARCH 28, 1753. I kept this day as the anniversary of my
Tetty's death with prayer & tears in the morning. In the evening I prayed for her conditionally if it were lawful.

APR. 3, 1753. I began the 2ᵈ vol of my Dictionary, room being left in the first for Preface, Grammar & History none of
them yet begun.

O God who hast hitherto supported me enable me to proceed in this labour & in the Whole task of my present state
that when I shall render up at the last day an account of the
talent committed to me I may receive pardon for the sake of
Jesus Christ. Amen.

———————

interesting since it gives the resolutions already referred to, which
Johnson made over Tetty's coffin. The New Style calendar, which
Johnson now follows, had been adopted the previous September
by Great Britain.

In the prayer on the first anniversary of Tetty's death, Johnson
voiced for the first time his uncertainty as to the propriety of
prayers for the dead, reflecting the tentative position of the English
Church on the subject: he wishes to pray for Tetty, if it is lawful.

The prayer on beginning the second volume of the *Dictionary*
shows with what speed Johnson completed that immense work.
He had already arranged the quotations under the words but had
still to revise and correct definitions and read proofs. The whole
was published almost exactly two years later, on 15 April 1755.

PRAYER ON EASTER DAY.

AP. 22. 1753. O Lord, who givest the grace of Repentance, and hearest the prayers of the penitent, grant that by true contrition I may obtain forgiveness of all the Sins committed and of all duties neglected in my union with the Wife whom thou hast taken from me, for the neglect of joint devotion,[4] patient exhortation, and mild instruction. And O Lord, who canst change evil to good, grant that the loss of my Wife may so mortify all inordinate affections in me that I may henceforth[5] please thee by holiness of Life.

And, O Lord, so far as it may be lawful for me I commend to thy fatherly goodness the soul of my departed wife, beseeching thee to grant her whatever is best in her present state, and finally to receive her to eternal Happiness.

All this I beg for Jesus Christs sake, whose death I am now about to commemorate, to whom &c. Amen.

This I repeated sometimes at Church.

4. for the ⟨sin of [undeciphered word] and for⟩ neglect of joint devotion, ⟨and⟩
5. may ∧henceforth∧

Again he is thinking of his talents in religious terms, as he had with the *Rambler*.

The next entry, 22 April, Easter Sunday, was written early in the morning before going to bed, perhaps about 1:00 A.M., since Johnson proposes to take the sacrament "in the morning," and on Monday says he received the sacrament "yesterday." Boswell did not print this, though he transcribed it, for the evident reason that he wished to create a picture of Johnson's marriage opposite from Hawkins's "dark uncharitable" interpretation of Johnson's relationship to Tetty. And Johnson's seeking a second wife less than thirteen months after Tetty's death Boswell apparently felt incompatible with his picture, though it could as well be argued that Johnson wanted a second marriage because his first was successful.

APRIL 22. 1753. As I purpose to try on Monday to seek a new wife without any derogation from dear Tetty's memory I purpose at sacrament in the morning to take my leave of Tetty in a solemn commendation of her soul to God.

APR 23. EASTER MONDAY. Yesterday as I purposed I went to Bromley where dear Tetty lies buried & received the sacrament, first praying before I went to the altar according to the prayer precomposed for Tetty and a prayer which I made against unchastity, idleness, & neglect of publick worship. I made it during sermon which I could not perfectly hear. I repeated mentally[6] the commendation of her with the utmost

6. Boswell's transcript: "mentaly ... l'arme a loeil"

The prayer for Easter Day, then, was composed as Johnson's farewell to Tetty, and used at the church at Bromley, Kent, where she was buried, to which Johnson made a special visit for this purpose, as the next entry shows. This prayer was printed by Strahan and Boswell, but without its context is much less meaningful.

The entry for Easter Monday Boswell omits also, though he had transcribed it. The prayer just printed looks like an amalgam of the two prayers Johnson refers to, since the first part mentions unchastity ("inordinate affections") and the second commends Tetty to divine mercy. It is not surprising that he should have commended her "tearfully," or that at home in the evening, his tears flowed. The sentence in the prayer for the Church Militant (in the Communion Service) where the dead are mentioned is: "And we also bless thy holy Name for all thy servants departed this life in thy faith and fear; beseeching thee to give us grace so to follow their good examples, that with them we may be partakers of thy heavenly kingdom."

The woman Johnson was considering as a second wife remains a mystery. The Hydes have canvassed the matter thoroughly in *Dr. Johnson's Second Wife* (privately printed, Princeton, 1953).

fervour larme à l'oeil before the reception of each element at the altar. I repeated it again in the pew, in the garden before dinner, in the garden before departure, at home at night. I hope I did not sin. Fluunt lacrymae. I likewise ardently applied to her the prayer for the Church militant where the dead are mentioned and commended her again to Eternal Mercy, as in coming out I approached her grave. During the whole service I was never once distracted by any thoughts of any other woman or with my design of a new wife which freedom of mind I remembered with gladness in the Garden. God guide me.

APR 29. 1753. I know not whether I do not too much indulge the vain longings of affection; but I hope they intenerate my heart & that when I die like my Tetty this affection will be

---

The most probable candidate is Hill Boothby, whom he had known and affectionately admired for thirteen years. None of his letters to her of this year survive, but in those two or three years later occur expressions which show deep emotion: "Dear Angel, do not forget me. My heart is full of tenderness," "I love you and honour you, and am very unwilling to lose you," "none but you on whom my heart reposes." But on 12 March 1753 Miss Boothby's close friend, Mrs. Fitzherbert, had died, and Miss Boothby fulfilled her promise of assuming management of the widower's household and his six children. It seems possible that in the six weeks since Mrs. Fitzherbert's death these arrangements had not been completed, or that Johnson had not heard of them. And if shortly thereafter he did, it would account for the fact that he never married her or mentioned the subject to anyone. It might also account for the fact that none of his letters to her of this year survive.

The entry for 29 April was printed by Boswell, but he altered the date to 23 April. The implications of the prayer correctly dated and following the entries about a second wife are quite

acknowledged in a happy interview & that in the meantime I
am incited by it to piety. I will however not deviate too much
from common & received methods of devotion.

1753? I do not remember that since I left Oxford I ever rose
early by mere choice, but once or twice at Edial, and two or
three times for the *Rambler*.

1754

Fl. Lacr.

MARCH 28. 1754. IN THE MORNING. O God who on this
day wert pleased to take from me my dear Wife, sanctify to me
my sorrows and reflections. Grant that I may renew and practise the resolutions which I made when thy afflicting hand

---

different. As Hill notes, "It was, no doubt, in his conditional
prayers for his wife that he deviated from 'common and received
methods of devotion.'"

The next brief undated entry, printed by Boswell, was "a note
in one of his little paper-books, (containing words arranged for
his Dictionary,) written, I suppose, about 1753" (*Life*, II.143).
The little book is not now known, but must have been, like some
others used by Johnson, stitched together by him from loose leaves.
Boswell's assumption that the date is about 1753 implies that the
words in the book are found in the second volume of the *Dictionary*, begun this spring. Johnson told his friend Dr. Maxwell that
Burton's *Anatomy of Melancholy* "was the only book that ever
took him out of bed two hours sooner than he wished to rise"
(*Life*, II.121).

During the rest of the year Johnson wrote some nineteen essays
for the *Adventurer*, the dedication of Charlotte Lennox's *Shake-
spear Illustrated*, and pressed ahead with the *Dictionary*. On the
next anniversary of Tetty's death, again in tears, he wrote prayers
both in the morning and evening. His resolutions were perhaps

was upon me. Let the remembrance of thy Judgements by which my wife is taken away[7] awaken me to repentance, and the sense of thy mercy by which I am spared, strengthen my hope and confidence in Thee, that by the assistance and comfort of thy holy spirit I may so pass through things temporal as finally to gain everlasting happiness, and to pass by a holy and happy death, into the joy[8] which thou hast prepared for those that love thee.

Grant this, O Lord, for the sake of Jesus Christ. Amen.

The melancholy of this day hung long upon me.

Of the resolutions made this day, I, in some measure kept that of breaking from indolence.

MARCH 28. 1754 AT NIGHT. [9]Almighty God vouchsafe to sanctify unto me the reflections and resolutions of this day, let not my sorrow be unprofitable; let not my resolutions be vain. Grant that my grief may produce true repentance,[1] so that I may live to please thee, and when the time shall come that I must dye like her whom Thou hast taken from me, grant me eternal happiness in thy presence, through Jesus Christ our Lord. Amen.

7. ₍by which my wife is taken away₎ 8. ⟨thy⟩ ₍the joy₎ 9. ⟨Almighty God by whose grace I have this day endeavoured⟩ 1. repentance, ⟨and⟩

---

the same ones which he had made at the time of Tetty's death.

In November and December 1754 Lord Chesterfield's two puffs for the *Dictionary* appeared in the *World*, and brought forth Johnson's famous letter, in which he characterized a patron as "one who looks with unconcern on a Man struggling for Life in the water and when he has reached ground encumbers him with help." Johnson's friends had already put in motion a plan which would please him more than Chesterfield's praise, and on 20 March 1755 Oxford conferred on him the degree of Master of Arts. Next month the *Dictionary* was published, with the degree after his name on the title page.

1755

The Annals of Literature, foreign as well as domestick. Imitate Le Clerc—Bayle—Barbeyrac. Infelicity of Journals in England. Works of the learned. We cannot take in all. Sometimes copy from foreign Journalists. Always tell.

SUNDAY JULY 13. 1755. Having lived hitherto in perpetual neglect of publick worship & though for some years past not without an habitual reverence for the sabbath yet without that attention to its religious duties which Christianity requires I will once more form a scheme of life for that day such as alas I have often vainly formed which when my mind is capable of settled practice I hope to follow.

1 To rise early and in order to [do] it to go to sleep early on saturday.

2 To use some extraordinary devotion in the morning.

3 To examine the tenour of my life & particularly the last week & to mark my advances in religion or recession from it.

4 To read the Scripture methodically[2] with such helps as are at hand.

2. Boswell's transcript: "methodicaly"

With that great task behind him, Johnson at once began to plan another major undertaking, a monthly review of English and European books, and wrote Thomas Warton that he expected it to start appearing the next winter. Boswell printed the extract here given, from "one of his little memorandum-books" now lost (*Life*, 1.284). The project apparently became the *Literary Magazine*, which Johnson largely wrote and supervised, beginning in May 1756.

The entry for 13 July, transcribed by Boswell from the burned journal, was printed by him in a mangled form. After the first two words, he omitted "hitherto in perpetual neglect of publick worship & though for some years past," and "I will once more

5 To go to church twice.

6 To read books of divinity either speculative or practical.

7 To instruct my family.

8 To wear off by meditation any worldly[3] soil contracted in the week.

ON THE STUDY OF PHILOSOPHY, AS AN INSTRUMENT OF LIVING.

JULY. O Lord, who hast ordained labour to be the lot of man, and seest the necessities of all thy creatures, bless my studies and endeavours; feed me with food convenient for me; and if it shall be thy good pleasure to intrust me with plenty, give me a compassionate heart, that I may be ready to relieve the wants of others; let neither poverty nor riches estrange my heart

3. Boswell's transcript: "wordly"

---

form . . . to follow." The purpose of these omissions is clear enough: they make Johnson's neglect of religious duty much less serious and less habitual. Johnson's full text has a note almost of despair—"perpetual neglect," "a scheme of life . . . I have often vainly formed," "when my mind is capable of settled practice." On the other hand, Boswell's emasculated text presents merely a pious man who realizes that his practice should be better. Some of the scheme Johnson was able to effect in time to come, particularly reading the Bible and books of divinity, but this was not done at once. He also later instructed his servant Frank Barber in religion, and at least on Easter often went to church twice. For the rest he succeeded only occasionally.

The prayer on the study of philosophy as an instrument of living is probably to be connected with the sixth part of the preceding, to read speculative and practical divinity; in other words, to supplement his spiritual instruction with ethical. But Johnson usually found his heart a reliable guide in directing his behaviour, and it is not surprising that he did not pursue the study. It is

from Thee, but assist me with thy grace so to live as that I may
die in thy favour, for the sake of Jesus Christ. Amen.

This study was not persued.

Transcribed June 26, 1768.

STUDY OF TONGUES.

Almighty God, giver of all knowledge, enable me so to persue the study of tongues, that I may promote thy glory and my
own salvation.

Bless my endeavours, as shall seem best unto Thee; and if
it shall please Thee to grant me the attainment of my purpose,
preserve me from sinful pride; take not thy Holy Spirit from
me, but give me a pure heart and humble mind, through Jesus
Christ. Amen.

Of this Prayer there is no date, nor can I tell when it was
written; but I think it was in Gough-square, after the Dictionary was ended. I did not study what I then intended.

Transcribed June 26, 1768.

---

possible that this temporary interest resulted in his edition of
Sir Thomas Browne's *Christian Morals*, with a life and notes,
which was published the following spring.

The prayer on the study of languages was composed between
April 1755, when the *Dictionary* was published, and March 1759,
when Johnson left Gough Square, if his recollection of the period
of composition is correct. It may be directly connected with his
proposed study of philosophy.

During the month in which the prayer on the study of philosophy was written Johnson's friend Zachariah Williams died in his
eighty-third year. Williams had been unable to put into acceptable
form his ideas on ascertaining the longitude at sea, and Johnson
did the work for him, publishing a small pamphlet with an
Italian translation by Baretti this year. As a further instance of

1756

JAN 1. 1756. AFTERNOON. Almighty and everlasting God, in whom we live, and move, and have our being, glory be to thee, for my recovery from sickness, and the continuance of my Life. Grant O my God, that I may improve the year which I am now begining, and all the days which thou shalt add to my life, by serious repentance, and diligent obedience, that by the help of thy holy Spirit[4] I may use the means of Grace to my own salvation, and at last enjoy thy presence in eternal happiness,[5] for Jesus Christ's sake. Amen.

HILL BOOTHBY'S DEATH.

JANUARY, 1756. O Lord God, almighty disposer of all things, in whose hands are life and death, who givest comforts and

4. ∧by the help of thy holy Spirit∧   5. happiness, ⟨by the assistance⟩

---

his charity, Johnson had taken Williams's blind daughter into his household, where she lived, except when Johnson was in lodgings, till her death in 1783. During the rest of the year Johnson's only published work was part of a preface to his friend Baretti's *Introduction to the Italian Language.*

The New Year's prayer for 1756 gives thanks for recovery from a cough so violent that Johnson once fainted from its convulsions (*Letters* 77). But he was most unhappy. Hill Boothby was very ill; he wrote her several times a week, urging her, "I beg of you to endeavour to live" (*Letters* 84). She died on the sixteenth, and Baretti later told Mrs. Thrale, "Johnson was almost distracted with his grief" (*Anecdotes*, p. 161).

In his prayer on her death, "I commend, &c." is his shorthand for his adaptation of his prayer for his wife on 22 April 1753: "I commend to thy fatherly goodness the Soul of my departed wife," itself a paraphrase of part of the Prayer for all Conditions of Men: "Finally, we commend to thy fatherly goodness all those

takest them away, I return Thee thanks for the good example
of Hill Boothby, whom thou hast now taken away, and implore thy grace, that I may improve the opportunity of instruction which thou hast afforded me, by the knowledge of her
life, and by the sense of her death; that I may consider the uncertainty of my present state, and apply myself earnestly to the
duties which thou hast set before me; that living in thy fear,
I may die in thy favour, through Jesus Christ our Lord. Amen.
  I commend, &c. W. and H. B.
  Transcribed June 26, 1768.

WHEN MY EYE WAS RESTORED TO ITS USE.

FEBRUARY 15, 1756. Almighty God, who hast restored light
to my eye, and enabled me to persue again the studies which
thou hast set before me; teach me, by the diminution of my
sight, to remember that whatever I possess is thy gift, and by
its recovery, to hope for thy mercy: and, O Lord, take not thy
Holy Spirit from me; but grant that I may use thy bounties
according to thy will, through Jesus Christ our Lord. Amen.

INTRODUCTORY PRAYER.

MARCH. 25. 1756. O God who desirest not the death of a
Sinner, look down with mercy upon me now daring to call
upon thee. Let thy Holy Spirit so purify my affections, and

---

who are any ways afflicted, or distressed, in mind, body, or estate"
(Book of Common Prayer). "W." probably stands for Zachariah
Williams, father of Anna Williams. After his death on 12 July
1755, Johnson had written a short memorial of him.
  In February, Johnson suffered an inflammation of his one good
eye, and when it was relieved, wrote the prayer of thanks given

exalt my desires that my prayer may be acceptable in thy sight, through Jesus Christ. Amen.

MARCH 28. —56, ABOUT TWO IN THE MORNING. Almighty God, our heavenly father whose judgements terminate in mercy, grant, I beseech thee, that the remembrance of my Wife whom thou hast taken from me, may not load my soul with unprofitable sorrow, but may excite in me true repentance of my sins and negligences, and by the operation of thy Grace may produce in me a new life pleasing to thee. Grant that[6] the loss of my Wife, may teach me the true use of the Blessings which are yet left me,[7] and that however bereft of worldly comforts, I may find peace and refuge in thy service through Jesus Christ our Lord. Amen.

6. that ⟨rememberi⟩   7. left me, ⟨that however solitary⟩

---

here. Four days later, as his letters show, the inflammation had returned.

Johnson's "Introductory Prayer" is in part an adaptation of the Absolution: "Almighty God . . . who desireth not the death of a sinner, but rather that he may turn from his wickedness and live" (*Book of Common Prayer*).

The prayer on the anniversary of Tetty's death is the last printed by Strahan for 1756, but among the undated prayers at the end of his book is one "On the study of Religion" which may belong to this year, for "About this period," says Boswell, "he was offered a living of considerable value in Lincolnshire, if he were inclined to enter into holy orders. It was a rectory in the gift of Mr. Langton, the father of his much valued friend" (*Life*, 1.320). Johnson did not accept it, perhaps from a sense of unfitness, and perhaps because he loved London, but he would have considered such an offer with care, and may have written this prayer on that occasion. It is also not far removed from his prayer on the study of philosophy of the previous July, and his resolution of the same month to study books of divinity.

PRAYER ON STUDY OF RELIGION.

Almighty God, our heavenly Father, without whose help, labour is useless, without whose light search is vain, invigorate my studies and direct my enquiries, that I may by due diligence and right discernment establish myself and others in thy holy Faith. Take not, O Lord, thy Holy Spirit from me, let not evil thoughts have dominion in my mind. Let me not linger in ignorance and doubt,[8] but enlighten and support me for the sake of Jesus Christ our Lord. Amen.

1757

JAN 1. 1757. AT TWO IN THE MORNING. Almighty God, who hast brought me to the beginning of another year, and by prolonging my life invitest to repentance, forgive me that I have mispent the time past, enable me from this instant to amend my life according to thy holy Word, grant me thy Holy Spirit that I may so pass through things temporal as not finally to lose the things eternal. O God, hear my prayer for the sake of Jesus Christ. Amen.[9]

8. ignorance ⟨and doubt⟩   9. ⟨grant . . . Amen⟩ then restored with *stet*

For the rest of 1756 Johnson brought out an abridged edition of his *Dictionary*, wrote a preface to Richard Rolt's *Dictionary of Trade and Commerce* and a dedication for Payne's *Game of Draughts*, wrote a few articles for his friend Smart's periodical the *Universal Visiter*, continued to supervise the *Literary Magazine*, and printed *Proposals* for his edition of Shakespeare, optimistically promising that the edition would be ready by Christmas 1757.

On the same day that Johnson wrote his New Year's prayer for 1757 was published the first number of the *London Chronicle*, with a "Preliminary Discourse" by Johnson. This was an auspicious beginning for a newspaper which became Johnson's favourite, and the best paper of its period. He received a guinea for his work.

EASTER EVE. 1757. Almighty God, heavenly Father, who desirest not the death of a sinner, look down with mercy upon me depraved with vain imaginations, and entangled in long habits of Sin. Grant me that grace without which I can neither will nor do what is acceptable to thee. Pardon my sins, remove the impediments that hinder my obedience. Enable me to shake off Sloth, and to redeem the time mispent in idleness and Sin by a diligent application of the days[1] yet remaining to the duties which thy Providence shall allot me. O God grant me thy Holy Spirit that I may repent and amend my life, grant me contrition, grant me resolution[2] for the sake of Jesus Christ, to whose covenant I now[3] implore admission, of the benefits of whose death I implore participation;[4] for his sake have mercy on me O God; for his sake, O God, pardon and receive me. Amen.

PRAYER.

SEPT. 18. 1757. Almighty and most merciful Father by whose providence my life has been prolonged, and who hast granted me now[5] to begin another year of probation, vouchsafe me such assistance of thy Holy Spirit, that the continuance of my life may not add to the measure of my guilt, but that I may so repent of the days and years passed in neglect of the duties which thou hast set before me, in vain thoughts, in sloth, and in folly, that I may apply my heart to true wis-

1. days ⟨which⟩   2. ₍grant me contrition, grant me resolution₎   3. ⟨humbly⟩
4. ₍of the benefits . . . participation₎   5. ₍and₎ who hast granted me ₍now₎

The only other prayers preserved for the year are those of Easter Eve and Johnson's birthday. He continued to write regularly for the *Literary Magazine* up to the fifteenth number, wrote a dedication for Lindsay's *Evangelical History* and for Charlotte Lennox's *Philander*, and helped Baretti with his *Italian Library*. By June he was far enough advanced with the Shakespeare to write

dom,[6] by diligence redeem the time lost, and by repentance obtain pardon for the sake of JESUS CHRIST. Amen.

Idleness intemperate sleep dilatoriness immethodical life
Lust
Neglect of Worship
Vain scruples.[7]

1758

EASTER DAY. MARCH 26. 1758. Almighty and most merciful Father, who hast created me to love and to serve thee, enable [me] so to partake of the sacrament in which the Death of Jesus Christ is commemorated that I may henceforward lead a new life in thy faith and fear. Thou who knowest my frailties and infirmities strengthen and support me. Grant me thy Holy Spirit, that after all my lapses I may now continue stedfast in obedience, that after long habits of negligence and sin, I may at last work out my salvation with diligence and constancy, purify my thoughts from pollutions, and fix my affections on things eternal. Much of my time past[8] has been lost in sloth, let not what remains, O Lord, be given me in vain, but let me for this time lead a better life and serve thee with a quiet mind through Jesus Christ, our Lord. Amen.

MARCH 28. 1758. Almighty and eternal God, who givest life and takest it away, grant that while thou shalt prolong my continuance on earth, I may live with a due sense[9] of thy

6. wisdom, ⟨and⟩ 7. ⟨Idleness . . . scruples⟩ 8. my ∧time∧ past ⟨life⟩ 9. takest it away, ⟨make me to enjoy the time for which⟩ thou shalt prolong my continuance ∧on earth∧ ⟨with the⟩ ⟨a⟩ due sense: ∧grant that while∧ thou shalt prolong my continuance ∧on earth I may live with a∧ due sense

---

Tom Warton that it was "printing." Shakespeare must have occupied most of his productive time during the year.

The prayers for Easter, for the anniversary of Tetty's death, and for Johnson's birthday are the only ones extant for 1758.

mercy and forbearance, and let the remembrance of her whom
thy hand has separated from me, teach me to consider[1] the
shortness and uncertainty of life, and to use all diligence to
obtain[2] eternal happiness in thy presence. O God enable me
to avoid sloth, and to attend heedfully and constantly to thy
word and worship. Whatever was good in the example of my
departed wife, teach me to follow, and whatever was amiss
give me grace to shun, that my affliction may be sanctified, and
that remembering how much[3] every day brings me nearer to
the grave, I may every day purify my mind, and amend my
life, by the assistance of thy holy Spirit, till at last I shall be
accepted by thee, for Jesus Christs sake. Amen.

SEPTR. 18. 1758. HORA PRIMA MATUTINA. Almighty and
most merciful Father, who yet sparest,[4] and yet supportest me,
who supportest me in my weakness, and sparest me in my sins,
and hast now granted to me to begin another year, enable me
to improve the time which is yet before me to thy glory and my
own salvation. Impress upon my soul such repentance of the
days[5] mispent in idleness and folly, that I may henceforward
diligently attend to the business of my station in this world,
and to all the duties which thou hast commanded. Let thy
Holy Spirit comfort and guide me that in my passage through
the pains or pleasures of the present state,[6] I may never be

1. consider ⟨how⟩ 2. ∧obtain∧ ⟨secure⟩ 3. ∧teach∧ ⟨enable⟩ me to follow . . .
give me ∧grace∧ ⟨power⟩ . . . remembering ∧how much∧ ⟨that⟩ 4. ⟨hast . . .
spared⟩ . . . supportest me, ⟨hear me, and pardon me⟩ . . . in ∧my∧ weakness
. . . sins, ⟨grant that they⟩ . . . enable ∧me∧ 5. the ⟨years⟩ ∧days∧ . . . attend
to the ⟨duties ∧employments∧ which thou shalt assign me, and to the duties
by which⟩ . . . and to ∧all∧ the duties 6. state, ⟨my⟩ I

During this year Johnson engaged in his usual miscellany of
projects, by far the most important of which was the *Idler*, which
began its weekly appearance on 15 April in Payne's *Universal
Chronicle*, for which Johnson also supplied two introductory
essays. He also wrote the *Proposals* for Bennet's *Ascham*, helped

tempted to forgetfulness of Thee. Let my life be useful, and my death be happy;[7] let me live according to thy laws and dye with just confidence in thy mercy for the sake of Jesus Christ our Lord. Amen.

This year I hope to learn diligence.

1759

JAN. 23. 1759. The day on which my dear Mother was buried; repeated on my fast with the addition.

Almighty God, merciful Father, in whose hands are life and death, sanctify unto me the sorrow which I now feel. Forgive me whatever I have done unkindly to my Mother, and whatever I have omitted to do kindly. Make me to remember her good precepts, and good example, and to reform my life according to thy holy word, that I may lose no more opportunities of good; I am sorrowful, O Lord, let not[8] my sorrow be without fruit. Let it be followed by holy resolutions and lasting amendment, that when I shall die like my Mother, I may be received to everlasting life.

7. death be ⟨useful⟩ ∧happy∧   8. ∧not∧

John Payne with the preface to his *New Tables of Interest*, and wrote the introductory paragraphs to his friend Saunders Welch's *Proposal to Render Effectual a Plan, to Remove the Nuisance of Common Prostitutes from the Streets*.

In January 1759 Johnson's mother died at Lichfield, two months before her ninetieth birthday. Though Johnson planned to see her during her last illness, he was unable to leave London before her death, and did not go to her funeral (less surprising then than now: Mrs. Thrale did not attend her children's funerals or her husband's). Even before her death he was negotiating with Strahan for the publication of *Rasselas*, which he now hurried to conclusion and published in April. He had paid off the mortgage

I commend, O Lord, so far as it may be lawful, into thy hands the soul of my departed Mother, beseeching thee to grant her whatever is most beneficial to her in her present state.

O Lord grant me thy Holy Spirit, and have mercy upon me for Jesus Christs sake. Amen.

And, O Lord, grant unto me that am now about to return[9] to the common comforts and business of the world, such moderation in all enjoyments, such diligence in honest labour, and such purity of mind, that amidst the changes, miseries, or pleasures of life, I may keep my mind fixed upon thee, and improve every day in grace, till I shall be received into thy kingdom of eternal happiness.

I returned thanks for my Mother's good example, and implored pardon for neglecting it.

I returned thanks for the alleviation of my sorrow.

The dream of my Brother I shall remember.

Jej.

MARCH THE 24. 1759   RATHER 25. AFTER 12 AT NIGHT.

Almighty God, heavenly Father, who hast graciously pro-

9. return ⟨to the cares an⟩

---

at Lichfield two years earlier, but there was need for the ready cash which *Rasselas* brought him, £100 for the first edition, and £25 for the second. He arranged for his stepdaughter Lucy to remain in the house with Catherine Chambers, his mother's maid, who was to carry on the business of the bookstore. Lucy was now his last close relative in Lichfield; his brother Nathaniel had died in 1737. The fast which Johnson mentions in the prayer on his mother's death was held on the night of 24/25 March, as the notation at the head of the next prayer shows.

On 23 March Johnson moved from Gough Square to Staple Inn, and made this the occasion of a prayer which Boswell cited

longed my life to this time, and by the change of outward
things which I am now to make, callest me to a change of in-
ward affections and to a reformation of my thoughts words and
practices. Vouchsafe merciful Lord that this call may not be
vain. Forgive me whatever has been amiss in the state which I
am now leaving, Idleness,[1] and neglect of thy word and worship. Grant me the grace of thy Holy Spirit, that the course
which I am now beginning may proceed according to thy laws,
and end in the enjoyment of thy favour. Give me, O Lord,
pardon and peace, that I may serve thee with humble confidence, and after this life[2] enjoy thy presence in eternal Happiness.

And, O Lord, so far as it may be lawful for me, I commend
to thy fatherly goodness, my Father, my Brother, my Wife, my
Mother. I beseech thee to look mercifully upon them, and
grant them whatever may most promote[3] their present and
eternal joy.

O Lord, hear my Prayers for Jesus Christs sake, to whom
with Thee and the Holy Ghost three persons and one God be
all honour and glory world without end. Amen.

O Lord let the change which I am now making in outward
things, produce in [me] such a change of manners, as may fit
me [for] the great change through which my Wife has passed.

[4]At the place where I commended her
At the place where she died
As much of the prayer as I can remember of Easter 17
Use the lines on this page[4]

1. Word obliterated.   2. life ⟨may⟩   3. ∧promote∧ ⟨tend to⟩   4. ⟨At the place
. . . this page⟩

---

as proof of Johnson's "orthodox belief in the sacred mystery of
the TRINITY" (*Life*, II.254). In the passage scored out at the bottom
of the prayer, "Easter 17" may be a slip for "Easter '57," when
Johnson wrote a prayer for amendment and contrition which
would be appropriate here. He may have misplaced the manu-

EASTER DAY. APR. 15. 1759. Almighty and most merciful Father, look down with pity upon my sins.[5] I am a sinner, good Lord, but let not my sins burthen me for ever. Give me thy Grace to break the chain of evil custom. Enable me[6] to shake off idleness and sloth; to will and to do what thou hast commanded, grant me to be chaste in thoughts, words, and actions; to love and frequent thy worship, to study and understand thy word; to be diligent in my calling, that I may support myself and relieve others.

Forgive me, O Lord, whatever my Mother has suffered by my fault, whatever I have done amiss, and whatever duty I have neglected. Let me not sink into useless dejection; but so sanctify my Affliction, O Lord, that I may be converted and healed;[7] and that, by the[8] help of thy Holy Spirit, I may obtain everlasting life through Jesus Christ our Lord.

And O Lord, so far as it may be lawful, I commend unto thy fatherly goodness my father, brother, wife and mother, beseeching thee to make them happy for Jesus Christs sake. Amen.

5. ⟨and misery⟩   6. ∧to shake off idleness and sloth;∧   7. ⟨Grant thou, O Lord,⟩
8. ∧and that by the∧

---

script in the usual confusion of his desk, and later have found it. The "lines on this page" which Johnson reminds himself to use make up the last paragraph of the prayer.

The Easter prayer is probably to be connected with the undated prayer on scruples. In both Johnson uses the "chain" metaphor from the *Book of Common Prayer*, and in both there is a very unusual request, that he may be diligent to support himself and relieve others. When his pension was granted in 1762, he no longer needed to support himself by his writing. His inability in 1768 to conjecture when the prayer was composed also suggests a rather early date.

During the rest of 1759 Johnson continued with the *Idler*, furnished a dedication for Mrs. Lennox's translation of Brumoy's

SCRUPLES.

O Lord, who wouldst that all men should be saved, and
who knowest that without thy grace we can do nothing acceptable to thee, have mercy upon me. Enable me to break the
chain of my sins, to reject sensuality in thought, and to overcome and suppress vain scruples; and to use such diligence in
lawful employment as may enable me to support myself and
do good to others. O Lord, forgive me the time lost in idleness; pardon the sins which I have committed, and grant that
I may redeem the time mispent, and be reconciled to thee by
true repentance, that I may live and die in peace, and be received to everlasting happiness. Take not from me, O Lord,
thy holy spirit, but let me have support and comfort for Jesus
Christ's sake. Amen.

Transc. June 26, 1768. Of this prayer there is no date, nor
can I conjecture when it was composed.

———————

Greek Theatre, and some parts of the translation as well, wrote an
advertisement for and the introduction to Newbery's collection
of voyages, *The World Displayed,* and contributed three letters to
the *Daily Gazetteer* on behalf of his friend John Gwynn's competition for the erection of Blackfriars Bridge.

The only extant prayer for 1760 is that on Johnson's birthday.
The unusually long series of resolutions, which "with God's help"
he would keep, has several points of interest. "Notions of obligation," Hill guesses, refers to Johnson's unwillingness to bind himself with a vow, and Hill further shrewdly ventures that Johnson
had at some time made vows. If so, they were assuredly broken,
and this would explain Johnson's horror of them, which he several
times expresses. "Your resolution to obey your father I sincerely
approve;" he wrote Boswell, "but do not accustom yourself to
enchain your volatility by vows: they will sometime leave a
thorn in your mind, which you will, perhaps, never be able to
extract or eject" (*Life,* II.21). And even more explicitly on another

1760

SEPT 18. 1760. Resolved D. j.
>To combat notions of obligation
>To apply to Study.
>To reclaim imagination
>To consult the resolves on Tetty's coffin.
>To rise early.
>To study Religion.
>To go to Church.
>To drink[9] less strong liquours.
>To keep Journal.
>To oppose laziness, by doing what is to be done.[1]
>To morrow
>>Rise as early as I can.
>>Send for books for Hist. of war.
>>Put books in order.
>>Scheme life.

9. To ⟨mak⟩   1. Period supplied.

---

occasion: "a vow is a horrible thing, it is a snare for sin" (*Life*, III.357).

"To reclaim imagination" is to be connected with "tumultuous imaginations" on 25 April 1752, "vain imaginations" of 6 May 1752, "depraved with vain imaginations," Easter 1757, "purify my thoughts from pollutions," Easter 1758, and probably with the prayer against unchastity on Easter 1753, when he was not "during the whole service . . . once distracted by the thoughts of any other woman." There seems little doubt that these imaginings were sexual fantasy; his language will scarcely fit anything else. It will be noted that no such expressions occur in prayers before Tetty's death.

The resolves on Tetty's coffin are all repeated here, to rise early, to lose no time, to keep a journal.

O Almighty God, merciful Father, who hast continued my
life to another year grant that I may spend the time[2] which
thou shalt yet give me[3] in such obedience to thy word and will
that finally[4] I may obtain everlasting life. Grant that I may
repent and forsake my sins before the miseries of age fall upon
me, and that while my strength yet remains I may use it to thy
glory and my own Salvation,[5] by the assistance of thy Holy
Spirit, for Jesus Christs sake. Amen.

2. time ⟨to⟩   3. yet ∧give me∧ ⟨grant and suffer me extend my life⟩   4. that
∧finally∧ ⟨my death⟩   5. glory ∧and my own Salvation∧

His resolution to drink "less strong liquours" is a new one. He
had apparently abstained throughout his marriage, but began
again sometime after 1757. Hill conjectures that it was in 1759
that "University College witnessed his drinking three bottles of
port without being the worse for it" (*Life*, 1.103 n.). In 1762, on
the other hand, he was intoxicated after three bottles. By 1767
he had had at least three more periods of abstinence, and thereafter he seems to have drunk little and rarely. The reason is reported by Hannah More in her *Memoirs*: "I can't drink a *little*,
child, therefore I never touch it" (1.251).

The last section was misread by Strahan and Hill. Johnson
decides to oppose laziness by action: "to morrow," on a line by
itself, introduces the last four resolutions and defines the actions
by which he will oppose laziness. Boswell assumed that by a history
of war Johnson meant the Seven Years War, then in progress; Hill,
perhaps more wisely, that it was to be a history of war in general.
At any rate, it remained only a project. Putting his books in order
was often necessary. Boswell described his doing so in 1776, with
clouds of dust flying around him, and was reminded of Dr. Boswell's description of him, " 'A robust genius, born to grapple with
whole libraries' " (*Life*, III.7). Planning his life, however, was
more troublesome than arranging his books, and Johnson never
accomplished it to his satisfaction.

During this year Johnson published little. The last number of
the *Idler* had appeared on 5 April. He wrote a short but excellent

1 7 6 1

EASTER EVE. 1761. Since the Communion of last Easter I
have led a life so dissipated and useless, and my terrours and
perplexities have so much encreased, that I am under great
depression and discouragement, yet I purpose to present myself before God tomorrow with humble hope that he will not
break the bruised reed.

Come unto me all ye that travail.

I have resolved, I hope not presumptuously, till I am afraid
to resolve again. Yet hoping in God I steadfastly purpose to
lead a new life. O God, enable me, for Jesus Christs sake.

My Purpose is

1^6

2 To avoid Idleness.

To regulate my sleep as to length and choice of hours.

To set down every day what shall be done the day
    following.

To keep a Journal.

3 To worship God more diligently.

To go to Church every Sunday.

4 To study the Scriptures.

To read a certain portion every week.

6. Line obliterated; the following numerals were altered from 2, 3, 4 to 1, 2, 3.
The last sentence of the prayer was added in pencil.

---

introduction to the *Proceedings of the Committee . . . for Cloath-
ing French Prisoners of War*, the dedication of Baretti's English
and Italian *Dictionary*, an extended and glowing review of Tyt-
ler's vindication of Mary Queen of Scots, and in December helped
Newbery with an introductory essay to a new paper, the *Public
Ledger*, to which he also contributed his last series of essays, the
Weekly Correspondent, only three in number. Boswell described
Johnson in this year as "either very idle, or very busy with his

Almighty and most merciful Father look down upon my misery with pity, strengthen me that I may overcome all sinfull habits, grant that I may with effectual faith commemorate the death of thy son Jesus Christ, so that all corrupt desires may be extinguished, and all vain thoughts may be dispelled. Enlighten me with true knowledge, animate me with reasonable hope,[7] comfort me with a just sense of thy love,[8] and assist me to the performance of all holy purposes, that after the sins, errours, and miseries of this world I may obtain everlasting happiness for Jesus Christs sake. To whom &c. Amen.

I hope to attend on God in his ordinances to morrow. Trust in God O my soul. O God let me trust in Thee.

1762

MARCH 28. 1762. God grant that I may from this day

Return to my studies.

Labour diligently

Rise early

Live temperately

Read the Bible

Go to Church[9]

7. hope, ⟨and⟩   8. love, ⟨that⟩ and assist me ⟨in⟩ ∧to∧   9. The next line and a fraction obliterated.

Shakspeare" (*Life*, 1.353). There is no evidence that he was busy with Shakespeare.

The next meditation, for Easter Eve 1761, ending with the quotation from St. Matthew xi.28, underscores in its acute distress Johnson's having done little during the previous year. The current year was, if anything, worse. At the beginning of January had appeared the short "Address" drawn up by Johnson for the "Painters, Sculptors, and Architects to George III on his accession to the throne." He also wrote some introductory paragraphs for Gwynn's *Thoughts on the Coronation*, and yet another

O God, Giver and Preserver of all life, by whose power I
was created, and by whose providence I am sustained, look
down upon me [with] tenderness and mercy, grant that I may
not have been created to be finally destroyed, that I may not
be[1] preserved to add wickedness to wickedness, but may so
repent me of my sins, and so order my life to come, that when
I shall be called hence like the wife whom Thou hast taken
from me, I may dye in peace and in thy favour, and be received
into thine everlasting kingdom through the merits and mediation of Jesus Christ thine only son our Lord and Saviour.
Amen.

1. not ⟨have⟩ be⟨en⟩

_____

dedication for Mrs. Lennox, this time for *Henrietta*. His only
substantial work for the year was the edition of *English Works of
Roger Ascham*, nominally by James Bennet, for which he wrote
the life of Ascham and probably did all the editorial work as well.
It was a typical piece of charity on behalf of a poor schoolmaster
without scholarly training.

The prayer on the anniversary of Tetty's death, 1762, shows
that Johnson's lassitude had continued, but apparently he soon
resumed work. By May he had written the preface to the *Catalogue
of the Society of Artists*, no doubt at Reynolds's request, and in
July he wrote to Baretti, "I intend that you shall soon receive
Shakespeare"—the first mention of his edition in years. And it
was none too soon, for in October Charles Churchill satirized him
in *The Ghost*:

> He for subscribers baits his hook,
> And takes their cash—but where's the book?
> No matter where—wise fear, we know,
> Forbids the robbing of a foe;
> But what, to serve our private ends,
> Forbids the cheating of our friends?

In three more years the eight volumes were ready. In the rest of
this year he wrote only the preface to Floyd's translation of du

1 7 6 4

Almighty and most merciful Father, who by thy Son Jesus
Christ hast redeemed man[2] from sin and death, grant that the
commemoration of his passion may quicken my repentance,
encrease my hope, and strengthen my Faith and enlarge my
Charity[3] that I may lament and forsake my sins and for the
time which thou shalt yet grant me, may avoid Idleness[4] and
neglect of thy word and worship. Grant me strength to be
diligent in the lawful employments which shall be set before
me. Grant me purity of thoughts, words and actions. Grant
me to love and study thy word, and to frequent thy worship
with pure affection.[5]

Deliver and preserve me from vain terrors,[6] and grant that
by the Grace of thy Holy Spirit I may so live[7] that after this
life ended, I may be received to everlasting happiness for the
sake of Jesus Christ our Lord. Amen.

2. ∧man∧ ⟨us⟩   3. ∧and enlarge my Charity∧   4. Next word crossed out. Johnson wrote the first five words of this prayer on a preceding page but began
again here.   5. affection, ⟨and grant that⟩   6. Several words deleted.   7. ∧that
. . . so live∧

Fresnoy's *Chronological Tables of Universal History* and the
dedication to Kennedy's *Astronomical Chronology Unfolding the
Scriptures*. But at least his financial difficulties were now over, for
this year he received his pension, £300 a year.

In 1763 Johnson's publications were all minor: a dedication
for Hoole's *Tasso*; a short character of the poet Collins for the
Poetical Calendar; and a review of Graham's *Telemachus* which
would be forgotten except that Graham was responsible for ma-
liciously dubbing Goldsmith "Dr. Minor" in contrast to Johnson,
"Dr. Major." But on 16 May an important event occurred when
the bookseller Davies introduced Boswell to Johnson.

The first prayer for 1764 is undated in the manuscript, but
immediately precedes the meditation for Good Friday, and Strahan was probably right in assigning it that date. In it Johnson

APRIL 20. 1764 GOOD FRYDAY. I have made no reformation, I have lived totally useless, more sensual in thought and
more addicted to wine[8] and meat; grant me, O God, to amend
my life for the sake of Jesus Christ. Amen.
    I hope,
    To put my rooms in order.*[9]
    I fasted all day
    *Disorder I have found one great cause of Idleness.

APRIL 21.[1] 1764 -3-M. My indolence, since my last reception of the Sacrament, has sunk into grosser sluggishness,
and my dissipation spread into wilder negligence. My thoughts
have been clouded with sensuality, and, except that from the
beginning of this year I have in some measure forborn excess
of Strong Drink my appetites have predominated over my
reason. A kind of strange oblivion has overspread me, so that
I know not what has become of the last year, and perceive that

8. to ⟨the⟩ wine   9. Next line obliterated.   1. 2⟨2⟩

_____

refers to his "terrors" for the second time; he had done so three
years earlier. It seems likely that this was a fear of insanity which
plagued him in his fits of melancholia.
    The Good Friday meditation again records Johnson's attempt
to bring order into his rooms. Hill quotes Hawkins's pompous
but appropriate remark: "we cannot but reflect on that inertness
and laxity of mind which the neglect of order and regularity in
living, and the observance of stated hours, in short, the waste of
time, is apt to lead men to: this was the source of Johnson's misery
throughout his life; all he did was by fits and starts, and he had
no genuine impulse to action, either corporal or mental" (p. 205).
    The next meditation was written early the next morning before
Johnson went to bed at his usual late hour. It is perhaps a little
misleading, for he had not been unusually inactive during the
past winter. (His last reception of the sacrament was presumably
the last Easter.) The Club had been founded, with Reynolds,

incidents and intelligence pass over me without leaving any impression.

This is not the life to which Heaven is promised. I purpose to approach the altar again to morrow. Grant, O Lord, that I may receive the sacrament with such resolutions of a better life as may by thy Grace be effectual, for the sake of Jesus Christ. Amen.

APRIL 21. I read the whole Gospel of St. John. The[n] sat up till the 22d.

My Purpose is from this time
1 To reject or expel sensual images, and idle thoughts.
  To provide some useful amusement for leisure time.
2 To avoid Idleness.
  To rise early.
  To study a proper portion of every day.
3 To worship God diligently.[2]
4 To read the Scriptures.
  To let no week pass without reading some part.
  To write down my observations.

I will renew my resolutions made at Tetty's death.

I perceive an insensibility and heaviness upon me. I am less than commonly oppressed with the sense of sin, and less affect-

2. Next line obliterated.

Johnson, Burke, Burke's father-in-law Dr. Nugent, Beauclerk, Langton, Goldsmith, Chamier (Secretary in the War Office), and Hawkins, meeting once a week. And early in the year Johnson had paid an extended visit to Langton, in Lincolnshire, where some time before he had been offered a living.

In the meditation on Easter Eve, Johnson's record that he had read the Gospel of St. John is the first statement of any extensive reading in the Bible. He did not read all of it till years later.

ed with the shame of Idleness. Yet I will not despair. I will pray to God for resolution, and will endeavour to strengthen my faith in Christ by commemorating his Death.

I prayed for Tett.

AP 22[3] EASTER DAY. Having before I went to bed composed the foregoing[4] meditation and the following prayer, I tried to compose myself but slept unquietly. I rose, took tea, and prayed for resolution and perseverance. Thought on Tetty, dear poor Tetty, with my eyes full.

I went to Church came in at the first of the Psalms, and endeavoured to attend the service which I went through without perturbation. After sermon I recommended Tetty in a prayer by herself, and my Father, Mother, Brother, and Bathurst in another. I did it only once, so far as it might be lawful for me.

I then prayed for resolution and perseverance to amend my Life. I received soon, the communicants were many. At the altar it occurred to me that I ought to form some resolutions. I resolved in the presence of God, but without a vow, to repel sinful thoughts, to study eight hours daily, and, I think, to go to church every Sunday and read the Scriptures.[5] I gave a shilling, and seeing a poor girl at the Sacrament in a bedgown, gave her privately a crown, though I saw Hart's hymns in her hand. I prayed earnestly for amendment, and repeated my prayer at home. Dined with Miss W. Went to Prayers at church. Went to Davies's, spent the evening not pleasantly.[6]

3. Ap 2⟨8⟩: Ap 2ᴧ2ᴧ   4. foregoing ⟨reflectio⟩   5. ⟨The Communicants were many.⟩   6. ⟨Came⟩

On Easter Johnson first wrote "28" for the date, no doubt still thinking of Tetty, whose death was on 28 March. His coming late at church, this time at the first Psalm, was habitual. Dr. Bathurst, Johnson's dear friend, had joined the British naval expedition against Cuba after ten years' unsuccessful practice in London,

Avoided wine and tempered a very few glasses with Sherbet.
Came home, and prayed.

I saw at the Sacrament a man meanly dressed whom I have
always seen there at Easter.

EASTER DAY   APRIL 22. 1764. AT 3. M. Almighty and most
merciful Father, who hast created and preserved me, have pity
on my weakness and corruption. Let me not be created to
misery, nor preserved only to multiply s[in].[7] Deliver me
from habitual wickedness, and idleness,[8] enable me to purify
my thoughts, to use the faculties which thou hast given me
with honest diligence, and to regulate my life by thy holy
word.

Grant me, O Lord good purposes and steady resolution, that
I may repent my sins, and amend my life. Deliver me from the
distresses of vain terrour and[9] enable me by thy Grace to will
and to do[1] what may please thee, that when I shall be called
away from this present state I may obtain everlasting happiness through Jesus Christ our Lord. Amen.

Against loose thoughts and idleness.

7. ⟨let me not be created to misery, nor preserved only to multiply s[in]⟩ 8.
ₐand idlenessₐ . . . to ₐuseₐ ⟨exert⟩ the faculties ⟨with⟩ which thou hast
ₐgivenₐ ⟨endowed⟩ me with honest ⟨and profi⟩ 9. Several words obliterated.
1. do ⟨wh those thing⟩ . . . ₐthatₐ ⟨and⟩ . . . state ⟨to a⟩

————————

and in October 1762 had died of fever before Havana, along with
thousands of the troops. Johnson's resolution to go to church every
Sunday, which he thinks he made in the morning but is not
certain, was little better kept than the others. The girl in a bedgown, a word not defined in Johnson's *Dictionary*, was perhaps
wearing "a kind of jacket worn by women of the working class
in the north" (*OED*, cited by Hill). J. Hart's *Hymns Composed
on Various Occasions* was highly evangelical and "enthusiastic"
in nature and therefore of a sort not acceptable to Johnson. He
did not let his disapproval interfere with his charity to the girl.

SEPT. 18. 1764 ABOUT 6. EVENING. This is my fifty sixth birthday, the day on which I have concluded fifty five years. I have outlived many friends. I have felt many sorrows. I have made few improvements. Since my resolution formed last Easter I have made no advancement in knowledge or in Goodness; nor do I recollect that I have endeavoured it. I am dejected but not hopeless.

O God for Jesus Christs Sake have mercy upon me.

7 IN THE EVENING. I went to Church prayed *to be loosed from the chain of my sins.*[2]

I have now spent fifty five years in resolving, having from the earliest time almost that I can remember been forming schemes of a better life. I have done nothing; the need of doing therefore is pressing, since the time of doing is short. O God

2. Five and a half lines obliterated.

Johnson no doubt dined with Miss Williams in a tavern; since March 1759, when he had given up his house in Gough Square to economize, he had lived successively in Staple Inn, Gray's Inn, and Inner Temple Lane, and Miss Williams had lived in lodgings (*Life*, I.421; III.535). The sherbet with which Johnson tempered his wine he defines as "the juice of lemons or oranges mixed with water and sugar." The poorly dressed man whom he saw at church re-enters the story the next Easter.

During the following summer Johnson spent almost two months visiting Percy at Easton Maudit, Northamptonshire, then returned to London, probably to work on Shakespeare. In the meditation on the night of his birthday, celebrated, strangely, by the Old Style calendar, he paraphrases part of the last of the Prayers . . . upon Several Occasions (in the American Prayer Book, in the Penitential Office for Ash Wednesday): "though we be tied and bound with the chain of our sins, yet let the pitifulness of thy great mercy loose us" (*Book of Common Prayer*). He had used a similar phrase on Easter 1759. After the prayer he paraphrases Statius's *Thebaid* v.535, *ad limina vita*, making it "the threshold

grant me to resolve aright, and to keep my resolution for Jesus Christs Sake. Amen.

Haec limina vitae. Stat.

I resolve

To study the Scriptures. I hope in the original Languages. Six hundred and forty verses every Sunday will nearly comprise the Scriptures in a year.

To read good books. To study Theology.

To drive out vain scruples.[3]

To treasure in my mind passages for recollection.

To rise early. Not later than six if I can, I hope sooner, but as soon as I can.

To keep a journal both of employment and of expenses. To keep accounts.

To take care of my health by such means as I have designed, as washing &c.[4]

To set down at night some plan for the morrow.

3. ⟨To drive out vain scruples.⟩   4. ⟨as washing &c⟩

---

of this life," probably referring to the shortness of time remaining to him.

Johnson's plan to read 640 verses of the Bible every Sunday in order to read the whole in about a year was not in itself formidable; the previous Easter he had read the Gospel of St. John, 879 verses, in a day. It was only the regularity of such reading which was an obstacle to him. He had made similar plans in college, and was to make them again.

Johnson's resolution to keep accounts is a new one. As has been seen (above, p. 8) he was surprised that his father had not kept accounts, but his own practice, as might be surmised, was irregular, and his advice on the matter capricious and contradictory. He told Boswell that Mrs. Boswell "should keep an account, because her husband wishes it; but I do not see its use" (*Life*, IV.177). On the other hand, he wrote Langton, "I am a little angry at you for not keeping minutes of your own *acceptum et expensum*, and think

Last year I prayed on my birthday by accommodating the Morning collect for Grace, putting *year* for *day*. This I did this day.

SEPT. 7.[5] 1764. O God, heavenly Father, who desirest not the death of a Sinner, grant that I may turn from my Wickedness and live. Enable me to shake off all impediments of lawful action,[6] and so to order my life, that increase of days may produce increase of grace, of tranquillity of thought, and vigour in duty. Grant that my resolves may be[7] effectual to a holy life, and a happy death, for Jesus Christs sake. Amen.

To morrow I purpose to regulate my room.

1765

JAN. 1. 1765. TUESDAY. 3 m., pr., a prayer composed; the Collect—to the beginning of this year, and evening prayer. Cb., m. d. with pain in face. Rose late; at 1 p. m. to Davis.

5. "18t" in the margin.   6. Several words obliterated.   7. be ⟨right, and may be [word obliterated]⟩ effectual to ⟨the⟩ a

---

a little time might be spared from Aristophanes, for the *res familiares*" (*Life*, IV.362).

The Collect for Grace, which Johnson altered for his use, is: "O Lord, our heavenly Father, Almighty and everlasting God, who hast safely brought us to the beginning of this day; Defend us in the same with thy mighty power; and grant that this day we fall into no sin, neither run into any kind of danger; but that all our doings may be ordered by thy governance, to do always that is righteous in thy sight; through Jesus Christ our Lord."

During the rest of 1764, Johnson's only published work was a review of Grainger's *Sugar Cane* and one of Goldsmith's *Traveller*. He was presumably working on Shakespeare.

In January 1765 Johnson began a more elaborate diary than any which survives up to that date. The manuscript is in the

Strange company. To Paterson; caen. At 2 m. came home having had much pain. L. 200 v of Juv.

2. L. 200 v. Juv.

3. L. 200 v. Juv. From this time pain and scruples impeded me. —Da veniam, Pater Aeterne, munus si periit tuum.

9 WEDN. At Mr Trails. Mrs Macaulays present. Began this book.

Hyde collection, and is now first published. Johnson did not begin it on New Year's Day, but on the ninth, as the entry for that day shows, writing retrospectively what he remembered of the first three days.

On the first he was still up at three, ate something, and used his adaptation of the collect mentioned on his last birthday. He lay down, but slept badly; rose late (as usual), and at one went to see Lockyer Davis (d. 1791), a bookseller and publisher at Lord Bacon's Head, near Salisbury Court, Fleet Street. Davis evidently knew Johnson fairly well, for on 21 December 1789 Boswell recorded in his Journal, "At home after visiting . . . Lockyer Davis for little Johnsonian particulars" (*Boswell Papers*, XVIII.12). Johnson then had dinner with Paterson, probably Samuel Paterson (1728–1802), bibliographer and author of *Coryat Junior*. Johnson was godfather to one of his sons (*Life*, II.175). Johnson's return at two in the morning was near his usual hour.

Of 2 and 3 January Johnson remembered only that he read two hundred lines of Juvenal each day, perhaps recollecting his earlier days when he had adapted the third and tenth satires. Then pain and religious doubts hindered him, and he apparently did nothing till the ninth.

The short ejaculation, "Have mercy, eternal Father, if thy gift has been wasted," reflects Johnson's religious concern over sloth and time misspent. On 18 September 1782 he used the same words.

"At Mr Trails" is Johnson's laconic record of perhaps the major event of his later years, his meeting the Thrales. Mrs. Thrale

10 TH. 2 cb. M 2. Floyd, Lucy, Coxeter, Beauclerc, Langton.
Took Floyd and Levet pr. Spent 6s. 9d. Gave to Coxeter 10s.
6d., to Lucy 5s 3d.⁸ which makes 1£. 3s. 9d. Floyd complained
of his Wife. I took physic about 8 p. m. Corrected a sheet.
Went to Lawrence, supped with Rider and his Wife. Invited
to their house. To W. at 4 p. m. n. cb.
8. ⟨5s. 9d.⟩

erroneously put the date as 1764 in her *Anecdotes*. But in *Thraliana*, writing in 1777, she said:

> It was on the second Thursday of the Month of January 1765.
> that I first saw Mr Johnson in a Room: Murphy whose In-
> timacy with Mr Thrale had been of many Years standing, was
> one day dining with us at our house in Southwark; and was
> zealous that we should be acquainted with Johnson, of whose
> Moral and Literary Character he spoke in the most exalted
> Terms; and so whetted our desire of seeing him soon, that
> we were only disputing *how* he should be invited, *when* he
> should be invited, and what should be the pretence. at last
> it was resolved that one Woodhouse a Shoemaker who had
> written some Verses, and been asked to some Tables, should
> likewise be asked to ours, and made a Temptation to Mr
> Johnson to meet him: accordingly he came, and Mr Murphy
> at four o'clock brought Mr Johnson to dinner—We liked each
> other so well that the next Thursday was appointed for the
> same Company to meet—exclusive of the Shoemaker, and
> since then Johnson has remained till this Day, our constant
> Acquaintance, Visitor, Companion and Friend [1.158–59].

One may guess that they dined together on Wednesday the ninth
and appointed the third Thursday for a second dinner.

On the same day as the dinner, Mrs. Catharine Macaulay, a
friend of Johnson's since 1752, and one of the best-known blue-
stockings of the period, gave him a present, perhaps the first
volume of her *History of England*, which had appeared in 1763.
It was at her house that Johnson, hoping to put down her repub-

13 SUND. Cb. at 2 p. m. n. M with the utmost difficulty. Ill.
At 2 p. m. to Gardiners, pr. coll. Levet invited. 10 n. to W.
Read Thomson's Missionary voyage. 2 home; read a book of
private devotions and resolutions which I pray that I may
keep. Gave at the theatr. 1d.

---

licanism, had said: "Madam, I am now become a convert to your
way of thinking. I am convinced that all mankind are upon an
equal footing; and to give you an unquestionable proof, Madam,
that I am in earnest, here is a very sensible, civil, well-behaved
fellow-citizen, your footman; I desire that he may be allowed to
sit down and dine with us" (*Life*, 1.447).

On Thursday, having gone to bed at two ("M" is his symbol
for defecation), Johnson saw a long list of people. Thomas Floyd
or Flloyd was the author of *Bibliotheca Biographica*, 1760, and
the translator of the *Chronological Tables* for which Johnson had
done a preface in 1762, of whom Boswell heard a report in 1776
that he "had been whipt as a thief at Moorfields" (*Boswell
Papers*, XI.274).

"Lucy" is ordinarily Lucy Porter, Johnson's stepdaughter, but
she lived in Lichfield, and even if she was visiting London at this
time, it is not easy to see why Johnson gave her small amounts
of money, as below. It is more likely that this is some unknown
recipient of his charity. The previous Easter he had given an unnamed girl five shillings.

Thomas Coxeter, son of the late antiquary (d. 1747), Johnson
described later as "slight and feeble, and worth nothing, but to
those who value him for some other merit than his own," that is,
his father's merit, and the fact that Mrs. Johnson had been fond
of the boy. In 1771 Johnson helped him when he was trying to
get a discharge from the East India service, and later tried to
get him admitted to Middlesex Hospital (*Letters* 245, 503).

Topham Beauclerk (1739–80) and Bennet Langton (1737–
1801) were intimate friends of Johnson.

Robert Levet (1705–82), a poor surgeon befriended by Johnson, later cared for the ills of the many dependents living in

14 MOND. M. rose late. J. Lucy 5s 3d which makes 1–9–0.
To Mrs Aheren 2s. 6d. Goldsmith, Beauclerc, Langton. Dined
with Langton. Cd. St. John. Club—2s. 6d., sugar 1s., in all
11s. 3.

27 SUNDAY. Gave Reid a guinea to free him from the Spung-
ing house, with 10. 6 before, in all 1–11–6.

Johnson's house. This entry means that Johnson took him and
Floyd to lunch at a cost of 6/9. The total of £1–3–9 is what Johnson had given Lucy over an unspecified period, as a later entry
shows.

In the evening Johnson corrected a sheet of his Shakespeare,
visited his physician and one of his closest friends, Dr.
Thomas Lawrence (1711–83), president of the College of Physicians, author
of a Life of Harvey and De Hydrope, and then supped with Rider
and his wife. This man may be William Rider (1723–85), a translator of Voltaire's Candide and perhaps the author of Lives and
Writings of the Living Authors of Great Britain, 1762. There were
two Riders in Lichfield in the 1730's, and this man may be related
to them. Johnson then went to Miss Williams, still living in lodgings, no doubt drank tea till very late, and retired at four.

On Sunday, having gone to bed late as usual, Johnson was ill,
but managed to go to lunch with Levet at the Gardiners', where
he dined also a year later. Gardiner was a tallow chandler on Snow
Hill. In the evening he went again to Miss Williams, read Thomas
Thompson's Account of two Missionary Voyages, 1758, and came
home late. He had probably gone to the theatre Friday or Saturday night, and belatedly remembered that he had given a penny
there.

Monday after breakfast ("J." stands for jentavi or jentaculum,
both of which Johnson uses) Lucy received another donation,
which added to the total mentioned on Thursday, made £1–9–0.
Mrs. Aheren (reading uncertain) is unidentified. Goldsmith is
referred to only twice in the diaries, the second time in April
of this year.

28 MOND. L. Ellibank. Lady Shelburne. 10–10– received quarter, lent Davies 25£. Received a guinea. Sulfor. Dined at Mr R.—Gave Mrs W. 2–2–0 which with 2–2–0 for coals and 1–1–0 is 5–5–0.

29 TUESDAY. Dined at Thrail's. Came to Club. No Wine. Expence sugar 1s, Coach 2s, club 2s 3d—in all 5s–3d.

Febr. omitted.

The abbreviations after "Langton" are uncertain. "Club" is The Club, founded a year earlier.

"Reid," to whom Johnson gave a guinea the following Sunday to free him from the sponging house (Johnson had had similar trouble) was probably Joseph Reed (1723–87), who read his tragedy *Dido* to Johnson some time before 1767. Johnson later said of him, "I never did the man an injury; but he would persist in reading his tragedy to me" (*Life*, IV.244 n.).

On Monday there were apparently two callers, Patrick Murray, fifth Baron Elibank (1703–78), of whom Johnson said, "I never was in Lord Elibank's company without learning something" (*Life*, III.24), and Lady Shelburne (d. 1780) née Mary Fitzmaurice, wife of John Petty (Fitzmaurice), first Earl of Shelburne. This must be the occasion Johnson wrote of in a letter to her son, 7 December 1778: "With Lady Shelburn I once had the honour of conversing, and entreat you, Sir, to let her know that I have not forgotten it." The sum of money following their names is not explained, unless one or both of the callers gave Johnson money for one of his charities. He would not have accepted anything for himself, and, indeed, at this date it would have been a brave and foolish man who offered him a gift. Of the quarterly payment of his pension, which he received this day, he lent Tom Davies £25; the trades of actor, bookseller, and hackwriter never paid Davies quite enough to live on. "Sulfor" may be meant for "sulphur," used, among other things, as a purge in the eighteenth century. Later in the day Johnson again dined with Rider (or Reynolds),

MARCH

15 FRID. Paid Mr Allen 6 guineas which I sent to my dying
Mother. From Davies received 3 Guineas.

16 SAT.

17 SUNDAY. Remembred, I think on the heavy day my dear
departed Wife. Went to Church in the afternoon. Came
home, recommended Tetty. Resolved or hoped to combat
sin and to reform life, but at night drank wine.

MONDAY 18. Eheu! M. 3 in bed in the morning with little
difficulty. At 5 p. m. at Trail's. Begged a Guinea for the
Widow with 4 children that sells herbs. Xp. Fr. 7s, Coach 2s,
Chariot 1; in all 10s.

---

and afterwards went to Miss Williams, no doubt for tea as usual,
and gave her her allowance.

Tuesday Johnson again dined with the Thrales (he is approaching the correct spelling of their name) and in the evening went
to the Club, where he avoided wine. He was at this time in the
midst of his struggle, in which he eventually succeeded, to give
up wine altogether.

Over six weeks later he resumed the diary, recording the repayment, more than six years after the event, of the loan from
his neighbour Edmund Allen to relieve the needs of his dying
mother. It is perhaps not coincidence that Davies repaid Johnson
three guineas on that day.

March 17, Old Style, 1752, Tetty had died, and Johnson usually
observed the New Style date, 28 March. This year, and on one
or two other occasions, he observed the earlier date.

Why Johnson begins the next day with "Alas!" is not easy to
say, unless he was still thinking of Tetty, or perhaps of his relapse
into drinking wine the night before. It does not refer to the state
of his bowels, with which he is satisfied. That afternoon he went
to the Thrales, no doubt for dinner, where we see that his charity

MARCH 19. TUES. 1765. Rose earlier than usual, having drunk n. v. at night. I did not sleep well. Corrected Blackrie's sheet. Pr. with Reynolds, then to Welch—meal—to Davies. 10 m c. to Williams, drank tea, n. v. Richardsons print—14s. Oranges 6d, box 8d—14–10.

APR. 1. MONDAY. Slept ill. M. 2. Rose late. Came Delaval, Maclin, Graham, Delap, Strahan. Pr. with Delap. 3s. C. at Allen's. Betty—1–1–0. Maclin's Poems.

---

was not limited to his own contributions, but that he solicited funds from his friends. The entry also shows how intimate he had become with the Thrales. His expenses that day were 7s. to Frank Barber, and for transportation.

The next entry heads a new page and so Johnson used a full date. He rose earlier than usual, having dosed himself with nux vomica. Since this is a stimulant, it is no wonder that he had not slept well. Blackrie may be one of the compositors working on Johnson's *Shakespeare*. After correcting a sheet for him, Johnson lunched with Reynolds, and then went to have another meal with his friend Saunders Welch, the magistrate. Afterwards to Davies and then to Miss Williams for tea. That night he took more nux vomica. "Richardsons print" is probably a framed and glazed print of his friend Samuel Richardson, who had died in 1761. In 1779 Johnson was collecting prints of his friends (*Letters* 634) and later extended his interest to famous authors. By his death he had 146; in the sale of his library the prices of some of the glazed ones equal this one. But this print may be by the painter Jonathan Richardson, who etched portraits of Milton and Pope, Dr. Mead, and himself.

After a lapse Johnson was recalled to his diary by Easter Week. On Monday there were several visitors. Delaval may be either Sir Francis Delaval (d. 1771) or John Hussey Delaval (ca. 1728–1808), neither mentioned elsewhere by Johnson. With the second, Boswell had a slight acquaintance many years later (*Boswell Papers*, XVIII.275).

APR. 5. GOOD FRIDAY. Slept ill. Rose. Mr Lye. To Church at the[9] lesson; heard ill. Graham. Sat at home. Read Nelson, then read Temple. In reading Nelson thought on Death cum lachrimis. To Miss Will. Came home, prayed several prayers for repentance. Eat nothing.

APR. 6. Slept not well—had flatulencies though I had eat nothing. I fasted till about five, yet not hungry. Supped with Williams.

EASTER DAY. APR. 7. 1765 ABOUT 3 IN THE MORNING. I purpose again to partake of the blessed Sacrament, yet when I consider how vainly I have hitherto resolved at this annual

9. ₍the₎ ⟨first⟩
_____

Of Charles Macklin (ca. 1697–1797), the actor, Steevens reported that Johnson called his conversation "a constant renovation of hope, and an unvaried succession of disappointment" (*Miscellanies*, II.317). Of his poems, referred to below, only one or two prologues are known to have been published. This entry seems to indicate that it was proposed to collect and publish his poems to augment his precarious income, as Johnson did the next year with Miss Williams's poems.

George Graham's *Telemachus* Johnson had reviewed in 1763.

John Delap, D.D. (1725–1812), poet and dramatist, was the clergyman whose prayers Johnson begged in the next year, when he feared for his reason (*Anecdotes*, p. 127).

William Strahan (1715–85), printer and M.P., was Johnson's friend for over thirty years, and during the latter part of his life his banker.

After his callers left, Johnson had lunch with Delap, and later dinner with Allen. The "Betty" to whom Johnson gave a guinea is not known.

On Good Friday the antiquarian Edward Lye (1694–1767) called. Johnson had met him the previous summer, and was taking an active interest in his forthcoming *Dictionarium Saxonico- et Gothico-Latinum*, 1772, to which several members of the Club

commemoration of my Saviour's death to regulate my life by his laws, I am almost afraid to renew my resolutions. Since the last Easter[1] I have reformed no evil habit, my time has been unprofitably spent, and seems as a dream that has left nothing behind. My memory grows confused, and I know not how the days pass over me.

Good Lord deliver me.

I will call upon God tomorrow for repentance and amendment. O heavenly Father let not my call be vain, but grant me to desire what may please thee, and fulfill those desires for Jesus Christs sake. Amen.

My resolutions, which God perfect, are:

1 To avoid loose thoughts.[2]

2 To rise at eight every morning.

I hope to extend these purposes to other duties, but it is necessary to combat evil habits singly. I purpose to rise at

1. Several words obliterated. 2. The next resolution obliterated and "3" altered to "2."

subscribed, and in which Johnson is listed as the "Rev. Samuel Johnson, LL.D." Then church, where Johnson was late again. Afterwards Graham came, and when Johnson was alone he read the appropriate part of the *Companion for the Festivals and Fasts of the Church of England*, by the nonjuror Robert Nelson (1656–1715), a book he recommended to his friend Daniel Astle (*Life*, IV.311), and a copy of which, annotated by Johnson, Boswell possessed (*Life*, II.458 n.). This Good Friday reading and meditation on death quite naturally brought Johnson to tears. Sir William Temple (1628–98), the other author Johnson read, was the one he told Boswell he had formed his style upon, the first writer who "gave cadence to English prose" (*Life*, I.218, III.257).

The first entries for Easter Day are from the Pembroke manuscripts. The resolutions which Johnson proposed to read at church are perhaps those he made at Tetty's death, and the persons for whom he would pray, besides Tetty, are his dead relatives, along with Bathurst, specified on the previous Easter. The collects which

eight because though I shall not yet rise early it will be much earlier than I now rise, for I often lye till two, and will gain me much time, and tend to a conquest over idleness and give time for other duties. I hope to rise yet earlier.

Almighty and most merciful Father, who hatest nothing that thou hast made, nor desirest the Death of a Sinner, look down with mercy upon me, and grant that I may turn from my wickedness and live. Forgive the days and years which I have passed in folly, idleness, and sin. Fill me with such sorrow for the time mispent, that I may amend my life according to thy holy word, strengthen me against habitual idleness[3] and enable me to direct my thoughts to the[4] performance of my duty:[5] that while I live I may serve thee in the state to which thou shalt call me, and at last by a holy and happy death be delivered from the[6] struggles, and sorrows of this life, and obtain eternal happiness by thy mercy, for the sake of Jesus Christ our Lord. Amen.

O God, have mercy on me.

At church I purpose

before I leave the pew to pray the occasional prayer, and read my resolutions

To pray for Tetty and the rest; the like after Communion.

3. Several words deleted.   4. ⟨attainment of eternal life⟩   5. ∧performance of my duty∧   6. A word obliterated.

---

he used are: "O God, the protector of all that trust in thee, without whom nothing is strong, nothing is holy; Increase and multiply upon us thy mercy; that, thou being our ruler and guide, we may so pass through things temporal, that we finally lose not the things eternal. Grant this, O heavenly Father, for Jesus Christ's sake our Lord." "O Lord, we beseech thee mercifully to receive the prayers of thy people which call upon thee; and grant that they may both perceive and know what things they ought to do, and also may have grace and power faithfully to fulfil the same; through Jesus Christ our Lord." "O God, who knowest us to be set in the midst

At intervals to use the collects of fourth after Trinity, and first and fourth after Epiph. and to meditate.

3 P. M.[7] This was done, as I purposed but with some distraction. I came in at the Psalms, and could not well hear. I renewed my resolutions at the altar. God perfect them. When I came home I prayed, and have hope; grant O Lord for the sake of Jesus Christ that my hope may not be vain.

I invited home with me the man whose pious behaviour I had for several years observed on this day, and found him a kind of Methodist, full of texts, but ill-instructed. I talked to him with temper, and offered him wine which he refused. I suffered him to go without the dinner which I had purposed to give him. I thought this day that there was something irregular and particular in his look and gesture, but having intended to invite him to acquaintance, and having a fit opportunity by finding him near my own seat after I had missed him, I did what I at first designed, and am sorry to have been so much disappointed. Let me not be prejudiced hereafter against the appearance of piety in mean persons, who, with indeterminate notions, and perverse or inelegant conversation perhaps are doing all that they can.

At night I used the occasional prayer with proper collects.

7. ⟨after church⟩ _____

of so many and great dangers, that by reason of the frailty of our nature we cannot always stand upright; Grant to us such strength and protection, as may support us in all dangers, and carry us through all temptations; through Jesus Christ our Lord."

After church Johnson invited home the "meanly dressed" man he had mentioned the previous Easter, and the man proved a disappointment: he was opinionated and a Methodist, and the combination was too much for Johnson's temper. But Johnson's behaviour was not so rude as it has been represented. Both Strahan and Hill read, "I . . . offered him twice wine," which looks as though Johnson pressed wine on him. The word "twice" is not

APR. 7. EASTER DAY. Rose about eight, prayed, drank tea. Went to church; at Sermon was sleepy but did not sleep. I had not been, I think, five hours in Bed, and had not slept well. Teeth bad. At church.

To rise at eight, if I well can. Dined at Mitre, tea at Strahan's, c. with W: went home about two. Gave 5–3 to the pue keeper, a shilling to poor woman, diner two shillings, collection for evening prayer two shillings. 10s 3d.

MONDAY 8. Rose about 7.

TUESDAY 9. Sx about 7; o. n. disturbed. Coals 3s–3d. Went to Goldsmith, dined at fouthers. 3s. Tea with W. Longitude. Mr Lye. Supper. 9d–2q. Read Adanson.

JULY 2. 1765. I paid Mr Simpson ten guineas, which he had formerly lent me in my necessity and for which Tetty expressed her gratitude.

---

in the manuscript. Johnson was merely being hospitable. After the man left, without his dinner, Johnson took himself to task for his impatience with mean persons who "perhaps are doing all that they can."

The diary resumes, with some additional facts for the same day: he had dined at the Mitre Tavern, a favourite with Johnson, had tea with Strahan, and supper with Miss Williams. He had also attended services again.

On Monday, in spite of having gone to bed after two, Johnson was able to keep his resolution and rise early, which he did again on Tuesday, though he had been disturbed all night, perhaps from the pain in his teeth mentioned on Easter. Then he visited Goldsmith, and dined at "fouthers," which remains unidentified. Tea with Miss Williams again, where they apparently discussed the little book on longitude which Johnson had written for her father ten years before. He saw Lye again, and after supper read in Michael Adanson (1727–1808), author of *Histoire naturelle du Sénégal*, 1757, not elsewhere mentioned by Johnson.

JULY. 8. I lent Mr Simpson ten Guineas more.

JULY 16. I received seventy five pounds. Lent Mr Davies twenty five. After Mich. 24–10–0 more.

SEPT. 1. In the morning M. Dined at the Mitre, treated Mr Levet. 3s 6p. Went to Mr Allens, went to church, gave pew woman a shilling. Supped at Mr Allens. No wine.

BEFORE THE STUDY OF LAW.

SEPT. 26. 1765. Almighty God, the Giver of wisdom, without whose help resolutions are vain, without whose blessing study is ineffectual, enable me, if it be thy will, to attain such

---

The three entries for July were printed from this diary by Boswell, except for the last payment to Davies in September. Joseph Simpson (b. 1721), a barrister, son of the Stephen Simpson of Lichfield who had been an early friend and encourager of Johnson, had married against his father's wishes and had been cut off (*Life*, 1.346). He was the author of a tragedy, *The Patriot*, published as by Johnson after both men were dead. The repayment of the debt and the further loan did not keep him from falling into dissipation and dying by 12 July 1773 (Reade, VIII.66–70, IV.155–58).

Johnson's lending Davies a third of his pension in July and September, as he had in January, is typical of his generosity.

The diary resumes in September with a single entry which is characteristic except for one thing: Johnson went to church on some other day than Easter or Good Friday. Perhaps his neighbour Allen was responsible.

The prayer "Before the Study of Law" introduces a new chapter in Johnson's life. His *Shakespeare* was finished, and another project was in order. Burke had in the previous spring ended his six years' service with William Gerard ("Single-Speech") Hamilton as fact-gatherer for that silent M.P., and Hamilton, whom Johnson

knowledge as may qualify me[8] to direct the doubtful, and instruct the ignorant, to prevent wrongs, and terminate contentions; and grant that I may use that knowledge which[9] I shall attain, to thy glory and my own salvation, for Jesus Christs Sake. Amen.

AT CHURCH OCTR.—65.

To avoid all singularity=*Bonaventura*.

To come in before service and compose my mind by meditation or by reading some portions of Scripture. *Tetty.*

If I can hear the sermon to attend it, unless the attention be more troublesome than useful; else to employ my thoughts on some religious subject.

To consider the act of prayer as a reposal of myself upon God and a resignation of all into his holy hand.

8. ∧may∧ qualify ∧me∧   9. ∧that∧ knowledge ∧which∧ : ⟨such⟩ knowledge ⟨as⟩

---

had known for several years, was looking for a successor, "who, in addition to a taste and an understanding of ancient authors, and what generally passes under the name of scholarship, has likewise a share of modern knowledge, and has applied himself in some degree to the study of the law." The stipend would be "an income, which would neither be insufficient for him as a man of letters, or disreputable to him as a gentleman," and later some kind of political post (*Life*, 1.519–20). The present prayer suggests that an agreement with Hamilton had been reached, and Johnson may even be looking forward to the possibility of an eventual seat in Parliament. Law had interested Johnson since his early years, but lack of a degree had kept him in literature. Here, perhaps, was a way of entering by a back door, in a vague collaboration with a man twenty years his junior, yet one of some distinction.

The October meditation exists in Boswell's transcript of the burned diary, and *Bonaventura* was annotated by him, "He was probably proposing to himself as a model this excellent person, who for his piety was named the Seraphick Doctor."

ENGAGING IN POLITICKS WITH H———N.[1]

NOV. 1765. Almighty God, who art the Giver of all Wisdom, enlighten my understanding with[2] knowledge of right, and govern my will by thy laws, that no deceit may mislead me, nor temptation corrupt me, that I may always endeavour to do good, and to hinder evil. Amidst all the hopes and fears of this world, take not thy Holy Spirit from me, but grant that my thoughts may be fixed on thee, and that I may finally attain everlasting happiness for Jesus Christs sake. Amen.

DEC. 8. 1765 TWO IN THE MORNING. I am going to rest with my rheumatism better, and a fire in my chamber. Fave, Deus mihi.

DEC. 30[3] I THINK. Had from Mr Davies five Guineas. The year is ended.

1. ∧With H–N∧   2. with ⟨good⟩   3. ⟨29⟩

The prayer on engaging in politics with Hamilton suggests that the work has begun, though nothing more of it is known in this year. But there may have been some work much earlier. On 3 August, Thomas Birch had written Lord Hardwicke about Hamilton's famous maiden speech on 13 November 1755, "which I hear to have been the performance of Sam. Johnson, with whom, I know, he is very intimate" (B.M. Add. MS 35,400; courtesy of Professor Clifford).

The *Shakespeare* had finally been published in October, and it had sold very fast, so that a second printing was needed. Johnson's only other work of the year was the dedication of Percy's *Reliques*, which he rewrote from Percy's draft. But the year had brought a new honour, when Trinity College, Dublin, had made him an honorary Doctor of Laws.

On 8 December he returned to his diary with a characteristic cry, "Protect me, O God," but he was perhaps feeling better than usual.

1766

JAN. 1. 1766, AFTER TWO IN THE MORNING. Almighty and
most merciful Father, I again appear in thy presence the
wretched mispender of another year which thy mercy has
allowed me. O Lord let me not sink into total depravity, look
down upon me, and rescue me at last from the captivity of
Sin. Impart to me good resolutions, and give me strength and
perseverance to perform them. Take not from me thy Holy
Spirit but grant that I may redeem the time lost, and that by
temperance and diligence[4] by sincere Repentance and faithful
Obedience I may finally obtain everlasting happiness for the
sake of Jesus Christ, our Lord. Amen.

Resolutions. God help me.
To read the Bible through in some language this year.
To combat Scruples.
To rise early.
To drink little wine.

JAN. 1. ☿ . After 2 m. prayed, after 3 wrote resolutions; had
almost no sleep. At 8 rose. λ. L. a little in Pearson; heavy for
want of sleep. Pr at Davies's. After diner slept an hour; at

4. ∧that by temperance and diligence∧

The last entry for the year was probably written on New Year's
eve, since Johnson is uncertain which day Davies gave him five
guineas, apparently a loan till the fifth, when his quarterly pension
was due.

After composing his New Year's prayer, Johnson returned to
his diary. After the date he has put the astronomical symbol for
Wednesday. He was able to keep one resolution, and rose at eight.
The lambda following is unexplained. Then he read in John
Pearson (1613–86), Bishop of Chester, whose *Exposition of the
Creed* had gone into eight editions by 1704. Pearson is now better
known as the editor of the *Golden Remains of John Hales*, 1659.

7 came home, read Norris. M. 2 c. drank tea. (Read Ovington
at Davies's.) λ. at 2 c. (read Nelson).
To write the History of Memory.

JAN. 2. Sx at 8. L. Pearson &c. Company. At 4 Thrale. 12 l.
Ovington.

3 ♀. No sleep till morning. Strongly tempted in a dream to
M. Καθ. Sx at 10 J. M. dined at Strahan's. 8 slept. C. l. Ovington.

4 SAT. M. d. Rose at 10, busied on trifles. Pr. at home. Slept.
Visited Putty. Drank wine for the first time this year.

After lunch at Davies's, where he also slept an hour as well as
reading in Dr. John Ovington, author of *A Voyage to Suratt*, 1696,
and *Christian Chastity; or, A Caveat against Vagrant Lust*, 1712,
he came home and read John Norris, author of *A Treatise Concerning Christian Prudence*, 1710, a copy of whose *Miscellanies*,
annotated by Johnson, is at Yale. To bed at 2 A.M., after tea and
more reading, this time in Nelson, whose *Festivals and Fasts* has
already been mentioned. Much of this reading seems in line with
the resolution to combat scruples.

Of the projected history of memory there is no further mention.
On Thursday, more reading of Pearson, and at four Thrale,
which probably means that he went there for dinner, since that
was his usual day for dinner there. At midnight more Ovington.

The symbol after "3" was perhaps meant for Friday, but it does
not look like the usual one. On this day Johnson's two-day habit
of early rising began to break: he breakfasted at ten after a purge.
It will be noticed that on almost every day of early rising, Johnson
slept or dozed during the day; it seems likely that he got quite
enough sleep at one time or another for an average man of fifty-six.
But he was disturbed that he did not work or sleep at conventional
hours.

Next day Johnson first wrote the symbol for Saturday, but then
wrote the abbreviation over it. He had slept badly, breakfasted

JAN. 5 SUNDAY. Slept not ill. Rose at 8, j., lay down on the bed sleepy. Dined at Hawkins's. Came to Allens, sleepy. Read in Hall, at 11. came home. After 1—c.

6 MONDAY. To Betty a guinea. Sx at 8. Sleepy all day. At club. Received 69£ 15s., returned Davies five Guineas. Drank wine.

7 TUESDAY rose at 9. Dined at Gardiners. Sleepy.

8 rose at 8. Dined at Welchs, carried Simpson's letter to Garrick.

9 at 8. Dined at Strahans.

---

at home, and visited "Putty," of which both reading and identification are uncertain. The fact that Johnson mentions a three-day abstinence from wine shows that he did not find abstinence easy.

Sunday Johnson rose early again, but, after breakfast, lay down. He dined with his old friend Hawkins, and then visited his neighbour Allen, where he read in Hall, perhaps Joseph Hall, Bishop of Norwich, the "English Seneca," author of *Meditations and Vows*, 1605. He went to bed after one.

On Monday Johnson continued his early rising, gave the unknown Betty a guinea (see 1 April 1765), drank wine at the Club in the evening, and having received his quarterly pension, repaid Davies his loan of the previous week, leaving himself £69 15s. This entry shows Johnson's usual habit of recording events in the order they returned to his mind, not in the order in which they occurred.

Tuesday he dined again with the Gardiners of Snow Hill (see 13 January 1765).

Wednesday, dinner with the Welches (see 19 March 1765). Simpson's letter to Garrick was probably that described by Percy Fitzgerald as "a piteous letter, asking his influence for reconciliation with the father," and also for a loan of a hundred pounds. Garrick "at once sent off the money, wrote down to Lichfield a

10   at 8, had much company. on all. In these days every day
sleepy. Least to day. Several times M. This day I put on a new
brown Wig.

11   at 8, less sleepy. Pr. at Reynolds, C. at Mitre, less sleepy
yet.

12   at eight. 21 pages in the 4to bible on Sundays, reading 6
verses a minute, may be read or more.

---

charming appeal to the offended father, but received back a gruff,
surly answer" (Garrick, 1868, p. 10). The letters are now lost.
This is the only mention of Garrick in the diaries.

On Friday, 10 January, the phrase "on all" is unexplained, unless Johnson started to write "on all these days," changed his mind,
and neglected to cross out the false start. A new wig was an occasion. Boswell had noted in 1763 that Johnson "had on a little
old shrivelled unpowdered wig, which was too small for his head"
(Life, 1.396). Perhaps the soft influence of young Mrs. Thrale was
making itself felt.

Next day lunch with Reynolds and supper at the Mitre.

Johnson's calculation on the next day that twenty-one pages
in a quarto Bible may be read in a day, at the rate of six verses a
minute, probably refers to a Greek Testament, since the rate
would be absurdly slow for English. His New Year's resolution to
read the Bible through "in some language" is relevant, and his
similar estimate, on 24 March 1771, mentions a Greek text. He is
at his old practice of breaking a large job into manageable units,
first noted in his Oxford studies and seen at intervals throughout
his life.

Two days later Johnson wrote to Boswell, who had been abroad
for a year and a half, urging him to come home: "I long to see
you, and to hear you; and hope that we shall not be so long
separated again" (Life, 11.4). In February Boswell reached London, and "found Dr. Johnson in a good house in Johnson's-court,
Fleet-street." They talked of Rousseau, Wilkes, and Corsica, before
Boswell returned to Scotland.

MARCH 2 —66 DD. Thought on writing a small book to teach the use of the Common Prayer.

MARCH 3. I have never, I thank God, since Newyears day deviated from the practice of rising.

In this practice I persisted till I went to Mr Thrale's some days before Midsummer; the irregularity of that family broke my habit of rising. I was there till after Michaelmas.

ENTRING N. M.

MARCH 7. 1766. Almighty and most merciful Father, who hast graciously supplied me with new conveniencies for study, grant that I may use thy gifts to thy glory. Forgive me the time mispent. Relieve my perplexities.[5] Strengthen my resolution, and enable me to do my duty with vigour and[6] constancy: And when the fears[7] and hopes, the pains and pleasures of this life shall have an end, receive me to everlasting happiness, for the sake of Jesus Christ our Lord. Amen.

5. A few words obliterated.   6. ‸and‸   7. Not in Johnson's hand; apparently replaces "doubts." A line following the end of the prayer is also obliterated.

On Sunday, "DD," 2 March, Johnson returned to his diary, thinking of writing an elementary book on the Common Prayer, which was not done, and next day congratulated himself on his adherence to early rising, which persisted for almost six months. No other such period of early rising is known in Johnson's life. Boswell thought this passage interesting enough to transcribe.

As Hill guessed, the next entry is not continuous with the foregoing but was clearly written in late September or October, after Johnson had returned from his summer's stay with the Thrales at Streatham.

The new study, which is the subject of the next prayer, was described by Hawkins (p. 452) as "An upper room, which had the advantages of a good light and free air" in the house in Johnson's Court.

GOOD FRIDAY. MARCH 28. 1766. On the night before I used
proper collects, and prayed when I awoke in the morning. I
had all the week an awe upon me, not thinking on⁸ passion
week till I looked in the almanack. I have wholly forborn
M[eat] and wine except one glass on Sunday night.
In the morning I rose, and drank very small tea without
milk, and had nothing more that day.
This was the day on which Tetty died. I did not mingle

8. ⟨of⟩

_____

The entries from 28 March through 4 May are from manuscripts
in the Bodleian, except the last half of that for 29 March,
which is in the Hyde collection. The collects which Johnson used
before retiring Thursday night are those for Good Friday: "Almighty God, we beseech thee graciously to behold this thy family,
for which our Lord Jesus Christ was contented to be betrayed, and
given up into the hands of wicked men, and to suffer death upon
the cross; who now liveth and reigneth with thee and the Holy
Ghost, ever one God, world without end." "Almighty and everlasting God, by whose Spirit the whole body of the Church is gov-
erned and sanctified; Receive our supplications and prayers, which
we offer before thee for all estates of men in thy holy Church, that
every member of the same, in his vocation and ministry, may truly
and godly serve thee; through our Lord and Saviour Jesus Christ."
"O merciful God, who hast made all men, and hatest nothing that
thou hast made, nor wouldest the death of a sinner, but rather that
he should be converted and live; Have mercy upon all Jews, Turks,
infidels, and heretics; and take from them all ignorance, hardness
of heart, and contempt of thy Word; and so fetch them home,
blessed Lord, to thy flock, that they may be saved among the remnant of the true Israelites, and be made one fold under one shepherd, Jesus Christ our Lord, who liveth and reigneth with thee
and the Holy Spirit, one God, world without end."
Hill makes the forceful point that Johnson's not realizing that
it was Passion Week till he looked in the almanac indicates that
he had "omitted church" of late.
"Small tea," an unusual expression, is not given in Johnson's

much men[tion] of her with the devotions of this day, because it is dedicated to more holy subjects. I mentioned her at church and prayed once solemnly at home.

I was twice at church, and went through the prayers without perturbation. But heard the sermons imperfectly. I came in both times at the second lesson, not hearing the bell.

When I came home I read the Psalms for the day, and one sermon in Clark. Scruples distract me, but at Church I had hopes to conquer them.

I bore abstinence this day not well, being at night insupportably heavy, but as fasting does not produce sleepyness I had perhaps rested ill the night before. I prayed in my study for the day, and[9] prayed again in my chamber. I went to bed very early, before eleven.

After Church I selected collects for the Sacrament.

Finding myself upon recollection very ignorant of Religion, I formed a purpose of studying it.

I went down, and sat below, but was too heavy to converse.

SATURDAY. 29. I rose at the time now usual not fully refreshed. Went to tea; a sudden thought of restraints hindred me. I drank but one dish. Took a purge for my health. Still uneasy. Prayed and went to dinner. Dined sparingly on Fish[1]

9. ⟨used⟩   1. ∧on Fish∧

———————

Dictionary, though he does give the common "small beer," defined as "weak."

Of Dr. Samuel Clarke (1675–1729), Johnson thought highly, though he would not admit his name to the Dictionary because of unorthodo.y as to the Trinity. He is frequently mentioned in the Life, and Johnson refers to his sermons often.

Johnson's intention to study religion goes back to July 1755. The undated prayer which we have placed at that time would be equally appropriate here. He had not done much methodical study in the meantime.

The first entries for Saturday are primarily medical; of the next,

about four. Went to Simpson. Was driven home by my Physick. Drank tea and am much refreshed. I believe that if I
had drank tea again yesterday I had escaped the heaviness of
the evening. Fasting that produces inability is no duty, but I
was unwilling to do less than formerly.

I had lived more abstemiously than is usual the whole week,
and taken Physick twice, which together made the fast more
uneasy.

Thus much I have written medically, to show that he who
can fast long must have lived plentifully.

I was yesterday very heavy; I do not feel myself to day so
much impressed with awe of the approaching Mystery. I had
this day a doubt like Baxter of my State, and found that my
Faith though weak, was yet Faith. O God strengthen it.

Since the last reception of the Sacrament, I hope I have no
otherwise grown worse, than as continuance in Sin makes the
Sinners condition more dangerous. Since last Newyear's day
I have risen every morning by eight; at least, not after nine.
Which is more superiority over my habits than I have ever
before been able to obtain. Scruples still distress me. My resolution, with the blessing of God, is to contend with them, and,
if I can, to conquer them.

My Resolutions are
To conquer Scruples. D.j.
To read the Bible this year.
To try to rise more early.
To study Divinity.
To live methodically.
To oppose Idleness.
To frequent Divine Worship.

---

primarily religious, Hawkins printed the second paragraph and
the resolutions, apparently from the original diary (p. 447).
Richard Baxter (1615–91), author of *A Call to the Unconverted*,

Almighty and most merciful Father, before whom I now
appear[2] laden with the Sins of another year, suffer me yet
again[3] to call upon thee for pardon and peace. O God, grant
me repentance, grant me reformation. Grant that I may be
no longer disturbed with doubts and harrassed with vain terrours. Grant that I may no more[4] linger in perplexity, nor
waste in idleness that life which thou hast given and preserved. Grant that I may serve thee with firm faith and diligent endeavour, and that I may discharge the duties of my
calling with tranquillity and constancy. Take not O Lord thy
Holy Spirit from me, but grant that I may so[5] direct my
life by thy holy laws, as that when thou shalt call me hence,
I may pass by a holy and happy death to a life of everlasting
and unchangeable joy, for the Sake of Jesus Christ, our Lord.
Amen.

I went to bed [at] one or later but did not sleep. Though
I know not why.

EASTER DAY. MARCH 30. 1766. I rose in the morning.
Prayed. Took my Prayer book to tea, drank tea, planned my
devotion for the church. I think prayed again. Went to
Church, was early. Went through the prayers with fixed attention. Could not hear the sermon. After sermon applied myself to Devotion. Troubled with Baxter's scruple, which was

2. ⟨gra[nt]⟩   3. ∧yet again∧ ⟨once more⟩   4. ∧that∧ I may no ∧more∧ ⟨longer⟩
5. ∧so∧ ⟨govern⟩ . . . ∧as∧ that . . . death ⟨I may pass⟩

---

an immensely popular book, had doubts as to his own salvation, which he described in *Reliquiae Baxterianae.* This was close
enough to Johnson's own situation to make him turn to Baxter's
solution of his "scruples."

On Easter Sunday Johnson was troubled by Baxter, but resolved
the matter to his satisfaction. The collect for the fourteenth Sunday after Trinity, which Johnson used at church, is: "Almighty
and everlasting God, give unto us the increase of faith, hope, and

quieted, as I returned home. It occurred to me that the scruple itself was its own confutation.

I used the prayer against scruples in the foregoing page in the pew, and commended (so far as it was lawful) Tetty, dear Tetty, in a prayer by herself, then my other friends. What collects I do not exactly remember. I gave a shilling. I then went towards the altar that I might hear the service. The Communicants were more than I ever saw. I kept back, used[6] again the foregoing prayer, again commended Tetty, and lifted up my heart for the Rest. I prayed in the collect for the fourteen S. after Trinity for encrease of Faith, Hope, and Charity, and deliverance from scruples; this deliverance was the chief subject of my prayers. O God hear me. I am now to try to conquer them. After reception I repeated my petition, and again[7] when I came home. My diner made me a little peevish, not much. After dinner I retired, and read in an hour and half the seven first Chapters of St Matthew in Greek. Glory be to God. God grant me to proceed and improve for Jesus Christs Sake. Amen.

I went to Evening Prayers, and was undisturbed.

At church in the morning it occurred to me to consider what example of good any of my friends had set me; this is proper in order to the thanks returned for their good examples.

6. ∧used∧ ⟨repeated⟩   7. ⟨ (I think)⟩

---

charity; and, that we may obtain that which thou dost promise, make us to love that which thou dost command; through Jesus Christ our Lord." After church, he broke his fast, but evidently ate too much, for after dinner he was "peevish."

Johnson's timing himself in reading the Greek New Testament is similar to his entry for 12 January, except that his speed is slower, since there are 201 verses in the first seven chapters of

My attainment of rising gives me comfort and hope. O God, for Jesus Christs sake bless me. Amen.

After church before and after dinner I read Rotheram on Faith.

After Evening Prayer I retired, and wrote this account.

I then repeated the prayer of the day with collects, and my prayer for night, and went down to supper at near ten.

MAY 4 —66. I have read since the noon of Easterday, the Gospels of St Matthew and St Mark in Greek.

I have read Xenophons Cyropaedia.

[SEPT.][8] 18. 1766. AT STREATHAM. I have this day completed my fifty seventh year. O Lord, for Jesus Christ's sake have mercy upon me. Amen.

Almighty and most merciful Father, who hast granted me to prolong my life to another year, look down upon me with pity. Let not my manifold sins and negligences avert from me thy fatherly regard. Enlighten my mind that I may know my duty; that I may perform it strengthen my resolution. Let not another year be lost in[9] vain deliberations: Let me

8. Ms torn.   9. One or more words obliterated.

St. Matthew. But he is encouraged that he has finally begun, and also that his early rising continues.

Rotherham's sermon *On the Origin of Faith*, which Johnson read, was preached at Oxford in 1761.

By 4 May Johnson had made reasonable progress with the Greek Testament. His reading of Xenophon's *Cyropaedia*, a work ostensibly dealing with the boyhood of Cyrus but actually a vehicle for Xenophon's ideas on education, was directly connected with his progress. For in 1783 he told Bowles that "In Greek . . . the *Cyropaedia* was the only author which he ever fairly red thro', and that was for the sake of the language" (*Life*, IV.524).

After the prayer on his birthday, Johnson added the collect

remember [that][1] of the short life of man a great part is already past,[2] in sinfulness and sloth. Deliver me, gracious Lord from the bondage of doubt and from all evil[3] customs, and take not from me thy Holy Spirit, but enable me so to spend my remaining days, that by performing thy will I may promote thy glory, and grant that after the troubles and disappointments of this mortal state I may obtain everlasting happiness for the sake of Jesus Christ, our Lord. Amen.

Added:

The fourteenth S. after Tr.

The Morning collect.

The beginning of this (day) year.

PURPOSES.

To keep a Journal. To begin this day.

To spend four hours every day in Study, and as much more as I can:

To read a portion of the Scriptures in Greek every Sunday

To combat scruples.[4]

To rise at eight.

1. MS torn.   2. past, (and past)   3. of (doubt and from all) evil   4. (To combat scruples)

---

which he had used at Easter, and apparently added two more, although Hill interprets the second and third as meaning the same collect. The morning collect for peace is: "O God, who art the author of peace and lover of concord, in knowledge of whom standeth our eternal life, whose service is perfect freedom; Defend us thy humble servants in all assaults of our enemies; that we, surely trusting in thy defence, may not fear the power of any adversaries, through the might of Jesus Christ our Lord." The third is that adapted by Johnson for his birthday in 1764, and printed under that date.

OCT. 3. —66. Of all this I have done nothing.

I returned from Streatham Oct. 1. —66, having lived there more than three months.

NOV. 8. 1766. I returned from Oxford, after a month's stay. At Oxford I rose regularly to early prayers.

Remember—Mother one Sunday between Church and supper lay with the children on the bed.

Mother after my Fathers death.

Christ did not dye in vain.

Lucy—There are six days in the week.

1767

JAN 1. 1767. 1ma mane scripsi. Almighty and most merciful Father, in whose hand are life and death, as thou hast suffered me to see the beginning of another year, grant, I beseech thee, that another year may not[5] be lost in Idleness or squandered

5. ∧not∧ . . . Idleness, [a few words obliterated] ∧or∧

On 3 October, having returned from his visit to the Thrales, Johnson recorded that his resolutions had been in vain, and as previously noted his early rising had lapsed also.

The diary resumes with the entry for 8 November.

In May, Johnson's young friend Robert Chambers had been elected Vinerian Professor of Law to succeed Blackstone, but in October he had not begun to lecture and was in some danger of being fined if the rules were enforced. During Johnson's stay of a month they probably discussed this, since the entry following that of 8 November (9 April 1767) is two pages out of chronological order, and must have been put here because Johnson associated his visit to Oxford with his later collaboration in the Vinerian lectures. On 11 December, Johnson wrote to Chambers: "Come up to town, and lock yourself up from all but me, and I doubt not but Lectures will be produced. You must not miss another term"

in unprofitable employment. Let not sin prevail on the remaining part of life, and take not from me thy Holy Spirit,[6] but as every day brings me nearer to my end, let every day contribute to make my end holy and happy.[7] Enable me O Lord to use all enjoyments with due temperance, preserve me from unseasonable and immoderate[8] sleep, and enable me to run with diligence the race that is set before me, that after the troubles of this life, I may obtain everlasting happiness, through Jesus Christ, our Lord. Amen.

JAN. 1. About[9] one in the morning composed a prayer and prayed; at 2 to bed, little rest. At 8 rose or a little after, lighted fire, prayed,[1] read 180 pages in Trap. Pr. with Davies; came home, prayed.

6. ∧and take not . . . Spirit∧   7. [several words obliterated] enable ∧me O Lord∧
8. ∧immoderate∧ ⟨intemperate⟩ ∧sleep∧   9. ⟨At⟩   1. ∧prayed∧

(*Letters* 187.2). During the next year or more Johnson helped Chambers, and the lectures were produced. The collaboration was kept secret, though Mrs. Thrale guessed at it and hinted in her *Anecdotes* that Johnson had written lectures as well as sermons, prefaces, and dedications for his friends.

The comparative incoherence of the jottings which follow seems to indicate considerable mental distress. There is nothing else on the page, and no indication of exact date.

During the past year, Johnson had written *Considerations on the Corn Laws*, the only known product of his work with "Single-Speech" Hamilton, had written dedications for Adams's *Globes* and Gwynn's *London and Westminster Improved*, and had edited, contributed to, and solicited contributions for his blind friend Miss Williams's *Miscellanies*.

The New Year's prayer for 1767, written at one in the morning as Johnson's note says, is followed by two entries in his diary. Just which author Johnson read before lunch with Davies is not clear. The word seems to be "Trap" (Trask?), perhaps Dr. Joseph Trapp

2. Rose before 9, trifled. Pr. with Reynolds. Used the new prayer both night and morning.

Uxbridge 13–9
Wicomb 10–6
Tetsworth 10–6

If my Mother had lived till March she would have been eighty nine.

AP. 9. 1767. I returned from helping Chambers at Oxford.[2]

On March 28, thought on poor dear Tetty by accident, and designed to reform but forgot it. This should have been on the other [page].

2. ⟨Ap. 9. 1767 I returned from helping Chambers at Oxford⟩

(1679–1747), first Professor of Poetry at Oxford, who had published four sermons against Whitefield, on the abridgement of which Johnson had written *Considerations on the Case of Dr. T.'s Sermons* in 1739.

On the second, Johnson "trifled," and lunched with Reynolds. The year had not begun very auspiciously, and the diary breaks off again.

In February Johnson had his famous interview with George III; at the end of March he thought by accident about Tetty, and recorded it out of place, two pages earlier, and near that date made a visit to Oxford to help Chambers, as he recorded on 9 April, when he had returned. On 11 May he was in Oxford again, as a letter shows, and very soon afterwards went to Lichfield, where he stayed till late in October with his stepdaughter Lucy Porter.

On the verso of a leaf facing the New Year's prayer, Johnson has jotted down expenditures at three towns on the road from London to Oxford. Uxbridge, Wycombe, and Tetsworth are about equidistant, and may have been coach stops. The fact that they are followed by a note about Johnson's mother suggests that they were made on his present journey to Oxford and Lichfield, when

³AUGUST 2. 1767. I have been disturbed and unsettled for a long time, and have been without resolution to apply to study or to business, being hindered by sudden snatches.

I have for some days forborn wine and suppers and have taken purges.⁴ Abstinence is not easily practiced in another's house, but I think it fit to try.

I was extremely perturbed in the night but have had this day, 5-24 p.m.⁵ more ease than I expected. D. gr. Perhaps this may be such a sudden relief as I once had by a good night's rest in Fetterlane.

The shortness of the time which the common order of nature allows me to expect is very frequently upon my mind. God grant that it may profit me.

AUGUST. 17. From that time by abstinence and purges⁶ I have had more ease. I have read five books of Homer, and

3. ⟨June 24 1767 I this day⟩ 4. ʌand have taken purgesʌ 5. ⟨5-24 p.m.⟩
6. ⟨and purges⟩

_____

his mother would be in his mind. Mrs. Johnson, of course, was eighty-nine when she died, and would have been ninety had she lived till March. Johnson did not make the same mistake in her epitaph, though there he put her place of birth in the wrong county.

In August Johnson made two isolated memoranda. On 2 August he notes that he has been "hindered by sudden snatches" from study. By this he apparently means interruptions, but such a meaning is not given in his *Dictionary*, where one definition of "snatch" is "a short fit of vigorous action," and another "a broken or interrupted action; a short fit." He may merely mean restlessness.

After thanking God for relief from pain, Johnson recalls a similar relief when lodging in Fetter Lane. Since this refers to the period 1741–49, one realizes how infrequent such relief was in Johnson's later years.

On the seventeenth, Johnson had made good progress with

hope to end the Sixth to night.[7] I have given Mrs LeClerc[8] a guinea.

By several purges taken successively and[9] by abstinence from wine and suppers I obtained sudden and great relief, and had freedom of mind restored to me, which I have wanted for all this year without being able to find any means of obtaining it.

AUGUST. 17. 1767. I am now about to receive[1] with my old Friend Kitty Chambers the sacrament preparatory to her death. Grant, O God, that it may fit me. I purpose temperance for my resolution. O God enable me to keep my purpose to thy glory.

5.32 p.m. I have communicated with Kitty, and kissed her. I was for some time distracted but at last more composed. I commended my[2] friends and Kitty. Lucy and I were much affected. Kitty is, I think going to Heaven.

O God, grant[3] that I may practice such temperance in Meat, Drink, and Sleep and all bodily enjoyments, as may[4] fit me for the duties to which thou shalt call me, and by thy blessing procure me freedom of thought, and quietness of mind,[5] that I may so serve thee in this short and frail life, that I may be received by Thee at my death to everlasting happiness. Take

7. ⟨I have⟩ [a few words obliterated]   8. ⟨Le Clerc⟩ a guinea.   9. ⟨By several purges taken successively and⟩   1. ⟨the⟩   2. An illegible Greek word deleted. 3. ⟨by the⟩   4. ⟨f[it] enable me⟩ fit ∧me for∧   5. ⟨O Lord⟩

Homer, but he never finished it in the original, as Windham noted in his *Diary* (p. 17).

The Mrs. Le Clerc to whom he gave a guinea is unidentified. She was almost certainly a Lichfield woman, perhaps a friend of Johnson's mother.

On the same date Johnson took communion with Catherine Chambers, his mother's old servant, who had been with the family over forty years. She was very ill, and was soon to die. In the second

not O Lord thy Holy Spirit from me, deliver me not up to vain fears[6] but have mercy on me, for the sake of Jesus Christ, our Lord. Amen.

O God who desirest not the Death.

O Lord grant us encrease.

O God.—pardon and Peace.

O God who knowest our necessities

Our Father.

OCT. 18. 1767 SUNDAY. Yesterday, Oct. 17 at about ten in the morning I took my leave for ever of my dear old Friend Catherine Chambers, who came to live with my Mother about 1724, and has been but little parted from us since. She buried

6. ⟨and doubts⟩?

---

paragraph of Johnson's memorandum, part of a Greek word is crossed out and illegible before "friends." Johnson was clearly thinking of his dead friends, and later used the symbol θ in similar circumstances (see 7 April 1776 and 4 April 1779).

After his prayer Johnson added the Introductory Prayer which he had adapted from the Absolution on 25 March 1756, the collect for the fourteenth Sunday after Trinity (see 30 March 1766), that for the twenty-first after Trinity, and the last but one in the Communion Service. These two last are: "Grant, we beseech thee, merciful Lord, to thy faithful people pardon and peace, that they may be cleansed from all their sins, and serve thee with a quiet mind; through Jesus Christ our Lord," and "Almighty God, the fountain of all wisdom, who knowest our necessities before we ask, and our ignorance in asking; We beseech thee to have compassion upon our infirmities; and those things which for our unworthiness we dare not, and for our blindness we cannot ask, vouchsafe to give us, for the worthiness of thy Son Jesus Christ our Lord." He ends with the Lord's Prayer.

Two months later, about to return to London, Johnson prayed

my Father, my Brother, and my Mother. She is now fifty eight years old.

I desired all to withdraw, then told her that we were to part for ever,[7] that as Christians we should part with prayer, and that I would, if she was willing, say a short prayer beside her. She expressed great desire to hear me, and[8] held up her poor hands, as she lay in bed, with great fervour, while[9] I prayed, kneeling by her, nearly in the following words.

Almighty and most merciful Father, whose loving kindness[1] is over all thy works, behold, visit, and relieve this thy Servant who is grieved with sickness. Grant that the sense of her weakness may add strength to her faith, and seriousness to her Repentance. And grant that by the help of thy Holy Spirit[2] after the pains and labours of this short life, we may all obtain everlasting happiness through Jesus Christ, our Lord, for whose sake hear our Prayers. Amen.

Our Father.

I then kissed her. She told me that to part was the greatest pain that she had ever felt, and that she hoped we should meet again in a better place. I expressed with swelled eyes and great[3] emotion of tenderness the same hopes. We kissed and parted, I humbly hope, to meet again, and to part no more.

7. ⟨and⟩ 8. ∧and∧ 9. ∧while∧ ⟨and⟩ I prayed ⟨nearly⟩, kneeling by her ∧nearly∧
1. ∧kindness∧ 2. ⟨we may all⟩ after the pains . . . short life, we may ∧all∧
3. ∧great∧

---

with Kitty for the last time. It is one of Johnson's most affecting prayers.

There are no further entries this year. Johnson's sole literary work, outside his assistance to Chambers in the law lectures, consisted in dedications to Payne's *Geometry* and to Hoole's translation of Metastasio, and some help to Fawkes in a translation of the *Idylliums* of Theocritus.

1 7 6 8

LENT 2. BED-TIME. Almighty God, who seest that I have no power of myself to help myself; keep me both outwardly in my body, and inwardly in my soul, that I may be defended from all adversities that may happen to the body, and from all evil thoughts which may assault and hurt the soul, through Jesus Christ our Lord. Amen.

This prayer may be said before or after the entrance into bed, as a preparative for sleep.

When I transcribed this Prayer, it was my purpose to have made this Book a Collection.

Ejaculation.

Imploring Diligence.

O God, make me to remember that *the night cometh when no man can work.*

JULY 26, 1768. I shaved my nail by accident in whetting the knife, about an eighth of an inch from the bottom, and about

---

The first prayer for 1768 is that for the second Sunday in Lent. Strahan notes that "this book" is "A parchment book containing such of these Prayers as are marked *transcribed.*" The prayer is an "accommodation" of the collect for that Sunday, substituting "I" for "we," etc.

The short ejaculation "Imploring Diligence" is undated but may belong to this year, since the quotation, St. John ix. 4, is the same as that inscribed on the dial of Johnson's watch, which was new this year (*Life*, II.57).

The entry for 26 July was printed by Boswell (III.398) from a diary now lost. Boswell compares it with notes on 7 August 1779 and 15 August 1783, when Johnson noted the length of time required to grow hair after shaving and the amount of weight lost by vine leaves while drying. Boswell suggests that these, with Johnson's experiments in chemistry, should be interpreted as filling "moments which admit of being soothed only by trifles." But it

a fourth from the top. This I measure that I may know the growth of nails; the whole is about five eighths of an inch.

SEPT. 18. 1768 AT NIGHT. Townmalling in Kent.

I have now begun the sixtieth[4] year of my life. How the last year has past I am unwilling to terrify myself with thinking. This day has been past in great perturbation. I was distracted at Church in an uncommon degree, and my distress has had very little intermission. I have found myself somewhat relieved by reading, which I therefore intend to practice when I am able. This day it came into my mind to write the history of my melancholy. On this I purpose to deliberate. I know not whether it may not too much disturb me.

I this day read a great part of Pascal's Life.

4. ∧sixtieth∧ ⟨fifty-ninth⟩

---

appears that they have a larger significance, for Johnson was interested in uncovering facts unknown to him, in examining manufacturing processes like Thrale's brewery and Santerre's in Paris, and in balloon ascents, among many others. It is all part of his wide and constant intellectual curiosity.

Johnson's next birthday prayer was written at the house of Francis Brooke, an attorney, to whom the Thrales had taken him in the course of a little tour for the benefit of his health (Clifford, p. 75). A few days later Mrs. Thrale, seeing the paper in a drawer, copied off the first three sentences. Johnson later wrote that Brooke's house "is one of my favourite places" (Letters 538).

His notion that writing a history of his melancholy might too much disturb him was surely sound. He later gave Boswell good advice on the subject: "Make it an invariable and obligatory law to yourself, never to mention your own mental diseases; if you are never to speak of them, you will think on them but little, and if you think little of them, they will molest you rarely" (Life, III.421).

Johnson's interest in Pascal extended to the Pensées, which on

O Lord who hast safely brought me &c.

Almighty and most merciful Father, Creator and Preserver of mankind, look down with pity upon my troubles and maladies. Heal my body, strengthen my mind.[5] Compose my distraction, calm my inquietude,[6] and relieve my terrours, that if it please thee, I may run the race that is set before me with peace, patience, and confidence. Grant this O Lord, and take not[7] from me thy Holy Spirit but pardon and bless me for the sake of Jesus Christ, our Lord.

LIBER MEMORABILIS. NOV. 14, 1768. To write to W, Lucy, Tolcher, Boswell.

DEC. 1768. The year is almost spent. God enable me to improve my time for Jesus Christs Sake. Amen.

I am now going to bed after two in the morning, being to rise by seven to go to Oxford.

5. ∧Heal . . . mind∧   6. ⟨when [a few words obliterated]⟩ ∧and∧ relieve my terrours ⟨and? [word obliterated] my Faith that I⟩   7. ∧not∧

2 April 1779 he handed to Boswell, "that he might not interrupt me."

Before his prayer, Johnson used his adapted collect, printed under 18 September 1764.

The memorandum of 14 November was lot 437 in Puttick and Simpson's sale of 16 March 1852. It is now lost. None of the letters Johnson mentions are known, if they were indeed written. "W" probably refers to Tom Warton or to Weston, with whom Johnson corresponded near this time. Alderman Henry Tolcher of Plymouth Johnson had described in 1762: "To see brisk young fellows of seventy-four is very pleasing to those who begin to suspect themselves of growing old" (Letters 146).

The next entry from the diary was probably written a few days before 14 December, when Johnson was at Oxford again helping Chambers with his lectures (Letters 211.1).

1 7 6 9

JAN 1. 1769. 24 AFTER 12. I am now about to begin another year. How the last has past, it would be in my state of weakness perhaps not prudent too solicitously to recollect. God will I hope turn my sufferings to my benefit, forgive me whatever I have done amiss, and having vouchsafed me great relief, will by degrees heal and restore both my mind and body, and permit me when the last year of my life shall come, to leave the world in holiness and tranquillity.

I am not yet in a state to form many resolutions; I purpose and hope to rise early in the morning, at eight, and by degrees at six; Eight being the latest hour to which Bedtime can be properly extended, and Six the earliest that the present system of life requires.

Almighty and most merciful Father who hast continued my life from year to year, grant that by longer life I may become less desirous of sinful pleasures, and more careful of eternal happiness. As age comes upon me let my mind be more[8] withdrawn from vanity and folly,[9] more enlightened with the knowledge of thy will, and more invigorated with resolution to obey it. O Lord,[1] calm my thoughts, direct my desires, and fortify my purposes. If it shall please thee, give quiet to my latter days, and[2] so support me with thy grace that I may dye in thy favour for the sake of Jesus Christ our Lord. Amen.

Safely brought us to the beginning of this year.

8. ⟨and more⟩   9. ⟨and⟩ more ⟨∧more and∧⟩   1. A few words obliterated.
2. ⟨let me dye at⟩

The meditation and prayer for New Year's Day 1769 record Johnson's ill health, which he refers to on his next birthday as "a slow progress of recovery," and his optimistic wish to achieve early rising. Hill notes that six years later he did once go to chapel at Oxford at six (*Letters* 399).

After his prayer, Johnson again used his adapted collect.

JAN. 1. SUNDAY. At 1 in the morning I composed a prayer and used it with the collect, *Safely brought us.* Went to Bed at Mr Thrale's. Sl[ept] not ill. Rose at 8, came home, went to Church. Pr. at Davies's. Murphy came in. At 8 went home; at 12 prayed, cub. God help me.

MAY 7. SUNDAY. Yesterday I was much disordered with looseness. To day I find myself recovered. D. G. I read the first homily of Theophanes, and one sermon of Clark.

Went to bed after one.

SEPT. 18. 1769. This day completes the sixtieth year of my age. What I have done and what I have left undone the unsettled state of my mind makes all endeavours to think improper. I hope to survey my life with more tranquillity, in some part of the time which God shall grant me.

The last year has been wholly spent in a slow progress of

The diary on the same day records lunch at Davies's, a visit from Murphy, to bed after midnight.

On 7 May a single entry in the diary gives thanks for recovery from diarrhoea. Feeling better, Johnson read in Theophanes Kerameus, archbishop of Rossano in Calabria (1129–52), whose sermons were famous for "lucid and unforced expositions of biblical texts" (*Catholic Encyclopedia*). Johnson's copy of the first edition, with a Latin translation, was lot 101 in the sale of his library and was bought by Dr. Edward Harwood, author of a "fantastical translation" of the New Testament (*Life*, III.39). This is Johnson's only reference to Theophanes. Samuel Clarke he read often.

Towards the end of May he went to Oxford for an extended stay, and much of August he spent in Lichfield and also Brighton, where he visited the Thrales. He was still there on his birthday.

The distress evident in Johnson's birthday prayer for the things he has left undone reflects not only his ill health but his lack of

recovery. My days are easier, but the perturbation of my nights is very distressful. I think to try a lower diet. I have grown fat too fast. My lungs seem encumbered, and my breath fails me, if my strength [is] in any unusual degree exerted, or my motion accelerated. I seem to myself to bear exercise with more difficulty than in the last winter. But though I feel all these decays of body, I have made no preparation for the grave. What shall I do to be saved?

Almighty and most merciful Father, I now appear in thy presence laden with the[3] sins, and accountable for the mercies of another year. Glory be to thee O God, for the mitigation of my troubles, and for the hope of health both of mind and body which thou hast vouchsafed me.[4] Most merciful Lord if it seem good unto thee, compose my mind, and relieve my diseases,[5] enable me to perform the duties of my station, and so to[6] serve thee, as that, when my hour of departure from this painful life shall be delayed no longer, I may be received to everlasting happiness, for the sake of Jesus Christ our Lord. Amen.

O Lord, without whose help all the purposes of man are vain, enable me to use such temperance as may heal my body, and strengthen my mind and enable me to serve thee. Grant this O Lord, for the sake of Jesus Christ our Saviour. Amen.

Who hast safely brought me to &c.

SEPT. 19. Yesterday having risen from a disturbed and wearisome night, I was not much at rest the whole day. I prayed

---

3. ∧the∧ sins, and ∧accountable for∧ ⟨blessed with⟩ 4. ∧which thou hast vouchsafed me∧ 5. ∧diseases∧ ⟨body [a few words obliterated] and⟩ enable ∧me∧ 6. ∧and so to∧ ⟨that I may so⟩

---

accomplishment. In the past eighteen months, outside of his work with Chambers, he had written only a prologue for Goldsmith's *Good-natur'd Man*, a dedication for Hoole's *Cyrus*, and a little "character" of the clergyman Dr. Mudge. But in spite of his illness

with the collect *to the beginning* in the night and in the morning. At night after diner late[7] I composed my prayer and wrote my resolutions. Reviewing them I found them both weakly conceived, and imperfectly expressed, and corrected the prayer this morning. I am glad that I have not omitted my annual practice. I hope that by rigid temperance, and moderate exercise I may yet recover. I used the prayer again at night, and am now to begin by the permission of God, my sixty first year.

NOV. 5. 1769. Almighty God, merciful Father, whose providence is over all thy works, look down with[8] pity upon the diseases of my body, and the perturbations of my mind. Give thy Blessing, O Lord, to the means which I shall use for my relief, and restore ease to my body, and quiet to my thoughts. Let not my remaining life be made useless by infirmities, neither[9] let health, if thou shalt grant it, be employed by me in disobedience to thy Laws, but give[1] me such a sense of my pains, as may humble me before thee, and such remembrance of thy mercy as may produce honest industry, and[2] holy confidence. And, O Lord, whether thou ordainest my days to be past in ease or[3] anguish, take not from me thy Holy Spirit, but grant that I may attain everlasting life, for the sake of Jesus Christ, our Lord. Amen.

This I found Jan. 11 —72. And believe it written when I began to live on Milk. I grew worse with forbearance of solid food.

7. ⟨after diner late⟩ I composed ⟨the⟩   8. ⟨upon⟩   9. ∧neither∧ ⟨and⟩ let ⟨not⟩
1. ∧give∧ ⟨enab grant⟩   2. ⟨blameless⟩   3. ⟨miser⟩

---

and his concern over his inactivity, his critical sense was undiminished, and on the day after his birthday he corrected and improved his prayer.

Back in London, Johnson was a character witness in Baretti's trial for murder in October, and with the rest of Baretti's friends

1770

PRIMA MANE JAN. 1. 1770. Almighty God by whose mercy I am permitted to behold the beginning of another year, succour with thy help, and bless with thy favour, the creature whom thou vouchsafest to preserve. Mitigate, if it shall seem best unto thee, the diseases of my body, and compose the disorders of my mind. Dispel my terrours[4] and grant that the time which thou shalt yet allow me, may not pass unprofitably away. Let not pleasure seduce me, Idleness lull me, or misery depress me. Let my remaining days be innocent and useful.[5] Let me perform to thy glory and the good of my fellow creatures the work which thou shalt yet[6] appoint me and grant that as I draw nearer to my dissolution, I may by the help of thy Holy Spirit feel my knowledge of Thee encreased, my hope exalted, and my Faith strengthened, that when the hour[7] which is coming shall come, I may pass by a holy death to everlasting joy[8] for the sake of Jesus Christ our Lord. Amen. Hora secunda mane. Beginning—year.[9]

JAN. 1. ☽. About one in the morning I composed a prayer, which I used and went to bed. Rose uncalled. Sent away

4. A few words obliterated.   5. ⟨Let . . . useful.⟩   6. ∧yet∧   7. ∧the hour∧
8. ∧joy∧ ⟨happiness⟩   9. ⟨hora . . . year.⟩

---

rejoiced in the acquittal. In his prayer of 5 November his ill health is still evident, but he was not too ill for charity, since on the same day he solicited a sermon from Percy to be given for a charity school.

At the beginning of his New Year's prayer for 1770, Johnson noted the hour, one in the morning; at the end he originally wrote the hour he finished, two A.M. But perhaps deciding that such "minute particularity" was foolish, he crossed out the second. It is interesting, however, as showing the time, and hence care, which he spent on the prayers.

The diary resumes, on the same day, with the astronomical

Steevens. Went to Church late. Read the four first Chapters of St. Matt. Dined with the Academy. Went to Mrs. Salusbury & to Club. Much disturbed. Came home read the fifth chapter. Slept indifferently.

JAN 2   ♂ . I Began to read, having used the prayer composed yesterday. Mrs Otway hindred me. Mrs Lucy Southwel got a thousand pounds in the Lottery. I read at night the 6th and 7th chapters of St Matthew.

FEBR. 4. ⊙ NEAR THREE IN THE MORNING. Yesterday the 3. I was weak of mind, but grew better after dinner.

FEBR. 5. ☽. ABOUT 2 IN THE MORNING. Yesterday I was pretty calm.

----

symbol for Monday. "Rose uncalled" vividly shows that the reverse was usual.

George Steevens (1736–1800), who was sent away, was then or within the next few weeks starting to help Johnson with the revision of his edition of Shakespeare which appeared in 1773.

In the afternoon Johnson dined with the Royal Academy, to which he was soon appointed Professor in Ancient Literature, an honorary post without emoluments or duties. Later he visited Mrs. Salusbury, Mrs. Thrale's mother.

Next day Johnson uses the astronomical symbol for Tuesday.

Mrs. Otway's identity is unknown, but that Johnson had some charitable interest in her family seems clear from a letter of 25 March 1773, where he says, "I am going this evening to put young Otway to school with Mr. Elphinston." She is mentioned again in an undated memorandum ("Easter Eve," p. 136) and in *Thraliana*, p. 66.

Lucy Southwell was apparently a daughter of Johnson's friend the second Lord Southwell. His letters show that he dined with her on occasion, and on 20 November 1782 he records her death.

The cryptic entry for 4 February means that Johnson is writing on Sunday (symbol) near three A.M., about the day just ended.

MARCH 28. WEDNESDAY. This is the day on which in —52 I was deprived of poor dear Tetty. Having left off the practice of thinking on her with some particular combinations I have recalled her to my mind[1] of late less frequently, but when I recollect the time in which we lived together, my grief for her departure is not abated, and I have less pleasure in any good that befals me, because she does not partake it. On many occasions I think what she would have said or done. When I saw the sea at Brighthelmston I wished for her to have seen it with me. But with respect to her no rational wish is now left but that we may[2] meet at last where the mercy of God shall make us happy, and perhaps make us instrumental to the happiness of each other. It is now eighteen years.

APRIL 14. This week is Passion week.

I have for some weeks past been much afflicted with the Lumbago, or Rheumatism in the Loins, which often passes to the muscles of the belly, where it causes equal, if not greater, pain. In the day the sunshine mitigates it, and in cold or cloudy weather such as has for some [time] past remarkably

1. ∧to my mind∧   2. ∧may∧ ⟨shall⟩

The next day the symbol for Monday recurs.

The meditation on Tetty's birthday is one of the most deeply personal of these years. Johnson remembers seeing the ocean at Brighton for the first time, and wishing that Tetty, who had never seen it, had been there. This apparently refers to the autumn of 1765, when Johnson had followed the Thrales to Brighton and had been angry that they had left (*Anecdotes*, p. 126). In October 1775, having seen the Palais Bourbon in Paris, he wrote in his diary, "As I entered my wife was in my mind; she would have been pleased."

Johnson was at Oxford again with Chambers during the first week in April, returning in Passion Week, on the eleventh. On Saturday the fourteenth he wrote an account of his rheumatism,

prevailed, the heat of a strong fire suspends it. In the night it is so troublesome as not very easily to be born. I lye wrapped in Flannel with a very great fire near my bed, but whether it be that a recumbent posture encreases the pain, or that expansion by moderate warmth excites what a great heat dissipates, I can seldom remain in bed two hours at a time without the necessity of rising to heat the parts affected at the fire.

One night between the pain and the spasms in my stomach I was insupportably distressed. On the next night, I think, I laid a blister to my back and took[3] opium, my night was tolerable, and from that time the spasms in my stomach which disturbed me[4] for many years, and for two past harrassed almost to distraction have nearly ceased. I suppose the breast is relaxed by the opium.

The blister relieved me but for one night. It rose and healed without pain, soreness or strangury. I sweated and bathed without effort. On Wednesday the 11th[5] I was cupped on my return from Oxford with four cups upon the part each applied to draw blood three times.[6] I scarcly felt the scarificator. Either the hot bath or the derivation by the cups eased me for two nights, but last night[7] the pain was great and the necessity of rising frequent.[8]

The narrative is continued after five pages.

I now

3. ⟨an⟩   4. ⟨have⟩ disturbed ∧me∧   5. ∧Wednesday the 11th∧ ⟨Thursday the 12th⟩   6. ⟨It eased. Either the⟩ I scarcly ⟨felt⟩ felt   7. ⟨it⟩   8. ⟨This I wrote⟩ the narrative . . . after five ⟨pages⟩ pages

---

which affected his stomach, and the treatment he had undergone. Hill, probably finding some details distasteful, omitted all the third paragraph except the single word "cupped," which he entered under 11 April.

The events of the week are not easy to follow. Apparently Johnson applied the blister and took opium at Oxford, and felt quick

Having passed Thursday in Passion Week[9] at Mr Thrales I came home on Fryday morning that I might pass the day unobserved. I had nothing but water once in the morning and once at bedtime. I refused tea after some deliberation in the afternoon. They did not press it. I came home late, and was unwilling to carry my Rheumatism to the cold church in the morning, unless that were rather an excuse made to myself. In the Afternoon I went to Church but came late, I think at the Creed. I read Clarks sermon on the Death of Christ.[1] and the second Epistle to Timothy in Greek, but rather hastily. I then went to Thrale's, and had a very tedious and painful night. But the Spasms in my Throat are gone[2] and if either the pain or the opiate which the pain enforced has stopped them the relief is very cheaply purchased. The pain harrasses me much, yet[3] many have the disease perhaps in a much higher degree with want of food, fire, and covering, which I find thus grievous with all the succours that riches and kindness can buy and give.

On Saturday I was not hungry and did not eat much breakfast. There was a dinner and company at which I was persuaded, or tempted, to stay. At night I came home, sat up, composed the prayer, and[4] having ordered the maid to make the fire in my chamber at eight went to rest, and had a tolerable night.

9. ∧in Passion Week∧ 1. Several words obliterated. 2. ∧are gone∧ 3. ⟨I⟩ many have ∧the∧ ⟨my⟩ 4. ⟨was going⟩

---

relief. On Wednesday, at home, he resorted to bleeding and hot baths, and had two comfortable nights, Wednesday at home, and Thursday at Thrale's in Southwark. On Friday he came home that he might fast unobserved. He was late, but not too late to go to church; nevertheless, he did not go, unwilling to expose his rheumatism to the cold church—unless, he honestly says, that was only an excuse. In the afternoon he did go, and returned to

EASTER DAY   APR. 15. 1 IN THE MORNING. Almighty and everlasting God, who hast preserved me by thy[5] fatherly care through all the years of my past Life, and now permittest me again to commemorate the sufferings and the merits of our Lord and Saviour Jesus Christ, grant me so to partake of this holy Rite, that[6] the disquiet of my mind may be appeased, that my Faith may be encreased, my hope strengthened, and my Life regulated by thy Will. Make me truly thankful for that portion of health which thy mercy has restored, and enable me to use the remains of Life to thy glory, and my own Salvation. Take not from me O Lord thy Holy Spirit.[7] Extinguish in my mind all sinful and inordinate desires. Let me resolve to do that which is right, and let me by thy help keep my resolutions. Let me, if it be left for me, at last know peace and comfort, but whatever state of life thou shalt appoint me let me end it[8] by a happy death, and enjoy eternal happiness in thy presence, for the sake of Jesus Christ our Lord. Amen.

1 IN THE AFTERNOON EASTER DAY. I am just returned from the communion having been very little interrupted in my duty by bodily pain.

I was very early at church and used this prayer, I think, before service, with proper collects. I was composed during the Service. I went to the table to hear the prefatory part of the office, then returned to my pew, and tried to settle some resolutions. I resolved to form this day some plan for reading the Scriptures.

5. ⟨providence⟩   6. ⟨my⟩   7. ∧Take not . . . Spirit. Extinguish . . . desires.∧
8. ⟨at last⟩

Thrale's for the night, which was a painful one. On Saturday he came home after dinner, wrote the first three paragraphs of the present account, composed his Easter prayer, and retired to "a tolerable night's sleep."

The line at the end of the third paragraph, "the narrative is

To confirm myself in the conviction of the truths of Religion.[9]

To rise by eight, or earlier.

To form a plan for the regulation of my daily life.

To excite in myself such a fervent desire of pleasing God as should suppress all other passions.[1]

I prayed through all the collects of meditation, with some extemporary prayers recommended my friends living and dead. When I returned to the table I staid till most had communicated, and in the mean time tried to settle my mind, prayed against bad and troublesome thoughts, resolved to oppose sudden incursions of them, and I think had ————[2] thrown into my mind at the general confession, when I went first to the table. The particular series of my thoughts I cannot recollect.

When I came home I returned thanks by accommodating the general thanksgiving, and used this prayer again with the collects after receiving. I hope God has heard me.

9. ⟨To confirm . . . Religion.⟩ 1. ⟨To repent of [illegible] in some fitting manner.⟩ ⟨To [rest of line illegible]⟩ 2. One word blotted.

———————————

continued after five pages," refers to the five pages which comprise the Easter prayer and meditation. The last pages of the medical narrative were probably written Easter night after his return from Evening Prayer.

In his meditation for Easter, Johnson mentions the "collects of meditation" he used at church. These were perhaps the same three that he used on Easter 1765. It is unlikely that he would use the word "collects" for prayers in books of private devotion like Taylor's *Worthy Communicant*, though one of his definitions is "any short prayer."

The General Thanksgiving Johnson adapted for use at home by substituting "I" for "we," etc.:

Almighty God, Father of all mercies, we, thine unworthy servants, do give thee most humble and hearty thanks for all thy

Shall I ever receive the Sacrament with tranquillity. Surely the time will come.

Some vain thoughts stole upon me while I stood near the table, I hope I ejected them[3] effectually so as not to be hurt by them.

I went to prayers at seven having first read the two morning lessons in Greek. At night I read Clarkes Sermon of the Humiliation of our Saviour.

1 SUNDAY AFTER EASTER. I have been recovering from my rheumatism slowly yet sensibly. But the last week has produced little good. Uneasy nights have tempted me to lye long in the morning. But when I wake in the night the release

3. ⟨so⟩

goodness and loving-kindness to us, and to all men; (particularly to those who desire now to offer up their praises and thanksgivings for thy late mercies vouchsafed unto them.) We bless thee for our creation, preservation, and all the blessings of this life; but above all, for thine inestimable love in the redemption of the world by our Lord Jesus Christ; for the means of grace, and for the hope of glory. And, we beseech thee, give us that due sense of all thy mercies, that our hearts may be unfeignedly thankful; and that we show forth thy praise, not only with our lips, but in our lives, by giving up our selves to thy service, and by walking before thee in holiness and righteousness all our days; through Jesus Christ our Lord, to whom, with thee and the Holy Ghost, be all honour and glory, world without end.

In the last paragraph of the meditation, Strahan and Hill have unfortunately read "first" as "fasted." The reading is certain; moreover, Johnson never fasted on Easter after receiving communion, and usually fasted only on Good Friday.

On 22 April Johnson reviewed his medical progress of the past week, which was moderate, and his progress in reading the Bible,

which still continues from the spasms in my throat gives me great comfort.

The plan which I formed for reading the Scriptures was to read 600 verses in Old Testament, and 200 in the New every week.[4] The Old Testament in any language, the New in Greek. This day I began to read the Septuagint but read only 230 verses, the nine first Chapters of Genesis.

On this evening I repeated the prayer for Easter day, changing the future tense to the past.

JUNE 1. Every Man naturally persuades himself that he can keep his[5] resolutions, nor is he convinced of his[6] imbecillity but by length of time, and frequency of experiment.[7] This opinion of our own constancy is so prevalent, that we always despise him who suffers his general and settled purpose to be overpowered by an occasional desire. They[8] therefore whom frequent failures have made desperate cease to form resolutions, and they who are become cunning do not tell them. Those who do not make them, are very few, but of their effect little is perceived, for scarcely any man persists in a course

4. ⟨On⟩   5. ⟨own⟩   6. ⟨own⟩   7. ⟨Nor can is it easy⟩   8. ᴧTheyᴧ ⟨Those⟩
... ᴧcease to formᴧ ⟨form no⟩ ... and ᴧtheyᴧ ⟨those⟩

---

which was poor. Since 13 July 1755 he had formed various plans for such reading, but so far had read only three of the Gospels and a little of Genesis.

Johnson's meditation of 1 June on keeping resolutions is interesting for the three people leading "regular" lives. Johnson's cousin Mrs. Harriots, mentioned in the "Annals" under 1710–11, extended her own regularity to her household. Dr. John Campbell (1708–75), a miscellaneous writer whose exactness Johnson knew only by the man's report, had been described by Johnson in 1763: "Campbell is a good man, a pious man. I am afraid he has not been in the inside of a church for many years; but he never passes a church without pulling off his hat. This shews that he has good

of life planned by choice, but as he is restrained from deviation by some external power. He who may live as he will, seldom lives long in the observation of his own rules. I never yet saw a regular family unless it were that of Mrs Harriots, nor a regular man except Mr Campbel whose exactness I know only by his own report, and Psalmanazar whose life was I think, uniform.

1771

PALM SUNDAY   MARCH 24. I purposed this day to begin my Greek Testament, but was unwilling to go to study, and hour stole away after hour. I did not go to Church. 12 pages

---

principles" (*Life*, 1.418). Hill appropriately quotes Reynolds on Johnson: "He was not easily imposed upon by professions to honesty and candour; but he appeared to have little suspicion of hypocrisy in religion."

Johnson's third example, George Psalmanazar (d. 1763) is most remarkable. He had passed his first forty years in an astounding series of impostures, culminating in his *Description of Formosa*, in which he passed himself off as a Formosan kidnapped by Jesuits and converted to Christianity. He eventually reformed to such a degree that Johnson, as Hill says, regarded him almost as a saint. Yet his posthumously published *Memoirs* have passages which sound boastful and even hypocritical.

During the rest of the year there are neither prayers nor diary entries. Johnson spent July in Lichfield and Ashbourne, seems to have spent a week in November visiting a friend on board H.M.S. *Ramillies* (*Life*, v.514), and wrote little. His major publication was *The False Alarm*, the first and his favourite of the political pamphlets. Presumably he worked intermittently revising his *Shakespeare*.

The first entry in the diary for 1771 is that on Palm Sunday. Johnson plans to read the New Testament by reading concurrently the Greek and the Latin translation by Theodore Beza (1519–

in 4to Gr. Test. and 30 pages in Beza's Folio comprise the whole in 40 days.

I began it on Easter Day, and have continued it in due proportions three weeks.

V. T.	588	19. Gen. 27
N. T.	188	3 Gen. 5
40/776/19		15 Gen. 24 V 30
40		
376		188
360		3
16		564

Apocr.   143   50/776/15
                        50
Pent.   150 pages   276
                        250
Hist.   196   26

Poet.   90   300/776/2
                        600
Proph.   152   176

                        776
                        143
                     300/919/3
                        900
                        19

1605), a French Protestant who also edited the New Testament. Four weeks later he has made good progress.

The calculations concerning the number of days needed to read through the Bible by doing a given number of pages a day are found at the end of the diary, out of chronological order. They may well belong here, though the calculations do not apply to the editions Johnson has just mentioned. They are preceded by

EASTER EVE. I rose and breakfasted, eat little; gave orders
that Mr *Stainesby the Clergyman who is to give dying Jenny
the Sacrament, should have 5s–3d. Steevens was with me. Watson paid. Mrs Otway. About Noon I grew faint by fasting,
then dined on Fish and eggs at the Mitre.
  *He came to Jenny very carefully.
  I then came home, and read two of Rogers's sermons.[9] Between ten and eleven I was very weary, I think, by fasting, and
a night rather unquiet. I was not much sleepy this day.
  O God for Jesus Christ's Sake have mercy upon me. Amen.[1]

9. A line deleted.   1. Two lines deleted.

---

the list of table linen bought in April 1771. It should be remembered that Johnson normally read the Bible only on Sundays, so
that his "40 days" really means forty weeks.
  We have moved the Easter prayer slightly out of chronological
order so that the material on reading the Bible might not be awkwardly interrupted.
  Of the undated prayers and meditations placed by Hill and
Strahan at the end of their collections, six may belong to the
spring of this year. All are on loose sheets, one or two to a sheet,
and are inserted in Book Six of the Prayers and Meditations, itself
consisting mostly of unbound leaves. All of the dated prayers in
Book Six fall between 1 January 1767 and 23 September 1771. The
prayer for Easter Eve is on paper and in ink matching dated
prayers for 1771, and it will fit in Easter Eve of that year, and in
no later years except 1780 or 1782. Mrs. Otway, Johnson had
mentioned on 2 January 1770, and in this year Steevens was working with Johnson on their edition of Shakespeare, which appeared
in 1773. The Reverend Richard Stainsby had been lecturer of
the church of St. Mary le Strand since 1755, and held the post till
his death in 1798 (*Gentleman's Magazine*, xxv, 44; lxviii, 447).
Jenny may have been a servant in Johnson's house in Johnson's
Court, Fleet Street, not far away from the church. Of Watson there
is no clue, unless he is the same as Watson the painter mentioned

[2]this reluctance, I shall break a long habit of self indulgence, and counteract by very frequent repulses that general indolence that preys upon my time. To read the New Testament once a year, in Greek.

RECEIVING THE SACRAMENT.

I profess my Faith in Jesus. I declare my resolution to obey him. I implore in the highest act of worship Grace to keep these resolutions.

I hope to rise to a new life this day.

I did not this week labour my preparation so much as I have sometimes done. My Mind was not very quiet; and an anxious preparation makes the duty of the day formidable and burdensome. Different methods suit different states of mind, body, and affairs. I rose this day, and prayed, then went to tea, and afterwards composed the prayer, which I formed with great fluency. I went to church, came in at the Psalms, could not hear the reader in the lessons, but attended the prayers with tranquillity.[3]

2. The beginning of this Meditation is not known.   3. ⟨I was afterwards⟩. The conclusion of this Meditation is not known.

---

in the diary under 11, 13 September and 20 October 1777. Rogers's sermons Johnson had read at Edial in 1736.

The next fragmentary meditation (Easter morning?), along with Johnson's moving profession of faith on receiving the sacrament, and the following meditation (Easter evening?) were printed in reverse order by Strahan and Hill by omitting the fragmentary sentences at beginning and end; in other words, they printed the verso of the leaf before the recto. There is at least one leaf missing before and another after. The resolution to read through the New Testament in Greek at least once a year is particularly appropriate at this date, for Johnson began to do so on this day,

[4]O Lord God, in whose hand are the wills and affections of men, kindle in my mind holy desires, and repress sinful and corrupt imaginations. Enable me to love thy commandments, and to desire thy promises; let me by thy protection and influence so pass through things temporal, as finally not to lose the things eternal, and among the[5] hopes and fears, the pleasures and sorrows, the dangers and deliverances, and all the changes of this life, let my heart be surely fixed by the help of thy Holy Spirit[6] on the everlasting fruition of thy presence, where true joys are to be found, grant O Lord, these petitions.

Forgive, O merciful Lord, whatever I have done contrary to thy laws.[7] Give me[8] such a sense of my Wickedness as may produce true contrition and effectual repentance, so that when I shall be called into another state, I may be received among the sinners, to whom sorrow and reformation have[9] obtained pardon, for Jesus Christs Sake. Amen.

4. ⟨Forgive⟩   5. ⟨manifold dan[gers]⟩ . . . ∧deliverances∧ ⟨escapes⟩   6. ∧by the help . . . Spirit∧ . . . ∧fruition∧ ⟨enjoy[ment]⟩   7. Two lines obliterated. 8. ∧me∧ . . . ∧when∧ I . . . ∧to∧ whom   9. ⟨∧made∧ restore⟩

---

and finished it this year for the first time. The relative tranquillity of these meditations fits the mood of Johnson's Easter prayer exactly.

The last three undated prayers we place here a little arbitrarily. The first is on a single sheet, the second and third on another, and inserted in the book ending in 1771. They are not distant in tone from those just above. They all lean rather heavily on the *Book of Common Prayer*. The first uses the collect for the fourth Sunday after Easter: "O almighty God, who alone canst order the unruly wills and affections of sinful men; Grant unto thy people, that they may love the thing which thou commandest, and desire that which thou dost promise; that so, among the sundry and manifold changes of the world, our hearts may surely there be fixed, where true joys are to be found; through Jesus Christ our Lord."

Almighty and most merciful Father whose clemency[1] I now presume to implore after a long life of carelessness and wickedness, have mercy upon me. I have committed many crimes.[2] I have neglected many duties. I have done what Thou hast forbidden, and left undone what thou hast commanded. Forgive, merciful Lord my sins, negligences, and ignorances, and enable me by thy Holy Spirit to amend my life according to thy holy word for Jesus Christ's sake. Amen.

O merciful God, full of compassion, long-suffering, and of great pity, who sparest when we deserve punishment, and in thy wrath thinkest upon mercy, make me earnestly to repent, and heartily to be sorry for all my misdoings, make the remembrance so burdensome and painful, that I may flee to

1. ∧whose clemency∧ ⟨before whom⟩ I now presume ⟨with all   to worship and⟩ ∧to∧ implore after a ∧long∧ life ⟨past in⟩ ∧of carelessness and∧ wickedness, have ⟨mercy for⟩ mercy upon ⟨my⟩ me.   2. ⟨crimes⟩ ∧trespasses∧

In the next, Strahan has heavily deleted Johnson's "crimes," probably feeling that it would be misinterpreted, and substituted the innocuous "trespasses." The prayer uses a distant paraphrase of part of the General Confession: "We have left undone those things which we ought to have done; And we have done those things which we ought not to have done," and a close paraphrase of part of the Litany: "That it may please thee to give us true repentance; to forgive us all our sins, negligences, and ignorances; and to endue us with the grace of thy Holy Spirit to amend our lives according to thy holy Word; We beseech thee to hear us, good Lord."

The last of the undated prayers uses part of the Commination (Penitential Office): "For thou art a merciful God, Full of compassion, Long-suffering, and of great pity. Thou sparest when we deserve punishment, And in thy wrath thinkest upon mercy." Then Johnson turned to the General Confession before Holy Communion: "We do earnestly repent, And are heartily sorry for these our misdoings; The remembrance of them is grievous unto

Thee with a troubled spirit, and a contrite heart; and O merciful[3] Lord visit, comfort, and relieve me, cast me not out from thy presence and take not thy Holy Spirit from me, but excite in[4] me true repentance, give me in this world knowledge of thy truth, and confidence in thy mercy, and in the world to come life everlasting, for the sake of our Lord and Saviour, thy Son Jesus Christ. Amen.

EASTER DAY. MARCH 31. —71. Almighty and most merciful Father, I am now about to commemorate once more in thy presence the redemption of the world by our Lord and Saviour, thy Son Jesus Christ. Grant, O most merciful God, that the benefit of his sufferings may be extended to me. Grant me Faith, grant me Repentance. Illuminate me with thy Holy Spirit.[5] Enable me to form good purposes, and to bring those purposes to good effect. Let me so dispose my time, that I may discharge the duties to which thou shalt vouchsafe to call me, and let that degree of health to which thy mercy has restored me be employed to thy Glory.[6] O God,[7] invigorate my understanding, compose my perturbations, recal my wanderings, and calm my thoughts, that having lived while thou shalt grant me life, to do good and to praise Thee, I may when thy call shall summon me to another state, receive mercy from thee, for Jesus Christs Sake. Amen.

De pedicis et manicis insana cogitatio.

3. ⟨visit⟩   4. ∧excite in∧ ⟨give⟩   5. Two and a half lines obliterated.   6. A few words obliterated.   7. ⟨and⟩

---

us; The burden of them is intolerable." He concludes with part of St. Chrysostom's prayer: "Fulfil now, O Lord, the desires and petitions of thy servants, as may be most expedient for them; granting us in this world knowledge of thy truth, and in the world to come life everlasting."

Johnson's "mad reflection on shackles and hand-cuffs" follows, in the diary, his comment on his progress in reading in the three

[Almighty and most merciful Father
whose clemency
before whom I now presume with
and to implore after a long life passed
of carelessness and
in wickedness, have mercy for mercy upon
my one. I have committed many trespasses

I have neglected many duties. I have done
what Thou hast forbidden, and left
undone what thou hast commanded
Forgive, merciful Lord my sins my
laziness, and ignorances, and enable me
by thy holy Spirit to amend my life
according to thy holy word for Jesus
Christs sake. Amen

Prayer, 1771?

APR 28 —71. I read some portion of my Greek Testament, not remembering that I read the same on the foregoing Sunday till I came to a remarkable passage. The same happened some years ago in reading Isocrates, or nearly the same.

Κρήματα

TABLE LINEN, BOUGHT, APR. 1771

4	Large Cloaths	4– 0–0
2	Middle ---	1–12–0
6	Napkins	
	6 yards $\frac{3}{8}$	0–17–6
2	Small cloaths ---	0–12–0
6	Napkins - -	0–12–0

Plate

Teapot	7– 0–0
Coffeepot	10– 0–0

bought

6 Table Spoons
Soop Ladle

bought

---

weeks since Easter. It is certainly related to Johnson's almost pathological melancholy. For one interpretation see Katharine Balderston's "Johnson's Vile Melancholy," in *The Age of Johnson.*

On a blank page opposite that on which Johnson mentions his inadvertently rereading some of the Greek Testament, he recalls doing the same earlier with the orations of Isocrates (436–338 B.C.). Johnson's copy of Isocrates was in lot 6 in the sale of his library.

The list of Johnson's "possessions" occurs near the end of the diary, preceding the calculations about reading given above. The

2 Salts with Spoons

bought

6 Desert Spoons
2 Small Salvers
2 Candle Sticks
2
2 Tea Spoons
Teatongs
2 Rings

AUGUST. 25 SUNDAY —71. 13 AFTER TR[INITY].
Since last Easter
I have gone to church once every Sunday except one.
I have added something to my evening devotions.
I have read my Greek Testament regularly, except while
I was in the Country.
I have M. once by accident.
I have used more corporal action.

SEPTEMBER 18. 9. AT NIGHT. I am now come to my sixty
third year. For the last year I have been slowly recovering
both from the violence of my last ilness, and, I think, from
the general disease of my life. My Breath is less obstructed,
and I am more capable of motion and exercise. My mind is
less encumbered, and I am less interrupted in mental employment. Some advances I hope have been made towards regu-

---

Greek word should be χρήματα, which Johnson has confused with
its synonym κτήματα.

Towards the middle of August Johnson returned from a visit
of six weeks or more to Lichfield and Ashbourne, and, as the diary
shows, on 25 August, the thirteenth Sunday after Trinity, he was
able to record regular progress in the Greek Testament, as well
as unusual regularity in church attendance. He had done no
writing since the publication in March of his second political

larity. I have missed Church since Easter only two Sundays
both which I hope I have endeavoured to supply[8] by attendance on Divine Worship in the following week. Since Easter
my Evening devotions have been lengthened. But Indolence
and indifference has been neither[9] conquered nor opposed.
No plan of study has been persued or formed except that I
have commonly read every week, if not on Sunday, a stated
portion of the New Testament in greek. But what is most
to be considered I have neither attempted nor formed any
scheme of Life by which I may do good, and please God.

One great hindrance is want of rest; my nocturnal complaints grow less troublesome towards morning, and I am
tempted [to] repair the deficiencies of the night. I think however to try to rise every day by eight, and to combat indolence
as I shall obtain strength. Perhaps Providence has yet some
use for the remnant of my life.

Almighty and everlasting God, whose mercy is over all thy
works, and who hast no pleasure in the Death of a Sinner,
look with pity upon me, succour, and preserve me; enable
me[1] to conquer evil habits, and surmount temptations. Give
me Grace so to use the degree of[2] health which thou hast
restored to my Mind and Body, that I may perform the task[3]
thou shalt yet appoint me. Look down, O gracious Lord upon
my[4] remaining part of Life, grant if it please thee that the

8. ⟨in the⟩ . . . Worship ₐin ₐ ⟨on⟩   9. ⟨improved⟩   1. A few words obliterated.
2. ₐdegree of ₐ   3. ⟨which ₐthat ₐ⟩ . . . appoint me, ⟨to thy Glory according to thy
will.⟩   4. ₐmy ₐ ⟨the⟩ . . . of ⟨my⟩ Life . . . ₐif it please thee ₐ

---

pamphlet, *Thoughts on the Late Transactions Respecting Falkland's Islands.* But now he began a major task, the revision of
his *Dictionary* for the fourth edition.

In Johnson's birthday meditation, perhaps his most noteworthy
comment is that Providence may yet have some use for the rest
of his life. The *Lives of the Poets* was still to come.

days few or many which thou shalt yet allow me, may pass in
reasonable confidence, and holy tranquillity. Withold not thy
Holy Spirit from me but strengthen all good purposes till
they shall produce a life pleasing to thee. And when thou
shalt call me to another state, forgive me my sins, and receive
me to Happiness, for the sake of Jesus Christ, our Lord.
Amen.

Safely brought us. &c.

SEPT. 23. 1771. On the 18th in the morning before I went
to Bed I used the general prayer (beginning of this year).
When I rose, I came home from Mr Thrale's that I might
be more master of my hours. I went to Church in the Morning, but came in to the Litany. I have gone voluntarily to
Church on the weekday but few times in my Life. I think to
mend. In the afternoon I was somewhat engaged one way or
other. I went with Macbean to dine.[5]

At night I composed and used the prayer, which I have used
since in my devotions one morning. Having been somewhat
disturbed, I have not yet settled in any plan, except that
yesterday I began to learn some verses in the Greek Testament for a Sundays recital. I hope by Trust in God to amend
my Life.

5. ⟨In the afternoon . . . dine.⟩

The collect with which he ends his prayer is that regularly used
on his birthday.

On 23 September he recalls using the same collect before retiring
on the eve of his birthday. Alexander Macbean, with whom Johnson dined, was an amanuensis who helped with the original
edition of the *Dictionary*. In 1773 Johnson wrote a preface for his
Dictionary of Ancient Geography. This sentence was deleted by
Strahan probably because it is secular material in the midst of
religious matter.

DR. 22. I have remitted much of my regularity, but am now in Hebrews. My purpose is to read two hundred verses every Sunday, if I can between Morning prayer and dinner.

PSALMUS 117.

Anni quà volucris ducitur orbita,
*Regem coelicolûm pe[r]petuo colunt
Quovis sanguine cretae
Gentes undique carmine.

blandior
*Regem, cujus amor laetior in dies
Mortales miseros servat, alit, fovet,
Omnes undique Gentes
Sancto dicite carmine.
In lecto.   *utrobique Patrem

1772

JAN. 1. 1772 2 IN THE MORNING. Almighty God, who hast permitted me to see the beginning of another year, enable me⁶ so to receive thy mercy, as that it may raise in⁷ me stronger desires of pleasing thee by purity of mind, and holi-

6. ⟨by thy grace⟩   7. ∧in∧

On 22 December Johnson records in his diary his good progress in reading the Greek Testament.

Following in the diary is the translation into Latin of Psalm 117, which was among the Latin poems collected and edited by Langton for the first edition of Johnson's *Works*. Langton replaced each "Regem" with "Patrem" as Johnson indicated. It was written in bed, probably in sleepless hours, as was much verse during Johnson's later years.

ness of Life. Strengthen me O Lord,[8] in good purposes, and reasonable meditations. Look with pity upon all my disorders of mind, and infirmities of body. Grant that the residue of my life may enjoy such degrees of health as may permit me to be useful, and that I may live to thy Glory; and O merciful Lord when it shall please thee to call me from the present state, enable me to dye in confidence of thy mercy, and receive me to everlasting happiness for the sake of Jesus Christ our Lord. Amen.

To rise in the morning.

EASTER EVE   APR. 18. 1772. I am now again preparing by Divine Mercy to commemorate the Death of my gracious Redeemer, and to form, as God shall enable me, resolutions and purposes of a better life.

When I review the last year, I am able to recollect so little done, that shame and sorrow, though perhaps too weakly, come upon me. Yet I have been generally free from local pain, and my strength has seemed gradually to increase. But my[9] sleep has generally been unquiet, and I have not been able to rise early. My mind is unsettled and my memory confused. I have of late turned my thoughts[1] with a very useless earnestness upon past incidents. I have yet got no command over my thoughts; an unpleasing incident is almost certain to hinder my rest. This is the remainder of my last ilness. By sleepless or unquiet nights and short days, made short by late

8. "O Lord," part of an obliterated line after "Life," is in the MS cued in at this place.   9. ₍But my₎ ⟨My⟩   1. ₍thoughts₎ ⟨mind⟩

After Johnson's New Year's prayer for 1772, the single resolution, to rise in the morning, does not sound confident.

In his meditation for Easter Eve, Johnson's comment that an unpleasant incident is liable to hinder his sleep, is enforced, Hill remarks, in a letter to Taylor (277) of the next August: "I had formerly great command of my attention, and what I did not

rising, the time passes away uncounted and unheeded. Life
so spent is useless.

I hope to cast my time into some stated method.

To let no hour pass unemployed.

To rise by degrees more early in the morning.

To keep a Journal.

I have, I think, been less guilty of neglecting publick worship than formerly. I have commonly on Sunday gone once
to church, and if I have missed, have reproached my self.

I have exerted rather more activity of body. These disposi-
tions I desire to improve.

I resolved, last Easter to read within the year the whole
Bible, a very great part of which I had never looked upon.
I read the Greek Testament without construing and this day
concluded the Apocalypse. I think that no part was missed.

My purpose of reading the rest of the Bible was forgotten,
till I took by chance the resolutions of last Easter in my hand.

I began it the first day of lent, and for a² time read with
some regularity. I was then disturbed or seduced, but finished
the old Testament last Thursday.

I hope to read the whole Bible once a year as long as I live.

2. ‸ᵃ‸

---

like could forbear to think on. But of this power which is of the
highest importance to the tranquillity of life, I have for some
time past been so much exhausted that I do not go into a company
towards night in which I foresee any thing disagreeable, nor
enquire after any thing to which I am not indifferent, lest something, which I know to be nothing, should fasten upon my imagination, and hinder me from sleep."

Johnson then notes that he has finally accomplished what he
has planned for years: he has read all the Bible except the Apocrypha (see 26 April below); the New Testament in Greek, the Old
probably in English, since he read that in just over five weeks,
including an extended interruption.

Yesterday I fasted, as I have always,[3] or commonly done, since the death of Tetty. The Fast was more painful than it has formerly been, which I imputed to some medicinal evacuations in the beginning of the week, and to a meal of cakes on the forgoing day. I can not now fast as formerly.

I devoted this week to the perusal of the Bible, and have done little secular business. I am this night easier than is customary on this anniversary, but am not sensibly enlightened.

EASTER DAY AFTER 12 AT NIGHT. The Day is now begun, on which I hope to begin a new course[4] ὥσπερ ἀφ᾽ ὑσπλήγγων.[5] My hopes are from this time

To rise early

To waste less time

To appropriate something to charity.

Almighty God, merciful Father, who hatest nothing that thou hast made, look down with pity on my sinfulness and

3. ⟨done⟩ ∧or∧   4. ∧course∧   5. Johnson has inserted η above a.

In commenting on his Good Friday fast, Johnson originally wrote "as I have always done," but before he went on, his scrupulous honesty made him delete "done" and continue "or commonly done."

Johnson made two versions of the meditation and prayer for Easter Eve, the first after midnight, and the second, on a separate and larger sheet, probably the next morning. This sheet was stitched to the others after the entries of the following Sunday. Strahan and Hill combined the two versions, using the meditation of the first and the prayer of the second. We print both of Johnson's versions together.

The Greek phrase in the first, "as from the starting line," occurs in several classical authors, among them Plato (*Phaedrus*, 254E). Johnson apparently quotes from memory, as he had trouble with one letter, and made another slight alteration.

Johnson's resolution to "appropriate something to charity"

weakness. Strengthen my mind, O Lord, deliver me from needless terrours.[6] Enable me to correct all inordinate desires, to eject all wicked thoughts, to break off all sinful habits and so to regulate my life, that when at the end of my days thou shalt call me hence, I may depart in peace, and be received to everlasting happiness for the sake of Jesus Christ our Lord. Amen.

EASTER 7 2. I hope from this time
  To rise more early
  To waste less time
  To appropriate something to Charity.

Almighty God, merciful Father, who hatest nothing that thou hast made, look down with pity upon my sinfulness and weakness. Strengthen, O Lord, my mind;[7] deliver me from needless terrours.[8] Enable me to correct all inordinate desires, to eject all evil thoughts,[9] to reform all sinful habits, and so to amend my life, that when at the end of my days thou shalt call me hence, I may[1] depart in peace, and be received into everlasting happiness for the sake of Jesus Christ our Lord. Amen.

9 IN THE MORNING. Glory be to Thee, O Lord God, for the deliverance which thou hast granted me from diseases of mind and body. Grant, O gracious God, that I may employ the powers which thou vouchsafest me to thy Glory, and the Salvation of my soul, for the sake of Jesus Christ. Amen.

6. Two and a half lines obliterated.   7. ⟨that⟩   8. Two and a half lines obliterated.   9. ⟨and⟩   1. ⟨dye⟩

———

was, for him, clearly superfluous, as the many instances of his charity noted up to this date demonstrate. They could be multiplied by both the evidence of the diary and testimony of his friends.

Johnson's recovery from illness, for which he gives thanks in

APR. 26. I was some way hindered from continuing this[2] contemplation in the usual manner, and therefore try at the distance of a week to review the last Sunday.

I went to Church early having first I think, used my prayer. When I was there I had very little perturbation of mind. During the usual time of Meditation, I considered the Christian Duties under the three principles of Soberness; Righteousness; and Godliness, and purposed to forward Godliness by the *annual perusal of the Bible*; Righteousness *by settling something for Charity*, and soberness *by early hours*. I commended as usual with preface of permission, and I think, mentioned Bathurst. I came home, and found Paoli and Boswel waiting for me. What devotions I used after my return home I do not distinctly remember. I went to prayers in the evening, and, I think, entred late. The Minister, a young man, read the lessons for the day of the month, instead of those for Easter day.[3] I have this week endeavoured every day but one to rise early, and have tried to be diligent, but have not performed what I required from myself.

On Good Fryday I paid Peyton without requiring work.

2. ⟨in the⟩   3. ⟨The Minister . . . Easter day.⟩

---

his prayer at nine on Easter morning, was not complete, but he was so much better that he might well speak of "deliverance."

A week later he reviewed the events of Easter Day. He had prayed for his dead relatives and friends, including Bathurst, who had now been dead for eight years. In the afternoon General Paoli and Boswell called. Recording the conversation, Boswell found Johnson cheerful and animated (*Life*, II.190).

The innocent sentence about the young clergyman who read the wrong lessons was too much for Strahan, himself a young clergyman, and he scored it out, protecting the cloth.

Peyton, whom Johnson had paid on Good Friday, had been an amanuensis for the original *Dictionary*, and was now helping

Since Easter –71 I have added a collect to my Evening devotion.

I have been less indulgent to corporal inactivity. But I have done little with my mind.

It is a comfort to me that, at last, in my Sixty third year, I have attained to know, even thus hastily, confusedly, and imperfectly, what my Bible contains.

May the good God encrease and sanctify my knowledge.

I have never yet read the apocrypha. When I was a boy I have read or heard Bel and the dragon, Susannah,[4] some of Tobit, perhaps all. Some at least of Judith, and some of Ecclesiasticus; and, I suppose, the Benedicite. I have some time looked into the Maccabees, and read a chapter containing the question *Which is the Strongest*, I think, in Esdras.

In the afternoon of Easter day, I read Pococke's commentary.[5]

---

with the new edition. Johnson seems to mean that he did not require him to work during Passion Week, when Johnson would not work himself, but paid him anyway. Peyton was extremely poor, and Johnson's act was a combination of fairness, humanity, and religion.

When Johnson says that he has never yet read the Apocrypha, he means that he has not read it through, for he mentions all but five of the fourteen books. The Benedicite is The Song of the Three Holy Children, from which the Benedicite in the *Book of Common Prayer* is derived. The question in I Esdras iii. 10 was proposed as a contest by three young bodyguards of the king. "The first wrote, Wine is the strongest. The second wrote, The king is the strongest. The third wrote, Women are strongest: but above all things Truth beareth away the victory."

Edward Pococke's *Commentary on Micah, Malachi, Hosea, and Joel*, 1677–91, was not his only work to interest Johnson. "At the time when Johnson's pension was granted to him, he said,

I have this last week scarcely tried to read, nor have I read any thing this day.

I have had my mind weak and disturbed for some weeks past.

Having missed Church in the morning I went this evening, and afterwards sat with Southwel.

Having not used the prayer except on the day of communion, I will offer it this night, and hope to find mercy.

On this day little has been done and this is now the last hour. In life little has been done, and life is very far advanced. Lord have mercy upon me.

1773

JAN 1. MANE 1.33'. Almighty God, by whose mercy my life has been yet prolonged to another year, grant that thy mercy may not be vain. Let not my years be multiplied[6] to encrease my guilt, but as age advances, let me become more pure in my thoughts,[7] more regular in my desires, & more obedient to thy laws.[8] Let not the cares of the world distract

6. ∧years be ⟨continued⟩ multiplied∧ ⟨life be prolonged⟩ 7. ⟨and⟩ 8. Several words deleted; ampersand inserted by Strahan before "more," and several words deleted after "Let not."

with a noble literary ambition, 'Had this happened twenty years ago, I should have gone to Constantinople to learn Arabick, as Pococke did' " (Life, IV.27).

"Southwel," with whom Johnson sat after church, was perhaps a brother of the Lucy Southwell who won at the lottery. Johnson was with them both the next January (Letters 294).

The prayer used by Johnson the same night was probably that composed a week earlier, on Easter Eve.

During the rest of the year Johnson continued with the revision of the Dictionary, visited Lichfield and Ashbourne for nearly two months, 15 October to 7 December, and published nothing.

Of the New Year's prayer for 1773, perhaps the most noteworthy

me, nor the evils of age overwhelm me. But continue and encrease thy loving kindness towards me,[9] and when thou shalt call me hence, receive me to everlasting happiness, for the sake of Jesus Christ, our Lord. Amen.

GOOD FRIDAY AP. 9. 1773. On this day I went twice to Church and Boswel was with me. I had forborn to attend Divine service for some time in the winter, having a cough which would have interrupted both my own attention and that of others, and when the cough grew less troublesome I did not regain the habit of going to church, though I did not wholly omit it. I found the service not burthensome nor tedious, though I could not hear the lessons. I hope in time to take pleasure in publick Worship.

On this whole day I took nothing of nourishment but one cup of tea without milk, but the fast was very inconvenient. Towards night I grew fretful, and impatient, unable to fix my mind or govern my thoughts, and felt a very uneasy sensation both in my stomach and head, compounded as it seemed of laxity and pain.[1]

From this uneasiness, of which when I was not asleep, I was sensible all night, I was relieved in the morning by drinking tea, and eating the soft part of a penny loaf.

This I have set down for future observation.

9. ∧towards me∧   1. Two lines deleted.

---

feature is Johnson's curious minuteness in recording the hour, 1:33 A.M.

By the end of February the revised *Dictionary* was printed. At the beginning of April, Boswell came to London and accompanied Johnson to church on Good Friday, where, he reports, Johnson's behaviour "was, as I had imaged to myself, solemnly devout. I never shall forget the tremulous earnestness with which he pronounced the aweful petition in the Litany: 'In the hour of death, and at the day of judgement, good Lord deliver us' " (*Life*, II.214).

SATURDAY AP. 10. I dined on cakes, and found myself filled and satisfied.

SATURDAY 10. Having offered my prayers to God, I will now review the last year.

Of the Spring and Summer I remember that I was able in those seasons to examine and improve my dictionary, and was seldom witheld from the work, but by my own unwilling-ness.[2] Of my Nights I have no distinct remembrance but believe that as in many foregoing years they were painful and restless.

A little before Christmas I had caught cold, of which at first, as is my custom, I took little notice, but which harrassed me, as it grew more violent, with a cough almost incessant, both night and day. I was let blood three times, and after about ten weeks, with the help of warm weather I recovered. From this time I have been much less troubled with nocturnal flatulencies, and have had some nights of that quiet and con-tinual sleep, which I had wanted till I had almost forgotten it.[3]

O God, grant that I may not mispend or lose the time which thou shalt yet allow me. For Jesus Christs sake have mercy upon me.

My purpose is to attain in the remaining part of the year as much knowledge as can easily be had of the Gospels and Pentateuch. Concerning the Hebrew I am in doubt. I hope

2. Three lines deleted.   3. This paragraph deleted.

Johnson's hope, in the meditation of the day, that he might in time take pleasure in public worship, makes evident what the reader must have suspected, that he went only as a duty.

On Saturday, Johnson again notes that moderate eating after a day's fast has relieved his troubled stomach.

Johnson's purpose to study the Gospels and the Pentateuch during the rest of the year is interesting because of his mention

likewise to enlarge my knowledge of Divinity, by reading at least once a week some sermon or small theological tract, or some portion of a larger work.

To this important and extensive study my purpose is [to] appropriate (libere) part of every Sunday, Holy day, Wednesday, and Friday, and to begin with the Gospels. Perhaps I may not be able to study the Pentateuch before next year.

My general resolution to which I humbly implore the help of God is to methodise my life; to resist sloth and to combat scruples.[4] I hope from this time to keep a Journal.

N B. On Friday I read the first of Mark, and Clarks sermon on Faith.

On Saturday I read little, but wrote the foregoing account, and the following prayer.

Almighty God, by whose mercy I am now about to commemorate the death of my Redeemer, grant that from this time I may so live as that his death may be efficacious to my eternal happiness. Enable me to conquer all evil customs. Deliver me from evil and vexatious thoughts.[5] Grant me light to discover my duty, and Grace to perform it. As my life advances, let me become more pure, and more holy. Take not from me thy Holy Spirit, but grant that I may serve thee with diligence and confidence; and, when thou shalt call me hence, receive me to everlasting happiness, for the sake of Jesus Christ our Lord. Amen.   Apr. 10. near midnight.

EASTER SUNDAY. APR. 11. I had more disturbance in the night than has been customary for some weeks past. I rose

4. ⟨and to combat scruples.⟩   5. A line and a half deleted.

---

of Hebrew. Apparently he proposed to read in his copy of the Polyglot Bible (perhaps that edited by Brian Walton, 1657), which he later bequeathed to Strahan. At any rate, there is no further mention of reading Hebrew. His following statement that

before nine in the morning, and prayed and drank tea.[6] I
came, I think, to church in the beginning of the prayers. I
did not distinctly hear the Psalms, and found that I had been
reading the Psalms for Good Friday. I went through the
Litany after a short disturbance with tolerable attention.

After sermon I perused[7] my prayer in the pew, then went
nearer the altar and being introduced into another pew, used
my prayer again, and recommended my relations with Bathurst and Boothby, then my Wife again by herself. Then I
went nearer the altar, and read the collects chosen for meditation. I[8] prayed for Salusbury and I think[9] the Thrales. I
then communicated with calmness, used the collect for Easter
day, and returning to the first pew, prayed my prayer the third
time. I came home, again used my prayer and the Easter
Collect. Then went in to the Study to Boswel, and read the

---

6. A few words deleted.   7. ∧perused∧ ⟨recited⟩   8. Several words deleted.
9. ∧I think∧

---

he intends to appropriate "freely" part of certain days for such
study seems to mean that he will not bind himself to particular
hours.

On Easter Day, Johnson, not hearing well, realized that he was
following the psalms for Good Friday in the Prayer Book, while
the clergyman was reading the correct ones. This is a reversal of the
previous Easter, when, hearing well, he realized that the young
minister was reading the wrong lessons. Strahan deleted the note
about the minister but left this one. Hill notes that Johnson's
pew was in the gallery, which may have had something to do with
his hearing poorly.

Bathurst and Tetty, Johnson prayed for as usual, but his mention of Hill Boothby, who had been dead for seventeen years,
is not usual, and confirms the deep loss he felt for her. Mrs. Salusbury, for whom he also prayed, was dying of cancer. In March
Johnson had written, "Part we must at last; but the last parting
is very afflictive. When I see her I shall torment her with caress-
ing her" (*Letters* 303).

Greek Testament. Then dined, and when Boswel went away ended the four first chapters of St Matthew, and the Beatitudes of the fifth.

I then went to Evening prayers, and was composed.

I gave the Pewkeepers each 5s 3d.

APR. 12 NEAR ONE IN THE MORNING. I used my prayer with my ordinary devotions and hope to lead henceforward a better life.

JUNE 18. 1773 FRIDAY. This day after dinner died Mrs Salusbury. She had for some days almost lost the power of speaking. Yesterday as I touched her hand and kissed it, she pressed my hand between her two hands, which she probably intended as the parting caress. At night her speech returned a little, and she said among other things to her Daughter— I have had much time, and I hope I have used it. This morning being called about nine to feel her pulse I said at parting God bless you, for Jesus Christs sake. She smiled, as pleased. She had her senses perhaps to the dying moment.

JULY 22 —73. This day I found this book with the resolutions, some of which I had forgotten, but remembred my

---

Boswell's dining at Johnson's house was an event: "To my great surprize, he asked me to dine with him on Easter-day. I never supposed that he had a dinner at his house; for I had not then heard of any one of his friends having been entertained at his table" (*Life*, ii.215).

In June Macbean's *Geography* was published, with Johnson's preface, and in the same month Johnson and the Thrales were saddened by the death of Mrs. Salusbury, whose epitaph Johnson wrote. Johnson's description is very close to that entered by Mrs. Thrale in her Children's Book (Clifford, p. 103).

A month later Johnson came upon the little book (No. 8 of those now at Pembroke) containing the Good Friday and Easter

design of reading the Pentateuch and Gospels, though I have not persued it.

Of the time past since those resolutions were made I can give no very laudable account. Between Easter and Whitsuntide, having always considered that time as propitious to study, I attempted to learn the low Dutch Language; my application was very slight, and my memory very fallacious, though whether more than in my earlier years, I am not very certain. My progress was interrupted by a fever, which, by the imprudent use of a small print, left an inflammation in my useful eye, which was not removed but by two copious bleedings, and the daily use of catharticks for a long time. The effect yet remains.

My memory has been for a long time very much confused. Names, and Persons, and Events, slide away strangely from me. But I grow easyer.

The other day looking over old papers, I perceived a resolution to rise early always occurring. I think I was ashamed or grieved to find how long and how often I had resolved,

---

meditations of this year, and remembered his forgotten plan to read the Pentateuch and the Gospels.

His remark that he considered the period between Easter and Whitsuntide favourable to study is opposed to one he had made in No. 11 of the *Idler*: "This distinction of seasons is produced only by imagination operating upon luxury." And later in his *Milton*: "The author that thinks himself weather-bound will find, with a little help from hellebore, that he is only idle or exhausted. But while this notion has possession of the head, it produces the inability which it supposes."

His study of Dutch, though it did not progress far this year, he seriously resumed in 1782. The inflammation in his one useful eye, which interrupted his study, was so serious that there was some fear that he might lose his sight.

what yet except for about one half year I have never done. My Nights are now such as give me no quiet rest; whether I have not lived resolving, till the possibility of performance is past, I know not. God help me, I will yet try.

1773. Inchoavi lectionem Pentateuchi—Finivi lectionem Conf. Fab. Burdonum.—Legi primum actum Troadum.— Legi Dissertationem Clerici postremam de Pent.—2 of Clark's Sermons.—L. Appolonii pugnam Betriciam.[9a]—L. centum versus Homeri.

9a. Appolonii, Boswell's MS. Betriciam, *Life*; Bebryciam, Boswell's MS.

Johnson still recalls the six-months' period in which he rose early, seven years before.

Boswell printed some scattered notes of Johnson's studies which "appear on different days in his manuscript diary of this year" (*Life*, II.263). Since the first of these mentions his beginning to read the Pentateuch, it is possible that Johnson did so soon after the memorandum just given, since his conscience was affected. The diary is now lost, and there is no clue to dating the rest of his reading.

That he finished reading the *Confutatio Fabulae Burdonum*, 1608, is less surprising than that he read it at all. It is J. J. Scaliger's attack on Scioppius's confutation of the Scaligers' assertion that they were descended from the family of La Scala—Scaliger's least successful and least important book.

His reading the first act of the *Troades* recalls his Oxford days, when, he told Boswell, he read Euripides (*Life*, I.70); and his diary in 1734 records his calculations of the length of *Medea* and *The Phoenician Maidens*. In 1784 he read Euripides again (*Life*, IV.311).

Samuel Clarke's last dissertation on the Pentateuch was probably joined with his reading the same books of the Bible.

Apollonius's *Argonautica*, Book II, contains the fight of Polydeuces with Amycus, king of the Bebryces (*Miscellanies*, I.69).

And finally, a hundred lines of Homer.

TALISKER IN SKIE. SEPT. 24. 1773. On last Saturday was my sixty fourth Birthday. I might perhaps have forgotten it had not Boswel told me of it, and, what pleased me less, told the family at Dunvegan.

The last year is added to those of which little use[1] has been made. I tried in the Summer to learn Dutch, and was interrupted by an inflammation in my eye. I set out in August on this Journey to Skie. I find my memory uncertain, but hope it is only by a life immethodical and scattered. Of my Body I do not perceive that exercise or change of air has yet either encreased the strength or activity. My Nights are still disturbed by flatulencies.

My hope is, for resolution I dare no longer call it, to divide my time regularly, and to keep such a journal of my time, as may give me comfort in reviewing it. But when I consider my age, and the broken state of my body, I have great reason to fear lest Death should lay hold upon me, while I am yet only designing to live. But, I have yet hope.

Almighty God, most merciful Father, look down upon me

1. ∧use∧ ⟨improvement⟩

On 6 August Johnson set out for Scotland and his tour of the Hebrides. On his birthday, he and Boswell were at Dunvegan, on the northwest coast of Skye, being entertained by Lady Macleod. A few days later, Johnson having thoroughly enjoyed himself, they went on to Talisker on the west coast, where their host, Colonel Macleod, proved equally pleasant. The gloom of Johnson's meditation on 24 September is partly offset by these facts.

Johnson's concern about his uncertain memory he had forgotten four years later, when he said of Boswell's father, "There must be a diseased mind, where there is a failure of memory at seventy" (*Life*, III.191).

As to dying "while yet only designing to live," Hill aptly cites *Rasselas*: " 'Those that lie here stretched before us,' said Rasselas, 'the wise and the powerful of ancient times, warn us to remember

with pity; Thou hast protected me in childhood and youth, support me, Lord, in my declining years. Deliver me from evil thoughts and scruples and[2] preserve me from the dangers of sinful presumption. Give me, if it be best for me, stability of[3] purposes, and tranquillity of mind. Let the year which I have now begun, be spent to thy glory, and to the furtherance of my salvation. Take not from me[4] thy holy Spirit, but as Death approaches, prepare me to appear joyfully in thy presence for the sake of Jesus Christ our Lord. Amen.

1774

JAN. 1. NEAR 2 IN THE MORNING. Almighty God, merciful Father, who hatest nothing that thou hast made, but wouldest that all should be saved, have mercy upon me. As thou hast extended my Life, encrease my strength, direct my purposes, and confirm[5] my resolution, that I may truly serve Thee, and perform the duties which Thou shalt allot me.

Relieve, O gracious Lord, according to thy mercy the pains and distempers of my Body, and appease the tumults of my

2. ⟨evil thoughts and scruples and⟩   3. ⟨good⟩   4. ∧me∧   5. ∧confirm∧
⟨strengthen⟩

the shortness of our present state, they were perhaps snatched away while they were busy like us in the choice of life' " (ch. 47).

At the end of November Johnson was back in London, where he found that what might be described as the first collected edition of his works had been published without his permission. In Tom Davies's *Miscellaneous and Fugitive Pieces* the first volume is wholly Johnson's, and three-quarters of the second is also. After a fit of anger, he forgave Davies. The work went into a second printing. Also during the year the new edition of Shakespeare appeared, in which Steevens had collaborated.

After the New Year's prayer for 1774, Johnson used the collect which he had adapted for that day and for his birthday, and added

Mind.[6] Let my Faith and Obedience encrease as my life advances, and let the approach of death incite[7] my desire to please thee, and invigorate my diligence in good works, till at last[8] when thou shalt call me to another state I shall lie down in humble hope, supported by thy Holy Spirit, and be received to everlasting happiness, through Jesus Christ, our Lord. Amen.

The Beginning. &c.

I hope

To read the Gospels before Easter
To rise at eight
To be temperate in Food.

This year has past with so little improvement, that I doubt whether I have not [rather] impaired than encreased my Learning. To this omission some external causes have contributed. In the Winter I was distressed by a cough, in the Summer an Inflammation fell upon my useful eye from which it has not yet, I fear, recovered. In the Autumn I took a journey to the Hebrides, but my mind was not free from perturbation. Yet the chief cause of my deficiency has been a life immethodical, and unsettled, which breaks all purposes, confounds and suppresses memory, and perhaps leaves too much leisure to imagination. Jan 9. 1774. O Lord, have mercy upon me.

6. Three lines deleted.   7. ∧incite∧ ⟨encrease⟩   8. ∧last∧ . . . lie down ⟨at last⟩
. . . Spirit, and ⟨pass⟩

---

three typical resolutions. He did not get round to his customary review of the past year till eight days later.

That Johnson's mind was not free of perturbation even during his tour of the Hebrides is doubtless true, but so is Boswell's statement: "He said to me often, that the time he spent in this Tour was the pleasantest part of his life" (*Life*, v.405).

JULY 5. TUESDAY. 11. a. m. We left Streatham. 1. p. m. 1.40'. Barnet. Price of 4 horses 2s a mile. At night to Dunstable. On the road I read Tully's Epistles.

6. To Lichfield 83 miles; to the Swan.

7. To Mrs Porters, to the Cathedral, to Mrs Astons. To Mr Greens.

On 5 July Johnson began his tour of North Wales with the Thrales, who were going to take possession of the estate of Bachy-Graig, which had fallen to Mrs. Thrale at the death of her uncle. Included in the party was the Thrales' ten-year-old daughter, Queeney.

Johnson's interest in the cost of travelling is characteristic, though academic, as Thrale was paying all ordinary expenses. After a forty-minute stop at the Mitre in Barnet, they went on to St. Albans, as Mrs. Thrale's diary shows, where they dined with Thrale's relatives, the Smiths, and then went on to spend the night at Dunstable. Johnson's reading Cicero on the road shows that he continued his usual travelling habit, even though this time he was with friends.

The distance the next day was exceptionally long, causing Mrs. Thrale to be concerned that it might affect Queeney's health. Johnson, however, was in high spirits and, as it grew late, cheerfully remarked "how much pleasanter it was travelling by night than by day" (Broadley, p. 160). He had looked forward to a trip with the Thrales and now he was about to have the opportunity of introducing them to his friends in Lichfield. It was shortly before midnight when they arrived at the Swan.

The next morning, when Mrs. Thrale came downstairs, Johnson did not like her costume, "a morning night gown and close cap," and made her change it, eager that she be well dressed. Johnson had a busy day planned for them, filled with places and people of obvious importance to him. Mrs. Thrale's diary makes clear that Johnson's order of events is not strictly chronological. First, they visited the museum of Richard Greene, an apothecary, who

8. To Mr Newton's, to Mrs Cobb. Dr Darwin's. Mr Greens
Museum was much admired, and Mr Newton's China. I went
again to Mrs Aston's. She was sorry to part.

9. Breakfast at Mr Garricks. Visited Miss Vise. Miss Seward.
Went to Dr Taylors. I read a little on the road in Tully's
Epistles and Martial.

---

claimed relationship to Johnson (*Life*, ii.465). The museum was
one of the sights of Lichfield, and Mrs. Thrale was greatly impressed. Boswell thought, when he saw it in 1776, that it was "a
wonderful collection, both of antiquities and natural curiosities,
and ingenious works of art." After dinner they attended service
in the cathedral and then Johnson took the Thrales to see his
birthplace. They later called upon Lucy Porter and finished the
evening in the handsome Stowe Hill house of Elizabeth Aston,
sister of Molly, whom Johnson had much admired.

On 8 July Johnson took them to breakfast in the fine house of
Dr. Erasmus Darwin, grandfather of Charles Darwin and pioneer
in biology. An eminent citizen though not a particular friend of
Johnson, Dr. Darwin later published an eccentric poem, *The
Loves of the Plants*. Mrs. Thrale was much impressed with his
rose tree. While Mr. Thrale went to see Lord Donegall at Fisher-
wick, the rest of the party visited Andrew Newton, a wealthy wine
merchant, brother of Thomas, Bishop of Bristol, who had a fine
collection of East Indian rarities. Later they had tea with Mrs.
Thomas Cobb, a widow, in her house, a curious old Friary, where
there were some painted glass panes. Peter Garrick, the eldest
brother of David Garrick, came for supper at the Swan.

Next day, while the gentlemen were dressing, Mrs. Thrale went
to take leave of Lucy Porter and upon her return they breakfasted
with Peter Garrick. Johnson then took them to call upon Mary
Vyse, the daughter of his friend, now dead, who had tried to
present him with a new pair of shoes at Oxford. The next call
was upon Anna Seward, "the Swan of Lichfield" and the grand-
daughter of Johnson's teacher, Hunter. Mrs. Thrale later wrote,

1774

July 5. Tuesday
 11 a.m. We left Streatham.
p.m. 1.40. Barnet.
at night to Dunstable
6. To Lichfield 83 miles. to
the Swan.
7 To Mrs Porters, to the Cathedral
to Mrs Astons. To Mr Greens.
8 To Mr Newtons. To Mrs Cobb.
    Dr Darwin.
I went again to Mrs Astons.
9 Breakfast at Mr Garricks.
Visited Miss Vyse. Miss Seward.
Went to Dr Taylors.
10 Morning at Church. Company
at Dinner.
11. Mr Flam, at Okeover
12 ..

Price of 4 horses 2s a mile,

On the road I read Bullys Epistles

Mr Greens Museum was much admired, and Mr Newtons China.

She was sorry to part.

I read a criticism on the rival of Bullys Epistles and Martial—

I was not pleased with Flam there I saw it first; but my friends were much delighted.

Welsh Diary, July 1774

10. Morning at Church. Company at Dinner.

11. At Ilam, at Okeover. I was less pleased with Ilam than when I saw it first; but my friends were much delighted.

12. At Chatsworth. The water willow, the Cascade, shot out from many spouts. The fountains. The water tree. The

---

"Dr. Johnson would not suffer me to speak to Miss Seward" (Croker, III.126), but it appears merely that Johnson monopolized her on this occasion. Then the party left for Dr. Taylor's in Ashbourne, in Derbyshire, dining at Sudbury on the way.

For the next eleven days Dr. Taylor was their host, either in his house or on excursions to places of interest near Ashbourne. The day after their arrival, being Sunday, was spent quietly, but on Monday the eleventh they went to Ilam, seat of the Port family, some four miles northwest of Ashbourne in Staffordshire. It was famous for its romantic scenery, especially for the emergence of the Manifold River from its underground course. Johnson refused to believe that it was the same river that went underground a few miles above (*Life*, III.188). During the day they passed by Okeover, about two and a half miles northwest of Ashbourne, on the Staffordshire side of the Dove. It was until recently the seat of the family of the same name.

On Tuesday they set out on a two-day excursion, mainly to see Chatsworth, the seat of the Duke of Devonshire, about sixteen miles northeast of Ashbourne. Johnson had seen it before in 1772, when he wrote to Mrs. Thrale: "They complimented me with playing the fountains, and opening the cascade" (*Letters* 288). The water willow Mrs. Thrale explained as "a water-work . . . with a concealed spring, which, upon touching, spouted out streams from every bough of a willow-tree" (Croker, III.126). It still operates. Mrs. Thrale said that the "smooth floors in the highest rooms" were "old oak floors polished by rubbing. Johnson, I supposed, wondered that they should take such pains with the garrets" (Croker, III.126).

smooth floors in the highest rooms. Atlas 15 hands inch and
half. Surly's Humours. River running through the park. The
porticos on the sides, support two galleries for the first floor.
My friends were not struck with the house. It fell below my
ideas of the furniture. The Staircase is in the corner of the
house. The Hall in the corner the grandest room, though
only a room of passage. On the ground floor only the Chappel,
and breakfast room, and a small library. The rest servants
rooms and offices.

A bad Inn.

13. At Matlock.

14. At Dinner, at Oakover, too deaf to hear or much converse.
Mrs. Gell.

————————

Atlas was a famous race horse, "very handsome and very gentle,
and attracted so much of Dr. Johnson's attention, that he said,
'of all the Duke's possessions, I like Atlas best'" (Duppa, cited
by Croker). Surley was another race horse in the stable, apparently
more capricious.

Mrs. Thrale was outspoken in her diary: "Dr. Taylor took us
to Chatsworth, where I was pleased with scarcely anything"
(Broadley, p. 166). The inn was at Edensor, and Mrs. Thrale
described it as "wretched." Their opinion was shared by Arthur
Young, who warned that a traveller "will find here nothing but
dirt and impertinence" (cited in Life, v.580).

The next morning the party drove on to Matlock Bath, about
ten miles southeast of Chatsworth in Derbyshire, principally
known for the gorge of the Derwent and the medicinal hot springs
not far away. Taylor was well known here and introduced his
friends to Edward Okeover, who promptly invited them to dinner
the next day. The party returned to Taylor's house, which Mrs.
Thrale now considered as "home."

On the next day, 14 July, the dinner at Okeover proved to be
a large one, but the host was unable to keep the evening from

The chapel at Oakover. The wood of the pews grossly painted. I could not read the epitaph. Would learn the old hands.

15. Mart 8 44. lino pro limo.

15.[9] At Ashbourne. Mrs. Diot and her daughters came in the morning. Mr Diot dined with us. We visited Mr Flint.

Τὸ πρῶτον Μῶρος, Τὸ δὲ δεύτερον ἦρεν εἶλεν Ερασμὸς,[9a]
Τὸ τρίτον ἐκ Μουσῶν στέμμα Μίκυλλος ἔχει.

9. ⟨16⟩   9a. Johnson forgot to delete ἦρεν.

---

being dull, says Mrs. Thrale. Mrs. Gell was no doubt the sixteen-year-old bride of Philip Gell of Hopton Hall, with whom they dined a few days later.

The small parish church near the Hall was known locally as the chapel. Powell conjectures that the inscription which Johnson could not read was one partially effaced, originally for Lord Zouch (d. 1447), "but altered to commemorate Humphrey Okeover" (d. 1538) (*Life*, v.581).

The fifteenth of July was a comparatively quiet day. Johnson found a typographical error in his Martial, *lino* instead of *limo*, Bk. VIII, No. 45 in modern editions: "Defluat, et lento splendescat turbida limo." On a blank page (35v) later in the diary, he noted: "There seem to be few books less depraved by transcription than Martial."

Mrs. Richard Dyott, wife of a wealthy Staffordshire man, called with her four daughters in the morning. Johnson later took his friends to tea with Thomas Flint, Taylor's confidential clerk, and Mrs. Flint, who was somehow related to Johnson.

The Greek distich praising the learning of Jacob Moltzer (1503–58), who adopted the name Micyllus from the dialogues of Lucian, has not been identified: "From the Muses, Sir Thomas More bore away the first crown, Erasmus the second, and Micyllus has the third." Johnson nowhere else refers to Moltzer. The excessive praise sounds like that of a contemporary of Moltzer.

16.[1] At Dovedale, with Mr Langley and Mr Flint. It is a place that deserves a visit, but did not answer my expectation. The river is small, the rocks are grand. Reynard's hall is a cave very high in the rock, [it][2] goes backward several yards, perhaps eight. To the left is a small opening through which I crept, and found another cavern perhaps four yards square; at the back was a breach yet smaller, which I could not easily have entered, and, wanting light did not inspect. I was in a cave yet higher called Reynard's kitchen. There is a rock called the Church, in which I saw no resemblance, that could justify the name. Dovedale is about two miles long. We walked towards the head of the Dove which is said to rise about five miles above two caves called the dog holes, at the end of Dovedale.

In one place where the Rocks approached I propose to build an arch from rock to rock over the stream, with a summerhouse upon it. The water murmured pleasantly among the stones. I thought that the heat and exercise mended my hearing.

I bore the fatigue of the walk, which was very laborious, without inconvenience. There were with us Gilpin and

1. ⟨17⟩   2. MS torn.

On the next day the party was off again sight-seeing. Taylor was occupied and so he sent Mr. Flint and the Reverend William Langley, headmaster of the Ashbourne Grammar School, to guide them. They went to Dovedale, that part of the valley of the River Dove forming the boundary between Derbyshire and Staffordshire north of Ashbourne, famous for its cliffs and caves, but more famous from having been fished by Izaak Walton and Cotton. It is curious that Johnson does not mention Walton here, one of his favourite authors.

What he heard as "Dog-holes" are Dove-holes.

Gilpin is probably William Gilpin, son of the author of several books on British scenery, though Mrs. Thrale later mistakenly

Parker. Having heard of this place before, I had formed some confused idea, to which it did not answer. Brown says he was disappointed. I certainly expected a larger river where I found only a clear quick brook. I believe I had imaged a valley enclosed by rocks, and terminated by a broad expanse of water. He that has seen Dovedale has no need to visit the Highlands. In the afternoon we visited old Mrs Dale.

17. SUNDAY. Morning at Church. Afternoon at Mr Dyot's. Καθ.

18. Dined at Mr Gell's.

---

said his father was a silversmith. He was an Oxford undergraduate. His friend, John Parker of Browsholme, in Yorkshire, was at Cambridge.

"Brown," who was disappointed with the site, Mrs. Thrale thought was Lancelot Brown (1715–83), nicknamed "Capability" from his saying that places were "capable of improvement." He was one of England's most celebrated landscape designers, specializing in natural landscaping. His opinion on Dovedale would therefore be important and was perhaps repeated to Johnson by Gilpin or Parker.

The Mrs. Dale whom Johnson saw was either the mother or the grandmother of Robert Dale, who had married the eldest of the Dyott girls (Life, v.581). The mother was about eighty.

The seventeenth of July was Sunday and another quiet day. Mrs. Thrale's diary shows that the party dined at "home" and spent the evening drinking tea at the Dyotts'. In the margin Johnson records taking a purge.

Next day the party dined at Philip Gell's. Mrs. Thrale recorded her opinion of him: "A man visibly impaired by age, and particularly ugly, talking largely and loudly on every subject, understanding none as I could find, foppish without elegance, confident without knowledge, sarcastic without wit and old without experi-

JULY 19. We went to Kedleston to see Lord Scarsdales new house, which is very costly but illcontrived. The hall is very stately, lighted by three sky lights; it has two rows of marble pillars dug as I hear from Langley in a quarry of Northamptonshire. The pillars are very large and massy and take up too[3] much room. They were better away. Behind the hall is a circular salon, useless and therefore illcontrived. The corridors that join the wings to the body, are mere passages, though segments of circles. The state bedchamber was very richly furnished. The dining parlour was more splendid with gilt plate than any that I have seen. There were many pictures. The grandeur was all below; the bedchambers were small, low, dark and fitter for a prison than a house of splendour. The Kitchen has an opening into the gallery, by which its heat and its fumes are dispersed over the house. There seemed in the whole more cost than judgement.

We went then to the Silkmil at Derby, where I remarked a particular manner of propagating motion from a horizontal to a vertical wheel. We were desired to leave the men only two shillings. Mr Thrales bill at the inn for dinner was 0–18–10.

3. MS: "two"

---

ence, a man uniting every hateful quality, a deist, a dunce, and a cotquean" (Broadley, p. 173).

The last day of their stay with Taylor was spent on a final excursion. The party visited Kedleston, the house recently built by Robert Adam for the newly created Baron Scarsdale, southeast of Ashbourne, towards Derby. Johnson was misinformed about the source of the marble; it was from a quarry in Nottinghamshire belonging to Scarsdale (*Life*, v.583). Mrs. Thrale's opinion of the house and its furnishings was like Johnson's. In 1777, talking to Boswell, Johnson was even more severe about the house.

At Derby, where the party dined before returning to Ashbourne, it is characteristic that Johnson remarked on the machinery of the

At night I went to Mr Langley, Mrs Wood, Captain Astle, &c.

2 0. We left Ashbourn, and went to Buxton, thenc[e] to Pool's hole, which is narrow at first, but then rises into a high arch, but is so obstructed with crags that it is difficult to walk in it. There are two ways to the end which is, they say six hundred and fifty yards from the mouth. They take passengers up the higher way and bring them back the lower. The higher way was so difficult and dangerous, that having tried it I desisted. I found no level part.

At night we came to Macclesfield a very large town in Cheshire,[4] little known. It has a silk mill. It has a handsome church, which however is but a chapel, for the town belongs

4. ⋏in Cheshire⋏

_____

silk mill, his usual interest in mechanical processes, and Mrs. Thrale on the quality of the silks.

At night there were farewell calls on friends. Captain Daniel Astle, who fought at Bunker Hill a little later, left the army in 1778 and took holy orders. Johnson prepared a list of reading for him, perhaps at this time, since one of the latest books in it is Goldsmith's *Roman History*, 1769. Astle's sister, Mary, was married to Ralph Wood, a nephew of Taylor's first wife (*Life*, IV.311, 537).

On 20 July the party bade farewell to Taylor and the portion of the tour which Johnson had carefully arranged was now over. Mrs. Thrale had thoroughly enjoyed it. The remainder of the journey was arranged by the Thrales, and the hospitality, in the main, was extended by Mrs. Thrale's relatives and their connexions. They drove twenty-five miles north to Buxton, where Mrs. Thrale tried the warm medicinal baths. Then they investigated the great limestone cavern at Poole's Hole nearby, and proceeded to Macclesfield, a few miles further on, now the centre of the English silk industry. The church which they saw was St. Michael's, an interesting one but not so striking as its mother

to some parish of another name as Stourbridge lately did to
Old Swinford. Macclesfield has a town hall and is, I suppose,
a corporate town.

2 1 . We came to Congleton, where there is likewise a silk mill.
Then to Middlewich, a mean old town, without any manufacture, but I think a corporation.

Thence we proceeded to Namptwich, an old town; from
the[5] Inn, I saw scarcely any but black timber houses. I tasted
the brine water, which contains much more salt than the sea-
water. By slow evaporation they make large crystals of salt,
by quick boiling small granulations. It seemed to have no
other preparation.

At evening we came to Combermere, so called from a wide
lake.

5. ⟨grist m⟩ _____

church, the thirteenth-century St. Peter's at Prestbury, two and
a half miles away. Johnson's guess that the town was incorporated
was correct: it received its first charter in 1261 and at the time of
Johnson's visit was operating under the charter of 1684.

The next morning the party proceeded on its way to visit Mrs.
Thrale's uncle, Sir Lynch Salusbury Cotton, at Combermere Hall,
now called Combermere Abbey, where they were to be entertained
for four days. They travelled by way of Congleton, where the silk
manufacture still continues. They detoured to see Middlewich,
not incorporated, though it had once been a borough of the
Palatinate. Why the party went out of its way in this displeasing
countryside is difficult to imagine. They had dinner in Nantwich,
to the south. The salt there was obtained from brine springs, the
brine being evaporated, as Johnson says. The springs are now
medicinal baths but the process is still used at Northwich, not
far away. They arrived in good time at Combermere Hall. It
had what was said to be the largest natural lake in a private park
in England. The lake formed an "L," not wide but about three-

22. We went upon the Mere, I pulled a bulrush of about ten feet.

23. We visited Lord Kilmurrey's house. It is large and convenient, with many rooms, none of which are magnificently spacious. The furniture was not splendid. The bed curtains were guarded. Lord K. showd the place with too much exultation. He has no park, and little water.

24. We went to a Chapel built by Sir Linch Cotton for his Tenants. It is consecrated and therefore, I suppose, endowed. It is neat and plain. The communion plate is handsome. It has iron pales and gates of great elegance, brought from Llewenny. "For Robert[6] has laid all open."

6. ᴧRobertᴧ ⟨Jack⟩

---

quarters of a mile long. Johnson may have been deceived as to its width by standing at the corner of the "L."

The first day of their visit was spent quietly, the morning being occupied by rowing on the Mere. But the next day, 23 July, the party was off again sight-seeing. They rode on horseback to Shavington Hall, the seat of the tenth Viscount Kilmorey, which was nearby in Shropshire. The "guarding" of the bed curtains is explained in Johnson's *Dictionary*: "to adorn with lists, laces, or ornamental borders." But this obsolete word had been used generally to apply to clothes only. Johnson's dissatisfaction with the house was shared by Mrs. Thrale, who was, as usual, more outspoken about its owner: "a character as the phrase is. A man who, joining the bluster of an Officer to the haughtiness of a Nobleman newly come to his estate—an estate which had held his Soul in suspense perhaps for twenty years—endeavours to swell the gay Jack Needham into the magnificent Lord Kilmorey, and is to me a man extremely offensive" (Broadley, p. 177).

The next day, Sunday, they all went to services at the chapel built by Sir Lynch at nearby Burleydam. It was consecrated in 1769 and endowed with £1000. As to its plate, the vicar wrote

25. We saw Hakeston, the seat of Sir Rowland Hill, and
were conducted by Miss Hill over a large tract of rocks and
woods, a region[7] abounding with striking scenes and terrifick
grandeur. We were always on the brink of a precipice, or at
the foot of a lofty rock, but the steeps were seldom naked; in
many places Oaks of uncommon magnitude shot up from the
crannies of stone, and where there were not tall trees, there
were underwoods and bushes. Round the rocks is a narrow
path, cut upon the stone which is very frequently hewn into
steps, but art has proceeded no further than [to][8] make the succession of wonders safely accessible. The whole circuit is somewhat laborious, it is[9] terminated by a grotto cut in the rock to
a great extent with many windings and supported by pillars,
not hewn into regularity, but such as imitate the[1] sports of
nature, by asperi[ties] and protuberances. The place is without any dampness, and would afford a habitation not uncomfortable. There were from space to space seats in the rock.
Though it wants water it excells Dovedale, by the extent of

7. ⟨with⟩   8. MS: "the"   9. ₍is₎ ⟨was⟩   1. A deleted word is illegible.

Dr. Powell in 1940 that "while the existing chalice and paten are
not particularly striking, the ewer is remarkable" (*Life*, v.584).
The pales and gates had been brought from Llewenny in Wales,
Sir Lynch's other estate, where his eldest son Robert was living,
and where the party was to visit later. These do not survive, "but
some handsome wrought-iron gate-posts remain." The remark
quoted by Johnson referred to family conversation, Mrs. Thrale
told Duppa. Croker noted that the rage for throwing down the
walls of estates, thus leaving the gates useless, was current at this
time.

On Monday the party went to one of the famous places in the
area, Hawkstone Park, the seat of Sir Rowland Hill, Bart., about
eight miles south of Combermere, in Shropshire. Miss Hill was
presumably Sir Rowland's daughter, showing the place in the

25 JULY 1774

5

its prospects, the awfulness of its shades, the horrors of its precipices, the verdure of its hollows and the loftiness of its rocks. The Ideas which it forces upon the mind, are the sublime, the dreadful, and the vast. Above, is inaccessible altitude, below, is horrible profundity. But it excells the Garden of Ilam only in extent. Ilam has grandeur tempered with softness. The walker congratulates his own arrival at the place, and is grieved to think that he must ever leave it. As he looks up to the rocks his thoughts are elevated; as he turns his eyes on the vallies, he is composed and soothed. He that mounts the precipices at Hawkeston, wonders how he came hither, and doubts how he shall return. His walk is an adventure and his departure an escape.[2] He has not the tranquillity, but the horrour of solitude, a kind of turbulent pleasure between fright and admiration. Ilam is the fit[3] abode of pastoral virtue, and might properly diffuse its shades over nymphs and swains. Hawkeston can have[4] no fitter inhabitants than Giants of mighty bone, and bold emprise, men of lawless courage and heroic violence. Hawkestone should be described by Milton and Ilam by Parnel.

Miss Hill showed the whole succession of wonders with great civility.

The House was magnificent compared with the rank of the owner.

2. ∧an escape∧   3. ∧fit∧ ⟨proper⟩ .   4. ∧have∧ ⟨proper⟩

---

absence of her father, who is not mentioned as present by either Johnson or Mrs. Thrale. The description which follows is so elaborate and so carefully revised that it amounts to a short essay on the effect of landscape on the emotions—a most unusual subject for Johnson. Croker was perhaps unduly suspicious: "The whole of this passage is so inflated and pompous, that it looks more like a burlesque of Johnson's style than his own travelling notes." "Giants of mighty bone and bold emprise" is quoted from *Paradise*

26. We left Cumbermere, where we have been treated with great civility. Sir L. is gross, the Lady weak and ignorant. The House is spacious but not magnificent, built at different times with different materials, part is of timber, part of stone or brick, plaistered and painted to look like timber. It is the best house that I ever saw of that kind. The Meer or lake is large with a small island, on which there is a summer house shaded with great trees. Some were hollow and have seats in their trunks.

In the afternoon we came to West Chester (my father went to the fair when I had the small pox). We walked round the walls which are compleat, and contain one Mile, three quarters, and[5] one hundred and one yards; within them are many

5. ∧and∧ one hundred ⟨an⟩ ∧and∧

Lost, xi.642. Mrs. Thrale was struck with Miss Hill, "an odd mixture of sublimity and meanness. . . . She is, however, by far the most conversible Female I have seen since I left home, her character, I hear, is respectable, and her address is as polite as can be wished. I shall never see her again probably, and I am sorry for it" (Broadley, p. 181).

On 26 July the visit to Combermere Hall ended. Johnson was more critical of his hosts than Mrs. Thrale had been of the hosts he had provided. However, Mrs. Thrale's note in her diary is almost a paraphrase of his: "I left them, too, liking them better than ever I liked them, though Sir Lynch's rusticity and his Wife's emptiness afforded nothing but a possibility of change from disgust to insipidity."

The party proceeded to "West Chester," a name Johnson used here to refer to Chester itself. Johnson's comment that he had smallpox when his father went to the fair at Chester supplies our only knowledge of either event, but it suggests that his father's visit here, probably to sell books, was an uncommon event, unlike his trips to Birmingham and Uttoxeter.

The city walls were the source of disagreement between John-

gardens. They are very high, and two may walk very commodiously side by side. On the inside is a rail; there are towers from space to space, not very frequent, and I think, not all compleat.

27. We staid at Chester, and saw the Cathedral, which is not of the first rank. The Castle, in one of the rooms the Assizes are held, and the refectory of the old abbey of which part is a Grammar School. The Master seemed glad to see me. The cloister is very solemn, over it are[6] chambers in which the singing men live.

6. MS: "a"

---

son and Mrs. Thrale, who wrote later: "He has since put me fairly out of countenance by saying, 'I have known *my mistress* fifteen years, and never saw her fairly out of humour but on Chester wall;' it was because he would keep Miss Thrale beyond her hour of going to bed to walk on the wall, where, from the want of light, I apprehended some accident to her—perhaps to him" (Croker, III.133). Of the five towers on or near the wall, one ruined one was rebuilt in 1894. Johnson's uncertainty whether they were all intact is probably the result of the falling darkness.

The next day was devoted to the sights of Chester. Johnson's itinerary might be paraphrased, "We saw the cathedral, the castle, and the refectory," but he did not see them in that order, as the refectory (of the Benedictine Abbey) is in the precincts of the cathedral, which was the abbey church of St. Werburgh until the dissolution of the monasteries. The King's School, founded by Henry VIII, now occupies a modern building, though the refectory is still used on ceremonial occasions. Of the ancient castle, some distance to the southwest in the corner of the city walls, only the tower and the museum remain. But the assizes are still held in the modern building on the site.

The schoolmaster who was glad to see Johnson was the Reverend Robert Vanbrugh (Powell); Johnson's welcome was probably due to his fame, as no connexion between the men is known,

In one part of the street was a subterranean arch very strongly built, in another what they called, I believe rightly, a Roman hypocaust. Chester has many curiosities.

28. We entered Wales, dined at Mold, and came to Llewenny.

---

and Johnson did not record his name. In spite of the Song School connected with the cloisters, Mrs. Thrale thought the performance of the "singing men" "below indifferent" (p. 180).

The subterranean arch which Johnson saw may perhaps have been in the ancient vaulted crypt at 34 Eastgate Street. The hypocaust is, of course, that part of the Roman bath in which the water is heated, and was the most considerable Roman ruin at Chester which had been excavated by the time of Johnson's visit.

This sight-seeing was done, Mrs. Thrale says, "with more haste than attention" (p. 180). In *British Synonymy* she mentions one crisis: "I have seldom seen him much more angry than he was with me, one morning, at West Chester; while some gentleman of the town was shewing us the curiosities of so ancient and respectable a place:—for our Doctor was slow, and heavy, and short-sighted; and by the time he had begun to examine and discuss one thing, our brisker Cicerone set us all going in chace of another. This went on a while; and I saw impatience struggling with civility in Johnson's countenance, when he suddenly asked me—in order to stop him, I suppose—'Pray what is this gentleman's name, who accompanies us so officiously?'—'I think they call him *Harold* (replied I); and perhaps you'll find him to be of the family of *Harold Harefoot*, he runs with us at such a rate.'—'Oh! madam, you had rather crack a JOKE, I know, than stop to learn any thing I can teach; so take the road you were born to run'" (1.323).

The following day, 28 July, the party spent travelling through beautiful country to Llewenny, about two miles northeast of Denbigh, said to have been one of the largest houses in the West. Here they were to visit Robert Cotton for three weeks. On the

29. We were at Llewenny.

30. We went to Bachycraig where we found an old house built 1567 in an uncommon and incommodious form. My Mistress chattered about tiring, but I prevailed on her to go to the top. The floors have been stolen; the windows are stopped. The house was less than I seemed to expect. The River Clwyd is a brook with a bridge of one arch about one third of a mile. The woods have many trees generally young, but some which seem to decay. They have been lopped. The house never had a garden. The addition of another story would make an useful house, but it cannot be great; some buildings which Clough the founder intended for ware houses would make storechambers and servants rooms. The ground seems to be good. I wish it well.

---

way they dined at Mold, in Flintshire, and Mrs. Thrale records that they saw the church there.

They were able to do little the first day of their visit because of rain, a disappointment because they had hoped to inspect Mrs. Thrale's inheritance, Bach-y-Graig, not far away, in Flintshire. Thrale, the businessman, and his host, Cotton, went over, but Mrs. Thrale did not wish to go out, and Johnson stayed with her. The next day they all examined Bach-y-Graig. The house had been built by Mrs. Thrale's ancestor, Sir Richard Clough, a merchant whose trading in Flanders was reflected in the architecture of the building, which had three large rooms on the ground floor, with the upper storeys tapering pyramidally to a lantern, with small dormers on the sides of the pyramid. The lantern, on the sixth storey, was reached by a ladder, as Mrs. Thrale said, and it is no wonder that she was unwilling to go to the top. Extending from the building in the shape of an "L" were the warehouses, and at the bottom of the meadow in front of the house was the river, and its bridge by Inigo Jones, according to Mrs. Thrale, facing the door of the house but obscured by the gatehouse. Johnson

31. We went to Church at St Asaph. The Cathedral though not large has something of dignity and Grandeur. The cross isle is very short. It has scarcely any monuments. The Quire has, I think thirty two stalls, of antique workmanship. On the backs were Canonicus, Prebend, Cancellarius, Thesaurarius, Praecentor. The constitution I do not know but it has all the usual titles and dignities. The service was sung only in the Psalms and hymns.[7] The Bishop was very civil. We went to his palace, which is but mean. They have a library, and design a room. Here lived Lloyd and Dodwel.

7. ʌThe service . . . hymns.ʌ

---

seems to mean that the river was a third of a mile away. He does not intend to suggest the addition of a storey in the present state of the house; Mrs. Thrale said that all above the ground floor might be removed and a storey built above that.

On Sunday 31 July the party went to service at the fifteenth-century cathedral of St. Asaph, in Flintshire, a few miles to the north, which is one of the smallest cathedrals in Great Britain. The choir was added in 1770. Johnson was familiar with the principal officers, omitting the dean: the precentor, next under the dean, in charge of music; next the chancellor, in charge of cathedral schools; the treasurer, in charge of the fabric of the cathedral; and the canons who with the prebends made up the chapter. He was unfamiliar with the constitution, since local history made variations in organization frequent among cathedrals. After service the bishop, Jonathan Shipley, whose civility to Johnson is noteworthy, since he was an ardent supporter of the Americans, invited the party to his palace, which he described, says Mrs. Thrale, as fit for "a good creditable Parsonage House in any of the less remote Counties" (Broadley, p. 185). By the "library" Johnson means the cathedral library, which is an important one; "they" would then refer to the chapter. The party saw the bishop again on 8 August, when he came to dinner at the Cottons'.

AUGUST 1. We visited Denbigh and the remains of its Castle. The town consists of one main street, and some that cross it which I have not seen. The chief street ascends[8] with a quick rise for a great length. The houses are built some with rough stone, some with brick, and a few are of timber. The Castle with its whole enclosure has been a prodigious pile, it is now so ruined that the form of the inhabited part cannot easily be traced. There are as in all old buildings said to be extensive vaults which the ruins of the upper works cover and conceal but into which boys sometimes find a way. To clear all passages and trace the whole of what remains would require much labour and expence.

We saw a church which was once the chapel of the castle but is used by[9] the town, it is dedicated to St Hilary and has an income of about

At[1] a small distance is the ruin of Church said to [have] been begun by the great Earl of Leicester, and left unfinished at his death. One side and I think the East end are yet stand-

8. ascend₍ₛ₎ ascend⟨ing⟩   9. MS: "byt"   1. ⟨Then⟩

William Lloyd was raised to the see of St. Asaph in 1680, went to the Tower in 1688 for refusing to permit the publication of James II's declaration for liberty of conscience, and died Bishop of Worcester in 1717. His friend Henry Dodwell, a nonjuror, visited him at St. Asaph.

Next day the party visited Denbigh Castle, built in the thirteenth century by the third Earl of Lincoln, who granted Denbigh its first charter. Nearly a mile around, it merits Johnson's "prodigious." The ruined church nearby was begun by Leicester in 1579, nine years before his death; it still stands. The story of the stone in its wall which would crush the best scholar in the diocese is paralleled by the Oxford legend which Johnson reported in a footnote to *The Vanity of Human Wishes*: "There is a tradition, that the study of Friar Bacon, built on an arch over the bridge,

ing. There was a stone in the wall over the doorway, which, it was said, would fall and crush the best scholar in the diocese. One Price would not pass under it. They have taken it down. We then saw the Chapel of   founded by one of the Salusburies. It is very complete, the monumental stones lye in the ground. A chimney has been added to it, but it is otherwise not much injured, and might be easily repaired.

We then went to the parish church of Denbigh which being near a mile from the town is only used when the Parish Officers are chosen.

In the chapel on Sundays the service is read thrice, the second time only in English, the first and third in Welsh.

The Bishop came to survey the Castle and visited likewise St Hilary's chapel which is that which the town uses.

N. In the lawn of Lleweney is a spring of fine water which rises above the surface into a stone basin, from which it runs to waste in a continual stream through a pipe. There are very large trees.

The Hay barn built with brick pillars from space to space, and covered with a roof. A mere elegant and lofty Hovel.

----

will fall, when a man greater than Bacon shall pass under it." Boswell told Johnson of a similar tradition in Edinburgh (*Life*, v.42).

The "chapel" of Llewenny (the name was evidently supplied to Duppa by Mrs. Thrale) was the Friary Church of the Carmelites in the outskirts of Denbigh, founded by Sir John Salusbury, who was buried there in 1289 (*Life*, v.587). It was not in use as a church, which accounts for Johnson's remark about the ease of repair; he clearly thought that it ought to be so used.

The parish church of Denbigh, Whitchurch, is again in regular use. The chapel next mentioned is St. Hilary's, as Johnson soon makes clear.

The note about the lawn and trees of Llewenny was transferred by previous editors, wholly or in part, to 29 July.

The rivers here are mere torrents which are suddenly swelled by the rain to great breadth and great violence but have very little constant stream. Such are the Clwyd and the Elwas. There are yet no mountains. The ground is beautifully embellished with woods, and diversified by inequalities.

AUGUST 2. We rode to a summerhouse of Mr C. which has a very extensive prospect. It is meanly built and unskilfully disposed.

We then went to Dimerchion Ch. where the old Clerk acknowledged his mistress. It is the parish Church of Bachycraig, a mean fabrick. Mr Salusbury was buried in it. Bachicraig has fourteen seats in it. As we rode by I looked at the house again. We saw Llanerk,[2] a house not mean, with a small park very well watered. There was an avenue of oaks, which in a foolish compliance with the present mode has been cut down. A few are yet standing. The owner's name is Davis. The way lay

2. ‸Llanerk‸ ⟨Clannar⟩

Johnson's disparaging remark about the hay barn perhaps reflects excessive praise by his host and Mrs. Thrale.

The Elwy is a tributary of the Clwyd.

On Tuesday the party went up the steep hill to the church at Tremeirchion, as the name is now written. The church overlooks the beautiful Vale of Clwyd. Some years later Mrs. Thrale, married to her second husband, Gabriele Piozzi, built Brynbella, a charming house less than a mile away, where they lived for many years. Both of them are buried in the church. Mrs. Thrale wrote that the church was "in a dismal condition, the seats all tumbling about, the Altar rail falling, the vessels for the consecrated elements only pewter, the cloth upon the table in a thousand holes, and the floor strewed with rushes" (Broadley, p. 186). The fact that her family had fourteen seats in the church had not led them to keep it up. But in later years, as Mrs. Piozzi, she contributed liberally to the church. The clerk's greeting to Mrs. Thrale, which John-

through pleasant lanes, and overlooked a region beautifully diversified with trees and grass. The old Clerk had great appearance of joy at the sight of his Mistress, and foolishly said, that he was now willing to die.

NOTES AND OMISSIONS.

In the parish Church of Denbigh is a bas relief of Lluyd the antiquary who was before Camden. He is kneeling at his prayers.

I saw no convenient boat upon Cumbermere.

At Dymerchion Church there is English service only once a Month. This is about twenty miles from the English Border.

The old Clerk had only[3] a crown given him by my mistress.

The Hall at Llewenny is 40 feet long and 28 broad.

The Gallery 120 feet long (all paced); the Library 42 feet long 28 broad.

3. ∧only∧ a crown ∧given . . . mistress.∧

---

son thought merely foolish, she took to be a direct quotation of the opening of Nunc Dimittis: "Lord, now lettest thou thy servant depart in peace: according to thy word." So used, it shocked her.

Llanerch, the home of John Davies, particularly interested Mrs. Thrale because her mother "loved the late Mrs. Davies dearly." Johnson's comment on the natural beauties of the site is one of many in the Welsh Diary which prove that he was not so insensitive to scenery as has been claimed. It may also suggest that at the moment Johnson may have had some thought of publishing a book on Wales, using the diary as a basis, as he had done the year before in Scotland.

Humphrey Llwyd, whose bust Johnson saw at Denbigh, was a physician and M.P. as well as antiquary.

When Mrs. Thrale (Piozzi) later read Johnson's remark about her giving the clerk at Tremeirchion only a crown, she commented: "The poor clerk had probably never seen a crown in his possession

The dining parlour 30 feet long 26 broad.

At Dymerchion Church, the Texts on the walls are in Welsh.

Ll is partly sashed and partly has casem[en]ts.

AUGUST 3. We went in the coach to Holywel. Talk with Mistress about flattery—Holywel is a Market town neither very small nor mean. The spring called Winifred's Well is very clear, and so copious that it yields one hundred tuns of water

---

before. Things were very distant A.D. 1774, from what they are 1816" (*Life*, v.440 n.).

The remark about the mixture of sash and casement windows at Llewenny reminds one that although sash windows were introduced almost a century before this, they were still in high fashion. As B. S. Allen says, "One may well suspect that a snobbish desire for display was frequently responsible for the installation of sashes, and that competition with one's neighbor doomed perhaps many a Gothic window" (*Tides in English Taste*, 1.44). And Robert Cotton's throwing down the gates here has shown that he was no lover of the old modes.

On 3 August the party decided to go to Holywell. The talk about flattery in the coach was reported later by Mrs. Thrale (Piozzi): "He said that I flattered the people to whose houses we went: I was saucy, and said I was obliged to be civil for *two*—meaning himself and me. He replied, nobody would thank me for compliments they did not understand. At Gwaynynog (Mr. Myddleton's), however, *he* was flattered, and was happy of course" (Croker, III.139). Fanny Burney tells the story nearer the event: "Mrs. T.— I remember, sir, when we were travelling in Wales, how you called me to account for my civility to the people; 'Madam,' you said, 'let me have no more of this idle commendation of nothing. Why is it, that whatever you see, and whoever you see, you are to be so indiscriminately lavish of praise?' 'Why I'll tell you, sir,' said I, 'when I am with you, and Mr. Thrale, and Queeny, I am obliged to be civil for four!'" (*Diary*, ed. Dobson, 1.130.)

in a minute. It is all at once a very great stream which within perhaps thirty yards of its eruption turns a mill and[4] in a course of two miles eighteen mills more. In descent it [is] very quick. It then falls into the sea. The Well is covered by a lofty circular arch supported by pillars, and over this arch is an old Chapel, now a School. The Chancel is separated by a wall. The Bath is completely and indecently open. A Woman bathed while we all looked on. In the Church, which makes a good appearance, and is surrounded by galleries to receive a numerous congregation, we were present while a child was christened in Welsh.

We went down by[5] the stream to see a prospect in which I had no part. We then saw a brass work where the lapis Calaminaris is gathred, broken, washed from the earth and the lead, though how the lead was separated I did not see, then calcined, afterwards ground fine, and then mixed by fire with the copper. We saw several strong fires with melting pots, but the construction of the fireplaces I did not learn.

At a copper work, which receives its pigs of copper, I think, from Warrington, we saw a plate of copper put hot between steel rollers, and spread thin. I know not whether [the] upper

4. ⟨before⟩   5. ₄by₄

At Holywell, in Flintshire overlooking the Dee estuary, the party naturally went first to St. Winifred's Well and its fine Gothic chapel, said to have been built by Margaret, mother of Henry VII. It is characteristic that Johnson was more impressed with the new church, built in 1769, than the "old Chapel," but perhaps that was because the chapel was no longer used as such.

The lapis calaminaris or calamine, called smithsonite in the United States, is zinc carbonate, still an important source of zinc. At Holywell it occurred in a lead mine. Johnson was probably right in thinking that the copper came from Warrington in Lancashire, since copper was an important industry in that city in

roller was set to a certain distance, as I suppose, or acted only by its weight.

At an iron work I saw round bars formed by a notched hammer and anvil. Then I saw a bar of about half an inch or more square, cut with sheers worked by water and then beaten hot into a thinner bar; the hammers,[6] all worked as they were by water, acting upon small bodies moved very quick, as quick as by the hand.

I then saw wire drawn, and gave a shilling. I have enlarged my notions. Though not being able to see the movements, and having not time to peep closely, I know less than I might. I was less weary, and had better breath as I walked further. I had $\text{Ka}\theta$ the day before, and had some of the effects this morning.

AUG. 4. Ruthlan Castle is still a very noble ruin. All the walls still remain so that a[6a] compleat platform, and elevations not very imperfect may be taken. It incloses a square of about thirty yards. The middle space was always open. The wall is I believe about thirty feet high, very thick, flanked with six round towers each about eighteen feet, or less, in diameter. Only one tower had a chimney. So that here was [no] com-

6. An inserted word deleted and illegible.
6a. ⟨very⟩

_____

his time. So Johnson at the factory enlarged his "notions." Ten years later he advised Susannah Thrale: "Look in Herschel's tele-scope; go into a chymist's laboratory; if you see a manufacturer at work, remark his operations. By this activity of attention, you will find in every place diversion and improvement" (*Letters* 944).

It appears that the Thrales did not find the problems of Bach-y-Graig demanding, for next day the party went sight-seeing again, first to Rhuddlan Castle in Flintshire, built by Edward I at the beginning of his conquest of Wales. It moved Johnson to measure-ment and Mrs. Thrale to rapture: "Wild in its situation, rude

modity of living. It was only a place of strength. The Garrison
had perhaps beds in the area.

Stapiltons house is pretty; there are pleasing shades about
it, with a constant spring that supplies a cold bath. We then
went to see a cascade; I trudged unwillingly, and was not sorry
to find it dry. The water was however turned on, and produced a very striking cataract. They are paid an hundred
pounds a year, for permission to divert the stream to the
mines. The River, for such it may be termed, rises from a
single spring which like that of Winifred is covered with a
buildi[ng].

We called then at another house belong[ing] to Mr Lloyd

---

in its appearance, the haunt of screaming gulls and clamourous
rooks . . ." (Broadley, p. 188).

The party next visited Mrs. Cotton's girlhood home, Bodrhyd-
dan, in Flintshire. Mrs. Cotton was Frances Stapleton, one of four
daughters. Mrs. Thrale says that the place was "hastening to decay
for want of a male heir" (p. 189), but as it was then occupied by
William Shipley, Dean of St. Asaph and the bishop's son, its condition may merely have been due to a tenant's neglect.

Johnson's ill-humoured remark about the cascade at Dyserth,
about two miles east of Rhuddlan, was paralleled later by his teasing Mrs. Cotton about it, wrote Mrs. Thrale (Piozzi), till "she was
ready to cry: the waterfall being near her maiden residence made
her, I suppose, partial to the place; for she sent us thither to be
entertained, and expected much praise at our return" (Croker,
III.141). Johnson's comment on the river, "for such it may be
termed," implies "in this country." His calling the Clwyd a brook
matches another remark about one of the Clwyd's tributaries, the
Ystrad: Mrs. Thrale (Piozzi) says that he asked, "Has this BROOK
e'er a name? and received for answer—Why, dear Sir, this is the
RIVER Ustrad.—Let us, said he, turning to his friend, jump over it
directly, and shew them how an *Englishman* should treat a *Welch*
RIVER" (*British Synonymy*, I.82, cited by Hill-Powell).

which made a handsome appearance. This country seems full
of very splendid houses.

Mrs T. lost her purse. She expressed so much uneasiness
that I concluded the sum to be very great, but when I heard
of only seven guineas, I was glad to find that she had so much
sensibility of money.

I could not drink this day either coffee or tea after dinner.
I know not when I missed before.

AUG. 5. Last night my sleep was remarkably quiet; little
flatus; I know not whether by fatigue in walking, or by forbearance of tea. I gave the Ipecacuanha—Vin. Emet. had
failed, so had tartar Emet. The Ipec. did but little.

I dined at Mr Middleton's of Gwaynynog. The house was
a Gentlemans house below the second rate, perhaps below the

The house visited next was probably, Powell says, Pengwern,
near St. Asaph, the seat of Edward Lloyd, sometime High Sheriff
of Flintshire.

Johnson's remark that the country was full of very splendid
houses is still true; almost all those of his time are still standing,
and many are inhabited by the same families.

The next day Johnson did not feel well. His omitting coffee
and tea suggests a seriously upset stomach. By "I gave the ipecacuanha" he apparently means that he gave the ipecac a chance by
not drinking. He cannot mean that he gave it up, as he immediately says that it had little effect, and ten days later he wrote to
Levet that he had taken "abundance" of ipecac pills "and hope
that they have done me good" (*Letters* 359). And here he goes on
to say that neither wine of antimony, another emetic, nor tartar
emetic has helped. Since these drugs are depressants, it is perhaps
remarkable that Johnson's disposition at this time was better than
bearish.

He was well enough, however, to join the rest for dinner at
Gwaynynog, near Denbigh, the house of John Myddelton, who

third, built of stone roughly cut. The rooms were low, and
the passage above stairs gloomy, but the furniture was good.
The table was well supplied, except that the fruit was bad.
It was truly the dinner of a country Gentleman. Two tables
were filled with company not inelegant. After diner the talk
was of preserving the Welsh language. I offered them a scheme.
Poor Evan Evans was mentioned as incorrigibly addicted to

---

had been to Oxford and knew of Johnson; Mrs. Thrale says, "Mr.
Johnson's fame has penetrated *thus* far" (Broadley, p. 190) in
explaining that the dinner was given in his honour and the
Thrales . The other guests were "genuine Welch folks" and Mrs.
Thrale did not think much of them. But the good dinner and the
talk of literature were quite enough to please Johnson.

How Johnson proposed to preserve the Welsh language may
perhaps be partly guessed by a letter (184) he wrote in 1766 to
William Drummond about translating the Bible into Erse: "My
zeal for languages may seem, perhaps, rather over-heated, even to
those by whom I desire to be well esteemed. To those who have
nothing in their thoughts but trade or policy, present power,
or present money, I should not think it necessary to defend my
opinions; but with men of letters I would not unwillingly com-
pound, by wishing the continuance of every language, however
narrow in its extent, or however incommodious for common purposes, till it is reposited in some version of a known book, that it
may be always hereafter examined and compared with other
languages, and then permitting its disuse." If it be objected that
the Bible and many other books had long since been translated
into Welsh, they were not very widely distributed. The British
and Foreign Bible Society was founded in 1804 partly because
of the dearth of Welsh Bibles. Or he may have proposed the establishment of a chair of Welsh at Oxford, as he had earlier supported
Warren Hastings's proposal to found a chair of Persian there
(*Letters* 353 n.).

Evan Evans, whose addiction to drink was either the cause or
the result of his failure to rise above a curacy in the church

strong drink. Worthington was commended. Middleton is the only man who in Wales has talked to me of literature. I wish he were truly zealous. I recommended the republication of David ap Rhees's Welsh Grammar. Two sheets of Hebrides came to me for correction to day. F. G.

AUG. 6. Καθ. δρ[αστικὴ]. I corrected the two sheets. My sleep last night was disturbed—Washing at Chester, and here— 5s–1d. I did not read. Atterbury's version a heap of barbarity.

(Powell), had come early to fame with his translations of Welsh poetry, particularly *Some Specimens of the Poetry of the Ancient Welsh Bards*, 1764, on which, while still in manuscript, Gray had based *The Bard*.

Reverend William Worthington, D.D., was the author of many works on religious subjects. Johnson and the Thrales visited him on 8 September.

The Welsh grammar of Dr. Siôn Davydd Rhys, *Cambrobrytannicae . . . Institutiones*, 1592, "the foundation of all later [Welsh] grammatical studies" was "an attempt to set out before the learned world regulations of bardic poetry and principles of the Welsh language" (*Encyclopaedia Britannica*). Johnson's recommendation that the book be reprinted (it was not) may be related to his scheme for preserving the language.

Johnson's receipt of proofs of sheets F and G of the *Journey to the Western Islands* shows that he had already corrected 64 pages (B–E).

Next morning he took a drastic purge.

Francis Atterbury's "version" is the last act of Beaumont and Fletcher's *Maid's Tragedy* as revised by Edmund Waller some years before his death in 1687 and published by Thomas Bennet in 1690 as the main piece in the second volume of Waller's poems. It is clearly taken from a poor manuscript, and seems to be the second draft of three that Waller wrote. The draft is preceded by a substantial unsigned preface containing an elaborate and appre-

The Καθ did not much, but I hope, enough. I saw to day more of the outhouses of Lleuwenny. It is in the whole a very spacious house.

———————————

ciative criticism of Waller's poetic career, which was later reprinted with some of Waller's poems and was included in Nichols's edition of Atterbury's *Letters* in 1783. But literary gossip had long connected Atterbury's name with the volume as Nichols suggests; hence Atterbury's "version." It may be that Atterbury gave the manuscript of the single act to the printer, or even subjected it to some editing. But it is very bad, not only structurally but in many details of verse and language, and in the same year Tonson issued a different version, much improved. A few samples will illustrate the "heap of barbarity":

Melantius. A brave Man rather than not take revenge,
          Just, or unjust, should the whole World unhinge.
                              (Atterbury, p. 14)
          —Rather than not accomplish my Revenge,
          Just, or unjust, I would the World unhinge.
                              (Tonson, p. 16)
Aspasia.   Oh! that some hungry Beast would come,
          And make himself *Aspasia's* Womb!
                              (Atterbury, p. 28)
          —And make himself *Aspasia's* Tomb!
                              (Tonson, p .33)
Aspasia.   But say we are to live elsewhere,
          What has the Innocent to fear?
          Can I be treated worse below,
          Than here? or more unjustly? No!
                              (Atterbury, p. 32)
          —But say we are to live elsewhere,
          What has the Innocent to fear?
          Can I be treated worse than here?
                              (Tonson, p. 36)

The sixth of August was not altogether the restful day Johnson

AUGUST 7. I was at Church at Botfarry. There was a service used for a sick woman, not canonically, but such as I have heard, I think, formerly at Lichfield, taken out of the visitation. Καθ μετριῶς.

The Church is mean but has a square tower for the bells, rather too stately for the Church.

OBSERVATIONS.

Bit and bridle Ps. 32. Southwel.

Dixit injustus. Ps. 36 has no relation to the English.

"Preserve us Lord" has the name of Robert Wisedome, 1618. Barkers Bible.

---

made it appear, for the Cottons entertained. Mrs. Thrale reported that this was true almost every day: "This is a place of great society and of tolerable good humour. . . ."

The following day was Sunday and the party went to church at Bodfari, not far from Denbigh, in Flintshire. The parson "gave out that service should be performed in English," Mrs. Thrale says (Broadley, p. 190), when their party entered. She reports that the church was "below many a stable for convenience or beauty." The service for the Visitation of the Sick in the prayer book is ordinarily performed in the home; hence Johnson's remark that using parts of it in the church service was not canonical.

He purged moderately this day.

Psalm 32 Johnson had perhaps read on Saturday, as it is one of the Psalms appointed for that date, as Psalm 36 is for the next day. His reference is: "Be ye not as the horse, or as the mule, which have no understanding: whose mouth must be held in with bit and bridle, lest they come near unto thee" (vs. 9). Reverend Robert Southwell, the Jesuit poet who went to the scaffold in 1595, aged twenty-four, uses a faintly similar phrase in *St. Peter's Complaint*: "A rack for guilty thoughts, a bit for wild" (line 376). Below, Southwell's thought of his own death may refer to any of

Battologiam ab iteratione recte distinguit Erasmus. Mod.
Orandi Deum p. 56.—144.
Southwells thought of his own death.
Baudius on Erasmus. Infinitum debet. q.

---

three poems on this subject, perhaps to "Upon the Image of
Death," one stanza of which reads:

> Before my face the picture hangs,
>   That daily should put me in mind,
> Of those cold names and bitter pangs,
>   That shortly I am like to find:
> But yet alas full little I
> Do thinke here on that I must die.

Few of Southwell's poems had been reprinted since 1636, and
except in some Roman Catholic circles he must have been almost
unknown at this time. It is most surprising to find Johnson reading him.

"Dixit injustus" ("the wicked saith"), the beginning of the
Latin version of Psalm 36, has no relation to the prayer book
(Coverdale) version: "My heart showeth me the wickedness of the
ungodly," but the King James version is closer: "The transgres-
sion of the wicked saith within my heart. . . ."

"Preserve us, Lord," says Croker (III.143), "alludes to 'A prayer
by R. W.' (evidently Robert Wisedom), which Mr. Ellis, of the
British Museum, has found among the Hymns which follow the
old version of the singing psalms, at the end of Barker's Bible
of 1639. It begins,

> 'Preserve us, Lord, by thy dear word,
> From Turk and Pope, defend us Lord!
> Which both would thrust out of his throne
> Our Lord Jesus Christ, thy deare son.' "

As Johnson says, Erasmus in *Modus Orandi Deum* justly dis-
criminates between "babbling or vain repetition" and repetition
caused by "ardent and vehement passion" in prayer, by pointing

8. The Bishop and much company dined at Llewenny. Talk
of Greek—and of the Army. The D. of M—s officers useless.
Read Phocyllides, distinguished the paragraphs.

9. Looked in Leland, an unpleasant book of mere hints. Lichfield School 10 L and 5 L from the hospital.

---

out that Christ's injunction, "But when ye pray, use not vain
repetitions, as the heathen do: for they think that they shall be
heard for their much speaking" (St. Matthew vi. 7) does not apply
to repetition like Christ's words on the Cross, "My God, my God."
Dominic Baudius's comment on Erasmus occurs in his *Epis-
tolae*, cent. ii, epist. xxvii (trans.): "He was more disposed to flee
than to follow. . . . But nevertheless posterity is infinitely indebted to him." The first sentence Johnson later applied to
Milton's never thinking "that he can recede far enough from
popery." But Johnson queries whether posterity is "infinitely" indebted to Erasmus, much as he admired his works.

On Monday the Cottons entertained again. Mrs. Thrale said
that there were twenty-four at tea and that they dined in separate
rooms. The Bishop, Dr. Shipley, with whom Johnson talked,
had been an army chaplain in 1747 and had perhaps heard some
anecdote to the effect that Marlborough took all responsibilities
into his own hands, and left his officers useless. Johnson later
described Shipley as "knowing and conversible" (*Letters* 483).

The poem once ascribed to Phocylides, Ποίημα νουθετικόν, was
translated by J. Hart in 1744 as *The Preceptive Poem*. It consists
of short precepts, each making up a paragraph of a few lines.
Johnson mentions it again on 18 August.

Tuesday 9 August was a quiet day, giving Johnson time for
reading.

That John Leland's *Itinerary* is a book of mere hints is not its
author's fault, since it consists merely of the notes he collected as
king's antiquary under Henry VIII in trying to preserve the manuscripts scattered at the dissolution of the monasteries. These were
published by Thomas Hearne in 1710–12. The part referred to

10. At Lloyds of Macemunnun, a good house, and very large walled garden. I read Windus's Account of his journey to Mequinez, and of Stuarts Embassy. I had read in the Morning Wasse's Greek trochaics to Bentley. They appeared inelegant and made with difficulty. The Latin Elegy contains only common places harshly expressed so far as I have read, for it is long. They seem to be the verses of a scholar, who has no practice of writing. The Greek I did not always fully understand.

---

by Johnson is: "B. *Smith* in H.K. 7 dayes, and last Bishop of *Lincolne*, beganne a new Foundation at this Place settinge up a Mr. there with 2. Preistes, and 10. poore Men in an Hospitall. He sett there alsoe a Schoole-Mr. to teach Grammer that hath 10. *l.* by the yeare, and an Under-Schoole-Mr. that hath 5. *l.* by the Yeare. King H. 7. was a great Benefactour to this new Foundation, and gave to it an ould Hospitall called Denhall in Wirhall in Cheshire" (cited in *Life*, v.445).

The last eight days of their stay at Llewenny were comparatively inactive. The Thrales had the problem of Bach-y-Graig, and there were several old friends to call upon. On 10 August they dined with Lloyd of Maesmynnan, Cotton's agent, who aspired to be Mrs. Thrale's. John Windhus's *Journey to Mequinez, the Residence of the Present Emperor of Fez and Morocco, on the Occasion of Commodore Stewart's Embassy Thither, for the Redemption of the British Captives, in the Year 1721* was published in 1725.

The Reverend Joseph Wasse's verses to Richard Bentley, the classical scholar, appeared in Jebb's *Bibliotheca Literaria*, 1723, No. 6, pp. 9–14. This periodical attempted to present "Inscriptions, Medals, Dissertations, &c." to a learned audience (a large part is written in Latin) but with such ill success that it expired after the tenth number. Its most interesting article is an anonymous essay, in No. 4, on English translations of the Bible. Wasse, an editor of Sallust, contributed a long essay on desiderata in editions of the classics, in which his survey of existing editions,

I am in doubt about 6 v. and last paragraph. Perhaps they are not printed right; for ἔντοκον perhaps ἔνστοχον. q.

The following days I read here and there. The Bibl. Literaria was so little supplied with papers that could interest curiosity, that it could not hope for long continuance. Wasse the chief contributor was an unpolished scholar, who with much literature, had no art or elegance of diction, at least in English.

AUGUST 14. At Botfarry I heard the second Lesson read, and the sermon preached in Welsh. The text was pronounced both in Welsh and English. The sound of the Welsh in a continued discourse is not unpleasant.

---

and his discussion of manuscript sources in English and Continental libraries, well justifies Johnson's description of him as having "much literature."

Johnson's suggested emendation of εὔτοκον "bringing forth easily" to εὔστοχον "hitting the mark" comes in line 4 of the sixth and last paragraph:

νοῦν ἰδοὺ τὸν εὔτοκον μὲν ὡς ἔπειτ᾽ ἐπομνύῃs/οὐδέν οἱ προαρπαγὲν.

Gennadius says that Johnson's criticism of the Greek verses is sound but that the emendation is unnecessary: "εὔτοκον stands as applied to a productive mind" (*Johnson Club Papers*, 1899, p. 36). Of the Latin verses urging Bentley to press some of his projects before it is too late, J. H. Monk says: "All that can be said in their favour is, that they are better than the generality of laudatory verses prefixed to books. The Latin copy contains some tolerable lines" (*Bentley*, 1830, II.170).

What troubled Johnson in line 6 of the Greek poem is not clear.

For the next three days Mr. or Mrs. Thrale, or both, went calling and once they rode through Bach-y-Graig, but had no key to get into the house. Johnson stayed at the Cottons'.

On 14 August the party again went to church at Bodfari, and the clergyman again offered to conduct the service in English, Mrs.

Βρῶσις ὀλίγη. Καθ. ἄ[νευ] φ[άρμακων].

The Letter of Chrysostom against transubstantiation. Erasmus to the Nuns, full of mystick notions, and allegories.

AUG. 15. Καθ. Imbecillitas genuum non sine aliquantulo doloris inter ambulandum, quem a prandio magis sensi.

AUG. 18. We left Llewenni, and went forwards on our Journey. We came to Abergeler a mean town in which little but Welsh is spoken, and Divine service is seldom performed in English. Our way then lay by the sea side at the foot of a Mountain called Penman ross. Here the way was so steep that we walked on the lower edge of the hill to meet the Coach that went upon a road higher on the hill. Our walk was not

---

Thrale reports, but the party preferred not. And Johnson ate sparingly and purged without a drug.

The *Letter to Caesarius* formerly attributed to Chrysostom contains a passage which seems to favour the theory of impanation, a heretical doctrine opposed to transubstantiation (*Catholic Encyclopedia*). It was printed in *Bibliotheca Literaria*, No. 4. In the canonical works, Chrysostom's position is orthodox.

Erasmus's *Sacris Virginibus* is Letter 497 in Leclerc's edition, Leiden, 1703.

On Monday Johnson felt "a weakness of the knees, not without some pain in walking, which I feel increased after I have dined" (trans. Duppa), and so he did not accompany Mrs. Thrale to see Myddelton's gardens at Gwaynynog. This was a fortunate call, for Myddelton invited the party to visit him later in their tour, an invitation which she accepted. It turned out to be a week's visit.

Apparently none of the party left Llewenny for the next two days. They were preparing to continue their journey.

On 18 August the party ended their considerable visit at Llewenny and set out for their tour of Carnarvonshire and Anglesey. Both Johnson and Mrs. Thrale had enjoyed the comforts of the large house, Mrs. Thrale particularly liking her hostess.

long nor unpleasant, the longer I walk the less I feel its[7] inconvenience. As I grow warm my breath mends and I think my limbs grow pliable.

We then came to Conway Ferry and passed in small boat[s], with some passengers from the Stage coach. Among whom were an Irish Gentlewoman with two maids and three little children of which the youngest was only[8] a few months old. The tide did not serve the large ferry boat, and therefore our Coach could not very soon follow us. We were therefore to stay at the Inn. It is now the day of the race at Conway and the town was so full of company, that no money could purchase lodging. We were not very readily supplied with cold dinner. We would have stayed at Conway, if we could have found entertainment, for we were afraid of passing Penmanmawr over which lay our way to Bangor but by bright daylight, and the delay of our coach made our departure necessarily late. There was however no stay on any other terms than of sitting up all night.

The poor Irish Lady was still more distressed. Her children wanted rest. She would have been content with one bed, but for a time none could be had. Mrs T. gave her what help she could. At last two gentlemen were persuaded to yield up their room with two beds, for which she gave half a guinea.

Our coach was at last brought and we set out with some anxiety but we came to Penmanmawr by day light, and found a way lately made, very easy and very safe. It was cut smooth and inclosed between parallel walls. The outer of which secures the [traveller] from the precipice which is deep and

7. ∧its∧ ⟨the⟩   8. ∧only∧ _____

They passed through Abergele, a little to the west of Rhuddlan, reached the sea a mile beyond, and passed by Penmaen Rhôs; then they ferried the River Conway, and were disappointed to find no accommodations at Conway, since Bangor was about fourteen

dreadful. This wall is here and there broken by mischievous wantonness. The inner wall preserves the road from the loose stones which the shatter[ed] steep above it would pour down. That side of the mountain seems to have a^9 surface of loose stones which every accident may crumble. The old road was higher and must have been very formidable. The sea beats at the bottom of the way. At Evening the Moon shone eminently bright, and our thoughts of danger being now past, the rest of our journey was very pleasant. At an hour somewhat late we came to Bangor, where we found a very mean Inn, and had some difficulty to obtain lodging. I lay in a room where the other bed had two men. I had a flatulent night.

NOTES.

Indidem=from the same place[1]

9. ∧have a∧ ⟨be consist⟩   1. Two or three words deleted.

---

miles further. They went on then past the 1550-foot rock of Penmaen Mawr, with its new road built just two years before (Powell). On the return trip Johnson revised his opinion that the breaks on the outer wall were caused by "mischievous wantonness." Finally they reached Bangor, where the mistress of the inn proposed, says Mrs. Thrale, that Johnson sleep "with Mr. Thrale and Queeney and I, who were all stuffed in one filthy room" (Broadley, p. 196).

The notes opposite this date were probably begun while Johnson was still at Llewenny, since he refers to the Greek verses he read there on the eighth, and entered at intervals till he was at Blenheim, when he saw the Greek grammar. He left no later blank spaces to accommodate such notes and naturally returned to this space when he did not wish to interrupt his narrative.

"Indidem," "from the same place," is a relatively uncommon word, though it occurs in Cicero. Apparently Johnson had not met it before.

Θαλιαὶς for Δολιαὶς in Phocylides.
To note down my Father's stock, expences, and profit.
Queeny's Goats 149 I think.
Potato set whole at the latter end of May produced Sept. 5,
7 lb 7 oz in a hundred potatoes great and small.
First Printed Book in Greek, Lascaris's Grammar 4to Mediolani 1476 per Dionysium Palivisinum q. Bowyer.

Johnson's emendation in the pseudo-Phocylidean poem already referred to, θαλιαὶς "make merry" for Δολιαὶς "act treacherously" concerns this distich:

καλὸν ξεινίζειν ταχέως λιταῖσι τραπέζαις
ἢ πλείσταις θαλίαισι βραδυνούσαις παρὰ καιρόν.

(lines 81, 82).

Hart had translated it in 1744 in accord with Johnson's notion:

Better to let a Stranger find, with Haste,
A hearty welcome to a mean Repast;
Than thro' an ill-tim'd hindrance make him wait
The formal Dainties of a gaudy treat.

Since Hart meticulously noted any departures from the received text, it is clear that the corrected reading must have been in print by this time. It is accepted by most modern editors.

Johnson's reminder to note down details of his father's business, which he mentions in the "Annals" (see above p. 8), he perhaps never accomplished.

"Queeny's Goats" Mrs. Thrale refers to 26 August, when the party, climbing Snowdon, saw goats, which Mr. Thrale, being nearsighted, asked Queeney to count, offering her a penny apiece with Johnson keeping the account (Duppa cited by Croker).

The note on the production of potatoes probably refers to Mrs. Thrale's tenant, who consulted with her on 5 September (Broadley, p. 207).

Johnson's query as to Lascaris's Greek Grammar, the first book printed in Greek, perhaps comes from his reading William Bow-

AUGUST 19. We obtained a boat to convey us to Anglesea, and saw Lord Bulkley's house and Beaumaris Castle. I was accosted by Mr Lloyd the Schoolmaster of Beaumaris who had seen me at University College, and he with Mr Roberts the Register of Bangor whose boat we borrowed, accompanied us. Lord Bulkeley's house is very mean, but his garden is spacious and shady, with large trees and smaller interspersed. The walks are strait and cross each other with no variety of plan but they have a pleasing coolness and solemn gloom, and extend to a great length.

The Castle is a mighty pile; the outward wall has fifteen round towers, besides square towers at the angles. There is then a void space between the wall and the castle, which has an area enclosed with a wall which[2] again has towers larger than those of the outer wall; the towers of the inner castle are I think eight. There is likewise a chapel entire, bui[l]t upon an arch as I suppose, and beautifully arch[ed] with a stone roof which is yet[3] unbroken. The entrance into the Chapel is about eight or nine feet high, and was I suppose, higher when there was no rubbish in the area.

This castle corresponds with all the representations of ro-

2. ⟨ha⟩   3. MS:"yet yet"

yer's *Origin of Printing*, which was published in June and contains the statement, p. 102. He may have made this entry before seeing the grammar at Blenheim on 22 September, following Bowyer's "Palavisinus" instead of the book's imprint, "Paravisinum."

The next morning the party set out for the Island of Anglesey in a boat of Thomas Roberts, the notary public and registrar of the Diocese of Bangor, whom Thrale had met in town. Upon reaching the island Roberts sent for William Lloyd to show the party the sights. Lloyd recognized Johnson, having seen him at Oxford, probably when Lloyd was an undergraduate between 1766 and 1769. Johnson was there in each of those years. After

mancing narratives. Here is not wanting the private passage, the dark cavity, the deep dungeon or the lofty tower. We did not discover the well. This is [the] most complete view that I have yet had of an old castle. It had a moat. The towers. We returned to Bangor.

AUGUST 20. We went by water from Bangor to Caernarvon, where we met Poali and Sir Thomas Wynne. Meeting by chance with one Troughton, an intelligent and loquacious wanderer, Mr T. invited him to diner. He attended us to the Castle, an Edifice of stupendous magnitude and strength. It has in it all that we observed at Beaumaris, of much greater dimensions; many of the smaller rooms floored with stone are entire; of[4] the larger rooms, the beams and planks are all lost; this is the state of all buildings left to time. We mounted the Eagle tower by 169 steps each of ten inches. We did not find the well, nor did I trace the moat, but moats there were I believe to all castles on the plain, which not only hindred

4. ∧of∧
_____

showing the party the house of the seventh Viscount Bulkeley, on a commanding site near the Castle, and the Castle itself, built by Edward I in 1293, Lloyd took Johnson to his school. Then they all returned to Bangor, where Roberts put them up for the night (Broadley, p. 197).

On 20 August, again in Roberts's boat, the party went through the straits to Carnarvon, stopping by the way. At Carnarvon the guns were firing for the Corsican General Paoli, who had just landed, said Mrs. Thrale (p. 198). Although Johnson had known and liked him for five years, he had not yet learned to spell his name. Sir Thomas Wynn, Bart., who was conducting him through the town, was M.P. and Lord Lieutenant of Carnarvonshire. Lieutenant Ellis Troughton, the "intelligent wanderer," was a half-pay naval officer. The dinner which he got, says Mrs. Thrale, was a bad one. Then to Carnarvon Castle, begun by Edward I, one of the most imposing mediaeval fortresses in Europe. They were

access, but prevented mines. We saw but a very small part of this mighty ruin. And in all these old buildings the subterraneous works are concealed by the rubbish. To survey this place would take much time. I did not think there had been such buildings. It surpassed my Ideas.

21. We were at Church; the service in the town is always English, at the Parish Church at a small distance always Welsh. The town has by degrees, I suppose, been brought nearer to the sea side. We received an invitation to Dr Worthington. We then went to diner at Sir T. Wynne's. The Dinner mean. Sir T. civil. His Lady nothing. Poali civil.

---

shown a small room in the Eagle Tower supposed to be that in which Edward II was born, after which he was shown to the people as a "prince of Wales who could speak no English." Troughton was properly sceptical of the room, remarking that "they had no other room left entire, and therefore they called this the Prince of Wales's birth Chamber." The party stayed the night at a "nasty Inn" in the town.

The next day, Sunday, they all went to church as usual. Johnson's guess that the town had been by degrees brought nearer to the sea is true at least in comparison to Roman times, when the town was half a mile to the east, and farther inland. Dr. Worthington, whom Johnson had heard commended on 5 August, sent them an invitation, of which they availed themselves on 8 September.

They dined with Sir Thomas Wynn. Mrs. Thrale was more outspoken than Johnson about Sir Thomas's wife and her dinner: she was "an empty woman of quality, insolent, ignorant, and ill bred, without either beauty or fortune to atone for her faults. She set a vile dinner before us, and on such linen as shocked one. . . . Mr. Johnson compared her at our return to sour small beer; she could not have been a good thing, he said, and even that poor thing was spoilt" (p. 200).

We Supped with Colonel Wynne's Lady who lives in one of the towers of the Castle.

I have not been very well.

AUGUST 22. We went to visit Bodville, the place where Mrs T. was born, and the churches called Tydweilliog and Llangynnidle[5] which she holds by impropriation. We had an invitation to the House of Mr Griffith of Brinoddle, where we found a small neat new built house, with square rooms. The walls are of unhewn stone and therefore thick, for the stones not fitting with exactness are not strong without great thickness. He had planted a great deal of young wood in walks. Fruit trees do[6] not thrive, but having grown a few years reach some barren stratum, and wither.

We found Mr Griffiths not at home, but the provisions were good. Mr Griffith came home the next day. He married a Lady who has a house and Estate at   over against Anglesea, and near Caernarvon, where she is more disposed, as it seems, to reside[7] than at Brinodl.

5. ∧called . . . Llangynnidle∧   6. ∧do∧ ⟨did⟩   7. ⟨and⟩

That evening the party supped with Sir Thomas's sister-in-law, the wife of Lieutenant Colonel Glynn Wynn, M.P.

Next day the party started down the Lleyn Peninsula towards Bodvil, having been invited by Mrs. Hugh Griffith, whom they had seen at her house at Llanfairisgaer on the twentieth, to make their headquarters at her other house, Brynodol, near Bodvil. They did not go to Bodvil till the next day. Johnson's remark may be paraphrased, "We set out to visit, etc." The churches Mrs. Thrale held by impropriation; that is, they were former monastic properties transferred to lay control.

Johnson's comment that Griffith "came home the next day" shows that he was writing at least two days after the event; this accounts for the differences between his chronology and Mrs. Thrale's.

I read Lluyds account of Mona which he proves to be Anglesea.

In our way to Br   we saw at Llanerk a Church built crosswise, very spacious and magnificent for this country; we could not see the Parson and could get no intelligence about it.

24. We went to see Bodvil. Mrs T. remembered the rooms, and wandered over them with recollection of her childhood. This species of pleasure is always melancholy. The walk was cut down, and the pond was dry. Nothing was better.

We surveyed the churches, which are mean and neglected to a degree scarcely imaginable. They have no pavement, and the earth is full of holes, the seats are rude benches. The altars have no rails; one of them has a breach in the roof. On the desk I think of each lay a Folio Welsh Bible of the black letter, which the Curate cannot easily read. Mr T proposes to beau-

---

Johnson could have read Humphrey Llwyd's "De Mona Druidum Insula," which shows that "the Mona of Tacitus, Pliny the Elder, and Dio Cassius was Anglesea and not the Isle of Man" in Ortelius, in Price's *Historiae Brytannicae Defensio*, or in Williams's *Humfredi Llwyd . . . Britannicae Descriptionis Commentariolum* (*Life*, v.592).

"Llanerk" is Clynnog, a seaside resort south of Carnarvon. The church, fifteenth–sixteenth century Perpendicular, is 138 feet by 70, one of the largest and handsomest in North Wales.

Johnson has mingled two days' events in this account. Mrs. Thrale says that they went to Bodvil on the twenty-third, also to Lloyd's, to the parish church, Llannor, where she was baptized, then to Pwllheli, where Johnson "could find nothing to purchase but a Primmer," and where Griffith overtook them and brought them home (pp. 201–3). Richard Lloyd, Mrs. Thrale says, "had played many a game at romps with me, and at draughts with my Father before I was seven years old." He had acted as Salusbury's business agent, was later High Sheriff of Carnarvonshire, and died in 1771 (*Life*, v.594). Johnson seems to have started to write "his

tify the Churches, and, if he prospers, will probably restore the tithes. The two parishes are Llangynnidle and Tydweilliog. The Methodists are here very prevalent. A better church will impress the people with more reverence of publick Worship. Mrs Thrale visited a house where she had been used to drink milk, which was left with an estate of 200 L a year, by one Lloyd to[8] a married woman who lived with him. We went to Pwlhely a mean old[9] town at the extremity of the country. Here we bought something to remember the place.

8. ⟨his⟩   9. ⟨Inn⟩

_____

mistress," and changed his mind. Mrs. Thrale says his "mistress or maid."

Mrs. Thrale's reaction to her birthplace was hardly melancholy. She says that she "looked at the old pond with pleasure, though it is now dry." And she adds, "The present possessors of the house were very civil, and indulged all my silly curiosity, letting me look into all their hiding-places. I saw and remembered them all." Johnson was perhaps remembering his own return to Lichfield in 1762: "I went down to my native town, where I found the streets much narrower and shorter than I thought I had left them, inhabited by a new race of people, to whom I was very little known. My play-fellows were grown old, and forced me to suspect that I was no longer young" (*Life*, 1.370). On 24 August the party saw the churches of which Mrs. Thrale had the impropriation, Tydweiliog and Llangwnadl. The condition of them shocked Mrs. Thrale as much as Johnson. Thrale's hope to restore the tithes was apparently not accomplished, as in 1809 the revenues were still very small (Duppa). During the day they visited John Griffith of Cefn Amwlch, about whom Mrs. Thrale says: "He found the place a ruin, and it is now a very habitable house; he found the demesne a waste; he has divided it into fields and gardens and has a hot-house and pinery" (Broadley, p. 203, corrected from MS), all this within a year. Johnson recorded his impressions of the visit, in retrospect, on 29 August.

2 5. We returned to Carnarvon where we eat with Mrs Wynne.

2 6. We visited with Mrs Wynne[1] Llyn Badarn and Llyn Beris, two lakes joined by a narrow strait. They are formed by the waters which fall from Snowden and the opposite Mountains. On the side of Snowden are the remains of a large fort, to which we climbed with great labour. I was breathless and harrassed. The lakes have no great breadth so that the boat is always near one bank or the other.

2 7. We returned to Bangor where Mr T. was lodged at Mr Roberts's the Register.

1. ∧with Mrs Wynne∧

On 25 August the party left Brynodol to return to Carnarvon. They dined in the coach on the meat Mr. Griffith of Brynodol had been kind enough to send along, for there was no decent inn on the way. After arriving in Carnarvon they spent the afternoon with Mrs. Wynn, who had invited Mr. Roberts, the vicar, to meet them. Mrs. Wynn proposed an excursion for the following day to see Snowdon.

The next morning this outing came off as planned, all those who had been at Mrs. Wynn's making up the group. They went to the beautiful Llyn Padarn and Llyn Peris to the northwest of Snowdon. From there they had a wonderful view of the mountain. They climbed up to Dolbadarn Castle, a solitary tower, above the town of Llanberis, the starting point for the easiest ascent of Snowdon. This was the day Queeney counted goats for her father, when Mrs. Wynn sang Welsh songs to a harper's accompaniment, and Roberts, the vicar, provided dinner at the far end of the lake. Mrs. Thrale sums up: "Mr. Johnson says he would not have the images he has gained since he left the vale erased for £100" (p. 205).

On 27 August the only plan was to return to Bangor, which, being a short trip, allowed time to have breakfast with Mrs. Wynn before making a leisurely start. In Bangor Mr. Roberts, the regis-

28. We went to worship at the Cathedral. The Quire is mean; the service was not well read.

29. We came to Mr Middleton's of Gyuannog. To the first place as my Mistress observed, where we have been welcome. N. On the day when we visited Bodvil, we turned to the house of Mr Griffiths of Kefnamwcl, a Gentleman of large fortune remarkable for having made great and sudden improvements in his seat and Estate. He has inclosed a large Garden with a brick wall. He is considered as a Man of great accomplishments. He was educated in literature at the University and served some time in the army, then quitted his commission, and retired to his Lands. He is accounted a good Man and endeavours to bring the people to church.

In our way from Bangor to Conway, we passed again the new road upon the edge of Penmanmaur, which would be very tremendous but that the wall shuts out the idea of danger. In the wall are several breaches made as Mr T. very reasonably conjectures by fragments of rocks which roll down the

---

trar, again put them up for the night, Mr. Thrale having made the arrangements.

The next day, Sunday, the party went to service at the Cathedral in Bangor, a small, plain building, in most part dating from the early sixteenth century. Johnson's disappointment probably derived from having seen Clynnog so recently, a much more impressive church. Mrs. Thrale says that they went to the Cathedral Library; it is a little surprising that Johnson did not mention it. The rest of the day was spent with the Robertses.

On 29 August the party set off for Myddelton's house. On the way they stopped at Conway Castle, which was built by Edward I in 1284 after designs of Henry de Elreton, who also planned the castles of Beaumaris and Carnarvon. The well is near one end of the Great Court. The party arrived at Gwaynynog, where a happy reunion took place. Mrs. Thrale amplified Johnson's state-

mountain, broken perhaps by frost, or worn through by rain.
We then viewed Conway.[2]

To spare the horses at Penman Ross, between Conway and
St. Asaph we sent the coach over the road cross the Mountain,
with Mrs Th. who had been tired with a walk some time
before, and I with Mr Th. and Miss, walked along the edge
where the path is very narrow, and much encumbred by little
loose stones which had fallen[3] down as we thought upon the
way since we passed it[4] before.

At Conway we took a short survey of the Castle, which
afforded us nothing new. It is larger than that of Beumarris,
and less than that of Caernarvon. It is built upon a rock so
high and steep that it is even now very difficult of access. We
found a round pit which was called the well, it is now almost
filled and therefore dry. We found the well in no other castle.
There are some remains of leaden pipes at Caernarvon, which,
I suppose only conveyed water from one part of the building
to another. Had the Garrison had no other supply, the Welsh
who must know where the pipes were laid could easily have
cut them.

2. ∧We . . . Conway∧   3. MS: "falled"   4. ⟨last⟩

———————————————

ment about their welcome: "This day was spent with Mr. Myddelton and his friends, and this seems to be the only place where we
have been received and treated with attention for our own value.
At other places we have been taken in because it was fit to take
us, and treated according to [our] rank, because it was right we
should be so treated. Here we are loved, esteemed, and honoured,
and here I daresay we might spend the whole Winter if we would"
(p. 206).

The days passed very pleasantly with the Myddeltons, though
without great activity. On 1 September Mrs. Thrale drove down
to Llewenny. On 3 September there were guests for dinner and
afterwards Mrs. Thrale rode over to Bach-y-Graig. On the way

AUG. 29. We came to the house of Mr Middleton (on Monday) where we staid to Sept. 6, and were very kindly entertained.[5] How we spent our time I am not very able to tell. We saw the wood which is diversified and romantick.

SEPT 4. SUNDAY. We dined with Mr Middleton the Clergyman at[6] Denbigh, where I saw the Harvestmen very decently dressed after the[7] afternoon service standing to be hired; on other days they stand at about four in the morning. They are hired from day to day.

5. ⟨we dined once with Mr Lloyd of⟩ 6. ⟨Caer⟩ 7. ∧very decently dressed∧ after ∧the∧ ... stand ∧at∧

she saw Bridge, her unsatisfactory agent, but could not bear to talk to him.

On Sunday, 4 September, for the first time neither Johnson nor Mrs. Thrale recorded going to church, but it is likely they did, for at dinner they faced the Reverend Robert Myddelton, rector of Denbigh from 1772 to 1797 and the younger brother of their host.

On 6 September the party left Gwaynynog. That the visit was as pleasing to the host as the guests was demonstrated three years later, when Myddelton erected an urn on his estate, inscribed:

This spot was often dignified by the presence of
SAMUEL JOHNSON, LL.D.
Whose moral writings, exactly conformable to the
precepts of Christianity,
Give ardour to Virtue and confidence to Truth.

But in spite of the flattering paraphrase from the last *Rambler* (*Life*, IV.554), Johnson was not pleased when he heard of the memorial: "Mr. Myddelton's erection of an urn looks like an intention to bury me alive. I would as willingly see my friend, however benevolent and hospitable quietly inurned. Let him think for the present of some more acceptable memorial" (*Letters* 548).

The travellers' destination was Wrexham, twenty miles away, but they did not arrive there until late, as they stopped to call

SEPT. 6, TUESDAY. We lay at Wrexham, a busy, extensive[8] and well-built town. It has a very large and magnificent Church. It has a famous fair.[9]

SEPT. 7. We came to Chirk Castle.

8. ∧extensive∧ ⟨large⟩   9. ∧It . . . fair.∧

---

upon Lloyd at Maesmynnan, where, after all these days in Wales, Mrs. Thrale said we "did as we sat in the coach all the business we came into this Country to do, ordered a Letter of Attorney for Cotton and his Agent, to receive my rents, etc., and so this affair is finished" (Broadley, pp. 207, 208).

At Wrexham they saw St. Giles's Church (1472) with its splendid tower. Perhaps, outside, they also saw the tomb of Elihu Yale, after whom Yale University is named.

On 7 September, going south from Wrexham the party passed through Ruabon, where, says Mrs. Thrale in her *Anecdotes*, Johnson was involved in this incident:

> It was impossible not to laugh at the patience he shewed, when a Welch parson of mean abilities, though a good heart, struck with reverence at the sight of Dr. Johnson, whom he had heard of as the greatest man living, could not find any words to answer his inquiries concerning a motto round somebody's arms which adorned a tomb-stone in Ruabon churchyard. If I remember right the words were,
>
>   Heb Dw, Heb Dym,
>   Dw o' diggon
> And though of no very difficult construction, the gentleman seemed wholly confounded, and unable to explain them; till Mr. Johnson having picked out the meaning by little and little, said to the man, "*Heb* is a preposition, I believe Sir, is it not?" My countryman recovering some spirits upon the sudden question, cried out, "So I humbly presume, Sir," very comically [p. 238].

But in her diary, Mrs. Thrale seems to place the same incident at

SEP. 8, THURSDAY. We came to the House of Dr Worthington at Llanrhaiadur. Our entertainment was poor though his house was not bad. The Situation is very pleasant by the side of a small river, of which the bank rises high on the other side[1] shaded by gradual rows of trees. The gloom, the stream, and the silence generate thoughtfulness. The town is old and very mean but has, I think, a market. In this house the Welsh translation of the old testament was made.

The Welsh Singing Psalms were written by Archdeacon Price. They are not considered as elegant, but as very literal and accurate.

1. side ⟨and⟩ ∧shaded∧   _____

Chirk Castle, a few miles farther on: "Here we saw the best Library we have been shewn in Wales, and a ridiculous Chaplain whose conversation with Mr. Johnson made me ready to burst with laughing" (p. 208). The castle was owned by Richard Myddelton, whose motto was the Welsh phrase on the tomb; the translation is, "Without God, without all. God is all-sufficient."

Johnson left a full column blank for comments on Chirk Castle, but did not return to fill it in. Perhaps he had described enough castles of the time of Edward I. This one was built by Roger Mortimer about 1300.

The next day by invitation the party proceeded to the home of Dr. Worthington, at Llanrhaiadr Mochnant, in the southern tip of Denbighshire. Mrs. Thrale says that the warmth of their welcome made up for the wretchedness of their accommodation. The town's market was a famous pony fair.

The first complete translation of the Bible into Welsh was made by the Reverend William Morgan while he was vicar of Llanrhaiadr, 1578–88, and published in 1588. He was assisted by Edmund Prys, archdeacon of Merioneth, whose metrical version of the Psalms was published as an appendix to the 1621 edition of the Welsh Book of Common Prayer. Both the Morgan Bible, revised, and the Prys Psalms have continued in use. Powell quotes the Venerable A. Owen Evans on Prys's Psalms: "His version is

We came to Llanrhaiadur through Oswestry, a town not very little nor very mean. The Church which I saw only at a distance seems to be an edifice much too grand for the present state of the place.

SEPT. 9. We visited the Waterfal which is very high, and in rainy weather very copious. There is a reservoir made to supply it. In its fall it has perforated a rock. There is a room built for entertainment. There was some difficulty in climbing to a near view. Lord Littleton came near it, and turned back.

When we came back we took some cold meat, and notwithstanding the Dr's importunities went that day to Shrewsbury.

SEPT. 10. I sent for Gwin, and he showed us the town. The walls are broken, and narrower than those of Chester. The town is large and has many Gentlemens houses, but the streets

---

a pleasing and correct translation and something more; it is a commentary and an exposition" (*Life*, v.454 n.).

On the way to Llanrhaiadr they had passed through Oswestry, in Shropshire, which had been a thriving centre of the woollen trade in the fifteenth and sixteenth centuries, perhaps accounting for the good appearance of the town. St. Oswald's Church, with its picturesque tower, was originally conventual and therefore more "grand" than one would expect of a mere parish church.

On 9 September the party went to Pistyll Rhaiadr, the highest waterfall in Wales, about five miles from Llanrhaiadr. Johnson's remark that the second Lord Lyttelton failed the climb probably reflects his pleasure in the fact that Lyttelton was only thirty, whereas he was almost sixty-five. Later in the day they pressed on to Shrewsbury.

Next day Johnson sent for the architect John Gwynn to show the party his native town. Mrs. Thrale implied that Johnson was imperious when she said that he "snubbed the poor fellow so hard that I half pitied him," but it should be remembered that the

are narrow. I saw Taylors library. We walked in the Quarry, a very pleasant walk by the river. Our inn was not bad.

SEPT. 11, SUNDAY. We were at St Chads, a very large and luminous Church. We were on the Castle hill.

12. We called on Dr Adams, and[2] travelled towards Worcester through Wenlock, a very mean place though a borough.

2. ∧called . . . and∧

---

two men had been friends for at least fifteen years, since Johnson wrote on Gwynn's behalf in the competition for the erection of Blackfriars Bridge.

Of the town walls only fragments remain. Dr. John Taylor, a classical scholar, had bequeathed his library of about 3500 volumes to the Shrewsbury Grammar School in 1766 (*Life*, v.594). The Quarry is a public park in the southwest quarter of the town in a bend of the Severn. Its fine lime-tree walk was planted by an ancestor of the eminent Johnsonian G. B. Hill.

On Sunday, 11 September, the party went to church at old St. Chad's, which was destroyed by the fall of its tower in 1788, though its large fourteenth-century Jesse window, which no doubt helped to make it luminous, was installed after the accident in the fine church of St. Mary's. Johnson and the Thrales saw Castle Hill in the northeast part of the town, where a modern watch tower now stands. Of the mediaeval castle, the keep and two towers remain.

On the following day, after breakfast with Johnson's friend Dr. Adams, perpetual curate of St. Chad's and the next year Master of Pembroke College—Mrs. Thrale did not enjoy either Dr. Adams or his breakfast—the party set off towards Worcester. The borough of Wenlock, disfranchised in 1885, includes the towns of Broseley, Madeley, and Much Wenlock, the last of which boasts a mediaeval priory, a Tudor guildhall, and ruins of the Cluniac church. But either Johnson did not see these, or he was not impressed. Mrs. Thrale says that they walked up Wenlock Edge, evidently following the coach up the steep hill on the road.

At noon we came to Bridgenorth, and walked about the town, of which one part stands on a high rock and part very low by the river. There is an old tower which being crooked leans so much that it is frightful to pass by it. In the afternoon we went through Kinver a town in Staffordshire, neat and closely built. I believe it has only one street.

The Road was so steep and miry, that we were forced to stop at Hartlebury, where we had a very neat inn, though it made a very poor appearance.

SEPT. 13. We came to Lord Sandys at Ombersley where we were treated with great civility. The house is large. The Hall is a very noble room.

––––––––––

At noon they saw the Norman tower at Bridgnorth, the surviving fragment of the castle, seventy feet high and leaning about thirteen degrees. Why the party passed through Kinver is difficult to guess. It is about three miles off the main road, which may have been under repair. But the town is also about three miles west of Stourbridge, and Johnson may have heard about it in his schooldays. Then they crossed into Worcestershire. But bad roads, broken tackle, and tired horses, says Mrs. Thrale, made them stop at the inn at Hartlebury, five miles short of Lord Sandys's house at Ombersley, where they were expected.

The inn proved so pleasant that the party stayed till noon of the next day and then went on to Lord Sandys, second Baron Sandys, an old friend of the Thrales. Mrs. Thrale says that they were received with all possible kindness and entertained "with a liberality of friendship which cannot be surpassed" (Broadley, p. 210).

On 14 September the Sandyses took the party to Worcester (Johnson is a day off here). There they saw the cathedral, where perhaps the most remarkable monument is that to King John, with what is said to be the earliest existing effigy of an English king. The first edition of Schedel's *Nuremberg Chronicle*, 1493,

15. We went to Worcester, a very splendid city. The Cathedral is very noble with many remarkable monuments. The Library is in the Chapter house; on the table lay the Nuremburg Chronicle, I think, of the first Edition. We went to the China Warehouse. The Cathedral has a cloister. The long isle is in my opinion neither so³ wide nor so high as that of Lichfield.

16. We went to Hagley, where we were disappointed of the respect and kindness that we expected.

3. ⟨long⟩

---

is still in the Cathedral Library. Johnson's opinion that the "long isle" (the nave?) of the cathedral is narrower and lower than that of Lichfield is wrong; perhaps he was deceived by the relatively much greater length of the nave at Worcester, 170 feet compared with 140 feet at Lichfield.

The next day was spent quietly. Mrs. Thrale stayed in, not feeling well, and she realized that she was again pregnant. They spent the evening among books and in literary talk, and Johnson was sorry that they were leaving.

On 16 September the party journeyed north to Hagley, a short distance from Stourbridge, where they stayed with William Henry Lyttelton, uncle of Lord Lyttelton, and his wife. Johnson had looked forward to the visit since 1771, when Lyttelton, who was a friend of Thrale's, had invited him. Johnson's early mentor Parson Ford had lived nearby at Pedmore, and Johnson hoped to talk about Ford and those early days. His disappointment was keen therefore to find his host and hostess boorish. Mrs. Thrale, still feeling sick, was forced "with an ill-bred but irresistible importunity" to play cards, and she reports that "Mr. Johnson sate to read awhile and then walked about, when Mr. Lyttelton advertised if he did not use his candle to put it out" (pp. 210, 211). In a later version of the story, she says that Lyttelton "took away Johnson's candle that he wanted to read by at the other end of the room" (Croker, III.157).

17. We saw the house and park which equalled my expectation. The house is one square mass. The offices are below. The rooms of elegance on the first floor with two stories of bed Chambers very well disposed above it. The Bedchambers have low windows which abates the dignity of the house.

The park has an artificial ruin, and wants water. There is however one temporary cascade. From the farthest hill there is a very wide prospect.

18. I went to Church. The Church is externally very mean, and is therefore diligently hidden by a plantation. There are in it several modern monuments of the Littletons.

The[re] dined with us Lord Dudley and Sir   Littleton of Staffordshire and His Lady, they were all persons of agreeable conversation.

I found time to reflect on my Birthday, and offered a prayer which I hope, was heard.

SEPT. 19. We made haste away from a place where all were offended. In the way we visited the Leasires. It was rain, yet

---

The next day the party visited Hagley Park, seat of Lord Lyttelton, the artificial ruin and cascades of which were more admired by Walpole: "There is a ruined castle, built by Miller, that would get him his freedom even of Strawberry: it has the true rust of the Barons' Wars. Then there is a scene of a small lake, with cascades falling down such a Parnassus! . . . and there is such a fairy dale, with more cascades gushing out of rocks!" (cited in *Life*, v.456).

The following day, Sunday, the party as usual went to church. Mrs. Thrale was more enthusiastic about the building than Johnson, who, remembering the night before, was in a mood to be critical of anything connected with his host. Fortunately, the second Viscount Dudley and Sir Edward and Lady Lyttelton came to dine and provided amusement for his birthday.

we visited all the waterfalls; there are in one place fourteen
falls in a short line. It is the next place to Ilam Garden. Poor
Shenstone never tasted his pension. It is not very well proved
that any pension was obtained for him. I am afraid that he
died of misery.

We came to Birmingham and I sent for Hector, whom I
found well.

On 19 September the party left Hagley, without regret, for
Birmingham. On the way they stopped at the Leasowes, near
Halesowen, the little estate developed by Shenstone, who had
died in 1763, described later by Johnson in his *Shenstone*: "He
began . . . to point his prospects, to diversify his surface, to entangle his walks, and to wind his waters; which he did with such
judgement and such fancy, as made his little domain the envy of
the great, and the admiration of the skilful; a place to be visited
by travellers, and copied by designers." Mrs. Thrale called the
place "this sweet seclusion," and would not subordinate it even
to Ilam: "The cascades . . . are so lovely, so unartificial to appearance, and so frequent that one must be delighted, and confess
that if one had to chuse among all the places one has seen the
Leasowes should be the choice to inhabit oneself, while Keddle-
stone or Hagley should be reserved for the gardener to show on
a Sunday to travelling fools and starers" (pp. 212, 213).

As to Shenstone's death, Johnson enlarges in his biography:
"He spent his estate in adorning it, and his death was probably
hastened by his anxieties. . . . It is said, that if he had lived a little
longer, he would have been assisted by a pension: such bounty
could not have been ever more properly bestowed; but that it
was ever asked is not certain; it is too certain that it never was
enjoyed." In a note on this passage Shenstone's friend Graves
pointed out that Johnson has perhaps exaggerated Shenstone's
distress, since he was able to leave some legacies and two small
annuities.

Immediately upon the arrival of the party in Birmingham, they

2 0. We breakfasted with Hector and visited the Manufacture
Papier machè. The paper which the[y] use is smooth whited
brown; the varnish is polished with rotten stone. Hector gave
me a tea board. We then went to Boltons, who with great
civility led [u]s⁴ through his shops. I could not [d]istinctly⁴
see his enginery.

Twelve dozen of Buttons for three [s]hillings.⁴ Spoons
struck at once.

2 1. Hector came to us again. We came easily to Woodstock.

4. MS torn.

_____

saw Johnson's boyhood friend Edmund Hector. Mrs. Thrale hoped
to get some anecdotes from him, but she was sick again.

On the next morning, however, she was well enough to go with
the party to Henry Clay's factory, where they saw his new process
of japanning, pressing sheets of paper together instead of using
paper pulp. The tea tray which Hector gave Johnson was probably
made this way. Then to Matthew Boulton's factory, two miles
north of town. Boulton is principally known for his partnership
with Watt in manufacturing the steam engine, but he also made
Sheffield plate, stamped out metal buttons in dies (and probably
the spoons Johnson saw), and a few years later produced coining
machinery.

On 2 1 September the party left early for the fifty-mile ride to
Woodstock on the way to Oxford. The road was good and they
arrived early enough to make plans to visit Blenheim in the morning. Johnson had never seen the palace and he had told Boswell
in the Hebrides that he would not go "just as a common spectator,"
but only if properly invited, that he might not give anyone on
the staff the power to say, "Johnson was here; I knew him, but
I took no notice of him" (*Life*, v.303). But though not invited,
Thrale clearly sent their names in ahead, since Mrs. Thrale writes,
"I hear the Duke and Duchess were very attentive and polite, and
said they would have asked us to dinner but that they were engaged abroad" (Broadley, p. 215).

22. We saw Blenheim and Woodstock park. The park contains 2500 Acres about four square miles. It has red deer.

Mr Bryant shewed me the Library with great civility.

Durandi Rationale. 1459.

Lascaris Grammar of the first edition, well printed, but much less than latter Editions. The first Batrachomyomachia.

The Duke sent Mr Thrale Partridges and fruit. At night we came to Oxford.

Next day they saw Blenheim as planned. Jacob Bryant, secretary to the fourth Duke of Marlborough, saw Johnson at least once again, when he dined with him in 1777 (*Letters* 505.3). William Gifford reported an exchange with Bryant many years later. Gifford had criticized Johnson's knowledge of Greek, and Bryant did not at once agree with him: " 'But, Sir,' said I, willing to overcome his scruples, 'Dr. Johnson himself . . . admitted that he was not a good Greek scholar.' 'Sir,' he replied, with a serious and impressive air, 'it is not easy for us to say what such a man as Johnson would call a good Greek scholar' " (cited in *Life*, v.458).

Another copy of the first edition of Durand's *Rationale* Johnson was to see next year in Paris. The copy of Lascaris's Greek grammar which Johnson saw was sold at the Sunderland sale, and later was bought by the Grecian-Johnsonian J. Gennadius, of the Johnson Society of London. The *Battle of the Frogs and Mice*, the first portion of the Homeric poems to be printed, is no longer attributed to Homer. It was printed by Laonicus Cretensis at Venice in 1486.

By nightfall the party arrived in Oxford for a four-day stay.

On 23 September, while Mrs. Thrale and Queeney were left to their own devices, Johnson took Thrale to see John Coulson. He was a senior Fellow of University College and in habit and appearance somewhat resembled Johnson, says Duppa; he "was considered in his time as an Oxford *character*" (Croker, III.159). When Johnson stayed with him the next year, Coulson was briefly insulted because he thought Johnson ridiculed him.

23. We visited Mr Colson. The Ladies wandred about the University.

24. Kαθ. We dine with Mr Colson. Van Sittaert told me his distemper.

Afterwards we were at Burke's, where we heard of the dissolution of the parliament. We went home.

———————

The next day the party spent in more sight-seeing at Oxford, including a visit to the Bodleian, and Coulson took them to dine at his College. It is remarkable that Mrs. Thrale was included, for such is not the twentieth-century custom. She described the dinner: "We dined in the Hall at University College, where I sat in the seat of honour as Locum Tenens forsooth; and saw the ceremonies of the Grace Cup and Butler's Book. Mr. Coulson entertained us with liberality and with kindness. . . . We drank tea in the Common Room, had a World of talk, and passed the evening with cheerfulness and comfort. I like Mr. Coulson much and pressed him to come to Streatham with a very honest importunity" (Broadley, p. 216).

On 25 September the party saw more colleges, halls, libraries, the picture gallery and museum. They dined with Dr. Robert Vansittart, Regius Professor of Civil Law, and for many years a friend of Johnson. He seems to have suffered from melancholia. Mrs. Thrale wrote of Vansittart that his "politeness and desire to oblige would be still more valuable than they are did one not easily observe that all is a mere effort to get rid of himself, not to oblige his friends" (p. 216).

The next day was their last full day in Oxford and the Thrales returned Coulson's hospitality with a dinner at their inn. Mrs. Thrale said: "The afternoon gave time for conversation and scope for argument in which poor Mr. Coulson was defeated and fretful" (p. 217).

On 27 September the party went on to Benson, about halfway to Henley, to see the Thrales' Crowmarsh farm, but the weather was so bad that a tour of inspection was not possible.

NOV. 27. ADVENT SUNDAY. I considered that this day, being
the beginning of the ecclesiastical year, was a proper time for
a new course of life. I began to read the Greek Testament
regularly at 160 verses every Sunday. This day I began the
Acts.

In this week I read Virgil's Pastorals. I learned to repeat
the Pollio and Gallus. I read carelessly the first Georgick.

The next morning, however, they drove over and were pleased
with the conditions they found. That night they came to Edmund
Burke's estate at Beaconsfield, where they "were received with
open arms."

The following day Burke was not able to be at home, and Mrs.
Thrale was not happy with the behaviour of the company provided. She was also displeased that Burke "came home at night
very much flustered with liquor."

On 30 September unexpected word came that Parliament was
dissolved; the tour was ended; the party immediately returned to
London.

Johnson quickly wrote a brief election address for Thrale, and
then helped his friend Dr. Thomas Talbot write an *Address* urging the establishment of an infirmary at Hereford, which was duly
accomplished (see *Huntington Library Quarterly*, III, 1940, 259).
He helped Thrale still further with the third political pamphlet,
The Patriot, also defending the conduct of the government in
America. And by the end of November he had corrected the last
proofs of his *Journey to the Western Islands*, the manuscript of
which he had almost completed before the Welsh tour. It had
been a busy year.

The entries for 27 November and for 2 January 1775 were
printed by Boswell from diaries now lost (*Life*, II.288, 289).

Johnson's memorizing Virgil's *Eclogues* VIII and X was no unusual feat for him, since both are short, 109 and 77 lines respectively.

1775

JANUARY 2. Wrote Charlotte's Proposals.

APR. 13 MAUNDY THURSDAY. Of the use of time or of my
commendation of myself I thought no more, but lost life in
restless nights and broken days, till this week awakened my
attention.

This year has passed with very little improvement, perhaps
with diminution of knowledge. Much time I have not left.
Infirmities oppress me. But much remains to be done. I hope
to rise at eight or sooner in the morning.

APR. 14 GOOD FRIDAY. Boswel came in, before I was up.
We breakfasted. I only drank tea without milk or bread. We
went to Church, saw Dr Wetherel in the pew, and by his desire
took him home with us. He did not go very soon, and Boswel

The new year began busily with composing *Proposals for Publishing the Works of Mrs. Charlotte Lennox*, a Johnsonian piece
which appeared in March. Boswell's copy, marked for quotation
in the *Life*, is at Yale. In January the *Journey to the Western
Islands* was published, and, by his violent denunciation of the
Ossianic poems of Macpherson, Johnson was plunged into im-
mediate controversy. In March he published an even more con-
troversial book, his last political pamphlet, *Taxation no Tyranny*,
and on 1 April Oxford followed Dublin, at a distance of ten years,
and awarded him an LL.D. Lord North's letter as chancellor of
the university does not mention Johnson's services to the government in recommending him for the degree, and it is possible that
they did not occur to him.

Johnson's meditation on 13 April, the day before Good Friday,
gives no indication of all this activity.

On Good Friday at church, Boswell and Johnson met Nathan
Wetherell, D.D., Master of University College, Oxford, and Dean
of Hereford, whom they visited in Oxford in the following year.

staid. Dilly and Miller called.[5] Boswel and I went to Church,
but came very late. We then took tea, by Boswels desire, and
I eat one bun, I think, that I might not seem to fast osten-
tatiously. Boswel sat with me till night; we had some serious
talk. When he went I gave Francis some directions for preparation to communicate. Thus has passed hitherto this aw⸗f⸗l
day.

$$10°\ 30'\ \text{p.m.}$$

When I look back upon resoluti[ons] of improvement and
amendments, which have year after year been made and
broken, either by negligence, forgetfulness, vicious idleness,
casual interruption, or morbid infirmity, when I find that so
much of my life has stolen unprofitably away, and that I can
descry by retrospection[6] scarcely a few single days properly
and vigorously employed, why do I yet try to resolve again?
I try because Reformation is necessary and despair is criminal.
I try in humble hope of the help of God.

As my life has from my earliest years been wasted in a morning bed my purpose is from Easter day to rise early, not later
than eight. $$11°\ 15'\ \text{p.m. D.j.}$$

AP. 15. EASTER EVE. I rose more early than is common after
a night disturbed by flatulencies though I had taken so
little. I prayed but my mind was unsettled, and I did not fix
upon the book. After the bread and tea I trifled, and about
three ordered coffee and bunns for my dinner. I find more

5. Several words deleted and illegible; then: ⟨Dilly and Miller called.⟩ 6.
⟨only a⟩

In the afternoon Edward Dilly, the publisher, called, bringing
with him John Miller, "a dilletanti man" with whom Johnson
had dined at Dilly's in the previous week (Life, II.338, 518).

Following the afternoon service, Boswell returned with Johnson. Part of their serious talk is given in the Life, II.357–59. When
Boswell went, Johnson gave Frank some religious instruction, and

faintness and uneasiness in fasting than I did formerly, perhaps the purges at the beginning of the week produced this.[7]
While coffee was preparing, Collier came in, a man whom
I had not seen for more than twenty years, but whom I consulted about Macky's books. We talked of old friends and past
occurrences, and eat and drank together.

I then read a little in the Testament, and tried Fiddes's B.
of Divinity, but did not settle.

I then went to Evening prayer, and was tolerably[8] composed. At my return I sat awhile, then retired, but found
reading uneasy.   1 1 . p.m.

These two days in which I fasted, I have not been sleepy,
though I rested ill.

                                                            1 2 ° 3 ′.

EASTER DAY. APR. 1 6. Almighty God, heavenly Father,
whose mercy is over all thy works, look with pity on my mis-

7. ⟨, perhaps the purges at the beginning of the week produced this.⟩   8. ⟨easy⟩

---

finally, at 10:30 was able to return to his own seasonal meditations.
At 11:15 he concluded with his usual resolution to rise early,
God aiding.

Next day "Collier" called. This is probably Joseph Collyer, a
translator of Klopstock's *Messiah* and other German works, who
died on 20 February 1776. "Macky" may be Spring Macky, another
hack writer, who translated Gueulette's *Chinese Tales*, 1725, and
other French works. One might guess that he had died and that
his widow had asked Johnson's help in disposing of his books.
The suggestion is strong that all three men had known each other
in the early fifties.

Richard Fiddes's *Body of Divinity*, two volumes folio, 1718–20,
was lot 599 in Johnson's library. The volumes are, respectively,
Theologia Speculativa and *Theologia Practica*.

The prayer for Easter was written on the same night as the pre-

eries and sins. Suffer me to commemorate in thy presence my redemption by thy son Jesus Christ. Enable me so to repent of my mispent time that I may pass the residue of my life in thy fear and to thy glory. Relieve, O Lord, as seemeth best unto thee, the infirmities of my body, and the perturbations of my mind. Fill my thoughts with aweful love of thy Goodness, with just fear of thine Anger, and with humble confidence in thy Mercy. Let me study thy laws, and labour in the duties which thou shalt set before me. Take not from me thy Holy Spirit, but incite in me such good desires as may produce diligent endeavours after thy Glory and my own salvation; and when after hopes and fears, and joys and sorrows thou shalt call me hence, receive me to eternal happiness for the Sake of Jesus Christ our Lord. Amen.

Collier is dead. Apr. 7. 1776

Transcribed from a former book with a slight emendation or two. With that book I parted perhaps unnecessarily by a Catch.

---

ceding comments, just after midnight. A year later, also Easter Day, when Johnson was looking over this prayer and his earlier remarks, he noted that Collyer had died. The following note, that he had parted with the original by a "catch," was written still later. "Catch" in a sense which would fit here is not in Johnson's *Dictionary*; Hill suggests that he may mean "by a sudden impulse, or by some scruple that caught hold of him."

In the summer Johnson made an extended visit to Oxford, Lichfield, and Ashbourne, and wrote a preface for Baretti's *Easy Phraseology*. Then on 15 September he left with the Thrales and Baretti for his only visit to the Continent.

The party landed at Calais on the seventeenth, and in the evening visited a Capuchin convent. Baretti, who was acting as courier, since he was the only one who spoke French well, got them up early in the morning of Johnson's birthday, and they went to the church of Notre Dame, built during the English

SEPT. 18. 1775. O God by whom all things were created
and are sustained, who givest and takest away, in whose hands
are life and death, accept my imperfect thanks for the length
of days which thou hast vouchsafed to grant me, impress upon
my mind such repentance of the time[9] mispent in sinfulness and negligence, that I may obtain forgiveness of all my
offences, and so calm my mind and strengthen my resolutions
that I may live the remaining part of my life in thy fear, and
with thy favour. Take not thy holy Spirit from me, but let
me so love thy laws, and so obey them, that I may finally be
received to eternal happiness through Jesus Christ, our Lord.
Amen.

Composed at Calais in a sleepless night, and[1] used before
the morn at Nôtre Dame. Written at St Omers.

9. ∧the time∧ ⟨a life⟩   1. ⟨uttered⟩

---

occupancy. There Johnson used the prayer he had composed the
night before. After further sight-seeing, they set off for St. Omer
on the Paris road. There Johnson had a chance to write down
his prayer. He was in a generally good humour, writing little coup-
lets at each stop ("St. Omer / Tout est cher"). He had already
observed that as a man at Calais had given the convent a ship-
model because he had grown more fond of it than it is fit to be
of any earthly thing, so Mrs. Thrale ought to give them Queeney,
her eldest daughter (French Journals, p. 71). He even wrote Levet
that he was going to try to speak French.

The party passed through Arras, Amiens, and Neufchâtel, stopping for a night at each, seeing the sights, and commenting on
the landscape and the manners of the people. At Rouen they were
joined by Mrs. Charles Strickland, an old friend of Mrs. Thrale's,
and they stayed a few days. Johnson had a chance to talk in Latin
with an abbé at the library of the Benedictines. On 26 September
they proceeded to Vernon, and on the next day to St. Germain-
en-Laye, worried but not much injured by an accident to the
coach. On 28 September they reached Paris, where they remained

OCT. 10. TU. We saw the *Ecole Militaire*, in which 150 young boys are educated for the army. They have arms of different sizes according to the age; [I] think of wood. The building is very large but nothing fine except the council room. The French have large squares in the windows; the[y] make good iron palisades. Their meals are gross.

We visited the[2] observatory, a large building of a great height. The upper stones of the parapet very large, but not cramped with iron. The flat on the top is very extensive, but on the insulated part, there is no parapet. Though it was broad enough, I did not care to go upon it. Maps were printing in one of the rooms.

We walked to a small convent of the Fathers of the Oratory. In the reading desk of the refectory lay the lives of the Saints.

2. ⟨infirmary⟩

———————————

through October. Johnson's diary for the first part of the trip has been lost, but Mrs. Thrale's gives a lively account of visiting churches and the theatre, engaging a tutor to teach Queeney French, and seeing the Queen. On 3 October Mrs. Strickland introduced them to the Benedictine convent, the prior of which, Father Cowley, came to dinner the next day. On 5 October they dined with Madame du Boccage, author of *Lettres sur l'Angleterre, la Hollande et l'Italie*; one dish was "a Hare not tainted but putrified" (*French Journals*, p. 103). On the sixth they saw the collection of the Duc d'Orléans at his palace, and, till the tenth, engaged in more sight-seeing.

The difference between Johnson's and Mrs. Thrale's entries for 10 October shows, as is stated later, that the party occasionally split into two groups for sight-seeing. Mrs. Thrale shopped and saw St. Roch church and the foundling hospital. Johnson (and Baretti and Thrale?) saw the relatively new Ecole Militaire (*Life*, II.523), commanded by Colonel Drumgould or Dromgold, of an emigrant Irish family. The party saw more of him later.

The "insulated" part of the observatory was the isolated or

OCT. 1 1. WED. We went to see *Hôtel de Chatelet* a house not very large, but very elegant. One of the rooms was gilt to a degree that I never saw before. The upper part for servants and their Masters was pretty.

Thence we went to Mr Monville's a House divided into small apartments furnished with effeminate and minute elegance.—Porphyry.

Thence we went to St Roque's Church which is very large, the lower part of the pillars incrusted with marble. Three Chapels behind the high Altar. The last a mass of low arches. Altars, I believe all round.

We passed through *Place de Vendôme* a³ fine square, about as big as Hanover Square, inhabited by the high Families. Louis XIV, on horseback in the middle.

Monville is the son of a Farmer general. In the house of Chatelet is a⁴ room furnished with Japan, fitted up in Europe.

We dined with Bocage, the Marquis Blanchetti, and his

3. a⟨n⟩   4. ₐaₐ
_____

exposed part; Johnson defines the word as "not contiguous on any side."

On 11 October they visited the house of the Duc du Châtelet, and then, according to Johnson, Monville's, son of a wealthy tax collector. The "we" in this case must mean Johnson and Thrale, since Mrs. Thrale makes it clear that she had not been there before the twelfth. Next day Johnson accompanied Mrs. Thrale as far as Monville's, whose house, says Mrs. Thrale, "seems to be contrived merely for the purposes of disgusting Lewdness, & is executed as I conceive on the model of some of the Roman Emperors' Retirements—the Ornaments are all obscene—and of no Value tha[t] I can conceive unless considered as [perfect] in that Character" (*French Journals*, p. 113).

The visit to St. Roch was perhaps the result of Mrs. Thrale's enthusiasm. She liked the church better than any she had seen on the Continent except Amiens Cathedral.

Lady—the sweetmeats taken by the Marchioness Blanchetti, after observing that they were dear. Mr Le Roy, Count Manucci, the Abbe, the Prior, and Father Wilson, who staid with me, till I took him home in the coach.

Bathiani is gone.

The French have no laws for the maintenance of their poor. Monk not necessarily a Priest. Benedictines rise at four, are at church an hour and half, at Church again half an hour before, half an hour after dinner, and again from half an hour after seven to eight. They may sleep eight hours. Bodily labour wanted in Monasteries. The poor taken to hospitals, and miserably kept. Monks in the convent fifteen, accounted poor.

OCT 12. TH. We went to the Gobelins. Tapestry makes a good picture, imitates flesh exactly. One piece with a gold ground. The Birds not exactly coloured. Thence we went to the Kings

---

In the evening, the Thrales' wedding anniversary, they gave "a grand dinner" to Mme. du Boccage; her niece Countess Blanchetti and her Italian husband, whom they liked; Julien-David Le Roy, architect and traveller, author of *Ruines des plus beaux monuments de la Grèce*; Baretti's Florentine friend Count Manucci, who visited them in England later; Abbé François, an agreeable man who often acted as their guide; Father Cowley, prior of the English Benedictines, who had assigned a cell for Johnson's use; and Father Wilson, another Benedictine, whom Mrs. Thrale called "an old stupid priest who could talk English once" (p. 82).

Bathiani, a young Hungarian nobleman, was returning to Vienna, where his father lived. He and Johnson had been much attracted to each other, and he had invited Johnson to visit him (pp. 107, 108).

Next day Abbé François conducted them through the Gobelin factory. Mrs. Thrale also commented on the colour of the birds: "they make a Pelican . . . Pink & Green, a Carp Purple & Yel-

Cabinet, very neat, not perhaps perfect. Gold ore.[5] Candles of
the candle tree. Seeds. Woods. Thence to Gagni's house, where
I saw rooms nine furnished with a profusion of wea[l]th and
elegance which I never have seen before. Vases—Pictures.
The dragon China, the lustre said to be of crystal and to have
cost 3500 L, the whole furniture said to have cost 125000 L.
Damask hangings covered with pictures. Porphyry. This house
struck me. Then we waited on the Ladies to Monville's. Capt.
Irwin with us. Spain country towns all beggars. At Dijon he
could not find the way to Orleans. Cross roads of France very
bad. Five soldiers—Woman—Soldiers estraped. The Colonel
would not lose five men for the death of one woman. The
magistrate cannot seize a soldier but by the Colonel's permission. Good inn at Nismes. Moors of Barbary fond of
Englishmen. Gibraltar eminently healthy; it has beef from
Barbary. There is a large Garden. Soldiers sometimes fall
from the rock.

5. MS "oar"

---

low—merely to shew the Strength of their Colours" (p. 116).
She also described the King's Museum, with its precious stones,
stuffed birds, and insects. The house of Gagny, Intendant des
Finances, impressed Mrs. Thrale as much as it did Johnson, particularly the pictures of the Dutch school, and she also mentions
the cost of the crystal lustre.

Captain Irwin, whose wife and daughter had also spent the
day with the party, is not elsewhere mentioned. Boswell ingeniously conjectured that "the rest of this paragraph appears to be
a minute of what was told by Captain Irwin." "Estraped" seems
to be Johnson's or Irwin's coinage from "estrapade," strappado;
the soldiers thus were given the military punishment of being
hoisted by the arms with a rope and then dropped. If handed
over to civil authority they would have been hanged. Johnson
had erroneously defined "strappado" as "chastisement by blows,"
which may account for the coinage here, not recognizing the two
words as the same.

OCT. 13.[6] I staid at home all day, only went to find the Prior who was not at home. I read some thing in Canus. *Nec admiror, nec multum laudo.*

OCT. 14. SAT. We went to the house of Mr Argensen, which was[7] almost wainscotted with looking glasses, and covered with gold. The Ladies closet wainscotted with large squares of glass over painted paper. They always place mirrours to reflect their rooms.

Then we went to Juliens the Treasurer of the clergy. 30000 L a year. The house has no very large room, but is set with mirrours and covered with gold. Books of wood here and in[8] another library.

At D Argensens I looked into the Books in the Lady's closet, and in contempt shewed them to Mr T—Prince Titi, Bibl. des Fées and other books. She was offended, and shut up, as we heard afterwards her apartment.

6. ⟨Th.⟩   7. ⟨glazed⟩   8. ∧an∧

On 13 October, while Mrs. Thrale wrote letters and took Queeney for a walk through the Luxembourg gardens, Johnson read in Melchior Canus, a Spanish Dominican, author of *De Locis Theologicis*. Johnson was unimpressed.

"Mr." Argenson was the Marquis de Paulmy d'Argenson, statesman and bibliophile. Mrs. Thrale remarked that his bed was reflected eight times by suitable mirrors. She is more specific than Johnson about the fairy tales, St. Hyacinthe's *Histoire du Prince Titi* and the *Bibliothèque des fées* (probably the *Cabinet des fées*, 8 vols., Amsterdam, 1731 ff.): "They would not let us see the upper apartments because they saw us laughing & handling their Books" (p. 117).

Next St. Julien showed them through his house, and though Johnson thought none of the rooms very large, Mrs. Thrale says that one of them was fifty feet long. Perhaps Johnson thought that not large for a man with an income of 30,000 livres (pounds?),

Then we went to Julien Le Roy the King's Watchmaker, a man of character in his business who shewed a small clock made to find the longitude. A decent man.[9]

Afterwards we saw the palais[1] marchande, and the courts of Justice civil and criminal. Queeney on the Sellette. This building has the old Gothick passages, and a great appearance of antiquity. Three hundred prisoners sometimes in the gaol.

Much disturbed, hope no ill will be. In the afternoon I visited Mr Freron the Journalist. He spoke Latin very scantily, but seemed to understand me. His house not splendid, but of[2]

9. A few deleted words: "minute and small"—Guppy; "His wife was"—Powell.
1. MS "plalais"   2. ∧of∧

though that was not a great sum, with the livre worth slightly less than a shilling. Mrs. Thrale also commented on the shelf of dummy books, which she thought the only unworthy feature of the house.

Then the party visited the famous horologist Pierre Le Roy (not Julien, his father, who was dead), brother of the architect. Mrs. Thrale says that he had "twice received the premium for facilitating the Discovery of the Longitude" (p. 117).

What Johnson calls the Palais Marchand consisted, as Croker says, of stalls along galleries of the Palais de Justice. There is still a Galerie Marchande in the building. The party then went into the building and, for sport, put Queeney on the *sellette*, the stool on which the prisoner sat while questioned by the court. That the building should have a great appearance of antiquity is not surprising, since the four north towers are Gothic. Curiously, neither Johnson nor Mrs. Thrale mentions the Ste. Chapelle, the gem of this group of buildings. The Conciergerie became even more famous during the Revolution.

Elie Fréron, critic and controversialist, had perhaps commended himself to Johnson by his attacks on Voltaire or by his life of Mary Stuart. The book which Johnson was to send to Fréron to translate was probably the *Journey to the Western Islands*, pub-

commodious size. His family Wife, son and daughter, not elevated but decent. I was pleased with my reception. He is to translate my book which I am to send him with notes.

OCT. 15. SUNDAY. At Choisi, a royal palace on the banks of the Seine about 7 m. from Paris; the terrace noble along the river. The rooms numerous and grand but not discriminated from other palaces. The Chapel beautiful but small.[3] China Globes, inlaid table. Labyrinth. Sinking table. Toilet tables.

OCT. 16. M. The Palais royal very grand, large and lofty, a very great collection of pictures. Three of Raphael.[4] Two holy family. One small piece of M. Angelo. One room of Rubens. I thought the pictures of Raphael fine.

The Tuilleries—Statues. Venus, Aen. and Anchises in his

3. ∧The Chapel ... small.∧   4. MS "Rapheal"

---

lished in January. No French translation is known before that which appeared in Geneva in 1785–86 in *Nouveau recueil de voyages au nord de l'Europe et de l'Asie*.

At Choisy Mrs. Thrale also commented on the table inlaid with varicoloured woods, at vast expense of time and money, and on the sinking table, lucidly described by Croker: "A round table, the centre of which descended by machinery to a lower floor; so that supper might be served and removed without the presence of servants" (Croker, III.272 n.).

Johnson's appreciation of the pictures in the Orléans collection at the Palais Royal was a late development. He had commented slightingly on painting in his earlier days (*Life*, I.363, n. 3). The 485 paintings were sold by Philippe Egalité in 1792 to further his revolutionary ambitions, and made their way to London. There were twelve Raphaels, seven probably genuine, including the *Holy Family with Palm* and several of the Virgin and Child. The two by Michelangelo, *Christ at the Mount of Olives* and a *Holy Family*, are not now listed in his works, and neither sounds small; the *Holy Family* might be a copy of that at the Uffizi, 43¼ inches

arms. Nilus, many more. The walks not open to mean persons. Chairs at night hired for two sous apiece. Pont tournant.

Austin Nuns. Grate. Mrs Fermor Abbess. She knew Pope, and thought him disagreeable. Mrs   has many books, has seen life. Their frontlet disagreeable. Their hood. Their life easy. Rise about five, hour and half in Chapel, dine at ten, another hour and half at chapel, half an hour about three, and half an hour more at seven. Four times in Chapel. A large garden. Thirteen pensioners. Teacher complained.

At the Boulevard saw nothing, yet was glad to be there. Rope dancing, and farce. Egg dance.

---

in diameter. It might seem small in comparison to many of the Rubenses, of which there were nineteen, including the *Judgement of Paris*, now in the National Gallery, London (G. F. Waagen, *Treasures of Art in Great Britain*, 1854, I.18–21, II.485–503).

Croker explains that the *pont tournant* was, before the Revolution, a kind of drawbridge between the Tuileries gardens and the Place Louis XV.

Mrs. Thrale had spent the day at the convent of the English Austin nuns, Notre Dame de Sion, and Johnson was not there till he came to fetch her at tea time, when he spent a short time with the nuns' confessor. Hence, most of his information comes from Mrs. Thrale, who talked at length with the prioress, a niece of Pope's Arabella Fermor, and with a Miss Canning, who had a good library, had "seen a great deal of the world," travelled, and read. Here Johnson probably made the remark to the prioress which he later related to Boswell: "Madam, you are here, not for the love of virtue, but the fear of vice" (*Life*, II.435). Still later, in his *Pope*, he said that the prioress "mentioned Pope's work with very little gratitude, rather as an insult than an honour," possibly with cause, for Arabella was immortalized as a vain "ideot."

The "easy life" of the nuns also comes from Mrs. Thrale: "Their Beds are soft, their Linnen fine, their Table plentiful & their House convenient." She mentions in addition their card and back

R. Near Paris whether on weekdays or Sundays the roads empty.

OCT. 17. T. At the palais marchand. I bought a snuffbox. 24 L 2–12–6.

6

Table book 15⁵

Scissars 3p   18

63   We heard the lawyers plead.
R. As many killed at Paris as there are days in the year. Chambre de question. Tournelle at the palais merchande. An old venerable building.

The Palais Bourbon belonging to the Prince of Conde. Only one small wing shown, lofty splendid, gold and glass.

5. A few words deleted.

gammon tables. In the large garden Queeney had run races with the pensioners, the boarding students (*French Journals*, pp. 121–23). In the evening the party went to the Boulevards and "saw a Boy dance among Rows of Eggs with surprizing Agility" (p. 123).

Johnson's comment on the absence of traffic on the roads near Paris had previously been made by Mrs. Thrale (p. 118), though Baretti disputed it. The "R" may stand for "remark." Johnson uses it consistently throughout the French diary where he would usually use "N" for "note."

On 17 October Johnson returned to the Palais de Justice, where he heard the pleadings, saw the torture chamber and the "tournelle"—the section dealing with criminal affairs—and also bought some souvenirs; he later gave the snuffbox to Lucy Porter. He summed up his expenditures in livres and then translated into pounds, shillings, pence. The note on the number of violent deaths in Paris probably comes from Count Manucci's telling the party that as many as seven bodies in a night, and seldom fewer than two, were brought to the morgue (p. 138).

The Palais Bourbon, built by the Prince's grandmother, im-

The battles of the great Conde are painted in one of the rooms. The present prince a Grandsire at thirty nine.

The sight of palaces and other great buildings leaves no very distinct images, unless to those who talk of them and impress them. As I entred my Wife was in my mind. She would have been pleased; having now nobody to please I am little pleased.

R.   In France there is no middle rank.

So many shops open that Sunday is little distinguished at Paris. The palaces of Louvre and Tuilleries granted out in lodgings.

In the palais de Bourbon gilt globes of metal at the fireplace. The French beds commended.

Much of the marble, only paste.

The Colosseum a mere wooden building, at least much of it.

OCT. 18. W. We went to Fontainbleau, which we found a large mean town crowded with people. The forest thick with woods, very extensive. Manucci secured us Lodging. The ap-

---

pressed Mrs. Thrale as the most magnificent in Paris. The Prince's grandson, Duc d'Enghien, born in 1772, was executed by Napoleon. The Prince lived to see his former mansion turned into the House of Parliament in 1815.

Johnson's statement that there was no middle rank in France was disputed at length by Croker, and indeed the Le Roys and Fréron, whom Johnson knew, were middle-class. But what he means is surely that, in comparison with the large and powerful middle class of England, that in France was relatively unimportant. He later told Boswell: "There is no happy middle state as in England" (*Life*, II.402).

The softness of French beds was commented on later by Mr. Thrale, but Prior Cowley reminded him that they were dirtier than the English ones (Guppy, p. 224).

The Colisée, a place of amusement, had been opened in 1771

pearance of the country pleasant. No hills, few streams, only one hedge. I remember no chapels nor crosses on the road. Pavement still, and rows of trees.

R.   Nobody but mean people walk in Paris.

OCT. 19. TH. At court we saw the appartments; the king's Bedchamber and council chamber extremely splendid. Persons of all ranks in the outward rooms through which the family passes, servants and Masters. Brunet with us the second time.

The Introductor came to us—civil to me. Presenting. I had scruples, not necessary. We went and saw the King and Queen at Dinner.[6] We saw the other Ladies at Diner. Madame Elizabeth with the Princess of Guimené. At night we went to a

6. Two lines and a fraction deleted.

———————

in imitation, says Mrs. Thrale, of the Pantheon in London. Neither survived the century.

At Fontainebleau Mrs. Thrale described the lodging as wretched, but they all slept soundly.

Johnson's comment that only mean people walk in Paris is in part borne out by Dr. Moore, who commented in 1779 that the only footways were on the Pont Neuf and the Pont Royal, and the quays between (cited by Hill). Elsewhere, walking was dirty and dangerous.

"Brunet" is unidentified.

The "introductor" came to explain the etiquette to the party. Custom required that only those who had been presented to their own sovereign be presented to another king, and Croker suggests that Johnson's scruples may have come from the fact that he had not formally been presented to George III. But since the party were only to see royalty dine, not to be presented, scruples were unnecessary.

Louis XVI's young sister, Madame Elisabeth, was executed during the Revolution. She was now attended by Mme. Guéméné, Princesse de Rohan.

comedy. I neither saw nor heard; drunken women. Mrs Th. preferred one to the other.

OCT. 20. FR. We saw the Queen mount in the forest. Brown habit, rode aside. One Lady rode aside. The Queens horse light gray—martingale. She galoped. We then went to the apartments, and admired them. Then wandered through the palace. In the passages stalls and shops. Painting in Fresco by a great master worn out. We saw the kings horses and dogs. The Dogs almost all English. Degenerate q.

The horses not much commended. The Stables cool, the Kennel filthy.

At night the Ladies went to the opera. I refused, but should have been welcome.

The king fed himself with his left hand as we.

The comedy which the party saw at night Mrs. Thrale described as a new piece full of old and new jokes, but incomparably performed.

On 20 October the party went to the forest in the morning to see the Queen mount for the hunt. She was accompanied, as Mrs. Thrale says, by the Duchesse de Luynes, both using side saddles. The Queen's horse, which Mrs. Thrale says was not gentle, was restrained with a martingale to keep him from rearing.

Mrs. Thrale comments on the shops in the palace: "In the great Gallery however which is adorn'd by Pictures of Primaticcio, & Sculptures of Cellini, & through which all the Family & their Attendants pass to & from Mass &c., there are Shops erected on each Side for Trinkets, Millinery, Books & all manner of things—particularly Trusses for Deformity . . ." (p. 127).

The worn fresco which Johnson saw was perhaps the series designed by Primaticcio and painted by Abate showing Francis I in episodes from the life of Alexander the Great. It was later restored by Pujol.

Mrs. Thrale thought the English staghounds in the kennels

SATURDAY 21. In the night I got ground. We came home to Paris.—I think we did not see the chapel. Tree broken by the wind.

The French chairs made all of boards painted.

R. Soldiers at the court of Justice. Soldiers not amenable to the magistrates. Dijon. Woman.

Fagot in the palace, everything slovenly, except in chief rooms. Trees in the roads some tall, none old, many very young and small.

Womens saddles seem ill made. Queen's Bridle woven with silver. Tags to[7] strike the horse.

SUNDAY OCT. 22. To Versailles, a mean town. Carriages of business[8] passing. Mean shops against the wall. Our way lay through Sevre, where the China manufacture. Wooden Bridge at Sevre in the way to Versailles. The Palace of great extent.

7. ⟨d⟩   8. ^of business^ ⟨of burdens⟩

---

beautiful, but she was more outspoken than Johnson about the horses; they were ugly, blind, lame, and vicious.

The opera which Johnson did not attend was in the private theatre of the palace. Mrs. Thrale says: "Johnson and Baretti thinking themselves not brilliant men enough to shine at such a Shew remained at the Lodging" (p. 128). The context makes clear that she means brilliance of dress and jewels.

Johnson's "I got ground" means that his health was better.

Johnson's note on Saturday concerning the Dijon woman and the soldiers is largely, if not all, a précis of his entry of 12 October.

Mrs. Thrale had commented on seeing a basket of firewood at the Palais de Bourbon, and had perhaps pointed out another to Johnson at Fontainebleau. She had also remarked disparagingly on the Queen's saddle.

Croker protested against Johnson's description of Versailles as a "mean" town, also applied to Fontainebleau. It may in part be explained by the business traffic and the shops against the

The Front long. I saw it not perfectly. The Menagerie. Cyg-
nets dark, their black feet, on the ground, tame. Halcyons, or[9]
gulls. Stag and Hind—young. Aviary very large, the net wire.
Black Stag of China, small. Rhinoceros. The horn broken,
and pared away which I suppose will grow. The basis I think
four inches cross. The skin folds like loose cloath doubled,
over his body, and cross his hips, a vast animal though young,
as big perhaps as four Oxen. The young Elephant with his
tusks just appearing. The brown Bear put out his paws. All
very tame. The lion. The tigers I did not well view. The
Camel or dromedary with two bunches, called the Highgeen
taller than any horse. Two Camels with one bunch. Among
the birds was a Pellican who being let out went to a fountain,
and swam about to catch fish. His feet were webbed. He
dipped his head, and turned his long bill sidewise. He caught
two or three fish but did not eat them. Trianon is a kind [of]
retreat appendant to Versailles. It has an open portico, the
pavement and, I think, the pillars of marble. There are many
rooms which I do not distinctly remember.

[1]A table of porphyry about five feet long and between two
and three broad given to Louis XIV by the Venetian State.
In the Council room almost all that was not door or Window
was I think looking glass. Little Trianon is a small palace like

9. ∧or∧   1. A word deleted.

---

walls, partly by the low site of the town, and partly by the relative
absence of spectacular buildings other than the palace.

Johnson was much more impressed with the menagerie than
was Mrs. Thrale, who saw nothing new to her. But it seems to be
Johnson's first visit to a real zoo. Boswell said that "Highgeen"
should apply to a camel with a single hump, but Powell notes
that at present "hagin" means simply "camel" in Egypt.

The Grand Trianon was the party's next stop, then the Petit
Trianon, which Mrs. Thrale calls "la petite Vienne," either from

a Gentleman's house. The upper floor paved with brick. Little Vienne. The court is ill paved. The rooms at the top[2] are small, fit to sooth the imagination with privacy. In the front of Versailles are small basons of water on the terrace and other basons I think[3] below them. There are[4] little courts. The great Gallery is wainscotted with mirrors not very large but joined by frames; I suppose the large plates were not yet made. The playhouse was very large.[5] The Chappel I do not remember if we saw. We saw one Chappel but I am not certain whether there or at Trianon. The foreign Office paved with bricks. The dinner half a Louis each, and I think a Louis over. Money given, at Menagerie 3 livres. Elsewhere 6 Livres.

OCT. 2 3. MONDAY. Last night I wrote to Levet.

We went to see the looking glasses wrought. They come from Normandy in cast[6] plates perhaps the third of an inch thick. At Paris they are ground upon a marble table by rub-

2. ⟨were⟩   3. ∧I think∧   4. ⟨many⟩   5. ⟨and⟩   6. ∧cast∧

---

a misunderstanding, or, more likely, from the fact that Louis XVI had given it to Marie Antoinette, his Viennese queen.

Then they saw the theatre, on the north end of the palace, the scene of the entertainment by the Gardes du Corps on 1 October 1789 which precipitated the march on Versailles. In the theatre Mrs. Thrale asked Johnson: "What Play shall we act?—[Foote's] the Englishman in Paris? No indeed, says he,—we will act Harry the fifth" (p. 131).

Next the party entered the chateau proper, where Johnson was impressed with its most famous feature, the Gallery of Mirrors, scene of more than one treaty-signing. Mrs. Thrale makes it clear that the chapel was the one in the chateau, but it is not surprising that Johnson, having seen miles of buildings and rooms during the day, could not remember which chapel it was. They returned to Paris after "finishing" the chateau.

That night Johnson wrote Levet, saying that he had run a

bing one plate on another with grit between them. The
various sands, of which there are said to be five, I could not
learn. The handle by which the upper Glass is moved has
the form of a wheel which may be moved in all directions.
The plates are sent up with their surfaces ground but not
polished and so continue till they are bespoken, lest time
should spoil the surface, as we were told. Those that are to
be polished are laid on a table covered with several thick
cloaths, hard strained that the resistance may be equal,[7] they
are then rubbed with a hand rubber held down hard[8] by a
contrivance which I did not well understand. The powder
which is used last seemed to me to be iron dissolved in aqua
fortis. They called it as Baretti said Mar de l'eau forte, which
he thought was dregs. They mentioned vitriol and saltpetre.
The cannon ball swam in[9] the quicksilver. To silver them,
a leaf of beaten tin is laid, and rubbed with quicksilver to
which it unites. Then more quicksilver is poured upon it
which by its mutual [attraction] rises very high. Then a paper
is laid at the nearest end of the plate, over which the glass
is slided till it lies upon the plate, having driven much of
the quicksilver before it. It is then I think[1] pressed upon
cloaths, and then set sloping to drop the superfluous mercury,
the slope is daily heightened towards a perpendicular.

7. ⟨it⟩ 8. ∧with a hand...hard∧   9. ∧The...in∧: a deleted phrase is illegible.
1. ∧I think∧ pressed ⟨I think⟩

---

race in the rain that day with Baretti, and beat him; his health
was much better, in spite of intensive sight-seeing.

On 23 October the men went to the mirror factory, while Mrs.
Thrale visited the Blue nuns. Johnson as usual was fascinated by
any process of manufacture, and rightly guessed that the final
polishing was with jewellers' rouge. Baretti's guess that "marc"
("mar" is phonetic) of nitric acid was "dregs" was also correct.

In the way I saw the Greve, the Mayor's house and the
Bastile.

We then went to Sansterre, a Brewer. He brews with about
as much malt as Mr T. and sells his beer at the same price
though he pays no duty for malt, and little more than half
as much for beer. Beer is sold retail at 6p a bottle. He brews
4000 barrels a year, there are seventeen brewers in Paris of[2]
whom none is supposed to brew more than he—reckoning
them at 3000 each they make 51000 a year. [3]They make their
malt, for malting is here no trade.

The moat of the Bastile is dry.

OCT. 24. TUESDAY. We visited the King's Library. I saw the
Speculum humanae Salvationis rudely printed with ink sometimes pale, sometimes black part supposed to be with wooden
types, and part with pages cut on boards. The Bible supposed

2. ∧of∧   3. ⟨He⟩ ... malting is ∧here∧ ⟨the[re]⟩

On the way they passed through the Place de Grève, now the
Place de l'Hôtel de Ville, saw the Hôtel de Ville ("the Mayor's
house"), burned in 1871, but rebuilt since in the same style, and
the Bastille.

Next, going east, they visited the Faubourg St. Antoine brewery
of Antoine-Joseph Santerre, immortalized by Carlyle in *The
French Revolution* as the "sonorous" brewer who advised that
the Bastille be fired by a "mixture of phosphorus and oil of tur-
pentine spouted up through forcing pumps." Santerre later commanded the troops at the execution of Louis XVI. Johnson's interest in the brewery was not academic: since 1772 he and Mrs.
Thrale had tried to restrain Thrale's disastrous experimenting
and occasional overproduction. In 1778 Thrale brewed 80,000
barrels, more than all the breweries of Paris (*Thraliana*, p. 333).

Next day, the party visited the Bibliothèque du Roi in the Rue
Richelieu. One edition of the *Speculum Humanae Salvationis*,
Holland?, 1470?, a block book of great typographical importance,

to be older than that of Mentz in 62; it has no date; it is supposed to have been printed with wooden types. I am in doubt;
the print is large and fair in two folios. Another book was
shown me supposed to have been printed with wooden types.
I think Durandi Sanctuarium in 58. This is inferred from the
difference of form sometimes seen in the same letter, which
might be struck with different puncheons. The regular simili-
tude of most letters proves better that they are metal. I saw
nothing but the *Speculum* which I had not seen, I think,
before.

Thence to the Sorbonne. The Library very large not in lat-
tices like the King's. Martene and Durand's, q. collection[4] 14

4. A word deleted.

------

contains twenty leaves of xylographic plates. The other forty-four
leaves are in movable type, but probably not wooden (Duff, *Early
Printed Books*, p. 12; *Life*, II.524). The Gutenberg Bible, which
Johnson next describes, he had known about since 1768, when he
wrote about this copy to Barnard, librarian to George III. One can
imagine his interest in seeing and handling this copy for the
first time, and also his doubt that it was printed in wooden type,
which it was not. The *Durandi Sanctuarium* must be Guil-
laume Durand's *Rationale Divinorum Officiorum*, several editions of which were printed in 1459. *Sanctuarium* was evidently
the title used on the binding; no early edition has a title page.
Johnson had already seen Durand's *Rationale* at Blenheim in
1774, when he gave it the correct title. But on 30 October, when
he saw the same book, he calls it the *Codex Divinorum Officiorum*.

Mrs. Thrale apparently had enough of incunabula at this point
and went shopping, but Johnson proceeded to the Sorbonne, the
great collection of which was broken up in 1795 and distributed
to other libraries. E. Martène and U. Durand's *Thesaurus Novus
Anecdotorum* (Paris, 1717, 5 vols., f°) and their *Veterum Scriptorum et Monumentorum Historicorum, Dogmaticorum, Mora-
lium, Amplissima Collectio* (Paris, 1724–33, 9 vols., f°) together
made the fourteen folios Johnson next mentions. The *Scriptores*

Fol. Scriptores de rebus Gallicis many Folios. Histoire geneal-
ogique of France 9 Fol.   Gallia Christiana, the first Edition
4, the last f. 12 Fol. The Prior and Librarian dined, I waited
on them home. This garden pretty, with covered walks, but
small, yet may hold many students. The Doctors of the Sorbonne are all equal, choose those who succeed to vacancies.
Profit little.

OCT. 25. W. I went with the Prior to St Cloud to see Dr
Hooke. We walked round the palace, and had some talk.
I dined with our whole company at the Monastry. In the

---

de Rebus Gallicis is probably a binder's title for the Recueil des
historiens des Gaules et de la France, published by the Benedictines of St. Maur (Guppy), since it is inconceivable that a work of
many folios should have perished or have remained unknown.
Next was the third edition, enlarged, of Père Anselme's Histoire
généalogique et chronologique de la maison royale de France, des
pairs, etc., (1726–33, 9 vols., f°).

The set of Gallia Christiana, a biographical dictionary of church
dignitaries which Johnson described as the first edition, was not
such, since Claude Robert's work, 1626, was a single folio. The
next edition, 1656, by Louis and Scévole Ste. Marthe, was the one
(4 vols., f°). Of the new edition, twelve folios had appeared (1715–
70) before Johnson's visit.

Prior Cowley and Dr. Luke Joseph Hooke, also a Benedictine
and librarian of the Mazarine, returned to the Thrales' lodgings
in the Rue Jacob nearby for dinner.

On 25 October, while Mrs. Thrale shopped, Johnson went to
St. Cloud with Father Cowley to see Hooke, and walked round
the palace, since burned. Returning to the city, the whole Thrale
party dined with the Benedictines, who persuaded Mrs. Thrale
to let Queeney have her dancing lesson there. Boswell guessed
that Johnson read in the library the works which follow, which
is probably correct, since Mrs. Thrale says that he stayed till bedtime, and all of the works are relatively short. Powell notes that

Library Beroald, Cymon–Titus, from Boccace Oratio Proverbialis. To the Virgin from Petrarch. Falkland to Sandys. Dry-
dens preface to the third vol. of miscellanies.

OCT. 26. TH. We saw the china at Sevre cut, glazed, painted.
Bellevue, a pleasing house not great, fine prospect. Meudon,
an old Palace. Alexander in Porphyry, hollow between eyes
and nose, thin cheeks. Plato and Aristotle. Noble terrace overlooks the town. St Cloud. Gallery not very high nor grand, but
pleasing. In the rooms, Michael Angelo drawn by himself,
Sir Thomas Moore, DesCartes, Bochart, Naudaeus, Mazarine.

---

all but the last two are found in a collection published in 1508
and frequently reprinted: *Orationes, Prelectiones, Praefationes
et Quaedam Mythicae Historiae Philippi Beroaldi.* It was surely
such a collection that Johnson read, for, though all had been
separately published, finding the separately published editions together is unlikely. The first two are translations from the *De-
cameron* (I, 5; VIII, 10); the third is Beroaldo's *Proverbialis
Oratio*; the fourth his translation of Petrarch's canzone, "Vergine
bella." The next seems to be Viscount Falkland's prefatory poem,
"To my Noble Friend, Mr. George Sandys," in Sandys's *Paraphrase
upon the Psalmes of David*, 1636 (Guppy, p. 182). The last is the
dedication, not preface, to the volume of Dryden's *Miscellany
Poems* which appeared in 1693.

Next day the party visited the porcelain factory at Sèvres and
the house Bellevue, built for Mme. de Pompadour in 1748 and
destroyed in the Revolution. Mrs. Thrale thought the site the
finest she had seen in France, overlooking Paris and not far from
the Bois. At Meudon, the "old palace" probably refers to the six-
teenth-century chateau, destroyed in 1803, not the newer castle,
burned later. Johnson's unusually close description of Alexander's
bust is the result of the tradition, reported by Mrs. Thrale, that
Alexander sat for this portrait. In describing the pictures, it is
noteworthy that, except for Michelangelo, Johnson mentions only
the subjects, whereas Mrs. Thrale, with one exception, mentions

Gilded wainscot so common that it is not minded. Gough and Keene. Hooke came to us at the Inn.—A message from Drumgould.

27 OCT.[5] FR. I staid at home. Gough and Keene and Mrs S——s Friend dined with us. This day we began to have a fire, the weather is grown very cold, and I fear, has a bad effect upon my breath, which has grown much[6] more free and easy in this country.

SAT. OCT. 28.[7] I visited the grand Chartreuse built by St Lewis. It is built for forty, but contains only twenty four, and will not maintain more. The Frier that spoke to us had a

5. ⟨26⟩   6. ⟨freer⟩   7. ⟨27⟩

---

only the artists. He was no doubt pleased to see scholars so honoured. Samuel Bochart was a distinguished orientalist, and with the bibliographical work of Gabriel Naudé, Cardinal Mazarin's librarian, Johnson was familiar (*Letters* 206).

Two new acquaintances were Sir Harry Gough, later Baron Calthorpe, and Keene, who may have been the Oxford architect, Henry Keene (Guppy, p. 143). Johnson had probably met Drumgould, commandant of l'Ecole Militaire, when he visited it. He later told Boswell that Drumgould was "a very high man . . . a most complete character" (*Life*, II.401).

On 27 October "Mrs. S——" is Mrs. Strickland. Guppy thought that her friend was Captain Killpatrick, an Irishman living in Paris, who had breakfasted with them the day before. But there is nothing to link him with Mrs. Strickland. That evening Mrs. Thrale felt too ill to go out, so, while the other men went to a play, "Mr. Johnson sat at home by me, & we criticized & talked & were happy in one another—he in huffing me, & I in being huff'd" (*French Journals*, p. 143).

On Saturday, while Mrs. Thrale said goodbye to her friends the English nuns and visited St. Sulpice, Johnson and Baretti visited the Chartreuse, a branch of the Grande Chartreuse at

pretty apartment. Mr Baretti says four rooms, I remember but three. His books seemed to be French. His garden was neat, he gave me grapes. We saw the place de Victoire with the Statues of the King, and the captive nations. We saw the Palace and Gardens of Luxembourg, but the Gallery was shut. We climbed to the top stairs. I dined with Colbrook who had much Company. Foote, Sir George Rodney, Motteux, Udson, Taaf. Called on the Prior and found him in bed.

Hotel a guinea a day. Coach 3 guineas a week. Valet de place 3 L a day. Avant-coureur a guinea a week. Ordinary

---

Grenoble. The Paris house had been installed by Louis IX in a chateau in the Rue d'Enfer, destroyed during the Revolution, and Louis had also begun the adjoining church. The statue of Louis XIV in the Place des Victoires, destroyed in 1792, has been replaced. The men continued to the Luxembourg, and then Johnson dined with "Colbrook," presumably Sir George Colebrooke, the bankrupt speculator who was living in France on an allowance from his creditors. Samuel Foote, the dramatist, later regaled Boswell with what sounds like an account of this dinner:

> He told me [says Boswell], that the French were quite aston-
> ished at his figure and manner, and at his dress, which he
> obstinately continued exactly as in London;—his brown
> clothes, black stockings, and plain shirt. He mentioned, that
> an Irish gentleman said to Johnson, "Sir, you have not seen
> the best French players." Johnson. "Players, Sir! I look on
> them as no better than creatures set upon tables and joint-
> stools to make faces and produce laughter, like dancing dogs."
> —"But, Sir, you will allow that some players are better than
> others?" Johnson. "Yes, Sir, as some dogs dance better than
> others" [Life, II.403].

The Irishman was perhaps "Taaf," who might have been, says Guppy, Denis Taaffe, an ardent nationalist. Rodney was the admiral; Motteux and Udson are unknown.

diner 6 L. a head. Our ordinary seems to be about five guineas
a day. Our extraordinary expences, as diversions, gratuities,
cloaths, I cannot reckon. Our travelling is[8] ten guineas a
day.

White stockens 18 L. Wig. Hat.

SUNDAY. OCT. 29. We saw the boarding school, the Enfans
trouvés. A room with about 86 children in cradles, as sweet
as a parlour. They lose a third, take in to perhaps more than
seven [years old], put them to trades, pin to them the papers
sent with them. Want nurses. Saw their chapel.

Went to St Eustatia, saw an innumerable company of girls
catechised, in many bodies, perhaps 100 to a Catechist. Boys
8. ⟨about⟩

Johnson's estimate of the party's expenses tends to confirm Mrs.
Thrale's statement that they were high. Thrale paid for all except
purely personal items. Smollett described the *valet de place*:
"There is always one ready in waiting on your arrival, who begins
by assisting your own servant to unload your baggage, and in-
terests himself in your own affairs with such artful officiousness,
that you will find it difficult to shake him off" (cited in *Life*,
II.398). "*Avant-coureur*" Croker judged to be a courier who rode
post.

On Sunday Mrs. Thrale went to St. Sulpice again, and Johnson
saw the foundling hospital, no longer standing, in the Faubourg
St. Antoine. Mrs. Thrale had seen it on 10 October, and agreed
with Johnson that it was clean but that the large number of
babies, 5200 admitted so far that year, made any real care impossible. The estimated mortality of one-third appears much
too low; Mrs. Thrale thought that few who were brought in
under eight months old would survive, and Benjamin Franklin
was told that nine-tenths died. Rousseau put his children here
(Guppy, p. 109; *Life*, II.398).

Next Johnson went to St. Eustache, near Les Halles. That evening the party had tea with Mme. du Boccage, and when the

taught at one time, girls at another. The Sermon, the preacher wears a cap, which he takes off at the name—his action uniform not very violent.

OCT. 30. MOND. We saw the library of St Germain. A very noble collection. Codex Divinorum Officiorum, 1459, a letter square like that of the Offices, perhaps the same. The Codex by Fust and Gernserhein. Meursius 12 v. Fol. Amadis in French 3 v. Fol. Catholicon sine colophone—but of 1460. Two other editions one by Latomis, one by Badius. Augustini

---

spout of the teapot became stopped the hostess put it into her mouth and blew it out, to Johnson's disgust (*French Journals*, p. 146; *Life*, II.403).

On Monday, while Mrs. Thrale looked at pictures in the Palais Royal, Johnson looked at books in the great library of St. Germain des Prés, near their hotel.

The first book is Durand's *Rationale Divinorum Officiorum*, which Johnson had seen twice before, a folio printed by Fust and Schoeffer. His guess that the type was perhaps the same as that in Cicero's *De Officiis*, 1465, by the same printers, is borne out by the *Gesamtkatalog*, a remarkable instance of Johnson's knowledge of printing and perhaps even more remarkable, of how well he used his poor eyesight. He does not say that he saw the *Offices* at this time, but he clearly knew this first edition of any Latin classic and the first book to use Greek type. The very copy of Durand that Johnson saw is probably that now in the Bibliothèque Nationale, with the stamp of St. Germain des Prés (*Life*, II.526).

The *Psalmorum Codex*, by the same printers (Gernsheim was Schoeffer's birthplace), was the first printed book with a complete date, 14 August 1457. In Johnson's letter to Barnard he said that "the annals of typography begin" with this book, noting that there were probably earlier undated books.

Next was the only complete edition, 1741–63, of the works of the Dutch classical scholar Meursius, edited by J. Lami.

de Civitate Dei. without[9] name, date, or place but of Fust's square letter as it seems.

I dined with Col. Drumgould had a pleasing afternoon. Some of the books of St Germains stand in presses from the wall like those at Oxford.

OCT. 31. TUES. I lived at the Benedictines, meagre day. Soup meagre, herrings, eels, both with sauce. Fryed fish. Lentils, tasteless in themselves. To the library, where I found Maffeus de[1] Historia Indica; *promontorium flectere, to double the cape.* I parted very tenderly from the Prior and Frier Wilkes.

9. ∧out∧   1. ⟨[Indecipherable word] Indicis⟩

Amadis de Gaula was translated at the desire of Francis I by Herberay des Essarts; the first three volumes, containing Books I–III, appeared 1540–42. In an undated letter (1145) Johnson asked Percy to lend him the book for a second time.

No copy of Balbus's *Catholicon,* Gutenberg?, 1460, is known to lack a colophon, but as Powell points out, "As the colophon occurs, not at the very end of the book, but before the 'tabula rubricarum,' it is possible that Johnson overlooked it" (*Life,* II.526).

The other editions of the *Catholicon* which Johnson saw were that printed by Lathomi, Johannis, and de Villa, 1494, and that by Badius Ascensius, 1510 (Guppy).

The only known incunable edition of Augustine's *De civitate Dei* without "name, date, or place" is that printed by Mentelin of Strasbourg, ca. 1468 (Powell). It used type different from the Durand. The edition of 1473 by Schoeffer does use the same type.

On Tuesday, while Mrs. Thrale looked again at the pictures in the Palais Royal, Johnson spent his last day with the Benedictines. The eve of All Saints' Day, it was a fast day. He should not have been surprised to find "*promontorium flectere,* to double the cape," in J. P. Maffei's *Historiarum Indicarum, Libri xvi* (ed. 1589, p. 4 [Powell]), for the same expression is used by Cicero,

Maitre es Arts 2 y. Bacc. Theol. 3.y. Licentiate 2 y. Doctor Th. 2 y. In all 9 years. For the doctorate three disputations, major, minor, Sorbonica. Several colleges suppressed, and transferred to that which was the Jesuite's College.

NOV. 1. We left Paris. St Denis a large town, the Church not very large, but the middle isle is very lofty and aweful. On the left are chapels built beyond the line of the wall which destroy the symmetry of the sides. The Organ is higher above the pavement than I have ever seen. The gates are of brass; in the middle gates is the History of our Lord. The painted windows are historical, and said to be eminently beautiful. We were at another church belonging to a Convent, of which the portal is a dome, we could not enter further, and it was almost dark.

NOV. 2. THURS. We came this day to Chantilly a seat belonging to the Prince of Conde. This place is eminently beautified by all varieties of waters starting up in fountains, falling in cascades, running in streams and spread in lakes. The water seems to be too near the house. All this water is brought from a source or a river three leagues off by an artificial canal which for[2] one league is carried underground. The House is magnifi-

2. ∧for∧

_____

De divinatione, 2. 45. 94. But then he did not have our reference books.

Johnson's tender parting with Father Cowley and Father Wilkes was not final. Wilkes came to London the next year, and Cowley in 1777.

The next day the party left Paris and spent the night at St. Denis. Johnson's comment that the glass in the Abbey is "said" to be eminently beautiful probably reflects some irritation from Mrs. Thrale's rhapsodies. She described the windows as "mighty beautiful" (*French Journals,* p. 150). The chapel they saw was that of the Carmelite convent.

cent. The cabinet seems well stocked, what I remember was the jaws of a hippopotamus, and a young hippopotamus preserved, which however is so small that I doubt its reality. It seems too hairy for an abortion, and too small for a mature birth. Nothing was in spirit, all was dry. The dog, the Deer, the ant bear with long snout, the toucan long broad beak.[3] The stables were of very great length. The Kennel had no scents. There was a mockery of a village. The menagerie had few animals. Two Fausans or Brasilian weasels, spotted, very wild. There is a forest, and, I think a park. I walked till I was very weary,[4] and next morning felt my feet battered and sore, with pains in the toes.

NOV. 3. FRYDAY. We came to Compiegne, a very large town with a royal palace built round a pentagonal court. The court is raised upon vaults, and has I suppose an entry on one side by a gentle rise. Talk of painting. The church is not very large, but very elegant and splendid. I had at first great difficulty to walk but motion grew continually easier. At night we came to Noyon an Episcopal City. The Cathedral is very

3. ∧the ant bear . . . toucan long   ∧ ∧broad∧ ∧   beak.∧   4. w∧e∧ary

---

At Chantilly Johnson perhaps remembered the filthy kennel at Fontainebleau when he commended the cleanliness of Condé's, particularly since it held three hundred dogs. The "mockery of a village" was on an island: "they think it in the English Style which is much prized among them" (p. 150). The fossas, were, as Boswell notes, from Madagascar, and not the same as Brazilian weasels. It is not clear just what the keeper of the menagerie showed Johnson, since according to modern writers neither animal is spotted, though the plate in Pennant shows the "fossane" so.

On Friday the party saw the palace built by Louis XV, described by Mrs. Thrale as "uninhabited, & not very grand" (p. 166), and Mrs. Thrale was impressed by pictures of Luther and Calvin. "Talk of painting" apparently consisted in Johnson's teasing Mrs.

beautiful, the pillars alternately Gothic, and Corinthian. We
entered a very noble parochial Church. Noyon is walled, and
is said to be three miles round.

NOV. 4. SAT. We rose very early, and came through St Quentin
to Cambray not long after three. We went to an English Nun-
nery, to give a letter to Father Welch the Confessor, who came
to visit us in the evening.

NOV. 5. SUNDAY. We saw the Cathedral. It is very beautiful
with chappels on each side. The Choir splendid. The Balus-
trade in one part brass. The Neff very high and grand. The
altar silver as far as it is seen. The Vestments very splendid.
At the Benedictines Church

Thrale about her use of such terms as "contour," "keeping,"
"grace," and "expression" until Thrale intervened to keep peace
(*Letters* 663, Guppy, p. 228).

In describing the alternating pillars and columns in the Cathedral of Noyon, Johnson is not far off in calling them Gothic and
Corinthian. The "Corinthian" columns have capitals with simple
crockets, and, at a glance, are similar to Corinthian capitals.

The parish church was probably the large, Gothic Eglise de la
Madeleine.

In Cambrai, as Mrs. Thrale says, Johnson delivered a letter
from Father Cowley to Father Welch, the confessor of the English
Benedictine nuns there.

Johnson gives both "nave" and "nef" in his *Dictionary*; apparently they had been used interchangeably for about a century.
But his use here is the last recorded by the *OED*.

The diary breaks off at the Benedictines' church, but what they
saw is supplied by Mrs. Thrale: grisaille paintings by Geeraerts in
imitation of bas-reliefs.

The party proceeded through Douai, Lille, and Dunkirk to
Calais, and landed at Dover on 11 November.

The rest of the year passed without incident.

1 7 7 6

JAN. 1. 1776. Almighty God, merciful Father, who hast permitted[5] me to see the beginning of another year, grant that the time which thou shalt yet afford me may be spent to thy glory and the Salvation of my own soul.[6] Strengthen all good resolutions. Take not from me[7] thy Holy Spirit but have mercy on me, and shed thy Blessing both on my Soul and body for the sake of Jesus Christ our Lord. Amen.

EASTER DAY

1776. APR. 7. The time is again at which, since the death of my poor dear Tetty, on whom God have mercy, I have annually commemorated the mystery of Redemption, and annually purposed to amend my life. My reigning sin, to which perhaps many others are appendent, is waste of time, and general sluggishness, to which I was always inclined and in part of my life have been almost compelled[8] by morbid melancholy and disturbance of mind. Melancholy has had in me its paroxisms and remissions, but I have not improved the intervals, nor sufficiently resisted my natural inclination, or sickly habits. I will resolve henceforth to rise at eight in the

5. ∧permitted∧ ⟨granted⟩   6. Three lines deleted.   7. Take not from ∧me∧
... ∧but have mercy on me,∧   8. ⟨with⟩

Johnson's New Year's prayer for 1776 lacks the review of the past year and the resolutions which often follow. During this month the first volume of Burney's *History of Music* was published, with Johnson's dedication.

In March Johnson visited Oxford, Lichfield, and Ashbourne with Boswell, but cut short his trip to return to console the Thrales for the loss of their last surviving son, Henry, the seventh child of Mrs. Thrale's to die, and the third within a year.

morning, so far as resolution is proper, and will pray that God will strengthen me. I have begun this morning.

Though for the past week I have had an anxious design of communicating to day, I performed no particular act of devotion, till on Friday I went to Church. My design was to pass part of the day in exercises of piety but Mr Boswel interrupted me; of him however I could have rid myself, but poor Thrale, orbus et exspes, came for comfort and sat till seven when we all went to Church.

In the morning I had at Church some radiations of comfort.

I fasted though less rigorously than at other times. I by negligence poured milk into the tea, and in the afternoon drank one dish of coffee with Thrale yet at night after a fit of drowsiness I felt myself very much disordered by emptiness, and called for tea with peevish and impatient eagerness. My distress was very great.

Yesterday I do not recollect that to go to Church came into my thoughts, but I sat in my chamber, preparing for preparation, interrupted I know not how. I was near two hours at dinner.

I go now with hope
    To rise in the morning at eight
    To use my remaining time with diligence.
    To study more accurately the Christian Religion.

Almighty and most merciful Father, who hast preserved me[9]

9. ∧me∧ by thy ∧tender∧ ⟨merciful⟩

Johnson's qualification of his Easter resolution to rise early, "so far as resolution is proper," stems from his unwillingness to bind himself by a vow, as we have seen.

On Good Friday Thrale called, "bereft and hopeless," but he managed to conceal his grief, for Boswell records that he "appeared to bear the loss of his son with a manly composure. There was no affectation about him; and he talked, as usual, upon in-

by thy tender forbearance, once more to commemorate thy
Love in the Redemption of the world, grant that I may so
live the residue of my days, as to obtain thy mercy when thou
shalt call me from the present State.[1] Illuminate my thoughts
with knowledge, and inflame my heart with holy[2] desires.
Grant me to resolve well, and keep my resolutions. Take
not from me thy Holy Spirit, but in life and in death have
mercy on me for Jesus Christs sake. Amen.

acts of forgiveness.

P.M.[3] In the pew I read my prayer and commended my
friends, and those that θ this year. At the Altar I was generally
attentive, some thoughts of vanity came into my mind while
others were communicating, but I found when I considered
them, that they did not tend to irreverence of God. At the
altar I renewed my resolutions. When I received, some tender

1. Two lines deleted.   2. ⟨designs⟩   3. Two lines deleted.

---

different subjects" (*Life*, III.18). Johnson's drinking coffee on
the day of his fast Boswell interpreted as a compliment to Thrale
(*Life*, III.24). But Johnson often broke his fast in such a manner
when guests were present, partly to avoid singularity.

After Johnson's Easter prayer the cryptic "acts of forgiveness"
is paralleled by "an act of contrition; an act of faith," cited by
Hill from Jeremy Taylor's *Holy Living*, as part of the preparation
for receiving communion. On the Sunday before celebrating communion, the clergyman admonishes the congregation "to forgive
others who have offended you, as ye would have forgiveness of
your offences at God's hand: for otherwise the receiving of the holy
Communion doth nothing else but increase your condemnation."
"Act" in this sense is defined as "a thing done as the . . . external
manifestation of any state, and, whence the state may be inferred"
(*OED*). In other words, a short prayer.

Johnson used the symbol θ for "dead" or "died" (see *Miscellanies*, 1.89). "Thoughts of vanity" may be paraphrased as "idle
or worthless thoughts."

images struck me. I was so mollified by the concluding address to our Saviour that I could not utter it. The Communicants were mostly women. At intervals I read collects, and recollected, as I could my prayer. Since my return I have said it.

2. P. M.

MAY 21. Those resolutions I have not practised nor recollected. O God grant me to begin now for Jesus Christ's Sake. Amen.

JULY 25. 1776. O God who hast ordained that whatever is to be desired, should be sought by labour, and who by thy Blessing bringest honest labour to good effect; look with mercy upon my studies and endeavours. Grant me, O Lord, to

---

The concluding address which so "mollified" or affected Johnson is:

> O Lord, the only-begotten Son, Jesus Christ; O Lord God, Lamb of God, Son of the Father, that takest away the sins of the world, have mercy upon us. Thou that takest away the sins of the world, have mercy upon us. Thou that takest away the sins of the world, receive our prayer. Thou that sittest at the right hand of God the Father, have mercy upon us.
>
> For thou only art holy; thou only art the Lord; thou only, O Christ, with the Holy Ghost, art most high in the glory of God the Father.

A week later Johnson went to Bath for a visit with the Thrales, and when he returned in May he realized that he had forgotten his resolutions. During that month also occurred Johnson's first meeting with Wilkes, arranged by Boswell at Dilly's house, where the two moral and political opposites found that they could at least agree on food.

Johnson's prayer of 25 July, when he intended to apply himself to the study of Greek and Italian, is interesting for his footnote, probably written a year later, suggesting that though he had not

design only what is lawful and right, and afford me calmness of mind, and steadiness of purpose, that I may so do thy will in this short[4] life, as to obtain happiness in the world to come, for the sake of Jesus Christ our Lord. Amen. Prevent—Our Father—[5]

When I purposed to apply vigorously to study particularly of the Greek and Italian tongues. Repeated July 3. 77. about 12 at night.[6]

MONEY RECEIVED

Sept. 22	I borrowed of Mr T.	3–3–0
27	. . . .	3–3–0
Oct. 28	. . . .	1–1–0
		7–7–0

EXPENDED

Paid to Mrs Thrale	
Miss Owen. &c	1–15–0
Given away at Tunbr. &c	0– 4–0
at Brighthelmston	
Booksellers and Rooms	1– 3–0
Given away	1–14–0
Sam: Bill	0– 7–4
neglected at the beginning	0– 3–0
Purloined by Mr T.	0– 2–0
	5– 8–4
In my pocket 1–19–0	1–19–0
	7– 7–4

4. ⟨and⟩   5. ⟨Prevent . . . Father⟩   6. ⟨repeated . . . night⟩

pursued the study he had not given up the hope of some kind of study.

The three words crossed out after the prayer refer to the Lord's Prayer, as often, and probably to the collect for the seventeenth

1777

JAN. 1. 1777. 2 P. M. Almighty Lord, merciful Father vouchsafe to accept the thanks which I now presume to offer thee for the prolongation of my life. Grant, O Lord, that as my days are multiplied, my good resolutions[7] may be strengthened, my power of resisting temptations encreased, and my struggles with snares and obstructions invigorated. Relieve the infirmities both of my mind and body. Grant me such strength as my duties may require and such diligence as may[8] improve those opportunities of good that shall be offered me. Deliver me from[9] the intrusion of evil thoughts.[1] Grant me true repentance of my past life, and as I draw nearer and nearer to the grave strengthen my Faith, enliven my Hope, extend my Charity, and purify my desires; and so help me by

7. ₐmay be strengthenedₐ . . . resisting ₐtemptationsₐ 8. ⟨not suffer⟩ opportunities of good ⟨to be⟩ offered me ⟨in vain⟩: ₐimprove ⟨such⟩ thoseₐ opportunities . . . ₐthat shall beₐ 9. A few words deleted. 1. A few words deleted.

Sunday after Trinity: "Lord, we pray thee that thy grace may always prevent and follow us, and make us continually to be given to all good works; through Jesus Christ our Lord."

In the autumn Johnson spent five weeks at Brighton with the Thrales, evidently stopping at Tunbridge Wells on the way. Of Margaret Owen, a distant cousin of Mrs. Thrale, Johnson later said, "She does not gain upon me, Sir; I think her empty-headed" (*Life*, III.48). Samuel Graves, the Thrales' footman, is mentioned later; he apparently paid a bill for Johnson.

Johnson's publications in the rest of the year were only a collected edition of his *Political Tracts* and a brief advertisement for an edition of the *Spectator*.

His New Year's prayer for 1777, which he repeated at night, begins a year of suddenly increased literary activity. In January the edition of Bishop Pearce's *Four Evangelists* appeared, with Johnson's dedication and numerous additions to the life of Pearce. In March he wrote *Proposals* for Shaw's *Galic Language*, in May

thy Holy Spirit that when it shall be thy pleasure to call me hence, I may be received to everlasting happiness for the sake of thy Son Jesus Christ, our Lord. Amen.

Our Father.

Recited 11 22′ p m

MARCH 28. This day is Good Friday. It is likewise the day on which my poor Tetty was taken from me.

My thoughts were disturbed in bed. I remembered that it was my Wife's dying day, and begged pardon for all our sins, and commended her; but resolved to mix little of my own sorrows or cares with the great solemnity. Having taken only tea without milk, I went to church, had time before service to commend my Wife, and wished to join quietly in the service, but I did not hear well, and my mind grew unsettled and perplexed. Having rested ill in the night, I slumbered at the sermon, which, I think, I could not as I sat, perfectly hear.

I returned home but could not settle my mind. At last I read a Chapter. Then went down about six or seven and eat two cross buns, and drank tea. Fasting for some time has been uneasy and I have taken but little.

At night I had some ease. L.D. I had prayed for pardon and peace.

I slept in the afternoon.

29. EASTER EVE. I rose and again prayed with reference to my departed wife. I neither read nor went to Church, yet can

----

a prologue for Kelly's *Word to the Wise*, in June papers for the condemned forger, the Reverend Dr. Dodd.

On Good Friday Johnson records that he had eaten two cross buns, easing his fast a little. He had defined "bunn" as "a kind of sweet bread." The last two paragraphs, written the next day, include his "praise God" for a better night's rest.

On Saturday he engaged with the booksellers to write prefaces

scarcely tell how I have been hindered. I treated with book-sellers on a bargain, but the time was not long.

30. EASTER DAY. 1ma MANE. The day is now come again in which,[2] by a custom which since the death of my wife, I have by the Divine assistance always observed, I am to re-new the great covenant with my Maker and my Judge. I humbly hope to perform it better. I hope for more efficacy of resolution, and more diligence of endeavour. When I sur-vey my past life, I discover nothing but a barren waste of time with some disorders of body, and disturbances of the mind very near to madness; which I hope he that made me, will suffer to extenuate many faults, and excuse many defi-ciences. Yet much remains to be repented and reformed. I hope that I refer more to God than in former times, and con-sider more what submission is due to his dispensations. But I have very little reformed my practical life, and the time in which I can struggle with habits cannot be now expected to be long. Grant O God that I may no longer resolve in vain, or dream away the life which thy indulgence gives me, in vacancy and uselessness.

9na MANE. I went to bed about two, had a disturbed night, though not so distressful as at some other times, having Kαθ[3] yesterday as I have done two other days in last week. I rose

2. ⟨I am⟩   3. ⟨the⟩

---

for the English poets, which developed into his major critical achievement, but the negotiations were brief. This suggests John-son's unwillingness to do business during Passion Week, and it also means that it was no excuse for his doing nothing else than business that day.

The first paragraph of the Easter meditation was written at one in the morning, the rest at nine. Strahan and Hill omitted the notation as to Johnson's purge, no doubt because it is in the

as it seems, about seven, so that I perhaps have not had more than four hours rest.

Almighty and most merciful Father, who seest all our miseries and knowest all our necessities, look down upon me and pity me.[4] Defend me from the violent incursion of evil thoughts, and enable me to form and keep such resolutions as may conduce to the discharge of the duties which thy Providence shall appoint me, and so help me by thy Holy Spirit, that my heart may surely there be fixed where true joys are to be found, and that I may serve Thee[5] with pure affection and a cheerful mind. Have mercy upon me,[6] O God, have mercy upon me; years and infirmities oppress me; terrour and anxiety beset me. Have mercy upon me, my Creatour and my Judge. In all dangers protect me, in all perplexities relieve and free me, and so help me by thy Holy Spirit, that I may now so commemorate the death of thy Son our Saviour Jesus Christ as that when this short and painful life shall have an end, I may for his sake be received to everlasting happiness. Amen.

APR. 6. By one strange hindrance or another, I have been witheld from the continuation of my[7] thoughts to this day, the Sunday following Easter day.

On Easter day I was at Church early, and there prayed over my prayer and commended Tetty, and my other Friends. I

---

4. Several words deleted.   5. ∧Thee∧   6. ∧upon me∧ . . . ∧up∧on me . . . ∧oppress me∧ ⟨press on⟩   7. ⟨medi⟩

---

middle of religious reflection. But it is a pity that they also omitted the following sentence, where Johnson says that he rose at seven: there are few records of his rising so early.

A week later Johnson returned to the events of Easter. At church, feeling better, he had written five resolutions in his prayer book: to order his life, to read the Bible, to study works of theology, to "serve and rejoice," and to resist scruples. When the

was for some time much distressed, but at last obtained, I
hope from the God of peace more quiet than I have enjoyed
for a long time. I had made no resolution, but as my heart
grew lighter, my hopes revived and my courage increased,
and I wrote with my pencil in my common prayer book.

Vita ordinanda.

Biblia legenda.

Theologiae opera danda.

Serviendum et laetandum.

Scrupulis obsistendum.[8]

I then went to the altar having I believe, again read my
prayer.[9] I then went to the table and communicated, praying
for some time afterwards, but the particular matter of my
prayer I do not remember.

I dined by an appointment with Mrs Gardiner, and passed
the afternoon with such calm gladness of Mind as it is very
long since I felt before. I came home and began to read the
Bible. I passed the night in such sweet uninterrupted sleep,
as I have not known since I slept at Fort Augustus.

On Monday I dined with Sheward, on Tuesday with Para-

8. ⟨Scrupulis obsistendum.⟩   9. About half a page deleted.

---

manuscript of this day was edited by Strahan he crossed off the
last so heavily that it cannot be read, probably as usual to play
down Johnson's religious doubts. This line was first printed in
the edition published at Lichfield in 1860. Johnson's copy of the
Book of Common Prayer, Edinburgh, Watson, 1720, with the
full entry in Johnson's hand, passed from Barber to Wright, and
is now at the Birthplace.

Easter afternoon Johnson dined with his old friend Mrs. Ann
Gardiner of Snow Hill, whom Boswell described as "not in the
learned way, but a worthy good woman" (*Life*, 1.242). And after
a quiet visit with this relaxing woman, he came home, read, and
was able to sleep.

dise; the mornings have been devoured by company, and one intrusion has through the whole week succeeded to another.

At the beginning of the year I proposed to myself a scheme of life, and a plan of study, but neither life has been rectified nor study followed. Days and months pass in a dream, and I am afraid that my memory grows less tenacious, and my observation less attentive. If I am decaying it is time to make haste. My nights are restless and tedious, and my days drowsy. The flatulence which torments me, has some times so obstructed my breath, that the act of respiration became not only voluntary but laborious in a decumbent posture. By copious bleeding I was relieved, but not cured.

I have this year omitted church on most Sundays, intending to supply the deficience in the week. So that I owe twelve attendances on worship. I will make no more such superstitious stipulations which entangle the mind with unbid[den] obligations.

My purpose once more, O Thou merciful Creatour, that

————————

"Sheward," with whom he dined on Monday, is probably William Seward (1747–99), later a member of the Essex Head Club. It may be a Mrs. Seward who was a friend of Mrs. Thrale, since Johnson does not always use Miss or Mrs. But it is not clear that he knew Mrs. Seward so early as this.

John Paradise (1743–95), with whom he dined on Tuesday, also became a member of the Essex Head Club. He was married to "a beautiful American," and Johnson dined with him several times.

Johnson's statement that in past weeks or months his breathing had sometimes been so difficult that it required a conscious and laborious effort is to be repeated frequently in his last years.

He had again involved himself in an obligation to go to church on Sunday, with poor results. Hill points out that there had been only fourteen Sundays so far in this year.

governest all our hearts and actions, βιοτῆς οἴηκα κυβερνῶν, let not my purpose be vain. My purpose once more is

1 To rise at eight
   To keep a journal.
2 To read the whole Bible in some language before Easter
3 To gather the arguments for Christianity
4 To worship God more frequently in publick.

AUGUST (TUESDAY) 5. I came from Oxford to Birmingham at eleven at night.

WEDNESDAY, 6. I saw Miss Hervey, Mr Hector, Mr Lloyd both Father and son, dined in the Square with Mr Lloyd, and came to Lichfield, then visited Mrs Aston.

I found Mrs Aston sick, as I expected. Whether she will recover I can not guess. She is old. At Birmingham I was told

---

The Greek phrase Hill translates "Steering the helm of life."

His purpose to gather the arguments for Christianity goes as far back as a conversation with Boswell in 1773, when Boswell urged him to "write expressly in support of Christianity," and Johnson replied, "I hope I shall" (*Life*, v.89).

At the end of July Johnson paid a short visit to Oxford, where he did some work in the Bodleian on the *Lives of the Poets*, leaving on 5 August for Birmingham.

The diary entries from this date to the ninth are found on two pages at the end of the Welsh Diary, to which they are not related. They were first printed, except for the last, in *Life*, III.492.

Miss Hervey, whom Johnson saw at Birmingham, is unidentified. She may be a sister of Johnson's late friends Henry and Thomas Hervey. When Johnson visited Birmingham in 1776 with Boswell, he had seen his childhood friend Edmund Hector, as well as Sampson Lloyd, the Quaker banker, and one of his sons. Of Lloyd's aunt Olivia, Johnson had been "much enamoured" when at Stourbridge (*Life*, 1.92).

that Mrs Roebuck, who was once Miss Camden, was dead, and at Lichfield I found Harry Jackson dead. I hoped sometime to have seen Miss Camden, and reckoned upon the company of Jackson. Miss Turton is dead too. De spe decidi. 7. I visited Mrs Aston. 8. I dined with the Ladies at Stowhil. I have had my mind perturbed, and my nights flatulent. 9. I have taken Physick. On the 8th I met Broadhurst with a Boy bundled in rags. I gave him three shillings. About the 20th I gave him 10s–6p. Faith in some proportion to Fear.

Elizabeth Aston, whom he saw at Lichfield, was an old friend, a year older than Johnson, sister of Molly Aston Brodie and Mrs. Gastrell.

Mrs. Elizabeth Roebuck, who had died in Birmingham, Johnson described as an old friend, in a letter the next day. In 1734 he had used her late father's Castle Inn at Birmingham as an accommodation address (Reade, IX.20–21).

Harry Jackson, who had also died, was another Lichfield schoolfellow. He had been entertained by Johnson and Boswell in Lichfield in 1776; Boswell described him as "a low man, dull and untaught" (*Life*, II.463).

Catherine Turton, also dead, was another friend whom Johnson had regularly seen on his Lichfield visits.

It is no wonder that he describes himself as "fallen from hope." On the eighth Johnson dined with Elizabeth Aston and Mrs. Gastrell, who had houses near each other on Stowe Hill, on the outskirts of Lichfield.

On the same day he met Broadhurst, whom he later described to Mrs. Thrale as his old friend, "—you know him—the play fellow of my infancy" (*Letters* 616). He was probably Walter Broadhurst, a watchmaker. The many references to him in this year

AUGUST 11. 1777.

Mrs Hinkley's jointure	18–0–0
Her own	35–0–0
In Cobbs hands 30 L	53–0–0

ARIOSTO = POPE

Ludovici Areosti humantur ossa
Sub hoc marmore, seu sub hac humo, seu
Sub quicquid voluit benignus haeres,
Sive haerede benignior comes, *sive* seu⁹ᵃ
Opportunius incidens Viator,;
Nam scire haud potuit futura,: sed nec

---

show Johnson's almost continuous assistance. Towards the end of the month Johnson added the note that he had given him 10*s.* 6*d.* about the twentieth.

The next entry is on the following page by itself without evidence of date. It sounds like an echo of some book Johnson was reading, or of a conversation. The connexion of faith and fear is not typically Johnsonian.

On 11 August Johnson returned to the 1765 Diary, in which he had made no entries since 1771. Mrs. Mary Bayley Hinckley (1718–88) was a Lichfield widow whose husband had been dead several years. She was a cousin and friend of Anna Seward. The entry seems to indicate that Johnson is again assisting widows and orphans in their affairs.

Francis Cobb (1724–1807) was a banker and brother-in-law of Johnson's friend Mrs. Cobb of Lichfield. The figures may mean that Mrs. Hinckley's jointure was worth, or had been sold for, £18, that she had £35 in addition, and that, of the total, £30 had been deposited with Cobb.

"Ariosto = Pope" goes back to May 1756, when, writing in the *Universal Visiter* on Pope's epitaphs, Johnson said, "In his last epitaph on himself, in which he attempts to be jocular upon one

Tanti erat vacuum sibi cadaver,
Ut urnam cuperet parare vivens,;
Vivens ista tamen sibi paravit,;
Quae inscribi voluit suo sepulchro
(Olim siquod haberet is sepulchrum)
Ne cum spiritus, exili peracto
Praescripti spatio, misellus artus,
Quos aegre ante reliquerit, reposcet,
Hac, et hac cinerem hunc, et hunc revellens,
Dum noscat proprium, vagus pererret.

---

of the few things that make wise men serious, he confounds the
living man with the dead:

Under this stone, or under this sill,
Or under this turf, &c.

"When a man is once buried, the question, under what he is
buried, is easily decided. He forgot that though he wrote the
epitaph in a state of uncertainty, yet it could not be laid over him
till his grave was made. Such is the folly of wit when it is ill
employed."

In this year Johnson had decided to append this essay to the
Life of Pope, which he was planning. He then realized, if not
earlier, that Ariosto had written a similar epitaph; this he copied
into the diary eight pages further on. It is printed here, instead
of later, for the convenience of the reader. When the *Life of Pope*
was published, he added the following to his discussion of the
epitaph: "The world has but little new; even this wretchedness
seems to have been borrowed from the following tuneless lines:
[The first 11 lines of Latin as above; translated:]
'The bones of Ludovico Ariosto are buried under this marble,
under this turf, or under whatever pleases his bountiful heir, or
more bountiful friend, or wayfarer who may appear at a very
timely moment; he could not know the future, nor had he such an
interest in his empty corpse as to make him prepare an urn in his

9a. So MS: Johnson is hesitating between alternates.

Keys in upper cupboard—Key of cupboard in a book in Thrale's desk.

Hope—Mother—never thought till Lately.

Wit's end Tetty—at Abels.

K. William could not breathe but in a Room many feet high.

She must founder. Easy to sit in one's parlour—

Walmsley—read prayers to the family every night—whether ever in a morning—uncertain. Studied the Scriptures. Blooded—lanced—thought not of death but the day before he died.

I gave Mr Levet at departure a note of ten pounds, a Guinea to Desmoulins.

------

lifetime. Yet in his lifetime he prepared these lines to be inscribed on his tomb, if such a tomb should ever be obtained.']

"Surely Ariosto did not venture to expect that his trifle would ever have had such an illustrious imitator."

The rest of the entries on this page of the diary show considerable perturbation and are hard to interpret. The keys which Johnson hid so carefully, since he was away from home, appear to have been household keys: the first to a drawer in which he kept money (on 3 September 1782 he took two guineas "from the drawer"), and the second to a cupboard where he presumably kept the plate which he listed in April 1771.

"Hope—Mother" may mean that he had only recently considered his mother's expressions of religious hope.

"Abels," if this is the correct reading, is unidentified.

The remark about King William III's breathing (he had asthma) sounds like an echo of reading or conversation, perhaps remembered because of Johnson's own difficult breathing. (This summer Johnson first suspected that he had asthma; see 20 April 1778.)

The rest of the page seems to concern Gilbert Walmesley, Johnson's early friend, who had died at Lichfield in 1751 and would naturally be discussed there.

—The tears each other sheds. Pope.

Fervidus—frigore membra.

ἄπο Μεροής.[9b]

Aug 5—I left Oxford.

Nogarola's judgment of Petrarch, &c Dante, and Boccace.

Ararim Parthus—Germania—

9b. So MS.

The next page is coherent again, recalling that when he left London he had given Levet ten pounds and Mrs. Desmoulins, to whom he allowed half a guinea a week, a guinea. He is trying, rather late, to account for his expenditures.

The quotation from Pope is from *Eloisa to Abelard*, which Johnson in his *Life of Pope* called "one of the most happy productions of human wit." The phrase which follows, "hot—a cold shudder," is a recollection of Aeneas's shivering with fear: "Aeneae solvuntur frigore membra" (*Aeneid*, 1.92). It may be connected with Pope.

The Greek phrase "from Meroë" refers to the ancient Ethiopian capital, mentioned by Herodotus and Strabo. It may have come to Johnson's mind from his reading Norden, below.

Luigi Nogarola (1509–59) was the Veronese author of *Epistola ad Adamum Fumanum*, where he says (translated): "In which vile medley of words, indeed, three men of our country excel, Dante, Petrarch, and Boccaccio, not, however, so absolutely and completely that no one can impute a fault to them. For that more splendid and ornate words are required of Dante; that subject matter and meaning subordinated to the words be sought in vain in Petrarch; that more intelligence is desirable in Boccaccio, is sufficiently clear" (Hamburg, 1709, p. 230). One may guess that Johnson had read or discussed Nogarola in his recent visit to Oxford.

The next line is a recollection of l. 63 of Virgil's *First Eclogue*, which Johnson had read about 27 November 1774: "aut Ararim Parthus bibet aut Germania Tigrim," "Sooner . . . shall the Parthian in exile drink the Arar [that is, Saône River, in France],

Norden found crocodiles in upper Egypt, one he thought
fifty feet long.
Free translation
Clipeus Hesiodi by
The Maid's groat.
I gave at Lichfield

to little Godwin	0–10–6
to Brodhurst	0–12–6
to Girl at door	0– 2–6
to Brodhurst	1–11–6
	2–17–0
Money given to strangers	
to Lucy's taxes	1– 1–0

Poor farmed at 1s 10d a week.

---

and Germany the Tigris, than that look . . . fade from my heart"
(trans. Fairclough).

The next line suggests that Johnson had been reading F. L.
Norden (1708–42), whose *Travels in Egypt and Nubia*, 1757, describes seeing at Sehenhuer several crocodiles, one of which "might
be thirty feet in length. We met also that day twenty other crocodiles, extended on banks of sand; and they were of different sizes,
namely, from fifteen to fifty feet" (II.43).

The next two entries may go together. The Latin means "shield
of Hesiod" and apparently refers to the *Shield of Heracles*, once
attributed to Hesiod, and evidently written in imitation of
Homer's Shield of Achilles in the *Iliad*. Johnson may mean that
the Latin poem is a free translation, and has left a blank for the
author, when he should remember or discover it. We have not
found it.

"The Maid's groat" may be an untraced literary reference. The
coin was not common at this date.

"Little Godwin" is unknown, perhaps the same as Nanny Godwin on 24 October, who received a shilling.

The blank after "money given to strangers" suggests one reason

SEPT.—77. That the stream of life may run forcibly it must be confined in Banks.

SEPT. 11. Watson the painters petition.

13. Scripsi.

14—Bis Templum, at night Boswel. On the 13th I sent Letters to Thrale, Aston, Porter, Davies, Levet, Williams, Watson.

SEPT. —77. I read Galba, Otho, Vitellius, in Suetonius.

---

why Johnson was unable to make his books balance: he gave away what was in his pocket, so long as it lasted.

The farming out of the poor for such small sums as Johnson mentions, though legal, was a frequent scandal in the middle years of the century. It was ameliorated, but not halted, by the Act of 1782.

On 30 August Johnson proceeded to Ashbourne to stay with Dr. Taylor, and wrote Boswell that he would be welcome too. The "stream of life" sounds like a quotation—it resembles several proverbs—but may be only a casual aphorism inspired by the stream at the bottom of Taylor's garden, about which Johnson wrote to Queeney on the fourth.

A Robert Watson entered the Royal Academy school of painting in 1775, and exhibited six works at the Academy in 1778 (W. T. Whitley, *Artists and their Friends*, 1.344). The entry for the thirteenth shows that Johnson wrote what he was asked. It is now lost.

On Sunday Johnson went twice to church and at night Boswell arrived. Of the eight letters that Johnson had sent on Saturday, the contents of only two are known (545, 546), a lively one to Mrs. Thrale and an encouraging one to Miss Aston, who had suffered a stroke. "Porter" is, of course, Lucy.

Johnson had been reading Suetonius's *Lives of the Roman Emperors*; he was again reading it in October 1782.

15 to Thrale—received none.

17. Partem concionis. I begged cloaths from Taylor for Brodhurst.

SEPT. 18. 1777. ASHBOURN. Almighty and most merciful Father, who hast brought me to the beginning of another year, grant me so to remember thy gifts, and so to acknowledge thy goodness, as that every year and every day which thou shalt yet grant me, may be employed in the amendment of my life, and in the diligent discharge of such duties, as thy Providence shall allot me. Grant me by thy Grace[1] to know and do what Thou requirest. Deliver and defend me from needless scruples and oppressive terrours and[2] give me good desires, and remove those impediments which may hinder them from effect. Forgive me my sins, negligences, and ignorances, and when at last thou shalt call me to another life, receive me to everlasting happiness, for the sake of Jesus Christ our Lord. Amen.

18. D. G. This day I gave a Guinea to buy linen for Brodhurst. I composed and said a prayer. My purpose is to rise in the morning by eight.

19. At Keddleston and Derby. Spent at Keddleston 6s; to Drivers 2s, turnpikes 2s.

1. ₐby thy Graceₐ ... to do ⟨my duty.⟩ ₐwhat Thou requirest.ₐ   2. ⟨Deliver ... terrours and⟩

In his letter to Mrs. Thrale on the fifteenth, he complained of her neglect: "Instead of writing to me you are writing the Thraliana" (547). She wrote on the two following days.

On the seventeenth he wrote "part of a sermon," no doubt for Taylor, which may be one of those published after Johnson's death. In return, he begged clothes from Taylor for Broadhurst.

Next day was his birthday, for which he gives thanks. The deleted sentence is restored from Boswell's transcript, evidence again of Strahan's editing.

21. At church.   Prayers before the Litany   24'
    Intermed. Psalm 4'   Litany   10
    Second Psalm   6   Communion   19
    ___   ___
                10   53
    Sermon 30'. The whole one hour, thirty three minutes.
    Afternoon, Prayers 20'.
Concio pro Tayloro.
Mrs Brodie had a paralytick stroke.

SEPT. 25. Pease for dinner.
Let[ter] from Mr Thrale

                    Linen for Brodhurst   1–1–0
                               more   2–4
                             making   2–6
                                             ___
                                             0–3
                                             ___
                                             1–6–1

After the birthday prayer, the diary resumes. Next day Johnson repeated a trip he had made with the Thrales. Taylor lent Johnson and Boswell his chaise to drive to Kedleston to see Lord Scarsdale's house, which Johnson thought better suited to be a town hall (*Life*, III.161). But he saw a copy of his *Dictionary* there, which pleased him. Then they went on to Derby to see the silk mills and the china works, which pleased Boswell (*Letters* 549). Johnson's note of his expenses shows that he tipped Taylor's coachman, as he no doubt did the other servants.

On Sunday Johnson's estimate of the time consumed by the parts of the morning service is a curious example of his love of calculation.

The following entry, "a sermon for Taylor," was printed by Hawkins, p. 392. Under the same date Boswell says that he "found upon [Johnson's] table a part of one which he had newly begun to write," doubtless this one.

"Mrs. Brodie" is probably a slip of the pen for Miss Aston, her sister, who had just had a stroke. Mrs. Brodie is said to have died about 1765.

29TH. 5s–1p for Brodhurst. The four shirts were made for half a crown. The cloath was 1s 2p a yard. I bought 20 yards; about 8 and half remain for the Wife.

30. Visi Kennedy.

OCT.—77.

1. Lavi capitis involucrum sericum, q. visio v.

5. At church. Preces quibus Vita emendatior petitur, de tempore per desidiam perdito praesertim intelexi.
The days grow short and cold.

12. Brachia satis setosa paulum a carpo rasi, ut notum sit quantum temporis pilos restituat.

———————

Johnson's reference to peas on the twenty-fifth implies surprise at their availability in September.

Thrale's letter enclosed a ten-pound note, which Johnson had asked for, since Boswell had spent more than he had expected and had borrowed from Johnson. On this same date he acknowledged receiving the note.

The £1–3–4 for Broadhurst's linen Johnson spent on cloth for shirts, with some left over for Mrs. Broadhurst, as the next entry shows. The half crown for making the shirts was extra and seems to have no relation to the sum of 5s. 1d.

On the thirtieth Johnson saw Kennedy, author of the *Astronomical Chronology* for which Johnson had written a dedication. Kennedy lived near Ashbourne.

Two days later Johnson "washed the silk wrapper for my head," the appearance of which had been noticed.

On 5 October, at church, Johnson "understood the prayers for an amended life, as referring especially to time wasted in sloth."

On the twelfth Johnson shaved his hairy arms enough "to see how much time would restore the hairs," a rather extreme example of his intellectual curiosity.

11. Finished the life of Cowley.

13. Finished the life of Denham.

Milton
Cowley	Sprat
Butler	Roscommon
Waller	Rochester
Dryden	Congreve
Prior	Fenton, Broome
Pope	

2 sermons. 2 more sermons 4 in all.

OCT. 20. Mem. When I come to London to write to Watson, Stockdale, Farmer. To visit Sir J. Hawkins.

Hat   –0–18–0

The day before, he had finished the life of Cowley, Johnson's favourite biography in the *Lives of the Poets* and one of the longest and most important. This is the first mention of a completed life. That *Denham*, though relatively short, was finished two days later, shows that Johnson is working at some speed.

The list which follows is in a very rough chronological order, if those in the right-hand column are inserted in the left. Except for *Cowley*, these may have been those Johnson proposed to work on next.

Taylor also was apparently keeping Johnson busy, with four more sermons.

On 20 October Johnson reminded himself to write to Watson, no doubt about the petition, and to Stockdale and Farmer. None of these letters are known. That to the Reverend Percival Stockdale was probably about Stockdale's life of Waller, from which Johnson quotes. Johnson had written to Richard Farmer, the Shakespearean scholar, for information which might be obtained at Cambridge about poets who had been students there, and he wrote again in 1780, without result (*Letters* 530, 673, 683).

OCT. 23. To Lichfield.

Barber	0-10-6
to Sedgewick	1- 1-0
to Walton	0- 1-0
Postilions	0- 4-0
to 24 to Brodhurst	0- 2-6
	1-19-0
24. Nanny Godwin	0- 1-0
	2- 0-0
25. for Brod.'s trimming	0- 3-0
	2- 3-0
Woman at door . . .	0- 1-0
Mrs Astons man . . .	0- 3-0
Physick	0- 0-6
Frank	0- 5-0
Maids Wine	1- 2-0
Paper and Letters . .	0- 2-6
to Frank before . . .	1- 2-0
	3-19-0

Johnson's note that he returned to Lichfield on the twenty-third is in error, since he wrote to Mrs. Thrale from there on the twenty-second (557).

In the list of Johnson's expenses, "Barber" is probably Johnson's barber Collet (*Boswell Papers*, XIII.210), who, still not named, received a guinea on 24 November, being in debt. Frank Barber can scarcely be intended, since Johnson usually refers to him as Frank or Francis. On 24 August 1782 Johnson records a loan of a guinea to Collet, this time naming him.

Sedgwick, a friend of Johnson's boyhood, is either Henry Sedgwick, baptized at Lichfield on 28 April 1709 and therefore Johnson's age, or Joseph Sedgwick, named in Court Leet Records of Lichfield in 1769. In 1776 Johnson wrote that "Sedgwick when I left him, had a dropsy" (*Letters* 455).

Nov.³ 2. To two Boys   0– 2–0
       3. To three women   0– 3–0
          Mrs A——s servants   0– 2–0
          Mrs Lowe   0– 5–0
       4. Lucy's servants   1– 1–0
       before) Brodh. Oct 31.   1– 1–0
          Hat. Oct.   0–18–0
                                     ――――――
                                     7–11–0
Mr Strahan owes me
    For Scotland   110–0–0
    For Pamplets
    For Edition of Polit.
    For Dictionary.
    For in hand   81–0–0
3. ⟨Sept.⟩
                                 ――――――――――――

Walton is unidentified. A William Walton married Elizabeth Cobb at Lichfield in 1762.

On 24 October Johnson gave a shilling to Nanny Godwin, who may be the same as "little Godwin" in August.

Next day he is still outfitting Broadhurst. Among other expenditures, his outlay of half a crown for paper and postage reminds one that the penny post was not among the blessings of the period, except in London.

The November expenditures which follow were put here by Johnson, out of order, because he is adding them to the sum above. The comparatively large sum of a guinea to Lucy Porter's servants is explained by the fact that Johnson was about to go home. Mrs. Lowe is probably Elizabeth, widow of Reverend Theophilus Lowe (1708–69), Johnson's schoolfellow.

On the next page Johnson transcribed the verses of Ariosto printed under 11 August. Below the poem he entered the sums Strahan owed him.

Johnson seems to have used Strahan as his banker at this time, as the phrase "in hand" suggests, although in 1779 he was using

OCT. 27. 1777. Lucy Porter is this day sixty three.

Mrs Esther Baily, aet. 77.

Taylors Cow's price — 126–0–0, sold to Mr Chaplin.

OCT. 31. To Broadhurst	1– 1–0
	0– 2–0
	0–10–6
	0– 0–6
	1– 1–0
Linen	0– 5–1
allowance	1–11–6
coals	0– 2–6
trimming	0– 3–0
	4–17–1

Thrale. He had been paid £100 so far for the *Journey to the Western Islands*, and did not receive the rest until 1784, when the amount was £150, the difference perhaps being given for the new edition which was to appear in 1785. "Pamplets" are the separate editions of the political pamphlets, and "Polit." the collected edition. No figure is given, because Johnson had left the determination of the amount to the "liberality" of the publishers (*Letters* 622, 713). Nothing certain is known about payments to Johnson for the fourth edition of his *Dictionary*, to which the next entry refers, and it is possible that, as with the pamphlets, he had left the matter to the publishers.

On 27 October, Johnson's statement that Lucy was sixty-three is in error, since she was born in 1715. She was entering her sixty-third year. Johnson had made similar mistakes on his own birthday.

Esther or Hester Bailey of Lichfield, a spinster, Johnson described as his old friend (*Life*, IV.143). She outlived him, and was buried on 2 October 1785.

Taylor bred fine cattle, and Johnson was naturally interested in the very high price paid by Chaplin, another breeder. He wrote

NOV. 6. I returned to London

    7. To Mr De Groot   -0-10-6
       To Mr Macbean   -1- 1-0
   L 10-0-0 From Mr Strahan
   L 3-3-0 borrowed of Mrs Gastrel.

    8. Casting weights . . . . -0- 4-0
      Tea and Sug 0- 4-0
      In Market 0-10-6
      To Miss Hern 8-11-0

Mrs. Thrale: "I really saw with my own eyes Mr. Chaplin of Lincolnshire's letter for Taylor's Cow, accompanied with a draught on Hoare for one hundred and twenty six pounds to pay for her" (557).

On 31 October Johnson totalled the sums he had given Broadhurst since he came to Lichfield. These have all been mentioned except the sixpence. Johnson forgot 3s. which he entered in the other diary on 8 August, on his first meeting Broadhurst after arrival.

After Johnson's return to London more pensioners appear. Isaac de Groot (d. 1779), great-grandson of Hugo Grotius, was "old, poor, and infirm, in a great degree." Johnson, who had known him many years, had applied in July to gain his admission to the Charterhouse, and succeeded, with the plea, "Let it not be said that in any lettered country a nephew of Grotius asked a charity and was refused" (*Life*, III.125).

Macbean, his old amanuensis, was always poor.

The three guineas borrowed of Mrs. Gastrell refers to Lichfield, where Mrs. Gastrell was caring for her sister Mrs. Aston. Either Johnson is noting it here so as not to forget it, or, more probably, he is repaying it, since it follows the ten guineas he has received from Strahan.

A casting weight is one which turns a balance when exactly poised. Those which Johnson bought were no doubt to be used in his weighing leaves a few days after this (see 10 December).

9. L20–0–0 From Mr Strahan
   to Mrs Desmoulins   1– 1–0
   to Miss Carmichael   1– 0–0
   to Frank   2–12–6
   to Brighthelmston f[ere]   3–15–6
                                  8–18–0
Mrs Inge N° 37 Welbeck Street.

NOV 24   Changed ten pound bill
         to Frank .   .   .   0–10–6
            Desmoulins . .   0– 9–0
            Levet   2– 2–0
         to Barber supposed to have been
         out of debt at Michaelmas 1– 1–0
            to Mrs Desmoulins   –0–10–6
                                 ──────
         Tea Sugar &c. forgotten.) 4–13–0

─────────────────

"Miss Hern" is Elizabeth, the lunatic daughter of Johnson's cousin Mrs. Phoebe Herne. Johnson was supporting the girl.

On the ninth Johnson received £20 more from Strahan, but the disbursements do not all belong to the same date, since he left for Brighton about the fifteenth, and returned on the eighteenth. It is characteristic that his disbursements there were "about" £3–15–6. And what is not at all characteristic, his addition is wrong.

Poll Carmichael, who received a pound, was a "stupid slut" living in Johnson's household, and the source of some friction there (Life, III.462).

Mrs. Henrietta Inge (d. 1790), whose address Johnson records, was the widow of Theodore Inge (d. 1753). Johnson no doubt saw or wrote to her about the story of Inge's father printed later in Johnson's Life of Ambrose Philips: " 'Philips,' said he, 'was once at table, when I asked him, How came thy King of Epirus to drive oxen, and to say I'm goaded on by love? After which question he never spoke again.' "

Lent Demosthenes to Mr Macbean.

to Mr Levett	0–13–3
Coach	0– 4–0
Frank (near)	0–12–6
De Groot	0–10–6
Mrs Desmoulins	0–10–6
Pocket	0– 6–6
	2–16–9
The rest unaccounted	4–13–0
	7– 9–9

6–6–0 D[ECEMBE]R 8 from Mr Strahan

To Frank for taxes.	2– 2–0

DEC. 10. 1777. An ounce weight of green laurel leaves, laid to dry weighed 139½ grains having lost about 17 in 24.

Betsey's Apron	–0– 9–0
to the Girls School	0–10–6
to Mrs Desmoulins	0–10–6
Coach	0– 5–6
to Herne	2– 2–0

10–0–0. From Mr Strahan

On 24 November Johnson changed a ten-pound note and in the next few days tried to keep track of it. He remembers five items totalling £4–13–0, but cannot remember what he spent on "tea, sugar, etc." This sum he adds to the six items in the next list, making £7–9–9: he cannot account for the rest.

"Barber," probably Collet, who should have been out of debt by the end of September, got a guinea more.

On 8 December Johnson received six guineas more from Strahan, and two days later made one of his experiments, finding that an ounce of laurel leaves when dried lost seventeen parts in twenty-four by weight. He made a similar test on 15 August 1783.

In the next list, "Betsey's apron" was for Frank's wife, Elizabeth (1756?–1816). The sum seems large.

Given to Mr Rann to whom four guineas were due—for
Thomas Johnson.

DEC. 17. in Pocket   –0– 6–0

    10– 0–0 ⎫
    20– 0–0 ⎪
     6– 6–0 ⎬ from Mr Strahan
    10– 0–0 ⎭
    ――――――
    46– 6–0   52–12–0
     6– 6–0   Thr[ale]   10– 0–0
    ――――――   3– 3–0
    52–12–0   ――――――
                         65–15–0
                          3– 3–0

         To Herne   1–1–0
         Desmoulins   1–1–0
    3–3–0– Strahan Dec 31

――――――――――

The girls' school was the Ladies' Charity School for Training
Girls as Servants, founded in 1702 under the auspices of the
Society for Promoting Christian Knowledge. Mrs. Thrale was one
of the managers, and Miss Williams later left it her small estate.

He gave another two guineas to Phoebe Herne.

The Reverend Joseph Rann, vicar of Holy Trinity, Coventry,
had interceded with Johnson on behalf of Thomas Johnson, his
cousin who had listened patiently to Johnson's recital of his
schoolboy lessons. Thomas, living at Coventry, had been helped
by Johnson since 1772, and in one period of sixteen months received £40. But Johnson felt that Thomas managed his money
badly, and there was some unpleasantness, which was resolved by
Rann. Johnson dined with Rann at Coventry in May 1779, and
saw Thomas, who died a few days later (*Letters* 365, 565.1, 616).
Johnson bequeathed half of his Lichfield property to Thomas's
daughter and grandchild.

A few days later Johnson recapitulates the sums he had received
from Strahan since his return from Lichfield, adds six guineas not

1778

JAN. 1. to Macbean   1–1–0
     Spent at Diner (circ)   1–1–6

1778. GOOD FRIDAY. APR. 17. It has happened this week, as it never happened in Passion Week before, that I have never dined at home, and I have therefore neither practised abstinence nor peculiar devotion.

This Morning before I went to bed I enlarged my prayers, by adding some collects with reference to the day. I rested moderately and rose about nine which is more early than is usual. I think I added something to my morning prayers. Boswel came in to go to church; we had tea, but I did not eat. Talk lost our time, and we came to Church late, at the second lesson. My mind has been for some time feeble, and impressible, and some trouble it gave me in the morning, but I went with some confidence and calmness through the prayers.

In my return from Church I was accosted by Edwards, an old fellow Collegian who had not seen me since —29. He knew me and asked if I remembered one Edwards, I did not

---

identified, ten from Thrale, and three more probably from Mrs. Gastrell (see 7 November).

Then another guinea to Phoebe Herne, and a final receipt of three more guineas from Strahan closes the year.

On New Year's Day 1778 Johnson made his last entry in this diary for five years, noting a guinea for Macbean and the large sum of £1–1–6 for dinner. He may have entertained Macbean and others.

During the next months Johnson continued to work on the *Lives of the Poets*; that of Waller was in proof by Good Friday, when Boswell saw it at Johnson's house.

After church on Good Friday, Boswell and Johnson were "accosted" by Oliver Edwards, whom Johnson did not at first re-

at first recollect the name, but gradually as we walked along recovered it, and told him a conversation that had passed at an alehouse between us. My purpose is to continue our acquaintance. We sat till the time of worship in the afternoon, and then came again late at the Psalms. Not easily, I think, hearing the sermon, or not being attentive, I fell asleep. When we came home we had tea and I eat two buns, being somewhat uneasy with fasting, and not being alone. If I had not been observed I should probably have fasted.

APR. 19. EASTER DAY   AFTER 12 AT NIGHT. O Lord have mercy upon me.

Yesterday (18) I rose late having not slept ill. Having promised a Dedication, I thought it necessary to write, but for some time neither wrote nor read. Langton came in, and talked. After dinner I wrote. At tea Boswel came in and wrote to Macaulay about his son.[4] He staid till near twelve.

4. ⟨and wrote . . . son⟩

---

member, for the excellent reason that their Oxford careers had overlapped only ten weeks. And then Johnson did remember their alehouse conversation about two lines of Latin verse (*Life*, III.304). Immediately after this, Edwards made the remark which has endeared him to posterity: "You are a philosopher, Dr. Johnson. I have tried too in my time to be a philosopher; but, I don't know how, cheerfulness was always breaking in."

On Saturday Johnson wrote a dedication, which was no doubt for Reynolds's *Seven Discourses*, published in May. Then Boswell came in and wrote the Reverend Kenneth Macaulay about a servitorship at Oxford which Johnson, when in Scotland, had promised to get for Macaulay's son. Johnson did as he promised, but the boy did not enter Oxford, apparently because his father thought a servitorship beneath his son, and entered the Marines as a lieutenant in the following February (*Life*, V.122, 505).

I purposed to have gone in the evening to Church but missed the hour.

Edwards observed how many we have outlived. I hope, yet hope, that my future life shall be better than my past.

From the year 1752, the year in which my poor dear Tetty died, upon whose soul may God have had mercy for the Sake of Jesus Christ, I have received the Sacrament every year at Easter. My purpose is to receive it now. O Lord God, for the sake of Jesus Christ, make it effectual to my salvation.

My purposes are

To study Divinity, particularly the Evidences of Christianity.

To read the New Testament over in the year with more use than hitherto of Commentators.

To be diligent in my undertakings

To serve and trust God, and be cheerful.

Almighty and most merciful Father, suffer me once more to commemorate the death of thy Son Jesus Christ, my Saviour and Redeemer, and make the memorial of his death profitable to my salvation, by strengthening my Faith in his merits, and quickening my obedience to his laws. Remove from me, O Lord, all inordinate desires, all corrupt passions & all vain

---

Johnson's remark that Boswell stayed till nearly midnight reflects his irritation earlier in the evening, when he gave Boswell a "horrible shock" by saying, "If your company does not drive a man out of his house, nothing will" (*Life*, III.315).

Edwards's remark that he and Johnson had outlived many of their contemporaries had been made on Friday, and displeased Johnson, who did not like to be reminded of old age. That he recollects it now shows how much it impressed him.

The last of Johnson's resolutions is almost a translation of one of the previous Easter, and is also, as Hill notes, a translation of the motto of Bishop Hacket of Lichfield: "Inservi Deo et laetare"

terrours;[5] and fill me with zeal for thy glory, and with confidence in thy mercy. Make me to love all men, and enable me to use thy gifts, whatever thou shalt bestow, to the benefit of my fellow creatures. So lighten the weight of years, and so mitigate the afflictions of disease that I may continue fit for thy service, and[6] useful in my station. And so let me pass through this life by the guidance of thy Holy Spirit, that at last I may enter into eternal joy, through Jesus Christ our Lord. Amen.

Having gone to bed about two I rose about nine, and, having prayed, went to Church. I came early and used this prayer.[7] After sermon I again used my Prayer,[8] the collect for the day I repeated several times, at least the petitions. I recommended my friends. At the altar I prayed earnestly, and when I came home prayed for pardon and peace, repeated my own prayer and added the petitions of the Collect.

O God have mercy upon me, for the Sake of Jesus Christ. Amen.

At my return home I returned thanks for the[9] opportunity of Communion.

5. About three words deleted; the ampersand is Strahan's.   6. ⟨that I may be⟩
7. More than three lines deleted.   8. ⟨read⟩   9. Word deleted.

———

—"serve God and be cheerful." Hill also remarks that Johnson may have been reminded of this by Edwards's comment on cheerfulness.

On Easter Day at church Johnson repeated "the petitions of the Collect," apparently the last one in the Communion Service: "We beseech thee mercifully to incline thine ears to us who have now made our prayers and supplications unto thee; and grant that those things which we have faithfully asked according to thy will, may effectually be obtained, to the relief of our necessity, and to the setting forth of thy glory; through Jesus Christ our Lord."

I was called down to Mrs Nollikens. I think nothing of her Sister.¹ Boswel came in; then Dinner. After dinner which I believe was late, I read the first Epistle to Thess: Then went to Evening prayers, then came to tea, and afterwards tried Vossius de Baptismo. I was sleepy.

MONDAY APR. 20. After a good night, as I am forced to reckon, I rose seasonably, and prayed using the collect for yesterday.

In reviewing my time from Easter —77, I find a very melancholy and shameful blank; so little has been done that days

1. ⟨I think nothing of her Sister⟩

———————————

Mrs. Nollekens, whom Johnson went downstairs to see, was the wife of the sculptor who had made a bust of Johnson in 1777. She was Mary, the elder daughter of Johnson's old friend Saunders Welch, now in Italy with his younger daughter, Anne. Johnson did not write Welch often, and relied on Mrs. Nollekens for news of him. His curious comment about Anne is heavily scored out. Johnson's only other known derogatory remark about Anne occurs in a letter to Mrs. Thrale: "his Daughter has powers and knowledge, but no art of making them agreeable" (857). That he liked Mary is clear from a statement in Smith's life of Nollekens: "I have heard Mr. Nollekens say that the Doctor, when joked about her, observed, 'Yes, I think Mary would have been mine, if little Joe had not stepped in'" (Oxford ed., p. 81).

After a relatively short visit from Boswell (he did not stay to dinner), Johnson dined, read the First Epistle to the Thessalonians, and in the evening tried one of the dissertations of G. J. Vossius (1577–1649), German classical scholar and theologian, many of whose works were in Johnson's library. The dissertations, in Latin, were in lot 423 in the sale of the library. On 18 November 1782 Johnson was reading him again.

On Monday, recalling the events of the past year, Johnson remarks that his breathing had been so constricted that he had

and months are without any trace. My health has indeed been very much interrupted. My nights have been commonly not only restless but painful and fatiguing. My respiration was once so difficult, that an asthma was suspected. I could not walk but with great difficulty from Stowhill to Greenhill. Some relaxation of my breast has been procured, I think, by opium, which though it never gives me sleep, frees my breast from spasms.

I have written a little of the lives of the poets, I think, with all my usual vigour. I have made sermons perhaps as readily as formerly. My memory is less faithful[2] in retaining names and, I am afraid, in retaining occurrences. Of this vacillation and vagrancy of mind I impute a great part to a fortuitous and unsettled life, and therefore purpose to spend my time with more method.

This year the 28th of March passed away without memorial. Poor Tetty, whatever were our faults and failings, we loved each other. I did not forget thee yesterday.

Couldest thou have lived—

I am now with the help of God to begin a new life.

2. ⟨with⟩

---

scarcely been able to walk between the two small hills on the outskirts of Lichfield, and that an asthma had been suspected. This disease made his last year miserable, and then, as now, he resorted to opium for treatment.

As to his quickness in writing sermons, he had told Boswell in 1773: "I have begun a sermon after dinner, and sent it off by the post that night" (*Life*, v.67). He is now referring to the sermons he had written for Taylor in October.

By July he had finished the *Life of Butler*, in addition to those already mentioned, and that of Dryden was "far advanced" (*Letters* 581). Perhaps because he was busy with these, he did not make his usual trip to Lichfield and Ashbourne. In September he spent a few days with Langton at Warley Camp, in Essex, observing the

1779

JAN 1. 1779. BEFORE ONE IN THE MORNING. Almighty God, merciful Father, who hast granted to me the beginning of another year, grant that I may employ thy gifts to thy glory, and my own salvation. Excite[3] me to amend my life:[4] Give me good resolutions, and enable me to perform them. As I approach the Grave let my Faith be invigorated, my Hope exalted, and my Charity enlarged. Take not from me thy Holy Spirit, but in the course of my life protect me, in the hour of death sustain me, and finally receive me to everlasting happiness for the sake of Jesus Christ. Amen.

GOOD FRIDAY. APR. 2. After a night restless and oppressive, I rose this morning somewhat earlier than is usual, and having taken tea which was very necessary to compose the disorder in my breast, having eaten nothing I went to church with Boswel. We came late, I was able to attend the litany with little perturbation. When we came home I began the first to the Thess. having prayed by the collect for the right use

3. ₳Excite₳ ⟨Enable⟩   4. Several words deleted.

---

militia and enjoying the experience, and later made a short visit to Winchester.

After Johnson's New Year's prayer for 1779 he soon set to work on the *Life of Milton*, and by 1 March was correcting proofs on it (*Letters* 603). At the end of March the first four volumes of the *Lives* were published, containing twenty-two biographies. About the same time Johnson wrote a preface for the Reverend Thomas Maurice's translation of the *Oedipus Tyrannus* (in Maurice's *Poems*) and perhaps helped with the dedication.

On Good Friday, at church with Boswell, Johnson was able "to attend the litany with little perturbation." He means physical distress, to which he has just referred, not mental, since a few lines below he says "I was again attentive."

of the Scriptures. I gave Boswel Les Pensées de Pascal that he might not interrupt me. I did not, I believe, read very diligently, and before I had read far, we went to Church again, I was again attentive. At home I read again, then drank tea with a bun and an half, thinking myself less able to fast, than at former times; and then concluded the Epistle. Being much oppressed with drowsiness, I slept about an hour by the fire.

11. P.M. I am now to review the last year, and find little but dismal vacuity, neither business nor pleasure; much intended and little done. My health is much broken; my nights afford me little rest. I have tried opium, but its help is counter ballanced with great disturbance; it prevents the spasms, but it hinders sleep. O God, have mercy on me.

Last week I published the lives of the poets written I hope[5] in such a manner, as may tend to the promotion of Piety.

In this last year I have made little acquisition, I have scarcely read any thing. I maintain Mrs. Desmoulins[6] and her

5. ∧I hope∧   6. ⟨Desmoulins⟩

At home he read the same epistle that he had the Easter before, and used the collect for the second Sunday of Advent: "Blessed Lord, who hast caused all holy Scriptures to be written for our learning; Grant that we may in such wise hear them, read, mark, learn, and inwardly digest them, that by patience and comfort of thy holy Word, we may embrace, and ever hold fast, the blessed hope of everlasting life, which thou hast given us in our Saviour Jesus Christ."

Johnson's handing Pascal's *Pensées* to Boswell to keep him quiet turned out to be a gift. Boswell had him inscribe it, and kept the book "with reverence" (*Life*, III.380).

Later Friday night, reviewing the past year, Johnson remarks that opium hinders his sleep. This fits Dr. Brocklesby's observation about Johnson, that an opiate was never destructive of his readiness in conversation (Hill, *Letters*, II.437).

daughter, other good of myself I know not where to find, except a little Charity.

But I am now in my seventieth year, what can be done ought not to be delayed.

EASTER EVE. APR. 3. 11. P.M. This is the time of my annual review, and annual resolution. The review is comfortless. Little done. Part of the life of Dryden, and the Life of Milton have been written; but my mind has neither been improved nor enlarged. I have read little, almost nothing, and I am not conscious that I have gained any good, or quitted any evil habit.

Of resolutions I have made so many with so little effect, that I am almost weary, but, by the Help of God, am not yet hope-

---

In stating that he has made little "acquisition" in the last year, Johnson means acquisition of knowledge, as the following phrase shows. The fact that he never acquired much money never bothered him.

The name of Mrs. Desmoulins's daughter, whom Johnson also supported, is not known. She may perhaps be an unidentified "Lucy" or "Jenny" in the diaries. Boswell says that the two women and Poll Carmichael all apparently slept in the room which had earlier been his (*Life*, III.222).

The "little charity" which Johnson gave, it should be remembered, included supporting Levet, Miss Williams, Phoebe Herne, Tom Johnson's family, and Broadhurst, besides those named.

On Easter Eve Johnson's statement that he had done little should be compared with his recent publication of four volumes of the *Lives*; his statement that he had read "almost nothing," is also comparative: almost nothing to what he thought he ought to have read. It is dangerous to assume that there were many books in Johnson's large library with which he was not well acquainted.

On Johnson's "Good resolutions must be made and kept," Hill aptly quotes from *Idler* 27: "I believe most men may review all

less. Good resolutions must be made and kept. I am almost seventy years old, and have no time to lose. The distressful restlessness of my nights, makes it difficult to settle the course of my days. Something however let me do.

EASTER DAY APR. 4. 1779. I rose about half an hour after nine, transcribed the prayer written last night, and by neglecting to count time sat too long at Breakfast, so that I came to Church at the first lesson. I attended the litany pretty well, but in the pew could not hear the communion service, and missed the prayer for the Church Militant. Before I went to the altar I prayed the occasional prayer. At the altar I commended my θ. ϕ. and again prayed the prayer. I then prayed the collects, and again my own prayer by memory. I left out a clause. I then received, I hope, with earnestness, and while others received sat down, but thinking that posture, though usual, improper I rose, and stood. I prayed again in the pew but with what prayer I have forgotten.

When I used the occasional prayer at the altar I added a general purpose

To avoid idleness.

I gave two shillings, to the plate.

Before I went I used, I think, my prayer and endeavoured to calm my mind. After my return I used it again, and the collect for the day. Lord have mercy upon me.

------

the lives that have passed within their observation without remembering one efficacious resolution, or being able to tell a single instance of a course of practice suddenly changed in consequence of a change of opinion, or an establishment of determination." But Johnson had stopped drinking, though in his last four years he did occasionally drink wine, punch, or, as medicine, rum.

At church on Easter Johnson commended his dead friends as usual.

His prayer for Easter Day, a fair copy, is marked "transcribed,"

I have for some nights called Francis to prayers, and last night discoursed with him on the Sacrament.

EASTER DAY. Transc. 1779.

Purposes Apr 4.

1 To rise at eight, or as soon as I can
2 To read the Scriptures
3 To study Religion.

Almighty God, by thy merciful continuance of my life, I come once more to commemorate the sufferings and death of thy Son Jesus Christ, and to implore that mercy which for his sake thou shewest to sinners. Forgive me my sins, O Lord, and enable me to forsake them. Ease, if it shall please thee the doubts[7] of my mind, and relieve the infirmities of my Body. Let me not be disturbed by unnecessary terrours, and let not the weakness of age make me unable to amend my life. O Lord, take not from me thy Holy Spirit, but receive my petitions, succour and comfort me, and let me so pass the remainder of my days, that when thou shalt call me hence I may enter into eternal happiness through Jesus Christ, our Lord. Amen.

AUG. 7, 1779. Partem brachii dextri carpo proximam et cutem pectoris circa mamillam dextram rasi, ut notum fieret quanto temporis pili renovarentur.

7. ∧anxieties∧ ⟨doubts⟩; "anxieties" not Johnson's hand.

---

that is, from the rough draft made the night before. In the third sentence, "anxieties," written above a word heavily scored out, is not in Johnson's hand. One may guess that Johnson wrote "doubts" and that Strahan softened this to a word not at all characteristic of Johnson's situation. See also the prayer for New Year's Day 1780.

On 21 May Johnson set off on his usual trip to Lichfield and Ashbourne, and by the end of June was back in London working on the last six volumes of the *Lives of the Poets*.

On 7 August Johnson made an experiment similar to the one he

SEPTEMBER 18   H.P.M.   12ma. Almighty God, Creator of
all things, in whose hands are Life and death, glory be to
Thee for all thy mercies, and for the prolongation of my
Life, to the common age of Man. Pardon me, O gracious God,
all the offences which in the course of seventy years I have
committed against thy holy Laws, and all negligences of those
Duties which Thou hast required. Look with pity upon me,[8]
take not from me thy Holy Spirit, but enable me to pass[9] the
days which thou shalt yet vouchsafe to grant me, in thy Fear,
and to thy Glory; and accept O Lord, the remains of a mispent
life, that when Thou shalt call me to another state, I may be
received to everlasting happiness for the Sake of Jesus Christ
our Lord. Amen.

EPSOM.

My Purpose is to communicate at least thrice a year.
To study the Scriptures.
To be diligent.
On the 17th Mr Chamier took me away with him from
Streatham. I left the Servants a guinea for my health, and was
content enough to escape into a house where my Birthday not
being known could not be mentioned. I sat up till midnight

8. Several words deleted ⟨enable me⟩   9. ⟨the re⟩

---

had made on 12 October 1778: he shaved part of his right arm
above the wrist and the hair around his right breast to see how long
it would take to grow hair again. Perhaps he had forgotten to keep
track of his October experiment, or thought that in summer the
hair would grow faster. The sentence was printed by Boswell
from a lost diary (*Life*, III.398 n.3).

  Johnson's next birthday prayer was written at midnight on
the night, not the eve, of his birthday, as the hour, 12:00 P.M., and
his later note make clear. He had been staying with the Thrales

was past, and the day of a new year, a very awful day, began. I prayed to God who had (safely brought me to the beginning of another year), but could not perfectly recollect the prayer, and supplied it. Such desertions of memory I have always had. I slept ill.[1]

When I rose on the 18th, I think I prayed again, then walked with my Friend into his grounds. When I came back after some time passed in the library, finding myself oppressed by sleepiness I retired to my chamber, where by lying down, and a short imperfect slumber I was refreshed, and prayed as the night before.

I then dined and trifled in the parlour and library, and was freed from a scruple about Horace. At last I went to Bed, having first composed a prayer.

19. SUNDAY. I went to Church, and attended the service. I found at church[2] a time to use my prayer. O Lord have mercy.

1780

JAN 1. H. 1 A.M. Almighty God my Creator and Preserver by whose mercy my life has been continued to the beginning

1. ⟨I slept ill.⟩   2. ∧at church∧

---

at Streatham, but had left on the seventeenth with Anthony Chamier, a member of the Club and Under Secretary of State, who had a house at Epsom. As usual, he used the collect which he had "accommodated" for his birthday, but forgetting part of it, substituted other words.

In the library Johnson was "freed from a scruple about Horace." This probably means that, not remembering a passage exactly, he looked it up. This is not his usual use of "scruple," but is justified by the first definition in his *Dictionary*: "doubt; difficulty of determination; perplexity; generally about minute things."

of another year, grant me with encrease of days, encrease of
Holiness, that as I live longer, I may be better prepared to
appear before thee, when thou shalt call me[3] from my present
state.

Make me, O Lord, truly thankful for the mercy which
Thou hast vouchsafed to shew me through my whole life;
make me thankful for the health which thou hast restored in
the last year, and let the remains of my strength and life be
employed to thy glory and my own Salvation.

Take not, O Lord thy holy Spirit from me,[4] enable me to
avoid or overcome all that may hinder my advancement in
Godliness, let me be no longer idle, no longer doubtful,[5] but
give me[6] rectitude of thought and constancy of action, and
bring me at last to everlasting happiness for the Sake of Jesus
Christ, our Lord and Saviour. Amen.

SUNDAY. JUNE 18. 1780. In the morning of this day last
year I perceived the remission of those convulsions in my
breast which had distressed me for more than twenty years.

3. ∧me∧   4. Several words deleted.   5. ∧sinful∧ ⟨doubtful⟩; "sinful" not Johnson's hand.   6. ⟨conviction⟩

_____

Johnson's scruples were more often about religion. On 28 August
1783 he used the word as here.

After a few days at Epsom, Johnson returned to London, where
the rest of the year passed much as usual.

The New Year's prayer for 1780, written at 1:00 A.M., appears
to have been altered by Strahan. In the last sentence "sinful"
is not in Johnson's hand and is written above a word heavily
scored out, which may have been "doubtful." The substitution
spoils Johnson's contrast and parallelism: idle—constancy of action; doubtful—rectitude of thought.

For the next nine months Johnson worked at the *Lives* in his
usual way. His note of 18 June that he has now had a full year
of relief from his difficulty of breathing brings him naturally to

I returned thanks at Church for the mercy granted me, which has now continued a year.[7]

THANKSGIVING.

Almighty God, our Creatour and Preserver, from whom proceedeth all good, enable me to receive with humble acknowledgment of[8] thy unbounded benignity, and with due consciousness of my own unworthiness, that recovery and continuance of health which thou hast granted me, and vouchsafe to accept the thanks which I now offer. Glory be to Thee, O Lord, for this and all thy mercies. Grant, I beseech Thee, that the health and life which thou shalt yet allow me, may conduce to my eternal happiness. Take not from me thy Holy Spirit, but so help and bless me, that when Thou shalt call me hence I may obtain pardon and Salvation, for the sake of Jesus Christ, our Lord. Amen.

SEPT. 18. 1780. I am now beginning the seventy second year of my life, with more strength of body and greater vigour of mind than, I think, is common at that age. But though the convulsions in my breast are relieved, my sleep is seldom long. My Nights are wakeful, and therefore I am sometimes sleepy in the day. I have been attentive to my diet, and have diminished the bulk of my body. I have not at all[9] studied; nor written diligently. I have Swift and Pope yet to write, Swift is just begun.

I have forgotten or neglected my resolutions or purposes

7. Several words deleted.   8. ∧acknowledgment of∧ ⟨confidence in⟩   9. ∧at all∧

---

a prayer of thanksgiving. In September he wrote a last election address for Thrale (*Life*, III.440), who lost the election, since his ill health prevented him from canvassing.

Johnson's birthday meditation shows that for once he is paying

[which] I now humbly and timorously renew. Surely I shall not spend my whole life with my own total disapprobation. Perhaps God may grant me now to begin a wiser and a better life.

Almighty God, my Creator and Preserver, who hast permitted me to begin another year, look with mercy upon my wretchedness and frailty. Rectify my thoughts, relieve my perplexities, strengthen my purposes, and reform my doings. Let encrease of years bring encrease of Faith, Hope, and Charity. Grant me diligence in whatever work thy Providence shall appoint me. Take not from me thy Holy Spirit but let me pass the remainder of the days which thou shalt yet allow me in thy fear and to thy Glory; and when it shall be thy good pleasure to call me hence, grant me, O Lord, forgiveness of my sins, and receive me to everlasting happiness, for the Sake of Jesus Christ, our Lord. Amen.   10.40′ P.M.

1781

JAN. 2. I was yesterday hindred by my old disease of mind, and therefore begin to day.

JAN. 1. Having sat in my chamber till the year began I used my accommodation of the morning prayer *to the beginning*

---

some attention to his weight. He had written Lucy Porter in April, "I have abated much of my diet" (*Letters* 656).

It is characteristic of Johnson that he does not say that he has *only* the lives of Swift and Pope to write out of the thirty-four lives making up the last six volumes. These two are lengthy, to be sure, but he had been working on them for some time. His only other literary work recently had been some help to Tom Davies in the *Life of Garrick*, which turned Davies from an unsuccessful bookseller into a successful author.

On New Year's Day 1781 Johnson wrote letters for Mrs. Des-

of this year, and slept remarkably well, though I had supped liberally. In the morning I went to Church. Then I wrote letters for Mrs. Desmoulins, then went to Streatham and had many stops. At night I took wine, and did not sleep well.

JAN 2. I rose according to my resolution, and am now to begin another year. I hope with amendment of life. —I will not despair. Help me, help me, O my God. My hope is

1 To rise at eight, or sooner,
2 To read the Bible through this year in some language
3 To keep a Journal
4 To study Religion
5 To avoid Idleness
6 To¹

Almighty God merciful Father, who hast granted me such continuance of Life, that I now see the beginning of another year, look with mercy upon me; as thou grantest encrease of years, grant encrease of Grace. Let me live to repent what I have done amiss, and by thy help so to regulate my future life, that I may obtain mercy when I appear before thee, through the merits of Jesus Christ. Enable me O Lord² to do my duty with a quiet mind; and take not from me thy Holy Spirit, but protect and bless me, for the sake of Jesus Christ. Amen.

APR. 13. GOOD FRIDAY 1781. I forgot my Prayer and resolutions till two days ago I found this paper.

Sometime in March I finished the lives of the Poets,³ which

1. ⟨6 To⟩ rest of line illegible. 2. A few words before and after "O Lord" deleted. 3. ₄of the Poets₄

---

moulins which are not known, but they were probably similar to that of 30 December, asking that she be made matron of the Charterhouse School. The application was unsuccessful. His having "many stops" after he reached the Thrales, Hill aptly glosses

I wrote in my usual way, dilatorily and hastily, unwilling to work, and working with vigour, and haste.

On Wednesday, 11, was buried my dear Friend Thrale who died, on Wednesday, 4, and with him were buried many of my hopes and pleasures.

APR. 14. On Sunday 1st. His Physician warned him against full meals, on Monday I pressed him to observance of his rules, but without effect, and Tuesday I was absent, but his Wife pressed forbearance upon him, again unsuccessfully. At night I was called to him, and found him senseless in strong convulsions. I staid in the room except that I visited Mrs Thrale twice. About five (I think) on Wednesday morning he expired. I felt almost the last flutter of his pulse, and looked for the last time upon the face that for fifteen years had never been turned upon me but with respect or benignity. Farewel. May God that delighteth in mercy, have had mercy on thee.

I had constantly prayed for him some time before his death.

The decease of him from whose friendship I had obtained many opportunities of amusement, and to whom I turned my thoughts as to⁴ a refuge from misfortunes, has left me heavy. But my business is with myself.

4. ∧to∧   _____

"obstructions or impediments in the mind," in other words, "my old disease of mind." His taking wine at night, most unusual in this period, may have been an attempt to break his depression.

By 5 March the *Lives of the Poets* were finished. In the first week of April Thrale died of a second attack of apoplexy. Johnson's Good Friday meditation naturally speaks of him.

By dropping "Apr. 14" Strahan and Hill have combined two days' meditations into one. The last sentence of this day might easily be misinterpreted: Johnson means that at the Easter season his religious duty is self-examination, not lamentation of Thrale.

There was too little space at the end of the page to begin that examination, and Johnson began another. But on his birthday,

SEPT. 18. My first knowledge of Thrale was in 1765. I enjoyed his favour for almost a fourth part of my life.

EASTER EVE APR. 14 1781. On Good Friday I took in the Afternoon some coffee and buttered cake, and today I had a little bread at breakfast, and potatoes and apples in the afternoon, the tea with a little toast, but I find my self feeble and unsustained, and suspect that I can not bear to fast so long as formerly.

This day I read some of Clark's Sermons.

I hope that since my last Communion I have advanced[5] by pious reflections in my submission to God, and my benevolence to Man, but I have corrected no external habits, nor have kept any of the resolutions made in the beginning of the year, yet I hope still to be reformed, and not to lose my whole life in idle purposes. Many years are already gone, irrevocably past in useless Misery; that what remains may be spent better, grant O God.

By this awful Festival is particularly recommended Newness of Life, and a new Life I will now endeavour to begin by more diligent application to useful employment, and more frequent attendance on publick worship.

I again with hope of help from the God of Mercy, resolve
    To avoid Idleness
    To read the Bible
    To study religion.

Almighty God, merciful Father, by whose Protection I have been preserved, and by whose clemency I have been spared,

5. ∧advanced∧ ⟨encreased⟩

---

when he reviewed his meditations for New Year's and Easter, he returned to this page and made the entry with that date. In other words, one should read continuously "My business is with myself. On Good Friday . . ." in order to keep Johnson's sense.

grant that the life which thou hast so long continued may be no longer wasted in idleness, or corrupted by wickedness. Let my future purposes be good, and let not my good purposes be vain.[6] Free me O Lord[7] from vain terrours, and strengthen me in diligent obedience to thy laws, take not from me thy Holy Spirit, but enable me so to commemorate the death of my Saviour Jesus Christ, that I may be made partaker of his merits, and may finally for his sake obtain everlasting happiness. Amen.

EASTER SUNDAY 1781. I rose after eight, and breakfasted, then went early to church, and before service read the prayer for the Church Militant.[8] I commended my θ friends as I have formerly done. I was one of the last that communicated. When I came home I was hindred by Visitants, but found time to pray before dinner. God, send thy Blessing upon me.

MONDAY APR. 16. Yesterday at dinner were Mrs Hall, Mr Levet, Macbean, Boswel, Allen. Time passed in talk after dinner. At seven I went with Mrs Hall to Church, and came back to tea. At night I had some mental vellications, or revulsions. I prayed in my chamber with Frank, and read the first

6. Several words deleted.   7. ∧O Lord∧   8. Over five lines deleted.

On Easter Day Johnson commended his dead friends at church as usual, and came home, where his "visitants" were Boswell and Dr. William Scott, the lawyer (*Life*, IV.91).

At dinner, besides those mentioned were Miss Williams and Mrs. Desmoulins. It was clearly an occasion, since Johnson brought out for the first time some silver salvers he had bought fourteen years earlier. Mrs. Hall, sister of John Wesley, and Johnson discussed the resurrection of the body, and Boswell decided to go to a meeting of a religious debating society to hear the same subject discussed, instead of to church, in spite of Johnson's disapproval.

Sunday in the Duty of Man, in which I had till then only looked by compulsion or by chance.

I paid the Pew Keepers.[9]

This day I repeated my prayer, and hope to be heard.

I have, I thank God, received the Sacrament every year at Easter since the death of my poor dear Tetty. I once felt some temptation to omit it, but I was preserved from compliance. This was the thirtieth Easter. Sept. 18.

JUNE 22. Almighty God who art the Giver of all good enable me to remember with due thankfulness the comforts and[1] advantages which I have enjoyed by the friendship of Henry Thrale, for whom so far as is lawful I humbly implore thy mercy in his present state. O Lord, since thou hast been pleased to call him[2] from this world, look with mercy on

9. ⟨I paid the Pew Keepers.⟩ 1. ∧advantages∧ ⟨conveniences⟩ . . . ∧enjoyed by∧ ⟨received from⟩ . . . ∧for∧ whom 2. ∧from this world∧ ⟨to another state⟩

At night Johnson's "old disease of mind" troubled him with "vellications or revulsions," which he had defined respectively as "twitchings, stimulation," and "drawing humours from a remote part of the body." He does not have a word for his condition which is satisfactorily descriptive.

He later read the first "Sunday," that is, the first part, of the *Whole Duty of Man*, which his mother had made him read on Sundays, without much profit (*Life*, 1.67). But he has forgotten that he quoted from it extensively in the *Dictionary*.

The last paragraph, on a separate page, was added on his next birthday.

In May Johnson and Wilkes met at dinner again, and their conversation was lively and friendly, Wilkes hinting that he was too poor to buy the *Lives of the Poets*, and Johnson later sending him a set.

By June Johnson's business as an executor of Thrale's estate had been largely settled with the sale of the brewery, and Johnson

those whom he has left, continue to succour me by such means as are best for me, and repay to his relations³ the kindness which I have received from him; protect them in this world from temptations and calamities, and grant them happiness in the world to come, for Jesus Christs sake. Amen.

AUGUST 9. 3.P.M. Aetat. 72 in the summer house· at Streatham.

After innumerable resolutions formed and neglected, I have retired hither to plan a life of greater diligence, in hope that I may yet be useful, and be daily better prepared to appear before my Creatour and my judge from⁴ whose infinite mercy I humbly call for assistance and support.

My purpose is
To pass eight hours every day in some serious employment.

11. Having prayed, I purpose to employ the next six weeks upon the Italian language for my settled study.

SEPT. 2. 1781. When Thrales health was broken for many months, I think before his death which happened Apr.   ,
I constantly mentioned him in my prayers and after his death have made particular supplication for his surviving family

3. ₐrelationsₐ ⟨family⟩   4. ₐfromₐ ⟨which⟩ . . . ₐcallₐ ⟨hope⟩

---

wrote his prayer on Thrale, correcting it, apparently, on 2 September, since that entry follows at once in the manuscript, and is written in the same ink as the corrections.

In the early summer Johnson paid two short visits to the country, but seems to have done little. On 9 August he is again resolving to work. Two days later he has again decided to give serious study to Italian.

On 2 September, Johnson left a blank after "Apr." to insert the day of Thrale's death, but neglected to do so. It was 4 April. The manuscript breaks off as shown, but one may conjecture that he meant that hereafter he would commemorate Thrale's death

to this day, but having now recommended them to God in this particular address, which though written

SEPT. 18. 1781. This is my seventy third birthday an awful day. I said a preparatory prayer last night, and waking early made use in the dark, as I sat up in bed of the prayer (beginning of this year). I rose, breakfasted and gave thanks at Church for my Creation, Preservation, and Redemption. As I came home I thought I had never begun any period of life so placidly. I read the second Epistle to the Thessalonians, and looked into Hammond's notes. I have always accustomed to let this day pass unnoticed, but it came this time into my [mind] that some little festivity was not improper. I had a Dinner and invited Allen and Levet.

What has passed in my thoughts on this anniversary is in stitched book K.

My purposes are the same as on the first day of this year, to which I add hope of

More frequent attendance on publick Worship.

Participation of the Sacrament at least three[5] times a year.

5. Substituted for a deleted word.

---

only on the occasions when he commended his other dead friends, such as at Easter.

On his birthday Johnson went to church; since it was a weekday, this was unusual. Later he read the Second Epistle to the Thessalonians and "looked into" Henry Hammond's notes on it in *A Paraphrase and Annotations upon the New Testament*, 1653, incorporated in the set of Hammond's *Works* which was lot 209 in the sale of his library.

Johnson's relaxation on this day is strikingly reflected in his decision to celebrate it with a dinner, the first time he has done so. It is too bad that "stitched book K," in which he recorded his thoughts, is not known.

His hope to participate in receiving communion at least three

SEPT 18. VESP. 10.40′ CIRC. Almighty and most merciful
Father, who hast added another year to my life, and yet permittest me to call upon thee, Grant that the remaining days
which thou shalt yet allow me may be past in thy fear and to
thy glory, grant me good resolutions and steady perseverance.
Relieve the diseases of my body and compose the disquiet of
my mind. Let me at last repent and amend my life, and, O
Lord, take not from me thy Holy Spirit, but assist my amendment, and accept my repentance, for the sake of Jesus Christ.
Amen.

OCT 14 SUNDAY. (PROPERLY MONDAY MORNING.) I am
this day about to go by Oxford and Birmingham to Lichfield
and Ashbourne. The motives of my journey I hardly know.
I omitted it last year, and am not willing to miss it again. Mrs
Aston will be glad, I think, to see me. We are both old, and
if I put off my visit, I may see her no more; perhaps she wishes
for another interview. She is a very good woman.

Hector is likewise an old Friend the only companion of my
childhood that passed through the school with me. We have
always loved one another. Perhaps we may be made better by[6]
some serious conversation, of which however I have no distinct hope.

At Lichfield, my native place, I hope to shew a good example by frequent attendance on publick worship.

At Ashbourne I hope to talk seriously with Taylor.

6. ⟨ano⟩

_____

times a year is a revision: a blotted and mostly illegible word
below "three" may be "four" or "six." He seems to have thought
he had better aim at a goal which he could reach.

Johnson's birthday prayer, written about 10:40 at night, also
shows his relative quietness of mind on this day.

On 14 October, about to go into the country, Johnson examined
the motives for his journey. It is noteworthy that he does not men-

1782

TU. JAN. 1. In the Bible at Streatham Genesis contains fifty pages. In the last are ten verses of Exodus.

JANUARY 20, SUNDAY. Robert Levett was buried in the church-yard of Bridewell, between one and two in the afternoon. He died on Thursday 17, about seven in the morning, by an instantaneous death. He was an old and faithful friend; I have known him from about 46. *Commendavi.*[7] May God have had mercy on him. May he have mercy on me.

7. Hawkins: *"commendari"*

---

tion his difficult stepdaughter, Lucy, but that is perhaps inadvertence. His hope of frequent churchgoing as a good example at Lichfield looks like a method of persuading himself to perform a duty which he never enjoyed.

The serious talk he intended with Taylor was probably an attempt to persuade that worldly clergyman of the seriousness of his state, though Taylor interpreted it otherwise in his *Letter to Samuel Johnson on the Subject of a Future State*, 1787.

The trip to see his friends was a long one, lasting till 11 December. He reached London to find that another unauthorized collection of his work had appeared, the *Beauties of Johnson*, a book of aphorisms published by Kearsley, which was twice reprinted within a year. The unknown editor perhaps mollified Johnson by the statement that he "has ever scorned to accommodate himself to the licentiousness and levity of the present age, but uniting the greatest learning with the greatest talents, has uniformly supported the cause of morality, 'by giving an ardour to virtue, and a confidence to truth'" (p. iv).

On 1 January the Bodleian diary begins with Johnson's entry about the Thrale's Bible at Streatham, where he may have been staying. The Bible, a gift from Johnson to the Thrales, is now in the Hyde collection.

The entry for 20 January was printed by Hawkins from a diary

MARCH 18. Having been from the middle of January, distressed by a cold which[8] made my respiration very laborious, and from which I was but little relieved by being blooded three times, having tried to ease the oppression of my breast by frequent opiates, which kept me waking in the night, and drowsy the next day, and subjected me to the tyranny of vain imaginations; having to all this added frequent catharticks, sometimes with mercury; I at last persuaded Dr Laurence on Thursday March 14 to let me bleed more copiously. Sixteen ounces were taken away, and from that time my breath has been free, and my breast easy. On that day I took little food, and no flesh. I had food [word illegible] and Friday March 15 had food twice again.[9] On Thursday night I slept with great tranquillity and had no call to οὐ which I have for some years had in the night wonderfully frequent. On the next night (15) I took diacodium and had a most restless night. Of the next day I remember nothing but that I rose in the after noon, and saw Mrs Lennox and Sheward.

8. ‸which‸ . . . from which I ‸was‸   9. ⟨I had food . . . twice again.⟩

now lost. Johnson's great distress at Levet's death, barely shown here, was transformed into one of his best poems. He commended him in his prayers, as he did his other dead friends.

On Monday, 18 March, Johnson recapitulated the events of the past few days. It is worth noting the connexion here between Johnson's use of opium and the "tyranny of vain imaginations" to which it subjected him. This must mean opium reveries, and may explain Hawkins's assertion that Johnson took opium for pleasure (pp. 320, 454).

Strahan and Hill omitted the passage after "tranquillity," probably out of delicacy, since "οὐ" is an abbreviation of the Greek word for urinate. It does not seem to have occurred to Johnson that the great quantities of tea he consumed acted as a diuretic.

On Friday he took diacodium, or syrup of poppies, and the opium disturbed him as before.

17 SUNDAY. I lay late, and had only Palfrey to dinner. d.
2s. 6.[1] I read part of Waller's Directory, a pious rational book,
but in any except a very regular life difficult to practice.
It occurred to me that though my time might pass unemployed, no more should pass uncounted, and this has been
written to day in consequence of that thought. I read a Greek
Chapter, prayed with Francis, which I now do commonly,
and explained to him the Lord's Prayer in which I find connection not observed, I think, by the expositors. I made punch
for Myself and my servant, by which in the night I thought
both my breast and imagination disordered.

MARCH 18. I rose late, looked a little into books. Saw
Miss Reynolds and Miss Thrale and Nicolaida, afterwards Dr
Hunter came for his catalogue. I then dined on tea &c then
I corrected Shaw,[2] read over part of Dr Laurence's book de

1. ⟨d. 2s. 6⟩   2. ∧I corrected Shaw.∧ ⟨I [illegible] for [illegible] and⟩

On Saturday he saw Charlotte Lennox and "Sheward," probably the William Seward with whom he apparently dined on
7 April 1777.
On Sunday he had "Palfrey" to dinner, identified as a woman
on 1 September, and gave her 2s. 6d. Then he read in William
Waller's *Divine Meditations upon Several Occasions with a Dayly
Directory*, 1680, in which "the day was strictly divided in the
Directory, with frequent private prayers and meditations, and
family prayers at noon and supper" (*Miscellanies*, 1.103 n.). It is
little wonder that Johnson felt that it was not for him.
Later, after attending to Frank's religious instruction, he made
punch for both of them, out of "spirit," water, sugar, and lemon
juice, as his *Dictionary* prescribes. It had the same effect on his
imagination as opium.
Next day the callers were Frances Reynolds (Sir Joshua's sister),
Queeney Thrale, and Nicolaida or Nicolaides, "a learned Greek,
nephew of the Patriarch of Constantinople, who had fled from a

Temperamentis, which seems to have been written with a troubled mind. I prayed with Francis.[3]

My mind has been for some time much disturbed. The Peace of God be with me.

I hope to morrow to finish Laurence, and to write to Mrs Aston and to Lucy.

19. I rose late. I was visited by Mrs Thrale, Mr Cotton, and Mr Crofts. To Pellé 5s.[4] I took Laurence's paper in hand, but was chill, having fasted yesterday. I was hungry and dined freely, then slept a little, and drank tea, then took candles and wrote to Aston and Lucy, then went on with Laurence of which little remains. I prayed with Francis.

3. ⟨I prayed with Francis.⟩   4. ⟨To Pellé 5s⟩

---

massacre of the Greeks" (Johnstone, *Life of Parr*, 1.84). Johnson, Boswell, and Langton had known Nicolaides since 1775 (*Letters* 398).

Dr. William Hunter, the famous anatomist, this year published a catalogue of his collection of coins, compiled by Charles Combe. Johnson was probably looking over the manuscript.

The "correction" which Johnson was doing for William Shaw was writing several paragraphs for the second edition of *An Enquiry into the Authenticity of the Poems ascribed to Ossian*, 1782, in which Johnson rose to the attack with his usual enthusiasm. Samples are given by Boswell (*Life*, iv.252).

After tea Johnson read in the manuscript of Dr. Lawrence's *De Temperamentis*.

On the nineteenth, Mrs. Thrale called with one of her cousins, probably Henry Cotton, described by Fanny Burney as "a young beau" (*Diary*, ii.103). The Reverend Herbert Croft, who wrote the *Life of Young* for Johnson's *Poets*, also came. Johnson called him "Crofts" again in a letter (828.1).

Mrs. Pellé, to whom Johnson gave 5s., is probably the "unhappy woman," known to Johnson many years, daughter of a clergyman

Mens sedatior, laus DEO.

To morrow Shaw comes. I think to finish Laurence, and write to Langton.

Poor Laurence has almost lost the sense of hearing, and I have lost the conversation of a learned, intelligent and communicative companion, and a friend whom long familiarity has much endeared. Laurence is one of the best men whom I have known.[5]

Nostrum omnium miserere, Deus.

20. D. b., non οὖ. Steevens came.[6] Shaw came. I finished reading Laurence, and ended with Shaw.[7] I dined liberally. Wrote a long letter to Langton, and designed to read but was hindred by Strahan. The Ministry is dissolved. I prayed with Fr. and gave thanks. 50 L. Plutarch.[8]

To morrow—To Mrs Thrale—To write to Hector. To Dr Taylor.

5. ∧Laurence is . . . known.∧   6. ∧D. b. . . . . came∧   7. ⟨and ended with Shaw⟩
8. ∧50L. Plutarch∧

---

of Leicestershire, and reduced by an unhappy marriage to solicit a refuge in the workhouse in 1783 (*Letters* 844).

The letter Johnson wrote to Lucy Porter is No. 768. That to Miss Aston is not known.

After prayer with Frank, Johnson gives thanks that his mind is more at ease, but on thinking of Dr. Lawrence's growing deafness he exclaims: "God have pity on us all."

On 20 March Johnson had slept well, but Steevens came at eight. Then Shaw, a long letter to Langton (770), and a call from Strahan. The "£50" in the margin seems to be a sum received from Strahan. "Plutarch" below it may refer to reading Plutarch, but may also somehow refer to the fall of Lord North's ministry, for which Johnson was glad. A few days later he wrote of the new ministry, "The men are got in, whom I have endeavoured to keep out, but I hope they will do better than their predecessors; it will not be easy to do worse" (*Letters* 776).

21. I went to Mrs Thrale. Mr Cox and Paradise met me at the door and went with me in the coach. Paradise's loss.[9] In the evening wrote to Hector. At night there were eleven Visitants. Conversation with Mr Cox.[1] D. b. When I waked I saw the penthouses covered with snow.

22. I spent the time idly. Mens turbata. In the afternoon it snowed.[2] I visited Ramsay; m̃ eggs. No little snow.[3] At night I wrote to Taylor about the pot, and to Hamilton about the Foedera.

9. ∧Mr Cox . . . Paradise's loss∧ 1. ∧Conversation . . . Cox∧ 2. ∧In the . . . snowed∧ 3. ⟨I visited . . . snow⟩

On 21 March Johnson drove to Mrs. Thrale's with Paradise, who was threatened with the loss of a large estate in Virginia, unless he claimed it in person (Teignmouth's *Sir William Jones*, p. 355). Also present was "Cox," probably Peter Coxe (d. 1844), a friend of the Thrales and Burneys, whom Fanny calls "a very cultivated man, a great scholar, a poet, a critic, and very soft-mannered and obliging" (*Diary*, II.104). He was a minor poet, less well known than his brother William, the historian.

In the evening Johnson wrote to Hector (*Letters* 771), and afterwards slept well. Next day he visited Allan Ramsay, the painter, of whom he told Boswell, "I love Ramsay. You will not find a man in whose conversation there is more instruction, more information, and more elegance, than in Ramsay's" (*Life*, III.336).

"In the morning, eggs," no doubt for breakfast. Johnson's mentioning this suggests that the event was unusual. His mind was perturbed, perhaps because he was idle. In the afternoon he wrote a letter now lost to Taylor about a silver coffee pot which Taylor had bought. Johnson, thinking the pot was for him, had sent the price, and the two old gentlemen were now arguing as to whether the pot was for someone else (*Letters* 767.1, 793).

He also wrote another letter, which is lost, to William Gerard Hamilton about a set of Rymer's *Foedera* which he was trying to sell for Davies.

23. I Came home, and found that Desmoulins had while I was away been in bed. I took Καθ. Corrected proofs for Shaw.[4] Letters from Langton and Boswel. M. d.[5] I promised Lowe[6] Six Guineas.

24, SUNDAY. I rose not early. Visitors Allen, Davies, Windham, Dr Horseley. Palfry 2s 6d. Dinner at Strahan's.[7] Came home, and chatted with Williams, and read Romans IX in Greek.

To morrow begin again to read the Bible; put rooms in order; copy Lowe's[8] Letter.

25 M. I Had from Strahan 78 L.[9] At night I read 11 p. of the Bible[1] and something more, in 55′.

4. ⟨Corrected . . . Shaw⟩ 5. ⟨M. d.⟩ 6. ⟨Lowe⟩ 7. Two lines deleted. 8. ⟨Lowe's⟩ 9. ⟨25 M . . . 78L.⟩ 1. ᴧof the Bibleᴧ

Next day at home he corrected proofs for Shaw, took a purge, slept badly, and saw the impecunious painter Mauritius Lowe, whom he promised six guineas. Lowe, the illegitimate son of Lord Southwell, had been supported by Southwell and later by Southwell's son, who had died two years before and had left Lowe without certain support.

On Sunday, besides Allen and Davies, visitors were the Right Honourable William Windham, later a member of the Essex Head Club, Dr. Samuel Horsley, later Bishop of Rochester and also a member of the Essex Head Club, and Mrs. Palfry (or Palfrey), who got another half-crown.

Johnson's copying Lowe's letter probably refers to his continuing effort to secure Lowe an allowance. He had written Lady Southwell, but apparently without result. In October, Lowe received the first payment from the new lord (*Letters* 705, 811).

On Monday Johnson continued his reading the Bible, apparently still in Greek, since in English or Latin eleven pages in fifty-five minutes would be too slow.

2 6 TU. I copied Lowe's Letter. I gave Desmoulins a guinea, and found her a gown. Paid Gardiner.[2] Then went to Mrs Thrale. Coxe visited me. I sent home Dr Laurence's papers with notes.

2 7 W. At Harley Street bad nights. In the evening Dr Bromfield and his Family. Merlins steelyard given me.

2 8. TH. Καθ.[3] I came home. Sold Rymer for Davies. Wrote to Boswel to dissuade him from his coming away.[4] Visitor Dr Percy. Mr Crofts. I have in ten days written to Aston, Lucy, Hector, Langton, Boswel: perhaps to all by whom my Letters are desired.

The Weather which now begins to be warm gives me great

2. ∧I gave Desmoulins . . . Paid Gardiner.∧   3. ∧TH. Καθ.∧   4. ⟨to dissuade . . . away⟩

On Tuesday the notes make a curious chronological mixture, because Johnson has added material in both margins as he remembered it. The events occurred something like this: he copied Lowe's letter; Coxe called; he gave Mrs. Desmoulins a guinea and "found" or supplied her with a gown; he returned Lawrence's manuscript, which he had annotated; he paid Mrs. Gardiner, perhaps the repayment of a loan; then he went to Mrs. Thrale's house in Harley Street which she had recently rented, where he spent two nights.

Wednesday evening, Dr. Robert Bromfield called with his family. He had attended Mrs. Salusbury and Thrale during their illnesses. John Merlin, a popular mechanic and piano maker, invented or improved many instruments. The steelyard, or Roman balance, presumably with improvements, would have been a welcome addition to Johnson's scales. Fanny Burney mentions Merlin often.

On Thursday Johnson came home, took a purge, sold Rymer's *Foedera* for Davies, wrote to Boswell (775) urging him not to come to London while his finances were strained, and then saw Dr. Percy and Croft, who called. His remark about the letters he

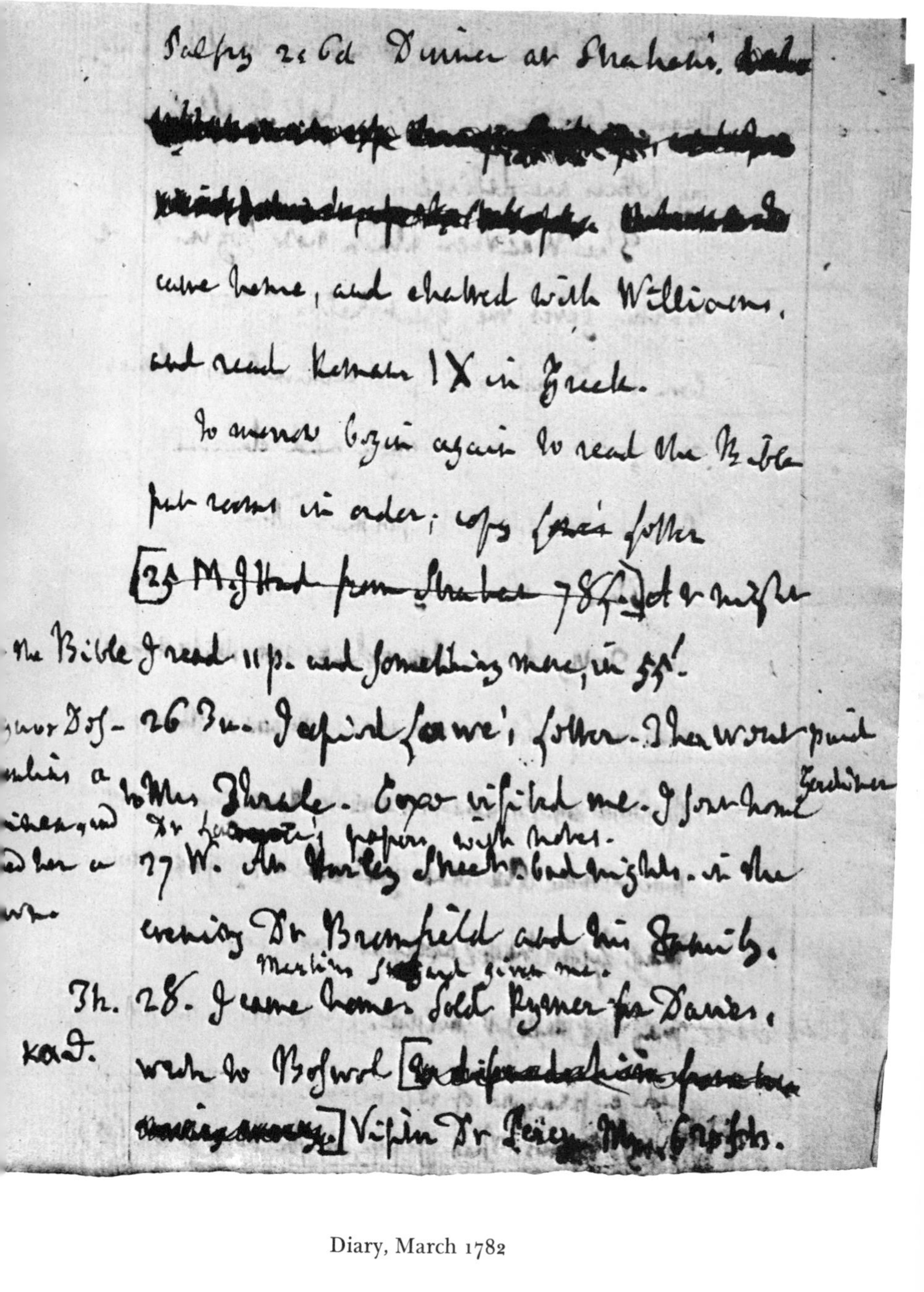

Diary, March 1782

help. I have hardly been at Church this year, certainly not since the 15 of Jan. My Cough and difficulty of Breath would not permit it.

This is the day on which in 1752 dear Tetty died. On what we did amiss, and our faults were great, I have thought of late with more regret than at any former time. She was I think very penitent. May God have accepted her repentance: may he accept mine.[5] I have now uttered a prayer of repentance and c[ontritio]n, perhaps Tetty knows that I prayed for her. Thou, God, art merciful, hear my prayers, and enable me to trust in Thee.

Perhaps Tetty is now praying for me. God, help me.[6]

We were married almost seventeen years, and have now been parted thirty.

I then read 11 p. from Ex. 36 to Lev. 7. The chapters named are included.[7] I prayed with Fr. and used the prayer for Good Friday.

29. GOOD FRIDAY. After a night of great disturbance and solicitude, such as I do not remember, I rose, drank tea, but

5. ⟨On what we did . . . accept mine.⟩ 6. ∧Perhaps Tetty . . . help me∧ 7. ∧The chapters . . . included∧

---

had written may need the qualification that others desired his letters when he was out of London, but while there he saw his friends with some frequency.

Then he turns to thoughts of Tetty. Strahan crossed out most of the passage, perhaps frightened by Johnson's "our faults were great." But Johnson is seldom more moving than in this meditation of contrition.

Johnson then uttered a prayer of repentance and contrition, read Exodus xxxvi to Leviticus vii, inclusive, and prayed with Frank.

On Good Friday after church Johnson read in Henry Hammond's *Paraphrase and Annotations upon the Psalms*, 1659, which

without eating, and went to Church. I was very composed, and coming home read Hammond on one of the Psalms for the day.[8] I then read Leviticus. Scot came in, which hindred me from Church in the afternoon.[9] A kind letter from Gastrel. I read on, then went to Evening prayers, and afterwards drank tea with Bunns, the[n] read till I finished Leviticus, 24 pages, et sup.[1]

Pr. with Fr.[2]

To write to Gastrel to morrow. To look again into Hammond. D. b.[3]

30. SAT. Visitors, Paradise and, I think, Horseley. γν *p* 11. *P* means pages of the Bible.[4] I was faint yet Καθ.[5] Dined on Herrings and potatoes. At Prayers, I think, in the Evening. I wrote to Gastrel, and received a kind letter from Hector. At night Lowe. Pr. with Francis. D. b.[6]

31. EASTER DAY. γν *p* 15. Caetera alibi.

8. A few words deleted. 9. ⟨which hindred . . . afternoon⟩ 1. Three lines and a marginal note deleted. 2. ⟨Pr. with Fr.⟩ 3. ∧D. b.∧ 4. ∧*P* means . . . Bible∧ 5. ⟨yet Καθ⟩ 6. ∧D. b.∧

––––––––––––

he evidently liked, as at the end of the day he reminds himself to do so again. In the afternoon his lawyer friend William Scott called, and he received a solicitous letter from Mrs. Gastrell about his health, which he answered the next day (776). By night-time he had finished Leviticus, more than twenty-four pages in a day, a good record. And he slept well.

The entry for Saturday was written several days later, since he cannot be sure that Horsley called, or that he went to church. But he does remember what he ate, the number of pages he read in the Bible (unless he marked each day's progress) and his praying with Frank. And he slept well again.

On Easter Day he entered only his reading: "The rest is elsewhere," but now lost.

During the next six weeks Johnson was still in bad health, and

SAT. MAY 18. From Streatham.

W. 22. Mrs Desm[oulins] 10s–6. Mrs Pelle 10s–6. Home.

TU. 28. To dine with Mrs Way.

TH. 30.   To the Washerwoman   –6–
            For tea to get change   –1–
            Bridge 1d. Jenny 1d   ––2
                                        ————
                                        –7–2

        In my Pocket gold   2–12–6
              at night   6–9
                    Silver &c   6–3½
                                     ————
                                    3– 5–6½

FR. 31. [Paid] Bridge – – 1.

---

the return of very cold weather made it worse. By the middle of May, however, he was able to go to Streatham for a week. The Bodleian diary resumes with his return.

On 21 May Johnson had apparently returned to Streatham for the night, since in a letter of that date he says that it is kind of Queeney to come for him.

Next day he is home again, and again helping Mrs. Pellé.

On 28 May Johnson was engaged to dine with Mrs. Benjamin Way, apparently the sister-in-law of his friend Lady Sheffield, a dinner which had been postponed because of his illness. Mrs. Way was very solicitous about Johnson's health during his last years, as Johnson's letters to her show.

On 30 May Johnson gave "Jenny" a penny. This may be his god-daughter Jane Langton, then five years old, whose father had called on Johnson a few days earlier (*Letters* 782.3). "Jenny" may, however, be some poor woman; an undated entry, which we have placed at Easter 1771, speaks of "dying Jenny," who appears to be an object of charity. The penny to "Bridge" seems to be a toll.

M. AUG. 5. γν 12 p. Corrected Lives. NB. 24 pp. of my B[ible],
to Gen. xxvii. 4. From Strahan 5–5–0.

TU. Steevens. Corrected lives at night.

To stock	1–1–0
To White (clear except wages	1–4–0
To Frank	7–0
To Williams to provide	1–1–0

W. γν 14 p. Corrected lives.[7]

TH. γν 16 p. Corrected lives. Alvus mota Cal. gr 8. Sleepy.

7. ⟨Cal gr 8 alvus probe mota⟩

In June Johnson spent a week at Oxford, and by the beginning
of August was working on a revision of the *Lives of the Poets*.

On 5 August he read in the Bible, which he had begun in late
winter, and had progressed into Numbers by Easter. He was now
in Kings, since, after some fifty pages more, he reached Chronicles
a few days later, and his calculation of this date tells us that in his
Bible the first twenty-six chapters of Genesis occupy just under
twenty-four pages. On New Year's Day he had noted that in the
Thrales' Bible, Genesis occupied fifty pages, which is almost exactly the same. He continues regularly through the Old Testament, omitting Psalms, which he knew well, and through the New
Testament thereafter.

The Bodleian diary is arranged in three columns (see plate),
not always exactly dated. These columns have been combined as
precisely as possible to make a single entry for each day. "Stock"
may be either a stock or stockings. Mrs. White, Johnson's house-
keeper, is being reimbursed for what she had spent, and Miss
Williams apparently for the same.

On Wednesday Johnson noted that he had taken eight grains
of calomel as a purge, and found it effective, but then he realized
that he had entered it on the wrong day, cancelled it, and entered
it on Thursday.

FR. γν 16 p. Corrected lives. Boileau contre des Femmes v. 738.
Cal. gr 8. Sleepy.

SAT. γν pp [blank] No meat. At home. Cal. gr 8 Καθ. This
night I slept well.

SUN. γν Chro[nicles] B[ook] I, except a few verses. Raasa,
Hoole. To Davies ten Guineas. This night d. b.   Cal gr 5.

M. 12. γν Chron. II. Dined. Gave Pelle 4s. D. b. Cal gr 5. From
Strahan 3–3–0.

TU. γν Chron II. Wrote to Taylor. I gave Crow a guinea. Mrs
Desm. 0–10–6. Cal gr 6 d. m.

To Frank	0– 7–0
To Wms. (about	0–17–0
To White (in full about	0–15–0
To Mr[s] Desm	0–10–6
	2– 9–6
Watch	4–0
Washer[woman]	0– 1–0
	2–14–6
In pocket	0– 7–0
	3– 1–6

On Friday Johnson read Boileau's Tenth Satire, *Contre des femmes*, which is 738 lines long. By the end of the month he had read all of the satires.

On Saturday he has read the Bible as usual, but did not remember the number of pages; evidently the entry was made some days later.

Sunday he read almost all of I Chronicles, saw Macleod of Raasay, whom he had met in the Hebrides (he wrote Boswell that they "dined cheerfully together," *Letters* 803), and John Hoole, for whom Johnson had written dedications. That night he slept well.

On 12 August he gave Mrs. Pellé 4s. again, slept well again,

w. γν Ezra and Nehemiah p. 21. Cal. gr 9. M. d.

TH. γν Esther and part of Job. Cator. Little dinner. Καθ. No water. D. med[iocriter].

FR. γν the rest of Job. Rose at 10. Cal. gr 5 circ[a].

SAT. γν Prov[erbs]. No dinner. Cal. puto gr 10.   Καθ besides.
Saturday [received from] Strahan 4–4–0
              [paid] Coddington   0– 2– 0
              Watch 4. Water 12   0–16– 0
              The whole   3–15–10
    Given 1–6.

SUN. Church m. γν Eccl[esiastes]. Cant[icum Solomonis].

---

and took a purge for the fifth day in succession. When he wrote to Taylor next day (798) he told him, "I have now had three quiet nights together, which, I suppose, I have not for more than a year before." He also urged against costiveness: "you will find that vexation has much more power over you, ridiculous as it may seem, if you neglect to evacuate your body."

On Tuesday he gave Crow a guinea; Johnson had lodged at Mrs. Crow's in Castle Street in London from 1738 to 1740. This person may be a relation. That night he slept ill, as he did on Wednesday also.

On Thursday he slept tolerably. He saw John Cator, M.P., with Johnson an executor of Thrale's estate.

The entry for Saturday was evidently not written that day, for Johnson is not sure of the calomel he took: he thinks it was ten grains. Coddington is unidentified; on 7 December Johnson again gave him 2s. The week's expenditures, continued from Tuesday, do not make the sum given, and it is not clear where Johnson made his mistake. He neglected to add the 4s. he gave to Mrs. Pellé and the guinea he gave Crow, but these do not balance the amount.

On Sunday, church in the morning.

M. 19. γν Isaiah. Dr Percy dined. D. b. Allen dined. From Strahan 3–3–0.

TU. 20.⁸ γν Isaiah. At Streatham d. b.⁹ Cator. Mrs Biron.

W. 21. γν Isaiah. I slept from 12 to four p.m. Cal. gr 5.

TH. 22. γν Jerem. Mrs Thrale told me her design of going abroad. 2 verses 2 Sat. Boileau. D. b. Slept a little.

FR. 23. γν Jerem. m. Rose at eight. Read Boileau. D. b. Wyndham. Sir Philip. Cal. gr. 6. Read Juv. Sat. 6.

8. MS: 21   9. ⟨I gave Crow a Guinea to Desmoulins ½ Guinea⟩

On Monday, 19 August, Johnson would appear to have dined twice, but he probably means that both Percy and Allen dined with him. On Tuesday Johnson erroneously entered and then crossed out the sums he had given Crow and Desmoulins on the previous Tuesday. He has also dated both Tuesday and Wednesday the twenty-first. He apparently entered the three guineas from Strahan and then erased, realizing that they belonged to the previous week also.

At Streatham on Tuesday Johnson saw Cator again and Mrs. John Byron, grandmother of the poet and wife of the admiral, "Foul-weather Jack." The Byrons were friends of the Thrales and the Burneys.

On Thursday Mrs. Thrale told Johnson of her plan to go abroad. His calm reaction to this announcement, reflected here, piqued Mrs. Thrale, since she had expected him to be upset, as her entry in *Thraliana* on this date shows (p. 540). He continued to read Boileau, but what "2 verses" means is not clear, since that is too small an amount to record normally.

On Friday Johnson's good friend William Windham called. Next spring, when he was about to set out for Ireland as Secretary to the Lord Lieutenant, he "expressed to the Sage some modest and virtuous doubts, whether he could bring himself to practise

SAT. 24. Rose at 7, read Boileau, Jerem. paulum. Wrote to
Boswel. Cal. gr. 10. Dined Beans and Ham. [From] Mr Strahan 4–4–0.

[To] White for bad money returned	0–10–6
To Frank	0– 7–0
lent to Collet	1– 1–0
To Mrs Pelle	5–6
washer[woman] about	2–6
	2– 6–6

SUN. 25. γν Jeremiah duas fere portiones. Church, Vesperi.
At Strahan's. Mrs Cooke and her son.

----

those arts which it is supposed a person in that situation has occasion to employ. 'Don't be afraid, Sir, (said Johnson, with a pleasant smile,) you will soon make a very pretty rascal' " (*Life*, IV.200).
    Another caller was a friend of the Thrales, Sir Philip Jennings-
Clerke, Bart., M.P. for Totnes. In May he had been making love
to Mrs. Thrale "quite openly & seriously" (*Thraliana*, p. 538),
but she was not interested.
    For the fourth day in succession Johnson records that he had
slept well: his health was much better, since his inability to sleep
was his only "great complaint," as he wrote Taylor (799).
    It is most remarkable that on Saturday he rose at seven, prob-
ably because he was returning to London, but this is also evidence
of his improving health. He read a little in Jeremiah, and wrote
Boswell (801), suggesting that they meet at Ashbourne or London.
    In his list of expenses, Johnson notes the return of a counterfeit
half guinea, a fairly common event, though counterfeiting was
punishable by death. He also records a loan of a guinea to Collet,
his barber, to whom he had also lent money in 1777.
    On Sunday Johnson read nearly all the "two parts" of Jeremiah,
considering the Lamentations as the second part, went to church
in the evening, and, apparently at Strahan's, saw a Mrs. Cooke.
She was probably the widow of John Cooke, bookseller, of Shake-

M. 26. γν Jerem. Streatham. Read Boileau. Wrote to Miss Laurence, Mrs Hervey, Taylor. In my pocket 2–5¹–0

TU. γν Ezech. 9. Read Boileau. Καθ. D.b.

| A light ½ Guinea Laid up | 0– 9–0 |
| To Fairy | 0– 1–0 |

W. γν Ezech. 20, Boileau a Son Esprit, at night l. Holliday. D.b.

TH. γν Ezech. 32. I rose late. Boileau sur Honeur. Cal. gr. 6. V. det. D. m. [To] Barber 0–1–0.

FR. I rose late. Mr Cator. I read Boileau's Equivoque, γν Ezechiel 42, read Boil. Art Poet. C[antos] 1. 2. I this day finished Boileau's Satires of which I had not read any one through before.

SAT. I went home. I read in the Bible paginas paucas. Καθ. Lowe had a letter from L. Southwel's Agent.

1. ⟨4⟩ ʌ5ʌ _____

speare's Head, Paternoster Row. Boswell's daughters had tea with her in 1793, and Boswell mentions her children (*Boswell Papers*, XVIII.218).

Next day Johnson returned to Streatham, where he wrote to Elizabeth Lawrence about her father, the doctor, who was very ill (*Letters* 802), and also to Taylor and the blind Mrs. Hervey, widow of Johnson's friend Henry Hervey, and sister of Elizabeth and Molly Aston. The last two letters are not known.

On Tuesday Johnson again had trouble with bad money, this time apparently clipped, not counterfeit as the week before. And he gave a shilling to "Fairy," unknown. He read Ezekiel through chapter ix.

Wednesday night he read in Barten Holyday, perhaps in his sermons or his *Survey of the World*, 1661. In *Idler* 69 Johnson had criticized his translations (Horace and Persius) as those of "only a scholar and a critick."

On Thursday, the abbreviation "V. det." is in doubt.

SUN. SEPT. 1. To Church. γν Bible. At diner, Mrs Hall, Macquin, Sastres, Palfry, Lowe. To Palfry 2s–6. Williams gave her 2s–6. To Palfry 0–2–6. Lent Lowe 10–6.

M. 2. γν Bible. To Greenwich. I was hurt in stepping from the coach. At night being very ill, Opium. I was blooded and took tinct. Ipeca. which operated well. To Desmoulins 0–10–6. Borrowed of Williams 2–6.

TU. γν Bible. To Streatham. Shelburne, Thomas to Strahan. Opium. Little flesh. I was ill in the coach. At night ejected opium. I took from the drawer 2–2–0. To White 10–0.

On Saturday, home again, Johnson read a few pages in the Bible, and was no doubt glad to learn that his efforts in behalf of Lowe were beginning to have effect, since Lowe had heard from Lord Southwell's agent, Paget. Money came a few weeks later.

On 1 September Johnson gave a very mixed dinner party: "lean, lank, preaching Mrs. Hall" (*Life*, IV.95); young Mackinnon from Skye (*Letters* 803); Francesco Sastres, the Italian master, author of *An Introduction to the Italian Language*, 1778; Mrs. Palfry, who received half a crown with her dinner as she had on 17 and 24 March; and Lowe, who got half a guinea. Also present, of course, were the members of his household.

On Monday Johnson made a short visit to Greenwich, where he had lodged during the summer of 1737. After his injury, he treated himself with his usual violence: blood-letting, opium, and ipecac as an emetic.

Next day Johnson went to Streatham, where he apparently stayed till Saturday. He saw Lord Shelburne, who had contracted to rent Streatham for three years, and probably Dr. Thomas, a schoolmaster at Streatham. The entry seems to mean that Johnson sent Thomas to Strahan, perhaps to mediate in the quarrel which young George Strahan was having with his father (*Letters* 800, 809).

w. Cambridge. Tinct. Ipec. D. b. Little flesh. Thomas. Mens fracta. γν Bible p. 6. D. b. To Williams borr: to lend Lowe, 10–6.

TH. Absolvi Vet Test. exceptis Psalm. γν Matt. 7. Cambridge and his son. Swinnerton. Little appetite. D. b. Borrowed of Sam: 0–1–0.

FR. I Read Cant. 3. Poetique de B[oileau]. Sidon Calm. γν Matt. 17. I read Cant 4 Poet. Boil. Καθ. I think myself recovered from the hurt. Sir Ph. Clark. Not much appetite.

SAT. 7. γν M[atthew] to the end. Mr Compton the Benedictine. Dined with appetite. D. b. Letter from Boswel θ π. I wrote to

---

On Wednesday Johnson saw Richard Owen Cambridge, author of *The Scribleriad*, 1751, and a contributor to the *World*, father of Reverend George Cambridge, prebendary of Ely, who came with his father on Thursday. Johnson writes that his mind is "crushed," but he was still suffering from his injury.

On Thursday he has finished the Old Testament, except for Psalms. Swinnerton called, a member of the family which lived at Hanley, twenty miles northwest of Lichfield. Fanny Burney calls him "a young beau," and a friend of Henry Cotton, Mrs. Thrale's cousin.

The man from whom Johnson borrowed a shilling was Samuel Graves, the Thrales' footman, whom Johnson helped in 1783 by instituting the Essex Head Club to meet in Graves's new tavern, the Essex Head.

Sidon Calm is unidentified.

On Saturday Johnson apparently returned to London, where Reverend James Compton called. He had recently left the Convent of the Benedictines in Paris, where Johnson had come to know him in 1775, and had "renounced the errors of Popery." Without funds, he had called on Johnson, who having heard his story "with the warmest expressions of tenderness and esteem,

Boswel. From Strahan 5–5–0. Returned to drawer one taken out, one fr[om] Strahan 2–2–0.

SUN. 8. Church M. γν Mark. Καθ. Dined with appetite. To White 1–1–0, to Frank 7[d].

M. 9. γν Luke 7. Wrote to Vyse about Compton. D. b. Compton came to tea.

TU. γν Luke 16. Jortins Serm. on prayer. I read Boileau Ep. 2. 3. Heavy and sleepy. I gave Williams two bo[o]ks of Lives. I ended the revisal of the lives.

W. γν Luke to the end and some of John. I read Boileau Ep. 4. 5. I think.

---

put into his hand a guinea, assuring him, that he might expect support from him till a provision for him could be found" (Hawkins, p. 531).

The letter from Boswell announced the death of his father, and Johnson's reply (803, dated "London") is a letter of condolence and advice about his affairs. The Greek symbol and abbreviation stand for "father, dead."

On Sunday Johnson went to church in the morning, feeling much improved.

On Monday he wrote to Dr. Vyse, whom he had used as an intermediary with the archbishop in 1777 to secure a place for De Groot. Though the letter is lacking, it no doubt asked for Vyse's help in securing ordination in the English Church for Compton, which was accomplished in the following January.

Dr. John Jortin's sermons, one of which Johnson read on Tuesday, had been published in 1771 (4 vols.) and in 1778 (7 vols.). Johnson thought them very elegant (*Life*, III.248). Jortin is now known chiefly for his *Life of Erasmus*, 1758.

The revised edition of the *Lives of the Poets*, which Johnson had just finished, was published in February.

Tuesday afternoon Johnson seems to have returned to Streatham.

TH. γν John. I read Boileau's Epistles 7. 8. 9. 10. 11. 12. Mrs [Thrale] went to Town. Paoli and Gentili dined a[t] Streatham.

FR. γν John in domuncula aestiva. Cum pr. I read Boileau's Lutrin. Lutrin one canto in the morning, the rest at night. Sastres, Swinnerton.

SAT. I came home. γν Acts c. 11, I saw Strahan, Compton, the American. I wrote for Lowe. M. d. emeticum egi. From Strahan 4–4–0

To Mrs Levet	1– 1–0
To Mrs White now clear	1– 2–4
To Mr Daniel	1– 1–0
To Frank	0– 7–
To Mrs Pelle (sometime	0– 3–0
To Mr Bright	0– 5–0
	3–19–4

On the twelfth, Mrs. Thrale went to town, and General Paoli and his fellow-Corsican Gentili came to dinner. Johnson knew both Count Gentili and General Antonio Gentili, but since all references to the Count are much earlier than this, the General is probably meant.

Next day Johnson read in the little summerhouse, where he also had lunch, and later saw Swinnerton and Sastres again.

On Saturday, at home again, Johnson saw an unidentified American. Although he had several American friends, none are known to have been in London this year. Furthermore, this sounds like a man Johnson did not know well; otherwise he would have used his name. He continued his efforts on Lowe's behalf, and, not having slept well, took an emetic.

Mrs. Levet, to whom he gave a guinea, is a problem. Levet had married a street-walker in 1762, but they had separated shortly afterwards, when she was tried as a pickpocket. It is possible that

SUN. γν Acts. At Church vesp. γν Romans. Dormitavi. Edwards. Non b. d.

M. 16. γν Cor. I. I read Boileau's Odes with preface and some epigrams. Dr Vyse about Mr Compton. No flesh. Slight diarrhoea. D. m. Mrs White owes of a Guinea left 0–9–2. Paid.²

TU. γν Cor. II. Gal. I read Boileaus Epigr. Swinnerton. Erdswick. These two days little flesh. D. m. Burney.

W. 18. Γ[ἔγονε] S. J. 1709.—Da veniam, Pater Aeterne, munus quod³ perijt tuum. γν Ephes. Phil. I went home, dined moderately, treated the family below. Pr. cub. at about 2. D. m. To treat the family 4–6, not all spent. Tea 0–9. To Frank lent 5–0.⁴ Paid.

2. ⟨Mrs White ... 0–9–2.⟩ ^Paid^   3. ^si^   4. ⟨5–0⟩ ^Paid.^

Johnson is extending her charity, but it is more likely that this woman is the wife of one of Levet's poor brothers in Yorkshire.

"Daniel" may be Dr. Samuel Daniel of Exeter, a friend of Boswell's, and "Bright" the Reverend Henry Bright, Master of Abingdon Grammar School, with whom Johnson had dinner at Oxford in 1775. In both cases the money might be a loan to cover a temporary shortage of cash for visitors to London.

On Sunday Johnson went to church in the evening, was sleepy, saw Oliver Edwards, the cheerful philosopher, and again did not sleep well. Next day he noted that Mrs. White still owed 9s. 6d. out of a guinea, and later crossed out the entry, marking "paid" against it. He did the same with a loan to Frank on Wednesday.

On Tuesday he is evidently back at Streatham, where he is more likely to have seen Swinnerton than at home, and was reading Sampson Erdeswicke's Survey of Staffordshire, 1723. "Burney" may be Dr. Burney but is more likely Fanny, to whom Johnson often refers in this way. She was frequently at the Thrales.

"S. J. was born 1709. Have mercy, eternal Father, even if thy gift has been wasted," the same words he had used on 3 January

TH. γν Coloss. Thess. 2. Tim 2. I read something in Boileau.
D. m. I returned to Streatham, dined on Soup and Fruit.
Slept before dinner. Swinnerton and Burney.

FR. γν. Titus, Philemon, to the Hebrews. I began Dutch. I
read Boileaus letter to Per[rault] and Arnaud's apol[ogy]. At
Mr Cators. Norman. Adair. Cator.

SAT. ἀναγνω̣ζεως.[4a] I went home late. Καθ. No meat. Compton,
Lowe. I wrote to Taylor and Boswel. D. m. I thought my self
faint and disordered by abstinence an[d] Καθ.

4a. So MS.

1765. Having eaten something late in the evening, he went to bed
at two, but did not sleep well.

On Friday Johnson resumed the study of Dutch, which he had
begun in the spring of 1773 for a short time. On his deathbed he
told Hoole why: "I feared that I had neglected God, and that
then I had not a *mind* to give him: on which I set about to read
Thomas a Kempis in Low Dutch, which I accomplished, and
thence I judged that my mind was not impaired, Low Dutch
having no affinity with any of the languages which I knew"
(*Miscellanies*, II.153).

Boileau's letter to Perrault, defending his satire on women
(X) from Perrault's attack, seems to have led Johnson to Antoine
Arnauld's defence of his friend Boileau. It seems unlikely that
Johnson is referring to Arnauld's *Apologie du clergé de France
et des catholiques d'Angleterre contre le ministre Jurieu*. But
Johnson knew enough of Arnauld to quote him on Boileau as
early as 1778 (*Life*, III.347).

Norman, whom Johnson saw the same day, was a timber merchant, as was Cator. James Adair, sergeant-at-law, was sometime
Recorder of London, and M.P. with Cator.

Why Johnson on Saturday used Greek to say that he was reading is curious, unless as practice. Then he wrote Boswell, urging
him to stay at home, and to Taylor (805, 806).

SUN. ἀναγ James. Peter. 2. John. 3. Jude. Revelations. At church, m. Dined Compton, Lowe, Macquin. Palfrey came and Macbean, and Allen. D. m.

M. 23. A little Dutch. D. m. To Mrs Hervey. With Mrs Desmoulins. Shebeare angry.

TU. A little Dutch. M. d. I caught a slight cold. To Streatham. Mr Crutchley gave me a Guinea for Lowe. From Mr Strahan 4–4–0.

W. A little Dutch. The cold continued. M. d. This week I have eaten mor[e] liberally than is usual and do not perceive that it has done me harm. Though I have had a cold and been costive, My Breath is not worse.

To Palfrey	0– 3–	0
To Desmoulins	10–	6
To Everet	5–	0
To Pelle	3–	0
To poor Woman	1–	0
To Fisher's Son	1–	0
To Frank	7–	0
To Coach	5–	6
To White (due 3s. 4d.)	1– 1–	0
To the Soldier	1–	0
	2–17–	6

On Sunday, he was at church in the morning, and later finished reading the New Testament. All the people who dined with Johnson that day or visited him were dependants, except his neighbour Allen and the young Scot, Mackinnon.

What John Shebbeare was angry about on Monday we do not know, but that violent political writer had once been sentenced to the pillory and was now enjoying a pension, which perhaps was late in arriving.

Betsy and Washer	4–11–2
	3– 2– 5–2
Jacob	1– 0
⊙. δχ. Given	1– 3– 6

TH. P[urgativum] egi. Cold still. Καθ. quinquies. Med. d.

FR. The cold continues.

SAT. Cold continues. Mr Compton. Mr Lowe.

SUN. MICHAELMAS DAY. At Church. V[esperi]. Davies in Afternoon.

M. 30. A little Dutch. Mr Compton and Mr Macbean dined with me. Mr Compton to Dr Vyse at ten in the morning, with his letters of ordination, and testimonials. To White 1–1–0. From Strahan 4–4–0.

On Tuesday, back at Streatham, Johnson begged a guinea for Lowe from Jeremiah Crutchley, Thrale's natural son and one of his executors. According to Fanny Burney, Johnson persuaded Crutchley to let Lowe paint his portrait; when Crutchley came for a sitting he was so appalled by the "dirt and filth, brats squalling and wrangling" that he left three guineas and departed in haste (*Diary*, I.494).

In the list of expenditures opposite the entry for Wednesday, "Everet" is perhaps the same as Mrs. Everet, otherwise unknown, to whom Johnson gave 5s. on 19 December. "Fisher's son" is either Thomas or Benjamin Johnson, sons of Fisher Johnson, a cousin, who had died in 1758. Both are named in the codicil to Johnson's will (*Life*, IV.403).

Betsey is Frank's wife, and Jacob Weston was the Thrales' coachman.

At the very bottom of the page, where there is no room for more names, Johnson's cryptic entry may be expanded, "On Sunday,

TU. OCT. 1. A little Dutch. I went to Streatham. Mr Cator will call. He called, and I put into his hands five hundred pounds.

To Frank for wages	2–10–0
To White	0– 5–0
for Coals	3–9

W. A little Dutch. Cold continues. Breath short. Packing to part. Barclay and Thornton dined at Streatham.

TH. I came home with Burney. Cold continues. A little Dutch.

FR. At home. A little Dutch. Cold continues.

---

apart [δίχα?], I gave £1–3–6," presumably to Compton, Lowe, and Macbean, who do not appear in his list.

On Thursday, still bothered by his cold, Johnson took a cathartic, evidently a violent one, since his subsequent evacuation was frequent. He slept tolerably.

On 1 October, at Streatham again, he put £500 into Cator's hands, perhaps for investment. If this seems a large sum for Johnson to have had on hand, it may be recalled that he had received a legacy of £200 from Thrale, and when Johnson made his will, he had £100 on hand. Perkins had had trouble finding his share of the purchase price of the brewery, and he and Barclay had £300 of Johnson's money in their hands at his death. Part or all of the sum given to Cator may have been used in this way.

Next day Robert Barclay, the new brewer, came to dinner, along with Henry Thornton, philanthropist and economist, who had been elected M.P. for Southwark, Thrale's constituency, in September. He was the first secretary of the Society for Missions to Africa and the East, and the first treasurer of the British and Foreign Bible Society.

The unusually large sum which Johnson drew from Strahan on Saturday is explained by the fact that Johnson was leaving for Brighton on Monday for an extended visit.

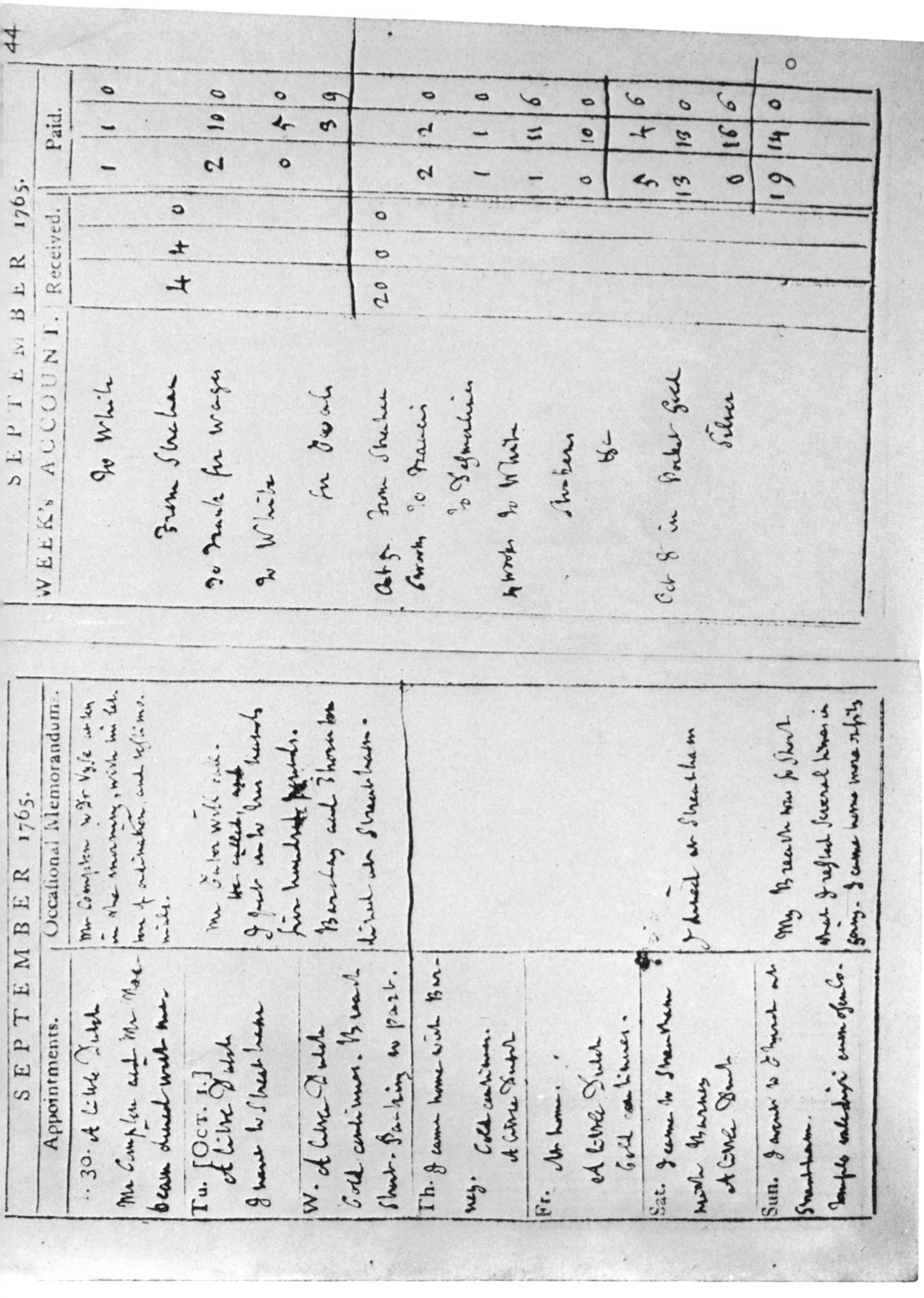

44

SEPTEMBER 1765.

Appointments.	Occasional Memorandums.
30. A little Dutch. Mr Compton and Mr Macbean dined with me.	Mr Compton to Dr Vyse at ten in the morning, with his letters of ordination and testimonials.
Tu. [Oct. 1.] A little Dutch. I went to Streatham	Mr Seton will call. He called, and I put into his hands five hundred pounds.
W. A little Dutch. Cold continues. Breath short. Packing in part.	Barclay and Thornton dined at Streatham.
Th. I came home with Barney. Cold continues. A little Dutch	
Fr. At home. A little Dutch. Cold continues.	
Sat. I came to Streatham with Barnes. A little Dutch	I dined at Streatham
Sun. I went to Church at Streatham. Templo valedixi cum osculo.	My Breath was so short that I rested several times in going. I came home more easily

SEPTEMBER 1765.

WEEK's ACCOUNT.	Received.			Paid.		
To White				1	1	0
From Strahan	4	4	0			
To Frank for Wages				2	10	0
To White				0	5	0
For Coals					3	9
Oct 5. From Strahan	20	0	0			
Coach To Francis				2	2	0
To Desmoulins				1	1	0
4 weeks To White				1	11	6
Strahans				0	10	0
&c				5	4	6
Oct 8 in Pocket Gold				13	13	0
Silver				0	16	6
				19	14	0

Diary, September 1782; written in an old memorandum book

SAT. I came to Streatham with Burney. A little Dutch. I dined
at Streatham. Oct. 5 From Strahan 20–0–0.

6 weeks To Francis	2– 2–0
To Desmoulins	1– 1–0
4 weeks To White	1–11–6
Stockens &c	0–10–0
	5– 4–6
Oct. 8 in Pocket Gold	13–13–0
Silver	0–16–6
	19–14–0

SUN. I went to Church at Streatham. Templo valedixi cum
osculo. My Breath was so short that I rested several times in
going. I came home more easily.

OCT. 6, DIE DOMINICA, 1782. Pransus sum Streathamiae
agninum crus coctum cum herbis (spinach) comminutis, far-
cimen farinaceum cum uvis passis, lumbos bovillos, et pullum
gallinae Turcicae; et post carnes missas, ficus, uvas, non admodum maturas, ita voluit anni intemperies, cum malis Per-

---

On Sunday Johnson "bade the church farewell with a kiss," an
indication of his feelings on leaving Streatham for the last time.
His saying that he "came home" more easily than he went is also
indicative, since "home" in this case is Mrs. Thrale's house.

To his moving prayer on this day, Johnson added his prayer
commending Thrale to divine mercy, in words similar to those
of his prayer on 22 June 1781.

On the same day, in a manuscript now lost, Johnson recorded
his feelings, and the menu for dinner (Croker, v.444): "I dined
at Streatham on a roast leg of lamb with spinach chopped fine,
the stuffing of flour with raisins, a sirloin of beef, and a turkey
poult; and after the first course figs, grapes not very ripe owing
to the bad season, with peaches—hard ones. I took my place in

sicis, iis tamen duris. Non laetus accubui, cibum modicè sumpsi, ne intemperantiâ ad extremum peccaretur. Si recte memini, in mentem venerunt epulae in exequiis Hadoni celebratae. Streathamiam quando revisam?

OCTOBER 6. 1782. Almighty God, Father of all mercy, help me by thy Grace that I may with humble and sincere thankfulness remember the comforts and conveniences which I have enjoyed at this place and that I may resign them with holy submission, equally trusting in thy protection when Thou givest and when Thou takest away. Have mercy upon me, O Lord, have mercy upon me.

To thy fatherly protection, O Lord, I commend this family. Bless, guide, and defend them. That they may so pass through this world as finally to[5] enjoy in thy presence everlasting happiness for Jesus Christs sake. Amen.

O Lord so far as &c—Thrale.

OCT. 7. I was called early. I packed up my bundles, and used the foregoing prayer with my morning devotions somewhat, I think, enlarged. Being earlier than the family I read St

5. ⟨live⟩

_____

no joyful mood, and dined moderately that I might not at the last fall into the sin of intemperance. If I am not mistaken, the banquet at the funeral of Hadon came into my mind. When shall I see Streatham again?" (trans. Hill).

Walter Haddon, who revised the Latin translation of the *Book of Common Prayer* for the use of the universities, died in 1571. We have found no reference to his funeral or any banquet. Johnson refers to him and Ascham in his *Milton* as "the pride of Elizabeth's reign."

On Monday morning Johnson did his packing (on the return trip he compliments himself on his secure packages), and then read in the library.

Some passages he read in St. Paul's farewell to the elders of

Pauls farewel in the Acts, and then read fortuitously in the Gospels, which was[6] my parting use of the library.

M. 7. I came to Brighthelmston. A little Dutch. My Breath was extremely difficult. I took Tinct. Ip. but it did not make me vomit, but yet, I think relaxed. My night better than the last. I rested four times between the Ship tavern and the house.

TU. Only broath and fish. I took a strong Καθ of salts and sen[n]a. Fuit X cop[iosus] then Καθ, 1 before dinner, 2 after dinner mod. 3 copiosiss. Sleepy, a good night. Dr Pepys told me that I did right.

W. A little Dutch. Only Broath and Fish. My Breath seems easier. Καθ. Purgatio copiosa. Not sleepy, little sleep.

6. ∧was∧

Ephesus, Johnson might have felt fitting to his departure from Streatham: "Ye know, from the first day that I came into Asia, after what manner I have been with you at all seasons, serving the Lord with all humility of mind, and with many tears. . . . I have coveted no man's silver, or gold, or apparel. Yea, ye your-selves know, that these hands have ministered unto my necessi-ties, and to them that were with me. I have shewed you all things, how that so labouring ye ought to support the weak, and to re-member the words of the Lord Jesus, how he said, It is more blessed to give than to receive" (Acts xx).

A little later Johnson set off with the Thrales for Brighton, and arrived the same day.

Next day, Johnson ate lightly, and purged heavily, with satis-factory results. He was confirmed in his treatment by Sir Lucas Pepys, M.D., a friend of Mrs. Thrale. She had taken Johnson to him earlier in the year. In the following March, Boswell heard Pepys tell Johnson, "If you were *tractable*, Sir, I should prescribe for you."

TH. Broath and Fish. A new cold. Spiritus expeditior. Not sleepy. Chapellain's letters. My eyes grew weary. Καθ. Purgatio copiosissima fuit. Somni parum. Tussis molesta. I wrote to Mr George Strahan—to make peace between him and his Father.

F. My cold is better. Broath and fish, alway[s] tart. No Καθ. Non bene dormivi. Though I do not sleep well in bed, yet I lie tolerably easy, and am not sleepy in the day.

SAT. Broath, Fish, tart, lettuce. Coals from Mr Barclay. Breath very easy. Καθ copiosissime. Tussis molesta est. Placidissime dormivi.

SUN. At church, m. Breath little obstructed. Kempis. Tussis nocte molesta.

On Wednesday, another cathartic, and good results.

On Thursday, his breathing was still easier, and he read the *Mélanges* of Jean Chapelain, dictator of French literary taste until the appearance of his execrable epic *La Pucelle* in 1656. Another cathartic and purge, but he had not had enough sleep, and his cough was troublesome.

On the same day he wrote to George Strahan (809), whose father was objecting to his expenses, urging him to settle the dispute at once, since "All quarrels grow more complicated by time, and as they grow more complicated, grow harder to be adjusted."

On Friday, he had again not slept well.

On Saturday Barclay, the brewer, sent coals, no doubt from the brewery stock. In May Johnson had asked Perkins to do so, unwilling to pay the high price on the open market (*Letters* 779.4). On the same day, though his breathing was easy, his cough troubled him. He slept very calmly.

On Sunday, Johnson attended church in the morning and later continued reading Thomas a Kempis. He found his cough troublesome at night.

M. 14. A little Dutch. Fish and tart. I walked out. Mr and Mrs Shelley. Not Miss. Night quiet. At the Ball. Selwyn, Sheward, Tidey, Metcalf, Pollard, Delap, Wade, Mrs Barwel, Whitbread.

To Thomas	0– 5–0
To Bowen	0– 5–0
Poor man	0– 0–6
Ball	0– 3–0
	0–13–6

On 14 October Johnson saw Mr. and Mrs. Shelley, probably the son and daughter-in-law of Sir John Shelley of Michelgrove, Sussex, a friend of the Thrales. Fanny Burney mentions a Mr. H. Shelley in company with the Thrales in December (*Diary*, ii.149). "Miss" is Queeney, who had been studying the classics with Johnson (*Thraliana*, p. 521). The frequent notes about her in the next weeks evidently refer to such lessons, one of which she omitted on this day. Since Johnson and the Thrales were living in the same household, these notes cannot refer to her mere presence or absence.

At the ball were Charles Selwin, a banker; William Seward, author of *Anecdotes of Some Distinguished Persons*, later a member of the Essex Head Club; Tidey (or Tidy), whom Fanny Burney met at the Thrales' in Brighton in 1779 and described as appearing "grave, reserved, quiet," but being in fact "sarcastic, observing, and ridiculing" (*Diary*, i.299); Philip Metcalfe, M.P., a wealthy malt-distiller; Pollard, unidentified; John Delap, D.D., poet and dramatist; William Wade, master of ceremonies at Brighton, said by Frederick Harrison to have stopped a violent dispute between Johnson and Reverend Henry Mitchell; Mrs. Barwell, perhaps the wife of a patron of Baretti; and Samuel Whitbread, the brewer.

Johnson's expenditures show that he patronized both booksellers of Brighton equally: R. Thomas, the fashionable one, and

TU. I Rose late. Pollard. Hurricane. Miss. Sheward. A little
Dutch. Broath, fish, κτλ. Καθ. satis. Delap. Sheward. D. b.

W. Carnium usus. Mr Metcalf's chaise I think. Alvus stricta.
D. b. Linen to wash: Shirts 4. Stocks 3. Handkercheif 1. Returned.

TH. A little Dutch. Dined at Whitbreads. M. Delap. Metcalf.
Alvus strictior. Pepys. Seward. The deaf man. D. b. Papers 14
[?s.]

FR. A little Dutch. Broath, fish. M. Delap. Metcalf's chaise.[7]
The Bucket. To Pepys. M. d., alvus clausa, respiratio facilis.
I wrote to George Strahan.

7. ⟨alvus clau⟩

J. Bowen, his rival, who had three shares in publishing the *Lives
of the Poets*.

Next day, for once, Johnson had an excuse for his late rising,
having attended the ball. He had slept well, had his usual broth,
fish, etc., and saw several visitors in spite of the hurricane.

On Wednesday Johnson had meat for the first time in several
days, but found his stomach constricted. "Mr. Metcalf's chaise I
think" suggests that this entry was written several days after the
event. Metcalfe had offered his carriage to Johnson a fortnight
before, but Johnson had "no desire of using Mr. Metcalfe's carriage, except when he can have the pleasure of Mr. Metcalfe's
company" (*Letters* 806.1).

On the same day, Johnson listed his laundry, and later added
"returned."

Thursday Johnson saw Delap and Metcalfe in the morning,
dined with Whitbread, and found his stomach rather constricted.

On Friday Johnson apparently used Metcalfe's chaise to go
to Pepys. "The Bucket" is explained in a letter a few days later:
"We have a deep Well, when I came I suffered so much in letting

SAT. A little Dutch. Rousseau. Broath, fish. Seward. Pollard. Whitbread. Καθ. Purg[amen]. durum 1, purg. molle 5. Tussis molesta. Spiritus liber. I wrote to Lowe about his money but I know not when.

SUN. M. at Church. Carnibus vescebar. Selwin. X οὐ. Burkitt. At Dr Pepys. Kempis. B. d.

M. 2 1. Hamilton. Metcalfe. Pr. parcum. Tydey. A little Dutch. Miss. X. At night, Rousseau. Parum d. Metcalf's man 0–1–0. Shirts 4. Stocks 3. Hand. 1. Returned.

---

down the bucket, that I never tried to pull it up. But I have done both to day with little trouble. By such experiments I perceive my own advances" (811.2). But he found today that his stomach was stopped up, though his respiration was easy. The letter he wrote to George Strahan is lost.

On Saturday Johnson was reading Rousseau, whom he had called "a very bad man" in 1766 (*Life*, II.12). Perhaps the book was Rousseau's *Confessions*, the first part of which had appeared this year, though not yet in English. At any rate, Johnson was interested enough to continue for ten days, probably reinforcing his earlier opinion.

On the same day, after a cathartic, he noted that his stools varied from hard to soft, that his cough was annoying, but that his breathing was free.

His comment about writing Lowe is entered opposite this date, but probably as much as a week later, since he wrote Lowe on 22 October congratulating him on receiving the first instalment of his pension from Lord Southwell (811), and is not likely to have written twice in so short an interval on the same subject.

On Sunday, after morning service, Johnson had meat again, but had no evacuation. Later he read in Reverend William Burkitt's *Expository Notes, with Practical Observations on the New Testament*, which he did again on the next Sunday, and once more in November.

TU. D. j. I began to rise. Ten pages of Answer. A little Dutch. Miss. To Lowe, pension paid him. Dine with Metcalf. X duriss. Muyt. Atkinson. Musgrave.

w. I rose early. Ten pages of answer. My eye inflamed. Pr. parcum. Rousseau. A little Dutch. Καθ copiosum. M. d. Miss.

TH. I rose late. Pr. parcum. 8 pages of answer. Miss. A little Dutch. X. Rousseau. Letters to Compton, to Strahan. I wound

---

Next day he saw Hamilton, presumably his old friend, now Chancellor of the Exchequer in Ireland. A light lunch that day, but he slept too little, unlike most of the past week. And he gave Metcalfe's man, probably the coachman, a shilling.

On Tuesday, "God helping," he began to rise more early. The "Answer" which Johnson was writing was probably a reply to Lady Salusbury's suit against Mrs. Thrale for the recovery of a loan—for the use of Mrs. Thrale's solicitors. Johnson had examined all the documents in the case and annotated them, but this "Answer" is now lost. See McAdam, *Dr. Johnson and the English Law*, 1951, p. 177.

During the day he saw Atkinson, probably Richard Atkinson, goldsmith, of London, who ran unsuccessfully for Parliament in 1784, became alderman in the same year, and died in 1785. "Muyt" (a Dutchman?) is unidentified. Richard Musgrave, whom Johnson also saw, was created first Baronet in this year. Fanny Burney described him as "an Irish gentleman of fortune, and a member of the Irish Parliament. . . . His manners are impetuous and abrupt; his language is high-flown and hyperbolical; his sentiments are romantic and tender; his heart is warm and generous; his head hot and wrong!" (*Diary*, II.27).

And the condition of Johnson's bowels was still of concern to him.

On Thursday Johnson wrote a letter to Compton (811.1) advising him about a book he was thinking of writing, and another to Strahan about his health, already quoted (811.2).

Bucket easily. Swinnerton. At night company. Pepysii cum conjugibus. L. Burgoyn. Sponsione facta de statura Selvinij et Pepysij perdidi 0–4–6.

FR. Prandium parcum. Rousseau (puto). Jal[ap] cum Cal-[omel] frustra. Ipec. M. d.

SAT. Rousseau. Pr. parum. Miss. A little Dutch. F. Burney came. Καθ copiose.

SUN. M. at Church. To the sea. At church I heard nothing. Pr. lautum. A little Dutch. Burkitt. Cotton and Swinnerton. At home alone. B. d. Miss. To an old Sailor 0–1–0.

M. 28. Sx. 9. Rousseau. I read in the remarks on Th's Suit. No help. Little comfort. Pr. lautum. X οὐ. Delap. Selwin. No

---

In the evening the Pepyses and their wives called. Johnson disliked the doctor's brother, Sir William Weller Pepys. Having made a bet on the height of Selwin and Pepys—is this Johnson's only known bet?—Johnson lost 4s. 6d. But he does not tell us which was the taller or who won. Another caller was Lady Burgoyne, wife of Lieutenant General Sir John Burgoyne, Bart., of Sutton Park.

On Friday Johnson thinks he read Rousseau, again showing that he is not writing on that day. He dosed himself thoroughly, with jalap and calomel, both cathartics, which had no effect, and then with ipecac. It is no wonder that he did not sleep well.

On Saturday Fanny Burney came, always welcome to Johnson.

On Sunday Johnson had a "splendid luncheon," saw Harry Cotton, Mrs. Thrale's cousin, and his friend Swinnerton, "the young beaux," and then was alone.

On 28 October he rose at nine, and then read in the remarks on "Th's Suit," which may be Thrale's suit, more business connected with the Salusbury lawsuit.

He then wrote to John Nichols about the forthcoming revision of the *Lives of the Poets* (812), and to Miss Williams. Her letter

dancing—at the Ball. A little Dutch. Nicol. Williams. Ball 0–3–0. Same puto 0–1–6.

TU. A little Dutch. Pr. mediocre. Letter from Williams. Miss. X bene. Hatsel. Pepys. Cox. L. Shelley &c. D. opt[ime]. Shirts 4 Stocks 2 Handk. 1.

w. A little Dutch. Felt ill. Metcalfe. Pr. med. K. tantum semel Καθ. Rose not late. T. Vesp. Suet. B. d. I have now for some time lain in Bed with very little disturbance, sometimes without sleep, but with no spasms. I commonly sit up once in the night.

TH. A little Dutch. Ride with Metcalfe. Mrs to Lewis. Pr. lautum. Galba in Suet. Mr Hamilton 5 p m. Metcalfe's chaise.

––––––––––––

is lost. Again he "thinks" he spent 1s. 6d. at the ball in addition to the subscription.

On Tuesday he had a letter from Miss Williams, probably written by Compton, as Johnson had asked in his last letter. "Hatsel," who called, was probably John Hatsell, chief clerk to the House of Commons, author of a *Collection of Cases of Privilege of Parliament*, 1778. Fanny Burney mentions Mr. and Mrs. Hatsell in her *Diary*, but does not identify them. She does, however, report a quarrel this day: "Mr. Pepys . . . joined Dr. Johnson, with whom he entered into an argument upon some lines of Gray, and upon Pope's definition of wit, in which he was so roughly confuted, and so severely ridiculed, that he . . . suddenly turned from him, and, wishing Mrs. Thrale good-night, very abruptly withdrew" (*Diary*, II.107).

"Cox" is Peter Coxe again. Lady Shelley was the second wife of Sir John.

Again he slept very well.

On Wednesday Johnson read Suetonius's life of Vespasian.

On Thursday Mrs. Thrale went to Lewes, in Sussex, and John-

Sir Lyndsay. Pepys. Hatsel. Miss Monkton. B. d. &c. Metcalfe's Man 0–1–0.

FR. NOV. 1. I rose not late. A little Dutch. Prandium lautum. Very sleepy. X. Mr Hamilton. Lees. Miss. Cotton, Swinnerton. D. med. My cough has left me, I know not how. It went, I suppose gradually away.

SAT. I rose not late. Dutch; sleepy. Prand. tenue. I wrote for Mistress. Pepys. Coxe. A storm. Καθ. M. d. Erdswick wet and dried. I am yet able to walk but a very little way without resting.

SUN. Sx. 9 puto. At Church but could not hear. Mrs and Burney staid away. X. Καθ. 2 p. m. op. gr. 2. Nox placida.

---

son stayed in Brighton. Fanny Burney says of this week that Johnson was "almost constantly omitted" in invitations, "either from too much respect or too much fear. I am sorry for it, as he hates being alone" (*Diary*, II.113). So he reread Suetonius's *Galba*, which he had read in 1777. Sir Lyndsay is unidentified. Another caller was the Honourable Mary Monckton, later Countess of Cork, who was in Brighton with her mother. She gave a party, amusingly described by Fanny Burney.

On 1 November, among the callers were the Lees, perhaps John Lee, lawyer and politician, who would have been known to Hamilton, and his wife.

On Saturday, Johnson had a light lunch, and wrote something for Mrs. Thrale, probably in connexion with the Salusbury case. During the storm, Johnson had evidently left Erdeswicke's *Staffordshire*, which he had been reading in September, in an exposed place, where it got wet. He later dried it.

On Sunday, having risen about nine (he thinks), Johnson went to church without Mrs. Thrale and Fanny Burney. Later he took two grains of opium, which, contrary to its usual effect on him, did not prevent a quiet night.

Next day he did not rise early. He saw George Townshend,

M. 4. Sx non sero. At Swinnerton's. De Ferrars. Prandium lautum. Alvus clausa. Mrs Scot, Coxe. Very sleepy. Arabian nights.

TU. Sx non sero. Prandium puto mediocre. Miss. D. b.

W. A little Dutch. Prandium med. Miss. Not sleep[y]. D. b.

TH. Sx non sero. Prand. lautum. A little Dutch. Ride with Metcalf. Not sleepy. Lett. to Ashburton, Perk[ins]. Dined with Hamilton. Lett. to Compton. Visited Monkton.

FR. With Mr Metcalfe to Arundel, and Chichester. My breath would not carry me to the old castle. Arundel gallery. Chichester Cathedral beautiful, the quire elegant, pews in body. Arundel 0–1–0, Chichester 0–2–0.

Lord De Ferrers, and later Mrs. Scot, Henry Thrale's sister. Later he read the *Arabian Nights*, his only reference to the work.

On Thursday, after riding again with Metcalfe, he wrote to John Dunning, Baron Ashburton, a famous lawyer and a member of the Club, no doubt about the Salusbury case, as a later letter (817.1) shows. A still later letter (817.4) tells of a fire in Ashburton's chambers, so that it is possible that Johnson's "Answer" was destroyed there. An unpublished letter to Compton about a book he was writing is in the Hyde collection. That to Perkins is still at the brewery. "Monkton" is Miss Monckton again.

On Friday Johnson set off with Metcalfe for a tour of western Sussex, stopping first at Arundel Castle, one of the seats of the Duke of Norfolk. By the old castle, Johnson probably means the twelfth-century keep; the rest of the castle was being restored, having been destroyed during the Civil War. He at least saw the gallery, but the climb into the keep was out of the question.

They then proceeded to Chichester, where Johnson admired the early Norman cathedral, and especially the choir, probably the retro-choir, starred by the guidebooks as "a charming example of the final transition from the massive Norman to the

SAT. To Cowdrey, and Petworth, through Midhurst. Petworth furniture magnificent. Cowdrey the pictures thought not genuine. The Chappel. Chappel at Petworth gloomy. Puto Cowdrey 0–2–0, Petworth 0–2–0.

SUN. Not at church. Home through Bramber and Steyning and Storrington. At home well received. At Cowdrey one of the galleries made lodging rooms.

M. 11. Dutch. Miss. Prand. modicum. Καθ. Did the French Skating. My Health seems much restored. I sleep well and have my mind tolerably calm. My breath is much mended.

---

lighter Gothic style" (Muirhead). By "pews in body" Johnson perhaps means that the nave was furnished with pews instead of the chairs common in cathedrals.

The men probably stayed at Chichester overnight, and in the morning went north to Midhurst and Cowdray House nearby, described by Walpole as "that loveliest and perfectest of all ancient mansions" (Letters, ed. Toynbee, xv.204). It was the property of Viscount Montagu, and destroyed by fire in 1793; its ruin is still impressive. The opinion that its pictures were not genuine perhaps comes from Reynolds, with whom Metcalfe had travelled in Flanders and Holland in 1781, but it may have been Metcalfe's own, since he was a member of the Society of Dilettanti.

Some time during the day Johnson wrote Mrs. Thrale (812.1) that Metcalfe had found so much to see that they would not reach Brighton that night. Then they went on to Petworth House, formerly belonging to the Percys but now the seat of the Earl of Egremont, where Johnson admired the furniture (perhaps he means the famous carving by Grinling Gibbons), but not the chapel, though Walpole thought it "grand and proper" (Letters, II.407).

On Sunday they drove southeast, through Storrington, Steyning, and Bramber to Brighton, where Mrs. Thrale made Johnson feel welcome.

TU. Dutch. Prandium modicum, alvus clausa. At Lord De Ferrars's. In the morning at Dr Delap's. D. med.

W. Dutch. Miss. Pr. lautum. Selwyn.[8] Kαθ. L. Ashburton. Reynolds palsy.

TH. Dutch. Pr. puto med. Wrote to Strahan and Reynolds.

FR. Dutch. Pr. lautum. Miss. I walked out with little trouble. Mrs At Sir J. Shelleys. D. b.   A Girl 0–0–6, Box 0–1–0.

SAT. Dutch. Prandium med. Selwyn. Kαθ with cal. D. b. Lady de Ferrars and her sisters.

SUN. At church, but have seldom if ever heard in this visit. De Salis. Kαθ. The pew. Kαθ ubertim. D. b. Mrs at Shelleys. Burkit a little.

8. MS: Selwy⟨a⟩n

On Monday Johnson did the translation of Roy's lines on skating, which Mrs. Thrale had begged from him (*Poems*, p. 202):

> O'er ice the rapid skaiter flies,
>   With sport above and death below;
> Where mischief lurks in gay disguise,
>   Thus lightly touch and quickly go.

He soon found out that Mrs. Thrale had begged translations from the Pepys brothers as well, and thinking their versions superior, he made another. Mrs. Thrale entered both versions in *Thraliana* under 4 November.

On Wednesday Johnson apparently had a letter from Ashburton telling him about an attack of palsy which Reynolds, a close friend of Ashburton's, had suffered, and on Thursday Johnson wrote Reynolds (813) that he had heard of it only the day before, and heard of his recovery also.

The letter to Strahan (814) mentions that Brighton is almost deserted, and wonders why his party stays so long.

M. 18. Dutch. Miss. Pransus sum pisces. I wind up the Bucket with little trouble. I lent Miss Vossius. B. d.

TU. Dutch. Pransus sum pisces. Compegi sarcinas non intutas. Mistress, sorrowful. We are now going away. D. med. Lord have mercy upon me. Washer 0–7–7, Barber 1–1–0, Gown 1–1–0.

W. 20. Dutch on the road. Fall of horses. Pr. lautum. Alvus strictior. D. med. Mrs Southwel dead. Mrs Gardiner ill. D. med.

On Saturday Johnson saw Lady De Ferrers, née Charlotte Ellerker, and her two unmarried sisters, all friends of Fanny Burney.

On Sunday Johnson saw Jerome, Count de Salis, whose mother was a daughter of the first Viscount Fane (*The Diary of John Baker*, ed. Yorke, 1931, p. 404). While Mrs. Thrale was at the Shelleys', Johnson read in Burkitt again.

On 18 November he lunched on fish, again found that he could manage the bucket easily, and lent Queeney one of Vossius's works, perhaps that on baptism, which he had read on Easter 1778.

On Tuesday, getting ready to return to London, he "put together not insecure packages," as he had done for the outward journey six weeks earlier. Mrs. Thrale was sorrowful because she had just told Queeney and Fanny Burney of her intention to marry Piozzi. She had begged her cold daughter to give her consent, but Queeney had been unsympathetic. Fanny "cried herself half blind" (*Thraliana*, p. 550). Johnson had not been informed.

And on Wednesday they left, Mrs. Thrale and her three daughters, Johnson, and Fanny Burney, Johnson reading Dutch on the way. The fall of the horses was evidently not serious, and they made the fifty-four miles to London without other trouble.

When Johnson reached home he found that Mrs. Southwell was dead, whether Lucy or her sister is not known. And Mrs. Gardiner of Snow Hill was ill, though she recovered.

TH. Dutch. Καθ. Mr Compton to dinner. Box and money. I gave Desm[oulin]s the gown. Dr Talbots letter. Lord Spensers letter. Sir A. Lever's letter. I gave Mrs Desmoulins who was sick, 1–1–0. Fund received from Mr Strahan for taxes &c. 3–3–0 of which remains 8–3½.

FR. To Argyle Street. Dutch. Prandium lautum. Mr Evans. Sastres. D. med. To Mrs White for house 0–14–5.

SAT. Dutch. Pr. pisc. Miss. No company. I came home. Corpus grave. Spiritus operosim agitur. To Mrs W. for Frank 1–1–0. Jacob 0–1–0.

M. 25. Tom Rose's Scales I returned.

TU. At Argyle St.

WEDNESDAY. Dined at home, I think. To Mr Compton 2–2–0.

TH. Καθ. Miss, I think.

On Thursday Johnson apparently received letters from Dr. Thomas Talbot, whom he had helped in promoting the Hereford Infirmary; from Earl Spencer, with whom Johnson had dined in 1781 (*Life*, IV.88 n.), whose son was a member of the Club; and from Sir Ashton Lever, of Alkerington, near Manchester, owner of a museum of natural history which Johnson thought should be purchased by the nation (*Life*, IV.335). No correspondence with any of these men is known.

On Friday Johnson went to Argyle Street, where Mrs. Thrale had rented a house for the winter, and found there Reverend James Evans, rector of St. Olave's, Southwark, a frequent guest at the Thrales' table, and Sastres, the Italian master.

On Saturday he had fish for lunch, and later came home, tipping Jacob, the coachman, as usual. He felt that his body was heavy and his breathing difficult.

FR. Καθ copiosa.

SAT. Home. Little dinner. Opium. Plate sold. Nox insomnis.

SUN. DEC. 1. Not at church. Dined at Strahan's. Greek. Dr Douglass. Mr Compton. Mrs Williams. To Mr Compton 1–1–0.

M. 2. Jejunium. Reynolds. Mr Pearson. Dutch. At Mr Perkins's. I brought away books. Macquin. D. opt. Coach 0–3–0.

TU. Metcalfe. To Argyle Str. To White for board wages, full 1–0–0. For house 13–0.

W. I came home.

On 25 November Johnson returned Tom Rose's scales, which he had probably been using for one of his experiments. A similar entry occurs in the next August. Tom is unidentified, unless he is the elder son of Dr. Rose of Chiswick, an old friend.

On 30 November Johnson's entry "plate sold" refers to selling Mrs. Thrale's plate, which she valued at £1400, to raise money to settle the Salusbury claim (*Thraliana*, p. 551). In a letter of the same day he urges Mrs. Thrale, who is clearly unhappy about the sale, "what is past is past. You have only turned uncoined silver into silver coined."

On Sunday Johnson saw John Douglas, D.D., a member of the Club and later Bishop of Salisbury, an old friend.

On Monday, fasting, he saw Reynolds and Reverend John Pearson, Perpetual Curate of St. Michael's, Lichfield, to whom Lucy Porter left her estate. Johnson once told Mrs. Thrale that when Pearson contradicted Lucy, she said: "Why, Mr. Pearson, you are just like Dr. Johnson, I think: I do not mean that you are a man of the greatest capacity in all the world like Dr. Johnson, but that you contradict one every word one speaks, just like him" (*Anecdotes*, p. 223).

On the same day Johnson visited Perkins and brought home books, apparently some that had been left at Streatham, or in

TH. At Reynolds's. Pr. lautum. Dutch. At Mrs Birons, Hunt-
ers. Coach 0–2–0.

FR. Pr. lautum. Miss. Dutch. Came home. Miss Burney. Swinnerton. Selwyn. D. m. Jacob 0–1–0.

SAT. With L. Ashburton. Καθ. At Mr Robsons. Rose early. I
walked not uneasily.* Sleepy. D. m. Mr Coddington 0–2–0.
Mrs Pelle 0–4–0. *I wrote to Mr Mrs Boswel, and Dr Taylor.

SUN. Not at church. A Dutch Chapter. Pr. lautum. Mr Crompton. At Monkton's. Metcalf. D. m. Pig 0–1–0. [From] Mr
Strahan 5–5–0.

Perkins's care, when Johnson went to Brighton. He seems to have
seen Mackinnon, the young Scot, at Perkins's, since on the following day he wrote to Perkins (814.2) asking him to get four volumes
Mackinnon had borrowed.

On Thursday, after a good lunch at Reynolds's, Johnson went
to Mrs. Byron's, where he apparently saw the Hunter brothers,
John and William, the doctors.

On Saturday he spent some time with Ashburton, doubtless in
connection with the Salusbury case, and then went to see Bateman
Robson, Mrs. Thrale's attorney, clearly on the same matter. Later
he gave the unknown Coddington 2s., as he had done in August.
His letter to Mrs. Boswell (804) declined an invitation to Auchinleck, and that to Boswell (815) gave an account of his health and
also urged Boswell to set his affairs in order. That to Taylor
(815.1) is largely devoted to an attempt to settle a legal struggle
between two young cousins, the Collier sisters, and their step-
father. And on the same day, though he does not mention it here,
he wrote another letter, trying to get the impecunious Collet a job
as toll-gatherer. It was a full day devoted to the troubles of his
friends.

On Sunday "Crompton" is probably a slip for Compton. Later
in the day he went to Miss Monckton's.

On 9 December Johnson wrote to Taylor (816) urging him

M. 9. Rose late. Steevens, Dr Bailey. Walker. Pr. med. I wrote to Taylor, and to Mrs Thrale. Querulous. M. d. To Miss Desmoulin 10–6. Lent to Collet 10–6. To Mrs Pelle 4–0.

TU. I rose late. Strahan. At Club. Pr. lautum. Hussey. Club numerous. Soft ans. from Thrale. Lort proposed. Academy Speech. To House 10–6. Poor Woman 1–0.

W. Mrs Pelle 4–0. From this time to the end of the year I made no regular registry, My life being unsettled between Argyle Street, and Bolt court, my body much disordered, and opium frequently taken. I did not wholly neglect Dutch. For some time I have lived much at home.

---

to take care of his health, and querulously to Mrs. Thrale, a letter now lost. Of his visitors, "Bailey" is probably Dr. Baillie, joint proprietor with Cruikshank of Hunter's Anatomical School after Hunter's death in 1783. John Walker, a lexicographer, dedicated to Johnson his *Elements of Elocution*, 1781, and his *Rhetorical Grammar*, 1785. Fanny Burney thought him "vulgar in conversation," though "modest in science" (*Diary*, II.181).

On Tuesday Johnson saw Hussey, probably the Reverend John Hussey, an old friend, who had gone to Aleppo in 1778 as chaplain to the English Factory there. Johnson also knew Dr. Thomas Hussey, but less well, and he would probably have distinguished him by his title or first name if he had seen him.

The "soft answer" which Johnson received from Mrs. Thrale is not known, but dealt with the Salusbury case, as Johnson's reply shows (817.1). Michael Lort, D.D., antiquary, and at this time a prebendary of St. Paul's, was proposed for the Club, but rejected a week later, when Johnson was absent.

The same day Johnson heard Reynolds deliver his twelfth "Discourse to the Students of the Royal Academy on the Distribution of the Prizes," and wrote Mrs. Thrale, "The king is not heard with more attention."

Johnson's statement that in the last three weeks of December

SAT. [From] Mr Strahan 5–5–0 I think.

TU. DEC. 17. Missed Club. Lort rejected.

W. Mrs Pelle 2–6.

TH. To Mrs Everet sometime 0–5–0.

SAT. [From] Mr Strahan 5–5–0 I think.

SUN. Not at Church.

W. 25. At church. Dined with Hoole. Very ill. To Desmoulines 1–1–0.

TH. To Mrs Thrales. This night, I think I translated part of Boetius into Greek but it was a very tedious night. To Frank, wages 2–10–0.

FR. [Received and paid] Two guineas due to the books 2–2–0.

------

his life was unsettled and his body disordered does not indicate what his letters show, that he continued working with Mrs. Thrale's lawyers on the Salusbury case, and tried again to reconcile George Strahan and his father.

On 19 December he gave a crown to Mrs. Everet, perhaps the same "Everet" to whom he gave a like amount on 25 September. In the intervening week he had stayed largely at home, not because Mrs. Thrale did not invite him to Argyle Street, but because his health was worse.

On Christmas Day he dined with Hoole and saw several friends, but in the afternoon, as he wrote Mrs. Thrale next day, he was "seized with a fit of convulsive breathlessness such as I think you have never seen" (819.1). Mrs. Thrale seems to have sent her carriage for him at once when she got this letter, since the same day he records going to her house. If her love for Piozzi was growing, her compassion for Johnson had not lessened.

The same night Johnson translated part of Boethius's *Con-*

SUN. Not at Church. Pr. Davies and his Wife. Lowe, Compton, Allen, Hoole. Wyndham, Hussey. Compton. Miss Thrale. &c.

M. Mrs. Thrale. A tolerable night without opium. Borrowed of Mrs Williams one Guinea for Angel before, and one which I gave him tonight. He goes this night. [Received and paid] 2–2–0.

TU. 31. Zaftanie. To Mr Wilson. Clithero and to Dr Taylor.

---

solations of Philosophy from Latin into Greek, apparently to avoid the tedium of sleeplessness, as he was translating part of the *Greek Anthology* into Latin for the same reason. Perhaps he was reminded that he had helped Mrs. Thrale translate part of Boethius into English in the first year of their acquaintance.

On Saturday Johnson was feeling much worse, and wrote Mrs. Thrale (819.2) that he was going home (perhaps she was out), but would return when he was better.

On Sunday Johnson saw many of his old friends; apparently he was better.

On Monday Johnson wrote Mrs. Thrale about attending a meeting of the executors (819.3), and gave "Angel" a guinea. This was perhaps "little George Angel," referred to by Mrs. Thrale in 1781 (*Letters* 741a). Johnson had asked that he be admitted to the grammar school of Christ's Hospital in 1778 (574.2), saying that he had once known George's grandfather, but that the boy "has hardly any friend left, but a Lady who happened to be his Godmother." Nothing else is known of him.

On Tuesday Johnson sat presumably for the portrait painter Johann Zoffany. The *Morning Herald* for 6 January 1783 said that Johnson had twice sat for the portrait, and such a picture is mentioned by Boswell, but it is not now known (*Life*, IV.421 n., 454).

On the same day Johnson wrote to Reverend Thomas Wilson of Clitheroe, Lancashire, acknowledging the dedication of Wil-

AT THE TABLE.

Almighty God, by whose Mercy I am now permitted to commemorate my Redemption by our Lord Jesus Christ; grant that this awefull Remembrance may strengthen my Faith, enliven my Hope, and encrease my Charity, that I may trust in Thee with my whole Heart, and do good according to my power. Grant me the help of thy holy Spirit, that I may do thy will with Diligence, and suffer it with humble Patience; so that when Thou shalt call me to Judgment, I may obtain Forgiveness, and Acceptance for the sake of Jesus Christ our Lord and Saviour. Amen.

AT DEPARTURE, OR AT HOME.

Grant, I beseech Thee, merciful Lord, that the Designs of a new and better Life, which by thy Grace I have now formed, may not pass away without effect. Incite, and enable me by thy Holy Spirit to improve the time which Thou shalt grant me; to avoid all evil Thoughts, Words, and Actions, and to do all the Duties which thou shalt set before me. Hear my Prayer, O Lord, for the sake of Jesus Christ. Amen.

These prayers I wrote for Mrs Lucy Porter in the latter end of the year 1782, and transcribed them Oct. 9. —84.

1783

APRIL 5th. I took leave of Mrs. Thrale. I was much moved. I had some expostulations with her. She said that she was

---

son's *Archaeological Dictionary*, just published, and to Taylor again about the Collier girls (820, 821).

The two prayers written for Lucy "at the latter end of 1782" are placed here for lack of a better date.

In the first months of 1783 Johnson's ill health continued, but

likewise affected. I commended the Thrales with great good will to God; may my petitions have been heard!

JUNE 16. I went to bed, and, as I conceive, about 3 in the morning, I had a stroke of the palsy.

17. I sent for Dr. Heberden and Dr. Brocklesby. God bless them.

25. Dr. Heberden took leave.

---

he busied himself with the Salusbury claim, which was finally settled in early spring, enabling Mrs. Thrale to move to Bath. Boswell had come to London in March, the final revision of the *Lives* was published, and Johnson, at the request of Burke and Reynolds, looked over the manuscript of an almost unknown poet, George Crabbe, made a few changes, and recommended *The Village* for publication.

The brief entry for 5 April, printed by Hawkins from a lost diary, records Johnson's parting with Mrs. Thrale. Johnson's ill health and the fact that Mrs. Thrale was going to Bath for an extended stay made the parting a serious one. Unless they saw each other in May (*Letters* 963), this was their last meeting. Johnson's expostulations probably concerned Piozzi, whose name had been coupled with Mrs. Thrale's in the newspapers, but she had not yet told Johnson of her determination to marry.

For the next few months Johnson remained in London, writing letters on behalf of Lowe, Compton, Mrs. Desmoulins's son, and others, dining out, missing Mrs. Thrale. Early in June his good friend Dr. Lawrence died, and on the sixteenth he suffered a stroke which temporarily deprived him of speech. Johnson's brief notes on the event were printed by Hawkins from a diary now lost. His letters give a full account.

Dr. William Heberden, Johnson had known for some years, and after Lawrence's final illness he was one of Johnson's doctors. After two days, Johnson's speech began to return, and in a week he was well enough to water his garden. By 1 July he was able to drive

JULY 10. Dartford. Northfleet.

11. On the Medway.

12. Barber 1s. Aylsford.
      Seston.⁹ Maidston.

13. Church—Taylor.

14. Καθ.   1– 6–6 expenses of journey
                   0–10–6 to Mr Wright
                   0– 5–0 to– Labourer
                   ―――――――
                   2– 2–0

15. Receipt for pension Apr. 5. 75 L.
      Salust imitates Plato. Longin. 13. and Xenophon. Longin.

9. That is, Teston.   ――――――――――――――

out to Hampstead for an airing, and to dine with the Club in the afternoon.

On 10 July Johnson went to Rochester, Kent, to visit Langton, who was stationed there with his regiment, and noted down in his diary two of the towns on the road. He had had some misgivings about the visit, since Langton had eight children, but next day, boating on the Medway River, he was satisfied. He later reported to Mrs. Thrale that on the boat were "four misses and their maid, but they were very quiet" (869). He also reported that they took "four little journies in a Chaise," and the entry for 12 July refers to one of these.

"Barber" does not refer to Frank, unless it is a letter to him. He was not with Johnson, since Johnson had to carry his portmanteau when he returned to London. Aylesford, Teston, and Maidstone, about four miles apart, are all on the Medway, forming a triangle.

On 14 July Johnson gave half a guinea to Mr. Wright, unidentified, but almost certainly the one referred to in a letter to Langton in the next year: "Mr. Wright . . . called on me lately. He looked well" (976).

30 JULY 1783

361

JULY. 30. Almighty God, Creator and Governor of the world who sendest sickness and restorest health, enable me to consider with a just sense of thy mercy the deliverance which Thou hast lately granted me, and assist by thy Blessing, as is best for me, the means which I shall use for the cure of the dis-

---

Next day Johnson sent the receipt for the second quarter's pension to Strahan, as usual acting as his banker. Hill comments on the frequent delays in payments in this period.

Hill also conjectures that Johnson had found Longinus's *On the Sublime* at Langton's (perhaps they merely discussed it, since Johnson owned Longinus at Oxford), and Hill also found the relevant passages: Longinus (sec. 13) quotes from Plato's *Republic* 9. 586A: "They who have no knowledge of wisdom and virtue . . . like beasts ever look downwards, and their heads are bent to the ground, or rather to the table; they feed full their bellies and their lusts" (trans. Havell). The imitation in Sallust (*Catiline* 1) is: "It behooves all men who wish to excel the other animals to strive with might and main not to pass through life unheralded, like the beasts, which Nature has fashioned grovelling and slaves to the belly" (trans. L. C. Rolfe).

The passage in Xenophon imitated by Sallust is perhaps that quoted by Longinus in section 28: "Labour you regard as the guide to a pleasant life, and you have laid up in your souls the fairest and most soldier-like of all gifts: in praise is your delight —more than in anything else." Sallust reads: "In very truth that man alone lives and makes the most of life, as it seems to me, who devotes himself to some occupation, courting the fame of a glorious deed or a noble career" (*Catiline* 2).

Johnson was probably working on his translation of Sallust, since two months later it was finished.

On 23 July Johnson returned to London by boat from Gravesend to Billingsgate, much improved from his holiday, except that a hydrocele, which had troubled him for some time, appeared to be worse. On 30 July he wrote to Cruikshank about it, asking for treatment.

ease with which I am now afflicted. Encrease my patience, teach me submission to thy will; and so rule my thoughts and direct my actions, that I may be finally received to everlasting happiness through Jesus Christ our Lord. Amen.

HINTS.

Tom Rose's Scales

1783   AUG. 15. I cut from the vine 41. leaves which weighed five oz. and half and eight scruples.[1]

I lay them upon my bookcase to try what weight they will lose by drying.

Almighty God, who, in thy late visitation, hast shewn mercy to me, and now sendest to my companion disease and decay, grant me grace so to employ the life which thou hast prolonged, and the faculties which thou hast preserved, and so to receive the admonition, which the sickness of my friend, by thy appointment, gives me, that I may be constant in all holy duties, and be received at last to eternal happiness.

Permit, O Lord, thy unworthy creature to offer up this prayer for Anna Williams, now languishing upon her bed,

1. Several words deleted: "... from ... six ... oz" are legible.

On the same day, his prayer refers to his recovery from the stroke and also to his new affliction.

On 15 August Johnson was at his old game of weighing leaves. Three weeks earlier he had written Sophia Thrale: "Nothing amuses more harmlessly than computation, and nothing is oftener applicable to real business or speculative enquiries. A thousand stories which the ignorant tell, and believe, die away at once, when the computist takes them in his gripe" (870).

During the next ten days Miss Williams was ill and clearly dying. Since Johnson was about to go into the country, he knew

and about to recommend herself to thy infinite mercy. O God, who desirest not the death of a sinner, look down with mercy upon her: forgive her sins, and strengthen her faith. Be merciful, O Father of mercy, to her and to me: guide us by thy holy spirit through the remaining part of life; support us in the hour of death, and pardon us in the day of judgment, for Jesus Christ's sake. Amen.

AUGUST 28. I came to Heale without fatigue.

30. I am entertained quite to my mind.
    To endeavour to conquer scruples, about
        Comedy
        Books in Garret
        Books on Shelves
        Hebrew.   Pollution
    Deus, juva.

---

that he might not see her again, and composed a final prayer for her.

On 28 August Johnson took the 6:00 A.M. coach for Salisbury to visit William Bowles of Heale House, later a member of the Essex Head Club. He arrived in about fifteen hours, "no more wearied with the journey, though it was a high hung rough coach, than I should have been forty years ago" (*Letters* 878).

On or after 30 August Johnson made a puzzling note about scruples. There is no other evidence that he had any scruples about comedy. In 1773 he had defined the "great end" of comedy as "making an audience merry" (*Life*, II.233), and he had said that Garrick's death had "eclipsed the gaiety of nations, and impoverished the publick stock of harmless pleasure" (*Life*, I.82). Whatever scruples he had of this kind were surely of short duration.

The note about his books probably refers to one of his recurrent attempts to put his study in order. If the word following "Hebrew" is "Pollution," Johnson may have in mind one of the many passages in the Old Testament about pollution and purifi-

SEPTEMBER 6. *I had just heard of Williams's Death.*

Almighty and most merciful Father, who art the Lord of life and death, who givest and who takest away, teach me to adore thy providence, whatever Thou shalt allot me; make me to remember, with due thankfulness, the comforts which I have received from my friendship with Anna Williams. Look upon her, O Lord, with mercy, and prepare me, by thy grace, to die with hope, and to pass by death to eternal happiness, through Jesus Christ our Lord. Amen.

SEPT. 8, 1783. Lex civ., lex canon.[2] Hales: "Duo gradus civiles faciunt unum canonicum."

Aquinas. Nullum, Domine nisi teipsum.

2. Conjectural reading.

cation. His "Help, O God," shows that the matter was serious, but further clues are lacking.

Early on Saturday morning, 6 September, Miss Williams died. Dr. Brocklesby wrote at once, and Johnson had the letter at Heale on the same night, whereupon he wrote his prayer on the death of his old friend, his "domestick companion for more than thirty years," as he wrote Reynolds (879.2). The letter to Reynolds implies that the news had been sent Johnson by messenger, or at least that the coachman had been instructed to get it to Heale from Salisbury at once.

Two days later Johnson made some entries in the Broadley diary, now lost. The references to civil and canon law occur in a letter "Concerning the Lawfulness of Marriages betwixt First Cousins, or Cousin-Germans" printed in the second edition of John Hales of Eton's *Golden Remains*: "Now *two Degrees* in the *Civil Law*, make but *one Degree* in the *Canon Law*, where the Rule is, that *in Linea aequali quoto gradu distant à stipite, toto distant inter se*: By which you see that *Second Cousins*, being in the *Third Degree* from the *Grandfather*, they are *three Degrees distant from each other*" (1673, p. 265). Since this letter does not appear in the first edition, one may guess that Johnson read

Chrysostom differs from Erasmus.
From Aleph to Tav.
Letters to Brocklesby, to Mudge, to Frank, to Susan.
6 Sh. 4 St.

10. Wells 8s.   Or. Sacra.[3] 1.   Heale[3] 11.s=L1–0–0.

3. Readings conjectural.

---

the second. The next reference to Aquinas also comes from the *Golden Remains*:

> He that doth God the greatest service, and receives here from him the least reward, is the *happiest* man in the world. There goes a story of Aquinas, that praying once before the Crucifix, the Crucifix miraculously speaks thus unto him, "Bene de me scripsisti Thoma, quam ergo mercedem accipies? Thou hast written well of me, Thomas, what reward dost thou desire?" To whom Aquinas is made to answer, "Nullam, Domine, praeter Teipsum; No reward, Lord, but thyself:" 'Tis great pity this Tale is not true, it doth so excellently teach, what to ask of God for our *reward* in his service [p.65].

Chrysostom's difference from Erasmus perhaps concerns transubstantiation; Johnson was reading them together on 14 August 1774, and noted the unorthodox position in a work once attributed to Chrysostom. Now Johnson was probably talking about them, for Bowles made a note at this time about Johnson's "Great regard for Erasmus" (*Life*, IV.524).

The two Hebrew letters, the first and last in the alphabet, may stand, we are informed, for "from first to last," like "from alpha to omega."

On 9 September Johnson wrote letters now lost to Brocklesby and Frank, perhaps about Miss Williams's funeral; to Mudge, a surgeon, about his sarcocele (874–1); and to Susannah Thrale (880), sending the news of Miss Williams's death. On the same day, he lists his laundry.

On 10 September Johnson made his only known visit to Wells,

1 1. I saw Stonehenge. Transoms, I think 1.

6. Saturday, at 3 in the morning, θ Anna Williams.

12 A. W. was buried.

Mournful conversation.

I do not know that I have any thing to forgive you. I have set my house in order.

Circle of a foot diameter=113 sq. inches. Cubick foot of water 1000 oz at end=C2 Lx½.

Aug. 28. I came to Heale. Sept. 16 I leave Heale tomorrow.

───────────

though Boswell had said some years earlier that he thought Johnson had seen all the cathedrals in England except Carlisle (*Life*, III.107).

Next day Johnson and Bowles visited Stonehenge, which Johnson compared later with Salisbury Cathedral as "the first essay, and the last perfection in architecture" (*Letters* 892). "Transom," for the lintel or impost of the triliths at Stonehenge is here the first recorded use in this sense. (Morse so used it in reference to Stonehenge in 1796 in his *Geography*.) In the letter just quoted Johnson speaks merely of the "transverse stones." Bowles pointed out to Johnson that these stones were mortised and not fixed with mortar, and Johnson deduced from this that they must precede the Danish invasion and were probably Druidical.

Next day Johnson records that Miss Williams had died on the sixth and was buried on the twelfth. His mournful conversation was perhaps with Bowles, who noted that Johnson seemed to bear Miss Williams's loss "with a laudable mixture of feeling & fortitude" (*Life*, IV.524). But it may refer to the following, which appears to be part of Miss Williams's last talk with Johnson before her death.

The calculations as to the area of a circle (correct) and the weight of a cubic foot of water (not very close) were perhaps stimulated by Johnson's observation during this visit of experiments at Salisbury in producing hydrogen, following Priestley's recent discoveries.

SEPT. 15.[4] I finished Sallust.

Andover	Bagshot
Whitchurch	Staines
Overton	Hounslow
Basingstoke	Brentford
Harford Bridge	

1784

JAN. 1   P. M. 11. O Lord God, heavenly Father, by whose mercy I am now beginning another year, grant, I beseech thee that the time which Thou shalt yet allow me, may be spent 4. ⟨16⟩

_____

Johnson again records the date he came to Heale, as he is about to leave. His translation of Sallust's *Catiline*, though finished, was never published. Apparently Johnson did it just for amusement. Twenty pages of manuscript survive (Hyde collection). Boswell thought the fragment had "no very superiour merit" (*Life*, IV.383 n.).

On 16 September Johnson wrote Frank saying that he would be home in time for dinner on his birthday, and asked that four guests be invited. His attitude towards celebrating his birthday is much more relaxed than it had once been.

On 17 September Johnson left for London, where he arrived at noon the next day. His list of towns on the road is written in pencil and is almost illegible; it was probably done in the coach. "Harford" for Hartford Bridge shows the pronunciation.

During the rest of the year Johnson remained in London, troubled with his sarcocele (which eventually healed without an operation), with gout, and at the end of December with spasmodic asthma. But he was well enough intermittently to establish the Essex Head Club, to beg a sermon for a charitable purpose, and to enjoy visits of his friends.

Johnson's New Year's prayer for 1784 reflects his continuing concern about scruples, but hardly suggests the serious state of

in thy fear and to thy glory, give me such ease of body as may
enable me to be useful, and remove from me all such scruples
and perplexities as encumber and[5] obstruct my mind, and
help me so to pass by the direction of thy Holy Spirit through
the remaining part of life that I may be finally received to
everlasting joy through Jesus Christ, our Lord. Amen.

EASTER DAY APR. 11. 1784. Almighty God, my Creator
and my Judge, who givest life and takest it away, enable me
to return sincere and humble thanks for my late deliverance
from imminent death. [6]So govern my future life by thy Holy
Spirit, that every day which thou shalt permit to pass over me,
may be spent in thy service, and leave me less tainted with
wickedness, and more submissive to thy will.

Enable me, O Lord, to glorify thee for that knowledge[7] of
my Corruption, and that sense of thy wrath which my disease
and weakness, and danger awakened in my mind. Give me
such sorrow as may[8] purify my heart, such indignation as may

5. ⟨perplex⟩ . . . ⟨help   so enable⟩ ∧help∧   6. ⟨Enable⟩   7. ∧knowledge∧ ⟨sense⟩
. . . sense of ∧thy wrath∧ ⟨my danger⟩   8. ⟨obtain thy⟩

---

his health. His asthma had kept him confined to his house since
the middle of December, and within a few days he began to be
troubled with dropsy, which grew dangerous as the winter advanced. He was not able to leave his house till 21 April, but he
saw his friends, wrote many letters, continued his efforts for impoverished friends, and even gave small dinner parties.

By Easter Johnson was much improved, but the severe winter
was still hanging on, and his physicians would not let him go to
church. He therefore received communion at home, after his
prayer for the day, which is marked with unusual serenity and
perhaps even confidence. When Boswell came to London in May,
Johnson told him "with solemn earnestness" of his recovery: "He
had shut himself up, and employed a day in particular exercises
of religion,—fasting, humiliation, and prayer. On a sudden he

quench all confidence in my self, and such repentance as may by the intercession of my Redeemer obtain pardon.

Let the commemoration of the sufferings and Death of thy son which I am now, by thy[9] favour, once more[1] permitted to make, fill me with faith, hope, and charity. Let my purposes be good and my resolutions unshaken, and let me not be hindred or disturbed by vain and useless fears,[2] but through the time which yet remains guide me by thy Holy Spirit, and finally receive me to everlasting life, for the sake of Jesus Christ our Lord and Saviour. Amen.

SUN. 16 MAY 1784. Afternoon spent cheerfully and elegantly, I hope without offence to GOD or man; though in no holy duty, yet in the general exercise and cultivation of benevolence.

9. MS: the   1. ⟨enable⟩   2. A few words deleted.

---

obtained extraordinary relief, for which he looked up to Heaven with grateful devotion. He made no direct inference from this fact; but from his manner of telling it, I could perceive that it appeared to him as something more than an incident in the common course of events" (*Life*, IV.272).

On Wednesday, 21 April, Johnson went to church to give thanks for his recovery: the dropsy was gone, and the asthma much better. For the next month he pursued all his usual activities, in one week dining out six nights.

The undated fragment printed by Boswell under 16 May from a diary now lost shows the extent of Johnson's recovery. As for the exercise of benevolence, his letters show that in a period of five weeks he asked Mrs. Thrale for two guineas for "a public charity," advised Frances Reynolds on the publication of a book, asked Ozias Humphrey to teach Johnson's godson Paterson painting, asked Reynolds for a contribution for "a poor man," and engaged Mrs. Gardiner to manage Mrs. Pellé's money (956–65). And he

8. JUNE—84. Very breathless, and dejected. Squills. X—at nigh[t] D. 52, in the night angustia et anhelitus. After some ease. Urinae fluxus.

9. Spiritus liberior. Squ.X. mane 4 pocula, prand. 2 poc. D 52³ caen. 1 p 52. Nox aestuosa, insomnis, turbatissima, surgendum fuit et sedendum. Sedens dormivi. Urinae satis.

10. Jent. hilare. Somnum qui defuit in cathedra recepi.

3. ₄D 52₄

---

contributed his own money as well, in spite of the fact that his pension was a year in arrears.

On 3 June Johnson went to Oxford with Boswell to spend a fortnight with Dr. Adams. His asthma was troublesome, and he was suspicious that the dropsy was returning.

On 8 June he noted in his diary that he took squills, as a diuretic, and that the dose was effective; he felt that if the intake and output of liquids were about equal, the dropsy was under control. And because the asthma distressed him at night, he took two drams of diacodium.

Next day his breathing was easier. He continued taking squills, four draughts in the morning, two at lunch, and one at supper, of two drams each, again with good results, repeating the diacodium as before. He was so very hot, sleepless, and disturbed at night that he got up and slept in a chair.

On 10 June he records that he breakfasted cheerfully, and made up for his restless night by sleeping in a chair.

During this visit Johnson was as lively as ever in conversation. He captivated Adams's thirty-eight-year-old daughter with his gallantry, and in another mood agreed to Adams's suggestion that he think of compiling a book of prayers. On 16 June he and Boswell returned to London, where, on the twenty-second, he dined with the Club for the last time.

On 30 June Boswell dined with Johnson for the last time and deeply touched the sick old man by his attempt to get an increase

AEGRI EPHEMERIS.

1784. C.

6. JULY. Crura et femora tument. Lactuca silvestris sumpta. Prandium e jusculo Testudines et pisi.³ᵃ f[aeces] copiosae nec durae nec liquidae, a prandio ejectae. Sudor multus. Somnus hesterna nocte fere nullus, hodie sedenti, qui satis esset.

3a. Testudines et pisi. So MS.·

7. Somnus brevis. Urinae vix satis. Pectus anhelitu tentatum. Sumsi suc[um]. lact. silv. A jentaculo bene dormivi. Prandium

---

in Johnson's pension so that he could spend the winter in Italy. On the same day Mrs. Thrale wrote him announcing her forthcoming marriage to Piozzi, and on 2 July Johnson wrote his dreadful reply—"God forgive your wickedness." On 4 July Mrs. Thrale answered with spirit and dignity—"God bless you"—and on 8 July Johnson had recovered himself enough to write a decent and affectionate letter. But their friendship of twenty years was over.

After his stroke in 1783 Johnson's letters to Mrs. Thrale had been in the form of a medical journal: "I think to send you for some time a regular diary. You will forgive the gross images which disease must necessarily present. Dr Laurence said that medical treatises should be always in Latin" (851). Now that he could no longer confide in Mrs. Thrale, he began, on 6 July, his "Sick Man's Journal," which he continued to 8 November, about five weeks before his death. Its purpose was to keep a record of his illness and the medications he used, and particularly, as time went on, to watch the balance of intake and output of liquids. On this day he realized that his shins and thighs were swelling. He took wild lettuce, probably the syrup, as a sleeping potion, had broth for lunch and apparently tortoise and peas, and found that his bowel movement afterwards was ample and of satisfactory quality. He sweated heavily (part of the output of liquid) and though he had had little sleep at night, made up most of it in a chair during the day.

Next day, after a short sleep, his urine was hardly adequate,

nimium fuit. f. durae. pectus graviter vellicatum. Mens prostrata. Ante lectum somni aliquid, in lecto somni nihil. Aestus
fuit supra modum molestus. Urinae, ut videtur, non satis, at
sudor magnus.

8. De somno dictum est in 7ᵐᵃ. Hora 7ᵐᵃ surrexi. dormivi in
sedili. Kαθ. jentavi. rursus dormivi. pectus graviter agitatum
panno laneo duplicato pene sedavi. aër enim, etiam canicula
aestuante laedit. Mens prostrata. Kαθ 3. Aceti squl. guttas 120.
Ventriculum paulum impeditum sensi. Ante prandium diacod. ℨss. Nox tolerabilis.

9. Nox, ut dictum est, tolerabilis. Pectus per dies aliquot lace-
ratum subito conquievit. aquae intercutis nimium.

Remissionis causa non apparet. Heri post diac. nec vesperi
nec nocte, nec mane melius habui. prandium fuit largum, mul-

---

but he sweated freely. For his troublesome asthma he took syrup
of wild lettuce, and slept well after breakfast. After an excessive
dinner, he found his faeces hard. His breast was severely convulsed,
and he was dejected. That night he had some sleep before bed,
but none in bed, where his panting was unutterably troublesome.

On 8 July he rose at seven and slept in a chair, took a purge,
breakfasted, and slept again. He almost quieted his heaving breast
with a woollen garment doubled, for the air hurt him, even in
the dog-days. He took 120 drops of vinegar of squills and thought
his stomach a little constricted. He also took half an ounce of
diacodium before dinner, and had a tolerable night as a result.
Even though he records that he was dejected, he managed to write
his final letter to Mrs. Thrale, one to Reynolds, and one to Lucy
Porter.

On 9 July Johnson noted that although the dropsy was excessive, his breast, tortured for some days, suddenly became quiet,
the cause of relief not clear. After the diacodium of the day before,
he had been no better, evening, night, or morning. (He has forgotten his "tolerable night.") He had eaten a liberal dinner and

tum fructuum devoratum. hodie in victu [non] mutatum est, nisi quod pro teâ, coffiam bibi. Subito jentanti cessavit anhelitus; at notandum quatuor squillarum grana sumpta fuisse, duo primo mane, duo, ut puto, ante jentaculum. At multae aceti squillati guttae heri hausa[3b] sunt nihil proficientis.

10. Nox satis turbata. Mane meliuscule habui. Pransus largiter, sub[4] noctem anhelitu laboravi. diac. 3ʒ2, dormivi, post somnum omnia graviora. diac. ʒss. In lecto parum quietis. mane sudor. Urinae non satis, omnia incommoda.

11.[5] Cultui sancto adesse volui, at lassis statim cruribus, spiritu impedito, reversus, aliquantulum dormivi. K. Sumsi squill. gr. 111. pransus. X. sedes liquida. pransus iterum dormivi. Sedes non admodum copiosa heri licet parum[6] ejecerim. Magna enim pars escae fructus et fraga. X2 liquida sedes nec admodum copiosa. Urinae fere satis.

3b. So MS.   4. ⟨noctem⟩   5. ⟨10⟩   6. pa⟨ulum⟩rum

---

much fruit. Today his diet was the same except that he drank coffee instead of tea. At breakfast, his panting had suddenly ceased. He notes that he had taken four grains of squills, two in the early morning and, he thinks, two before breakfast. But the squills had done no good the day before.

He had a restless night, but felt a little better in the morning. He had a hearty lunch, but towards night his asthma troubled him, and he took two drams of diacodium. He slept, but was worse on awaking and doubled his dose of diacodium. Even so, he had little rest, everything was uncomfortable, and his sweating did not make up for inadequate urine. He was, however, able to write a cheerful letter to Bowles (972.2).

On Sunday he started to church, but his legs tired at once, and his breathing was obstructed. So he returned and slept a little. Later he took a purge and squills, dined, slept again, and was more nearly satisfied with the balance of liquids. Indeed, he says,

12.⁷ Nox turbatissima. caelum frigidius me male habet. X commode. pectus vexatum. duos calices sp sacchar. sumsi, at vix quidquam profeci. dormivi sedens, nec tamen placide. virtutem electricam et cruri et lumbis adhibui. Pransus largiter aliquantulum dormivi. X iterum commode.

13. Vehiculum meritorium conscendi, in aliam regionem contendens.

14. Licfeldiam veni. In rhedâ placide legi.

20. Asburniam.

24. Squillarum usu crura detument. Somni tamen in lecto pene nihil. Diacodij heri ℥ss anhelitus levior. hodie nihil diac.

7. ⟨11⟩

---

a large part of his food was fruit and strawberries. He was feeling well enough to write Boswell and Dr. Adams (973, 974).

That night was most disturbed, because of cold weather. He took two cups of rum to quiet his breast, without much relief, and got some fitful sleep in a chair. Next day he applied electricity to his legs and loins, a treatment he had urged for Dr. Lawrence's paralysis (*Letters* 802). After an ample dinner he slept a little more.

On 13 July Johnson left for Lichfield by coach, reading calmly on the way Erasmus's *Ciceronianus*, which large treatise he finished on the second day just as he reached Lichfield (*Letters* 979). The journey did not fatigue him unduly, though he "could not have born such violent agitation for many days together." He found everyone glad to see him, and stayed for five days.

On 20 July he went on to Ashbourne to visit Dr. Taylor, whom he found rebuilding his house, spending his days in his fields, and continuing his usual unpleasant practice of going to bed at nine, which did not suit Johnson at all.

On 24 July Johnson found that the swelling in his legs was yielding to the squills, but he was still getting almost no sleep

25. Nox turbatissima. ante prandium X commodissima sine catharsi. Prandium mediocre, femora tumere visa. mane squil g. 40. totidem vesperi. diac 311 et ultra. meliuscule habui. decubiturus sumpsi squil. g. 40—Squillarum summa gtt. 120. Urina, ut videtur, aliquanto abundantior.

25. At church twice. In the morning a foolish heat. Dining in the evening.

26. Nox turbida et insomnis. squil. gr. 3. ab hora 7ma ad 9^m sedens dormivi. In rheda ad captandas auras[8] vectus, aliquantulum dormivi. Prandium solito minus. A prandio anhelitus molestus, tristitia gravissima. Diac. 36. pectus sedatius. potus exiguus, urina copiosior. X sine Καθ. decumbens sumsi gr Opij unum.

27. Nox sedata sed pene insomnis. Corpus doloris expers. Men[s][9] recreata. Mane opij gr unum. Gestatio d[u]arum hora-

8. ⟨gestatus⟩   9. ⟨recrea⟩

---

in bed. He had taken half an ounce of diacodium the day before, none today, and his asthma was easier. The night was most restless.

Next day, since his thighs seemed worse, he took squills morning, evening, and on going to bed, 120 drops in all. His bowels acted normally, for a change; he had a moderate lunch; on the whole he felt a little better. The squills seemed effective.

On Sunday Johnson's "foolish heat" perhaps refers to a dispute with Taylor. It can hardly mean that he had foolishly got himself physically hot, since he complains in his letters of the coldness of the summer and his difficulty in keeping warm. The night was sleepless and disturbed.

On Monday, after sleeping in a chair from seven to nine, he drove out to take the air, and slept a little more. After a light dinner, his asthma was troublesome, and he was severely depressed.

rum. Prandium lautum. A prandio somnus. Potus modicus.
Cremor fecit crudum. Spiritu sacchari me curavi.

2 8. Nox tranquilla, at somni vix satis. urinae minus quam
vellem. Mane squill. gr. 3. Καθ copiose. sumsi op. gr. 1. levior
et laetior factus. Liquidi parum, escae non multum. a prandio
longus ante opium somnus.

S E P T E M   A E T A T E S .

Prima parit terras aetas; siccatque secunda;
Evocat Abramum dein tertia; quarta relinquit
Aegyptum; templo Solomonis quinta superbit;[1]
Cyrum sexta timet; laetatur septima Christo.

1. ⟨Cyrum sexta vocat,⟩ laetatur
⟨Sexta dolet Babylona, et gaudet⟩

———————

Six drams of diacodium quieted his breast somewhat. He drank
very little, but a dose of squills had effect, and his bowels were
normal. On retiring he took one grain of opium, and spent a quiet
but almost sleepless night without pain.

In the morning, his mind refreshed, he took another grain of
opium. After a two-hour drive, he had an excellent dinner without
much drink, but broth gave him indigestion, which he cured with
rum. The night was quiet, but with hardly enough sleep.

On Wednesday, not satisfied with the flow of urine, he took
squills and a large purge. He felt lighter and more cheerful, had
very little liquid and not much food. A long sleep after dinner
he followed with a grain of opium.

"The Seven Ages" was printed by Langton in the booksellers'
edition of Johnson's *Works*, 1787, and in the 1941 edition of
Johnson's *Poems* it was printed from this manuscript. It has no
connexion with the context and is not mentioned in Johnson's
letters.

On 29 July, after a quiet but sleepless night, Johnson found
his legs less swollen. He took a grain of opium before dinner, and

29. Nox placida sed insomnis. crura detument. Ante prandium op. gr. 1. A prandio somnus.

30. Nox insomnis. Pectus laborans opij gr. ss. Sedatum est. opium in tenebris per digitos quaesivi. Ante prandium somnum. Ventriculo quod gustui placet, gratum; οὐ X. crura tenuantur. opij. gr. 1. Acet. squil. g. 80.

31. nox turbatissima, horâ 6ta sx. in cathedra ad 9^{nam} d. X duriter. Gestatio. Prandium abundantius. cerasorum et uvarum crisparum nimium. Somnus.

AUGUST 1, 1784, ASHBOURN. O God, most merciful Father who by many diseases hast admonished me of my approach to the end of life, and by this gracious addition to my days hast given me an opportunity of appearing once more in thy presence to commemorate the sacrifice by which thy son Jesus

———————————

slept after dinner. Again he had a sleepless night, during which he took half a grain of opium, in the dark, to quiet his breast.

Next day he slept before dinner, and noted that his stomach welcomed what pleased his palate. His legs were getting thinner. Another grain of opium and more squills. No evacuation.

On 31 July, after a most disturbed night, he rose at six and slept in a chair till nine. The opium was making him costive. Later he went driving again. He ate a rather large dinner and too many cherries and gooseberries, the Latin phrase for which he has remembered from his schooldays, when his tutor Holbrooke did not know its meaning. Johnson had written Dr. Brocklesby a week earlier, "I have a voracious delight in raw summer fruit, of which I was less eager a few years ago" (979). He slept after this ample meal.

On Johnson's prayer for Sunday, 1 August, Hill comments: "By the note which Johnson made at the word 'Repentance' it is clear that he wished to recall certain faults when he was using the prayer; it is no less clear that in employing abbreviations in

Christ has taken away the sins of the world, assist me in this commemoration by thy Holy Spirit that I may look back upon the sinfulness of my life past with pious sorrow, and efficacious Repentance,* that my resolutions of amendment may be rightly formed and diligently exerted, that I may be freed from vain and useless scruples, and that I may serve thee with Faith, Hope, and Charity for the time which Thou shalt yet allow me, and finally be received to Everlasting Happiness for the sake of Jesus Christ, our Lord. Amen.

To work as I can.

To attempt a book of prayers.

To do good as occasion offers itself.

To review former resolutions.

At * may be mentioned μ.χ. ἀισχ-νο κεν. β. M.

AUG. 1. Nox inquietissima. In stomacho ardor. sx. bene mane. In cathedra somnum cepi. Jentaculum sine esca. X natura agente. Prandium modicum. Languor molestus, anhelitus gravis. Peractis post meridiem sacris, sumpsi opij gr. 2. quod mihi nuper insolitum est. Molestiae mihi haec scribenti inter-

---

Greek he wished to secure secrecy, in case the prayer should fall into a stranger's hands. My friend Mr. W. R. Morfill . . . ingeniously conjectures that the first three entries are μέλαινα χολή; αἰσχρὰ νοήματα; κενὰ βουλεύματα—melancholy; shameful thoughts; vain resolutions. His melancholy if he had indulged it, or if he had not taken the proper means to subdue it, he would have looked upon as sinful" (Miscellanies, 1.117 n.). "M" is perhaps "memento," "remember."

Johnson had had a very restless night, with heat in the stomach, and so he rose very early and slept in a chair. He had breakfast without solids, found his bowels normal, had a light dinner, and then was troubled with lassitude and severe panting. Following church in the afternoon, he took two grains of opium, not his practice of late. But as he was writing, his pains had an intermis-

quiescunt. Quid sit futurum velle et scire Dei est; Me, Summe
Pater, miserare.

2. Nox insomnis, et lenta, sed pectus sedatum. Mane, post
brevem in sedili somnum Mil Pass. 24. gestatio. nec fames,
nec fatigatio. Prandium e piscibus et pisis et fructibus non
satis modicum. parum profeci. sumsi opij. gr. 1. tristis et
timidus.

3. Nox molesta. ab 11 ad 2 puto dormivi. postea rarus et frac-
tus somnus. Nona jentavi. Squill gr 3 et Καθ prius sumptis, in
sedili, ab 10 ad 1. fere, dormivi² placidissime. Καθ³ feliciter,
levior factus sum. sine carnibus pransus sum, mihique tenui
victu satis placui, an diu sim sic placiturus nescio. Sumsi op.
gr. 1. Spiritus expeditior.

2. ⟨in sedili⟩   3. That is, X.

---

sion, impelling him to say, "To wish and know the future is for
God. Almighty Father, have mercy on me."

That night was as usual, except that his breast was calm. In the
morning, after a short sleep in a chair, he went for a twenty-four
mile drive, without hunger or fatigue. Indeed, he wrote Burney,
he could have gone forty-eight more (984). He then dined rather
freely on fish, peas, and fruit, and comments, a little inconsistently,
that he has made little progress. Another grain of opium. He was
sad and fearful, but in the same letter to Burney he promised a
dedication, his last, for the *Commemoration of Handel*.

On 3 August, Johnson had had another troublesome night,
sleeping, he thinks, between eleven and two, with a little broken
sleep thereafter. In the morning he took squills and a purge, breakfasted at nine, and from ten to about one slept peacefully in a
chair. He had an easy evacuation and felt lighter. Dinner without
meat, a meagre diet, pleased him, but he was not sure that the
pleasure would last. One grain of opium; his breathing was more
free. But that night was poor again.

4. Nox insomnis, nec inturbata. Sumpsi diluculo op. gr ss. placide decubui, parum tamen dormivi. a jentaculo gestatio.⁴ Spiritus minus difficilis, c[r]ura minus gra[v]ia. Prandium sine carnibus, a prandio somnolentia. Sero vesperi op. gr 1. Bene vertat Deus. Hodie Cantharidum tincturam experturus gtt. mane 8, vespere 10 sumsi.

5. Nox insomnis. Tinct. Can. gtt. 10. Kaθ. pr. mod. ex fabis cum lardo. X 4 puto. parum potus, nulla sitis. toto die somno gravor. languens vespere opij gr. 1 sumsi. In cathedra unam horam, ab 8. ad 9 altissime dormivi. Ves. Cantharid. gtt. 10.

6. FR. At prayers and sermon.

7. SAT. At Snelston in the Chariot. Very languid.

4. ⟨Pran⟩

———————

At dawn he took half a grain of opium, lay down peacefully, but slept little. On a drive after breakfast he found his breathing easier and his legs lighter. After a meatless dinner he was drowsy; in the late evening a grain of opium. "May God help me." This day he began to try tincture of cantharides as a diuretic, eight drops in the morning, ten in the evening.

On 5 August, after a sleepless night, he wrote Brocklesby (985) about his condition, saying that there was no change, and telling him of the cantharides, of which he took twenty drops this day. He had a light dinner of bacon and beans, drank little, but was not thirsty. He was drowsy all day, and, feeling languid in the evening, took a grain of opium, after which he slept soundly in a chair from eight to nine.

On Friday Johnson went to church because it was the Feast of the Transfiguration.

On Saturday he drove to Snelston, a village about three miles from Ashbourne. He was feeling well enough to write affectionately and almost cheerfully to Hoole (986) and Bowles (986.1).

On Sunday, after a restless night but one without pain, he

8. Nox turbatior, at sine pectoris dolore. Canth gtt 20. Jent. e lacte. Prandium modicum. Ca[n]th. gtt 30 urina non videtur cohiberi, at nec femora detument. opij gr. 2. caveatur. Canth. gtt 30. Caena panis ex lacte. Tumetur.

9. Nox insomnis. Tumetur. E lecto pulsus, dormivi, ut puto, horas tres. Jentavi e lacte et pane. Καθ cum Canth. gutt. 80 in potionem injectis. Vi tanta cantharidum territus, poculum dimidium ante jentaculum, dimidium hausi post jentaculum, hausi, unde factum credit,[4a] ut nihil profuerit. Non multo post ad prandium accersitus, pastus sum carne ferina, gallinacea, suilla, anserina, cum bellarijs quibusdam. Quaerens cur non essem escae avidior, causas habui caenam hesternam, hodiernum jentaculum cum medicamento quod ventriculum turbasse potuerit. Paulo post alvum gravem sentiens in hortum, ut levarem, secessi; faeces vero in molem tam duram et magnam concreverant ut postica exire non possent. per clysteram rem agendum con[stitui], et postquam una plus hac vice lat-

4a. So MS.

---

increased his dosage of cantharides, noting that it seemed effective, but that the swelling of his thighs did not subside. He breakfasted on milk, dined lightly, and had a supper of bread and milk. After taking two grains of opium, he warns himself: "Careful!" More swelling of his legs, and again a sleepless night.

On Monday, driven from bed by discomfort, he slept about three hours. Because the swelling continued, he took eighty drops of cantharides in a drink, with a purge, but afraid of such a large dose, he drank half a cup before his milk breakfast and half afterwards. And that is why, he thinks, it did no good. A little later he was called to dinner and had venison, fowl, pork, goose, and some dessert. But he was not very hungry and thought that his supper the night before and his breakfast with a drug, which might have upset his stomach, were the reasons.

A little later, feeling a need for evacuation, he went to the privy, but was unable to move the large and hardened faeces, and de-

rinam intrassem, et nisus magno cum cruciatu, saepius vanos, ingeminassem. Pharmacopolam accersi jubeo. Multae erant morae, magna molestia, dolor obtusus quidem sed qui maxime gravaret. Injectum tandem est, ingens vis faecium emissa. Omnia melius continuo habuerunt. Καθ iterum. X 2.

10. Nocte ter X=5. Urina affatim fluit, nec tamen tumor subsidet. Mane opij gr. 1. Gestatio cum socio non injucundo. Squill gr 4 nec opio nec squillis quidquam sensi effectum. Animus jacet. Victus hodie satis tenuis. parum liquidi, carnium nihil. Somnus parvus.

11. Nox insomnis, suffocatio gravis. Haustulus aquae aliquantulum dedit levaminis. X bis, sine pharmaco, quid nuper vix contigit. Prandium modicum, liquidi parum. sub noctem sumpsi Acet Squill. gtt 100. quo eventu, nondum liquet.

---

cided to use an enema. Repeated trips to the privy were fruitless though agonizing. He then sent for an apothecary. There was long delay and great discomfort, the pain not acute, but very oppressive. At last the enema produced an immense evacuation, and everything was at once better. He took another purge, with effect. That night three more evacuations. (No more will be noted unless exceptional, since the reader will find them in the text with the symbol "X.")

On 10 August Johnson notes that the swelling does not subside, although the urine flows freely. A grain of opium and a dose of squills seemed ineffective, but he had a drive with a pleasant companion, probably Taylor. But Johnson's spirits were low. His diet was meagre, with little liquid and no meat. Little sleep during the day, and a sleepless night, with severe breathlessness, but a little drink of water gave some relief.

On Wednesday, without a purge, his bowels moved twice, very unusual lately. A light dinner with little drink, and at night squills again, with what result not yet apparent.

The night was dreadful. He rose at five and slept in a chair.

12. Nox misera. Quinta mane surrexi et in cathedra somnum cepi. Urina ut videtur, potum superat. Καθ. jentavi lacte. ante jentaculum X, quod cathartico non tribui. post jentaculum[5] Acet. Squill. gtt 40 et 40 successu hactenus nullo. —40– 40– 40– 40 = 240. X5. urina, ut spero, fluit. nihil prandij.

AGAINST INQUISITIVE AND PERPLEXING THOUGHTS.

AUG. 12 —84. O Lord, my Maker and Protector, who hast graciously sent me into this world, to work out my salvation,[6] enable me to drive from me all such unquiet and perplexing thoughts as may mislead or hinder me in the practice of those duties which thou[7] hast required. When I behold the works of thy hands and consider the course[8] of thy providence, give me Grace always to remember that thy thoughts are not my thoughts, nor thy ways my ways. And while it shall please thee to continue me in this world where much is to be done and little to be known,[9] teach me by thy Holy Spirit[1] to withdraw my Mind from unprofitable and dangerous enquiries,[2] from

5. ⟨X 3⟩ 6. ⟨by obedience to thy laws⟩ . . . drive from ∧me∧ ⟨my mind⟩ 7. thou⟨gh⟩ hast ⟨com⟩ required. ⟨Let⟩ 8. ∧the course∧ of thy providence, ⟨defend ∧preserve∧ me O Lord, from enquiries vainly and curious and from doubts impossible to be solved⟩ 9. ⟨make me to remember that of a ∧the∧ short life of man⟩ 1. ∧by thy Holy Spirit∧ 2. ⟨to fix it upon those ∧to be a∧⟩

He was pleased that he seemed to expel more liquid than he drank. A breakfast of milk, and again his bowels seemed normal. More squills, but no results so far. Later still more, 240 drops in all, and his urine seemed to flow. No dinner.

On the same day, still troubled with religious doubts, Johnson composed his prayer "Against inquisitive and perplexing thoughts." He was well enough to write a letter of advice to Queeney Thrale (988.1), another letter as a "voucher" for two guineas to Heely (988), the indigent widower of one of Johnson's

difficulties vainly curious, and doubts impossible to be solved.³
Let me⁴ rejoice in the light which thou hast imparted, let me
serve thee with active zeal, and humble confidence, and wait
with patient expectation for the time in which the soul which
Thou receivest, shall be satisfied with knowledge. Grant this,
O Lord, for Jesus Christs sake. Amen.

1 3. Nox insomnis, non tamen aliter gravis. Primo mane sumsi
opij gr. 2. Urina fluxit. Opium vero nihil profuit.⁵ Surgens
Squill aceti gtt 120. Jent. Gestatio. corpus leve, spiritus liber,
mens hilarior. Prandium modicum, potus parcus. Sq. Acet.
gtt 120. Somnolentia solita minor. Ante lectum Opij gr. 1.

1 4. Nox insomnis, at non gravis. Καθ. cum squill gtt. 120,
purgatio parum processit. Καθ iterum cum squil. gtt. ut puto
80. Prandium parcum sine carnibus. X4. Tertium effusissime.

3. ∧from difficulties . . . solved∧ 4. ∧Let me ⟨to⟩ rejoice in the∧ . . . ⟨and to⟩
∧let me∧ 5. ⟨Jent⟩

cousins, and a third to Brocklesby (987), detailing his medications
and asking for advice. It should be noted that Johnson is not
haphazardly experimenting on himself, but consults with his doctors and reads medical authorities about his treatment.

On 13 August Johnson began a period of considerable improvement. After a sleepless night, not otherwise troublesome, he took
two grains of opium, which did no good. The heavy dose of squills
of the day before was effective, and on rising he took more. After
breakfast a drive, and his body felt light, his breath free, and his
mind more cheerful. A light dinner, with little drink, followed
by more squills. He was less drowsy than usual, and took another
grain of opium. The night was sleepless but not painful.

Next day Johnson was so encouraged that he wrote Brocklesby
(990), Davies (991), and Lucy Porter (991.1) about his improvement. And in the letter to Lucy is a clue to his earlier depression:
"In this place I have every thing but company, and of company
I am in great want. Dr Taylor is at his farm, and I sit at home."

15. D. Nox insomnis. Dies laetior solito. Prandium largius, e bubula et alijs escis, etiam cum ferina in furno coctâ.

16. Mane paululum somni.[6] Jentaculum lacteum. Prandium largum. Sumpsi Jal. gr 10 Cal. gr. 5. X. 1 nihil liquidi. Dormivi, crudus et gravis a prandio, horas tres.

17. Nox insomnis et tristis. X 1 nihil liquidi. Hesterna cruditas vinci videtur. Sump. pil. Squil. 3. X 1. n[ihil] liq[uidi]. tumetur. Diac. ℥ss.

18. Nox misera. quiddam opis attulisse visus est Spiritus sacch. Jentaculum lacteum. Καθ. prandium tenue. X3 op. gr. 1. anhelitus non gravis.

6. ⟨Pran⟩

─────────────────────

Today he took two purges, with eventual results, two doses of squills, and had a sparing dinner with no meat.

On Sunday, after a sleepless night, he had a happier day than usual, and dined on beef and other things, including baked venison. In his letter to Brocklesby next day (992), he says that he walked to church after this liberal dinner, without any inconvenience, and was so delighted that he did not despair of "another race upon the Stairs of the Academy."

On Monday he had a little sleep in the morning, breakfasted on milk, and had a liberal dinner. As a purge, he took ten grains of jalap and five of calomel. His stool was without liquid on this and the next day. After dinner, heavy and suffering from indigestion, he slept three hours.

On Tuesday, after a sad, sleepless night, at least his indigestion was gone, and he took more squills, since he was concerned with swelling in his legs, and half an ounce of diacodium.

On Wednesday Johnson eased a wretched night somewhat by drinking rum. He had a milk breakfast and a light dinner; his asthma was not severe. A grain of opium.

On 19 August after a tedious night, with some broken sleep in the morning, he had a hearty milk breakfast. His mind was not

19. Nox taedij plena. Mane somnus, at non placidus. Jentaculum e lacte largum. Mens non admodum tristis. pectus non penitus quietum. Prandium modicum. Mens tristior. Diac. ℥ss. Quid sit futurum cras fuge quaerere. Mens post Diacod. turbatior, quam op. gr. 1 sedavit. X nullum.

20.[7] Nox insomnis. Mane somni aliquantulum. Sx sero. Καθ cum tanta vi acet. squill. ut emeticam agerem. ventriculo multum moto. Profuit tamen, ut puto, aegrotasse. Squillarum maxima parte rejecta pars urinam ciebat, crura enim videntur minus tumere,[8] minus certe nitent. urina vero, ni me vota fallunt, fluxit copiosior. Prandium fere nullum. Liquidi pauxillum. Sub noctem op. gr. 2. Somnus in sedile placidus.

21. Somni parum. Pectus quietum. Jent. e lacte parcum. Gestatio longa. Prandium[9] parcum sine carnibus. Urina hesterna

7. ⟨Mox⟩   8. tumere⟨nt⟩   9. MS: Pranndium

---

immoderately sad, but his breast was not wholly quiet. After a light dinner, he was sadder and took half an ounce of diacodium. He quotes Horace, *Odes* 1. 9. 13: "Ask not what tomorrow will bring." But his mind was more troubled after the diacodium, and he soothed it with a grain of opium. This is the first clear evidence that Johnson was taking opium to relieve his depression, but a week later he expands on this in a letter to Brocklesby (1000): "I have here little company and little amusement, and thus abandoned to the contemplation of my own miseries, I am sometimes gloomy and depressed, this too I resist as I can, and find opium, I think useful, but I seldom take more than one grain." This perhaps confirmed Hawkins's impression that Johnson took opium for pleasure (pp. 320, 454).

On 20 August, after a sleepless night Johnson slept a little in the morning and rose late. Then he took a purge with so much squills that he vomited most of the dose. But though his stomach was much disturbed, he thought the sickness did good, since the

die et tota nocte feliciter fluxisse videtur, a prandio sumpsi
squil pulv. gr 3. dormivi sumpsi squillarum altera gr 3. spero
quiddam magnum, metuo quiddam grave. Deus juvet.

22. D. Somnus in lecto solito longior altiorque quem opium
nondum penitus ejectum, cum jejunio dedisse puto. Tumor
vero aquosus non minuitur, quod me terret. Animus jacet.
Deus miserere. Vespere, Pectore laborante, identidem licet in
sedile dormirem, sumpsi gr. 1. pectus requievit. In lecto tamen
bene parum dormivi.

23. Nox insomnis. Mens turbata, at urina, ni fallor, potum[1]
longe superabat. Sx. 8ᵛᵃ. Sumsi squillarum gr. 4. Jentaculum
1. ⟨multum⟩

---

squills stimulated urination, and his legs seemed less swollen, at
least less shiny. He had hardly any dinner, with little liquid. At
night, two grains of opium, and he had a calm sleep in a chair.

On 21 August he had had little sleep, but his breast was still
quiet. After a scanty milk breakfast, he went for a drive, and
later had a light dinner without meat. Satisfied that the squills
were still working, he took more, and slept. "I hope for something
great, fear something bad. God help me." But he was well enough
to write Brocklesby (997) not only about his illness but about a
projected balloon ascent to which he had subscribed, and to
write Sastres (998) about a proposed dictionary, with a lively
aphorism out of his own experience: "Dictionaries are like watches,
the worst is better than none, and the best cannot be expected to
go quite true."

That night he had a longer and deeper sleep than usual, which
he attributed to the opium, not yet all evacuated, and to fasting.
But the dropsy was no better, and that frightened him. "My
spirits are low. God have mercy." In the evening, though his breast
was convulsed, he managed to get some sleep at intervals in a
chair. A grain of opium quieted his breast, but in bed he hardly
slept.

On Monday his mind was troubled, but he was inclined to

e lacte. post Jentaculum sumsi squill. gr 3. Squillas enim
habeo consensu medicorum maxime commendatas. Lactis un-
cias octodecim credo jentâsse. Opium urinam ciet potius
quam cohibet. Prandium ex ovis, cum placenta. Vesperi alvus
faecibus induratus¹ᵃ onusta. Καθ. post jentaculum nihil potus
praeter tres Teae parvos cyathos.

24. Nox'satis injucunda. Post medicamentum purgans, dormivi sedens, undecima fere decubui, in lecto iterum dormivi.
tertiâ alvus mota, quinta quoque, et ut puto septimâ. X 4.
Jentavi lactis ʒi8. Urina potum superare videtur, nec tamen
detumeo. Mens admodum tristis. Soletur Deus. Ab 11ᵐᵃ ad
1ᵐᵃᵐ in subsellio altum dormivi, ita ut, recedente somno, in
lecto esse viderer. X iterum nunc quintum. Aeger animi
sumpsi diacod. 36. recreatus sum.

25. Longa Nox et gravis. Mens ita turbata ut ad opij gr. 1.
Mane esset confugiendum, inde mens sedatior. cubui ad 10ᵐᵃᵐ.

1a. So MS.
_____

believe that his urine, stimulated by opium, greatly exceeded what
he drank. He rose at eight, took squills before and after his milk
breakfast, for "The Squills have every suffrage" of physicians (*Letters* 993), and dined on eggs and a cake. Except for about 18 ounces
of milk in the morning, he drank nothing but three small cups of
tea. In the evening he needed a purge, and took one. He then slept
sitting till about eleven, when he went to bed and slept again. But
the night was unpleasant.

On Tuesday the purge took effect in the early morning and
during the day. He breakfasted as on Monday, but was rather depressed, since the swelling did not go down, even though his urine
seemed more than his drink. "God comfort me." From eleven till
one he slept so soundly on a sofa that while he was awaking he
thought he was in bed. In low spirits, he took six drams of diacodium and felt better. But it was a long, heavy night.

On 25 August his mind was so disturbed that he had recourse

Jentacu. e lacte copiosum. Gestatio longa. Mens erectior. Prandium sine carnibus, sine crudis fructibus. a prandio somni aliquantulum. p. m. 11ma Op. gr. 1. Acet. Squil gtt 110. Potus ʒ30² fere.

26. Nox lenta. Kaθ cum gr 3 Squill. Potus ʒ ut puto 24. Urina ʒ ut puto 36. Prandium largum e ferina, et majali. Sensi, aut sentire visus sum, in vesica stimulos squillarum. Crura videntur mollescere, moles vero nescio an minuatur. X ex Kaθ 4.

27. Mane X ex hesterna Kaθ. Jentaculum ʒ12. Prandium sine carnibus, nisi quod pisciculi pauci comesti sunt. Squill. gr. 3. potus fere ʒ8=20 urina 48.

28. Nox misera. Squil gr 3. Jent. ʒ12. prandium sine carnibus. Coff. ʒ12. Op gr 1 X. multum languoris. refectior.

2. ⟨circ⟩

to a grain of opium, and felt more settled. He lay in bed till ten, then had an ample milk breakfast, and went for a long drive, which cheered him. He dined without meat or raw fruit, and slept a little afterwards. At eleven he took another grain of opium with squills, and estimated his drink during the day as 30 ounces.

After a tedious night Johnson took a purge and squills, estimated that his urine was half again as much as his drink, and felt, or thought he felt, the action of the squills in his bladder. His legs seemed softer, but he doubted that they were less bulky. An ample dinner of venison and pork.

On Friday it is noteworthy that Johnson does not comment on his sleep. He had 12 ounces of liquid at breakfast and about eight later, but his urine was more than double that. For dinner no meat, but a few small fish.

On Saturday, after a miserable night, he breakfasted as on Friday, took squills, dined without meat, and had 12 ounces of coffee. He took a grain of opium, feeling much lassitude, but soon was better.

Almighty and most merciful Father, who afflictest not willingly the children of Men, and by whose[3] holy will now languishes in sickness and pain, make I beseech this punishment effectual to those gracious purposes for which thou sendest it, let it, if I may presume to ask, end not in death but in repentance, let him live to promote thy kingdom on earth by the useful example of a better life, but if thy will be to call him hence, let his thoughts be so purified by his sufferings,[4] that he may be admitted to eternal Happiness.

And, O Lord, by praying for him, let me[5] be admonished to consider my own sins, and my own danger,[6] to remember the shortness of life, and to use the time which thy mercy grants me to thy glory, and my own Salvation, for the Sake of Jesus Christ our Lord. Amen.
AUGUST 28. —84. Ashbourn.

29. D. Nox jucunda. Urina ante cubitum pellucida, colore carens. Potus fere ℥28, urina 48. moles femorum minuta. Spiritus solutior. Jent ℥12. Sq. gr 1. ventriculum laborabat. X. prandium carnes furno coctae. Pransus sum large. X. Squl. gr 2. Op. gr. 1. Teae ℥10. Potus 24, Urina 36, credo 40.

3. ∧whose∧ . . . effectual to those ⟨p⟩ . . . presume ∧to ask,∧ end ∧not∧ . . . live to ⟨show⟩ . . . kingdom on earth by ⟨a bet⟩   4. ∧sufferings∧ ⟨pain⟩   5. A letter or two deleted.   6. ⟨and enable me⟩

On the same day Johnson composed a prayer for Taylor, whose name must be inserted in the blank left in the manuscript. A few days earlier, Johnson had written, "My friend is sick himself, and the reciprocation of complaints and groans affords not much of either pleasure or instruction" (*Letters* 994). Johnson's leaving a blank in the manuscript perhaps indicates that he intended using the prayer in his projected collection.

Sunday: a pleasant night. This was so unusual that Johnson quoted the Latin phrase in a letter to Brocklesby (1000.2) the next day, where he says, "My last two nights have been better."

30. M. Nox mediocris. Sero sx. Jentaculum ℥12. Ad templum eunti spiritus aliquanto minus expeditus. Prandium e carnibus in furno coctis, cum fructibus satis largum. X molle et postea liquidum, copiose. Potus post meridian. ℥ fere 18. de urina non constat.⁷ exigua non fuit. femora mollescunt.

31. Nox felix somno. Jent. ℥12. Prandium fere sine carnibus. Alvus solutior. X2. p. m. somnus. Post somnum languor. Potus ℥10 caena ℥6.=f. 34. de urina non constat.

1. SEPTEMBER. W. Nox placida cum somno. Urina ℥36 praeter id quod effusum est. inferiora ut puto quotidie quiddam ejiciunt. Jentac. ℥20. prandium, pullus, &c. de caeteris non constat.

7. ⟨parva⟩

His urine at bedtime had been clear and colourless and had been, on Saturday, almost double his drink. The bulk of his thighs was less, as Frank had told him (*Letters* 1000.2), and naturally he was in better spirits. After his usual breakfast and squills, he had a stomach-ache, but he dined liberally on baked meat, followed by more squills, a grain of opium, and tea. Again his urine was at least half again as much as his drink.

On Monday, after a middling night, Johnson rose late and breakfasted as before. He notes that as he went to church his breath seemed a little less free, but this probably refers to Sunday, since Johnson rarely attended church on weekdays. His bowels were loose, his thighs softening, and he forgot to make a record of his urine, except that it was ample, which suggests that he was worrying less about it.

On Tuesday, after a night "made happy by sleep," he dined with hardly any meat, slept in the afternoon, and was weary later. His stomach was looser, his drink about 34 ounces, and again he did not record his urine.

On 1 September, a placid night with sleep. Dinner, a chicken; what else, he has forgotten. Urine 36 ounces, besides what he spilt

2. Nox placida, sed partim insomnis. Squill 3 gr quae cum gr. 2. hesterna nocte sumptis alvum laxarunt. X3 minimum. Prandium e jusculo crasso, et anate. liquidum fortasse ℥30. op. gr. 1.

3. De urina non constat. Somni parum, opio renitente, nihil tamen doloris. X nullum. Jent. ℥12. vectatio longa. Prandium e carnibus lautum cum fructibus. potus f. ℥18 Squill gr 2.

4. Nox propitia. Urina timeo ne deficiat, X. Gestatio. Jent ℥18. prandium sine carnibus. potus f. ℥10. Vires prostratae; quiddam febrile.

---

when measuring it. He thinks his thighs and legs lose some liquid daily. Johnson had gone to church in the morning with Windham, who had paid him a most welcome two-day visit and had relieved his boredom with such conversation as he would not have again "till I come back to the regions of literature" (*Letters* 1001; *Life*, IV.544).

On Thursday, though the past night had been placid but partly sleepless, he wrote to Brocklesby (1001) about the two nights preceding: "Such Nights it is long since I have known." He also wrote Ryland (1003.1), who had been concerned about Johnson's use of opium, that he had taken only two grains in the last six days, showing how careful he was to avoid addiction. He took another grain this day. The squills which he took, along with those of the night before, loosened his stomach, but with little result. He drank about 30 ounces of liquid. For dinner, thick soup and duck.

On Friday the opium had kept him from sleeping much, but he had no pain. He went for a long ride, had a liberal dinner of meat and fruit, with about 18 ounces of liquid other than his breakfast, but he made no note of his urine.

On Saturday, after a good night, he was afraid that his urine was deficient. He took a drive, dined without meat, and found his spirits low. A little feverish. Another fairly good night.

ASHBOURN SEPT. 5. 1784. Almighty Lord and merciful
Father, to Thee be[8] thanks, and praise for all thy mercies, for
the awakening of my mind, the continuance of my life, the
amendment of my health, and the opportunity now granted
of commemorating the death of thy Son Jesus Christ,[9] our
mediator and Redeemer. Enable me O Lord to repent truly
of my Sins*—Enable me by thy Holy Spirit to lead hereafter
a better life. Strengthen my mind against useless perplexities,
teach me to form good resolutions and assist me that I may
bring them to effect, and when Thou shalt finally call me to
another state, receive me to everlasting happiness, for the sake
of our Lord Jesus Christ, Amen.
  *To shun idleness.
  To study the Bible.

5. D. Nox satis prospera. de urina non constat, timeo ne deficiat. Jent. ʒ12. Prandium e ferina lautum. Potus ʒ16.

6. De urina non constat. Detumere mihi videor. Sx 6ᵗᵃ. Iter
feci curru Chatsvortham. Pransus ferinam lautissime redij.
Ambulavi non male. Spiravi facile. potus ʒ24.

8. ₍be₎ ⟨by⟩ thanks, ₍and₎   9. ⟨for⟩

On Sunday Johnson composed a prayer for his reception of
communion, and as on 1 August he indicates, by footnotes, a
particular sin, idleness, which he repents, and a curative course
for the future, to study the Bible. One phrase, "the awakening
of my mind," is unusual, but if one supplies "to the truths of
religion" it is in keeping.

On the same day he dined liberally on venison. He drank 28
ounces during the day, kept no record of urine, but was afraid
that it was deficient.

On Monday Johnson rose at six and drove to Chatsworth, where,
he wrote Reynolds (1007), "I met young Mr Burke [Richard],
who led me very commodiously into conversation with the Duke

7. Urinae satis. Nox ita gravis ut Opij gr. 2. sumerem. somni parum. jent ʒ24. Spiritus liber. hydropis restat parum tumoris, ut videtur, vix quidquam. Καθ. prandium¹ e jusculo cum pauxillo ovillae. medicinalis potus nihil egit. Καθ iterum, jam alvus mota sed faeces durae, clysterem requirebant, post clysterem purgatio tota nocte copiosa.

8. Omnia meliora, prandium modicum. de potu et urina non constat.

9. Nox singultu molesta. Mane jent. ʒ28. X. prandium nullum. potus ʒ10. op. gr. 1. Rheumatismo humerus dexter dolet.

10. Nullus fere somnus. Nox caeterum placida. Jnt. ʒ18. Opium prohibuit somnum. de urina non constat. Ambulavi

1. ⟨sine carnibus⟩

---

and Dutchess. We had a very good morning. The Diner was publick." They dined very elegantly on venison, and Johnson came home. He walked pretty well and his breath was easy. His swelling seemed to go down. No record of urine, and for the next fortnight it was either adequate or not recorded. Drink 24 ounces.

That night was so bad that he took two grains of opium, but he had little sleep. His breath was free, there seemed little left of the dropsy, hardly anything of the swelling. Johnson first wrote that he had dined without meat, but before he finished writing the line he remembered that he had had broth and a little mutton. He took two purges during the day, and eventually, aided by an enema, they were efficacious, even through the night.

On 8 September, everything was better, and he had a moderate dinner.

On 9 September he had had a night disturbed by gasping and so omitted dinner. He took a grain of opium, perhaps to relieve rheumatism in his right shoulder. But he wrote Brocklesby on the same day that "Every thing has run smoothly," even though his nights were not so pleasant as they had been a few days earlier.

commode, meque ultronea de ambulatione oblectavi. Potus 18ʒ=36 f 40.

11. Nox commoda. de urina non constat. Jent ʒ18. Gestatio. Prandium lautum e carne vitulina furno coctâ. a prandio Mens prostrata. ante prandium pruna et pyra aliquot, fortasse nimis multa devoraveram. X2. Sub vesperam Diac. 32. melius habitum est. potus ʒ14.

12. D. Nox insomnis et turbatissima, puto, ex diacodio. Hydropici tumoris vix quidquam restat. Jent. ʒ18. Spiritus non difficilis. Prandium lautum.

13. Καθ. X saepius. Prandium satis magnum.

14. Jent. ʒ20. Prandium parcum. Nox satis placida. Mens perquam tristis. diac. 32 potus ʒ12. mane X.

That night he had almost no sleep, because of the opium, but the night was otherwise peaceful. He walked easily in the evening, and enjoyed walking of his own free will. As he wrote Brocklesby (1010), "I felt what I had not known for a long time, an inclination to walk for amusement, I took a short walk, and came back neither breathless nor fatigued."

After a comfortable night he had a drive. Before dinner he ate some plums and pears, "perhaps too many," then dined liberally on baked veal, after which he was low-spirited. In the evening two drams of diacodium, and he was better.

On Sunday, after a sleepless and very disturbed night, probably from the diacodium, he found hardly any dropsical swelling left. His breathing was easy. A liberal dinner.

Next day, after a purge, he had rather frequent evacuations. An adequate dinner.

On 14 September, after a calm enough night, the purge continued effective. A light dinner; then he was extremely depressed. Two drams of diacodium gave him a sleepless night.

15. Nox insomnis ex diacod. Mane somnus brevis. Jentaculum ℥18. spiritus facilis. potus f ℥12. m. X tenue.

16. Nox placida, multum somni. Prandium crassum.

17. Nox placida, at somni non satis. Jent ℥18. Prandium parcius. pot. ℥18. Alvus per se solutior. X3.

ASHBOURN, SEPTEMBER 18, 1784. Almighty God, merciful Father, who art the giver of all good, enable me to return Thee due thanks for the continuance of my life, and for the great mercies of the last year, for[2] relief from the diseases that afflicted me, and all the comforts and alleviations by which they were mitigated; and, O my gracious God, make me truly thankful for the call by which thou hast awakened my conscience and summoned me to Repentance. Let not thy call, O Lord, be forgotten, or thy summons neglected, but let the residue of my life, whatever it shall be, be passed[3] in true contrition, and diligent obedience. Let me repent of the sins of my past years,[4] and so keep thy laws for the time to come that when it shall be thy good pleasure to call me to another state, I may find mercy in thy sight. Let thy Holy Spirit support me

2. ⟨my⟩   3. ᴧbe passedᴧ   4. ᴧyearsᴧ ⟨life⟩

Next day he had a small evacuation and some sleep in the morning. His breath was easy.

On Thursday, after a calm night with much sleep, he had a solid dinner. On this day Johnson wrote Brocklesby (1011), who had charged him, "somewhat unjustly with luxury" in eating. Johnson pointed out that he ate but once a day, excluding his milk breakfast, that he was not growing fatter, and that his digestion was good, except when he took a purge. The diary generally bears him out.

On Friday, after a quiet night, but not enough sleep, he dined rather sparingly. His bowels were normal.

in the hour of death, and O Lord[5] grant me pardon in the day of Judgement, for the sake of Jesus Christ, our Lord. Amen.

18. Nox bona. X. Jent. ʒ18. Prandium largum e vitulina et suilla. Potus, ut puto, largus.

19. DOM. Nox benignior. Jent. ʒ12. Prandium mediocre. multum potus. Gestatio vesperi. Sub noctem gravis somnolentia. X.

20. Nox somno caruit. jent. ʒ12. Καθ. prandium exiguum. X5. sub noctem op. gr. 2. A prandio somni pauxillum. Teae nihil.

21. Somnus fere nullus. jent. ʒ18. corpus leve.[6] Prandij nescio quid* multis cum fructibus.

*Pisa cum lardo, et pullus Gal.

5. ᴧO Lordᴧ   6. ⟨Prandium ex assa Bubula largum⟩ . . . ᴧPisa . . . pullus Gal.ᴧ

The birthday prayer reflects, in its unusual calmness, Johnson's improved health.

His birthday was appropriately begun with a good night, and continued with an ample dinner of veal and pork, at which he drank freely, not at the moment worried about dropsy. The day was enlivened with three letters about Lunardi's balloon ascent: "I could have been content with one," he wrote Reynolds (1013). Johnson was seventy-five.

On Sunday, after a more pleasant night, he dined moderately, with much drink. Then a drive in the evening and heavy drowsiness afterwards.

Next day, after a sleepless night, he took a purge after breakfast. He dined very sparingly and then slept a little. No tea. Two grains of opium at night.

On Tuesday he had had almost no sleep, but his body felt light. The next entries show that Johnson was writing on the following day: he first wrote "dinner of roast beef with much fruit," then

22. Jent. ʒ18. Prandium ex assa bubula, multis etiam per totam diem fructibus devoratis. Alvus solutior.

23. Nox turbatissima. pil. squil. 4. jent e teâ. prandium tenue sine carnibus. X saepius. vesperi op. gr. 1. pectus vellicatum.

24. Nox fere insomnis. jent. ʒ18, prandium ex anate. pil. squill. 2. caput insomnia aliquantulum gravatum. pil. squill. 2. nocte praeterita multum urinae parum coloratae effusum, quam squillas movisse visum est.

25. Jent. ʒ18. Nox inquieta. Prandium e vitulina. Pectus vexatum. 34. [diac.] Pectus sedatum.

26. DOM. Nox insomnis et inquieta. ʒ Jent. 18. redeunti a templo per pluviam, incessus, celer, expeditior, facilis. D. G. ad vesperam pectus vexatum. Diacod. 32. requievi.

---

realized that he had had that on the twenty-second, crossed out the beef and wrote "dinner, I know not what"; remembering, he inserted "peas with bacon, and a young cock."

Next day Johnson had his roast beef, and much fruit all day. His stomach was looser.

On Thursday, 23 September, after a most disturbed night, he took squills, and had only tea for breakfast. A light dinner without meat. His bowels continued loose. In the evening, finding his breast convulsed, he took a grain of opium.

On Friday he had had an almost sleepless night, during which the squills moved a large discharge of almost colourless urine. More squills today. He dined on duck, and found his head somewhat oppressed from sleeplessness.

On Saturday, after a restless night, he had veal for dinner. Four drams of diacodium quieted his troubled breast.

On Sunday, he had had a sleepless, restless night, but returning from church in the rain, he found his gait free and easy. "God be praised." Towards evening he took two drams of diacodium and eased his troubled breast.

27. Nox non admodum turbata. Urinae multum. Jent. ℥18.
diac 32. Iter facile et commodum. Prandium e bubula. Alvus
constrict[a]. Καθ. faeces induratae ut enemate essent solvendae.
Enema parum effecit, altero opus erat. Enema secundum in-
testinum acriter stimulavit, ut alvum in horto cum ad lat-
rinam pervenire non sustinuerim, exonerarem. ita egit ca-
tharsis ut X puto septies.

28. Nox inquieta. Somnus matutinus[7] placidus. ambulavi non
leviter, at Stoae collim tamen perveni. tota die. X.

29. Nox inquieta. a prandio Op. gr. 1. (Jent. ℥24) Prandium
e vitulina. Spiritus impeditus.

30. Nox insomnis. Καθ. X2 feliciter. Jent. ℥24. multum fructuum. Prand. mediocre. corpus grave.

7. MS: matietinus

On Monday the night had not been very disturbed. There was
much urine; for the next fortnight it was either adequate or not
mentioned by Johnson. He left Ashbourne for Lichfield, and
found the trip easy and pleasant. After dining on beef, he was
costive, took a purge, which was ineffective, and finally resorted
to two enemas, which operated so well that he was unable to reach
the house and had to relieve himself in the garden privy.

On Tuesday, after a restless night, he had a peaceful sleep in
the morning, and later walked, with some difficulty, to Stowe Hill.
The purge continued effective all day.

Next day, after a restless night, he had veal for dinner, and
afterwards a grain of opium. His breathing was hindered. This
day Johnson wrote to Brocklesby (1015) that his health had held
reasonably well for a month, with perhaps a little decline in the
last day or two.

On Thursday, after a sleepless night, he had much fruit and a
moderate dinner. Then a purge; his body was heavy.

The first four nights of October were wretched. He did not

OCTOBER. 1.2.3.4. Noctes miserae. virium nullum incrementum. Anhelitus molestus, non tamen ad extremum gravis. Diac aut op. saepius.

4.[8] L. Faeces durae. Ad noctem sumpsi ol Cast.

5. MART. Καθ. X4.

6. MERC. Anhelitus molestus. Somnolentia gravis. Prandium largum e vitulinâ. potus non parcus. Diacodij 34.

7. JOVIS. Nox insomnis. 4 Pil. Scill. Lac cum pane. Prandium e piscibus et fructibus. alvus astrictior. Spiritus mane expeditior. 2 Pil. scil.

8. VEN. Nox insomnis et molesta. Καθ. X saepius satis commode. Prand. parcum. a prandio somnus placidus, anhelitus gravis. Urinae satis.

9. SAT. Morbus ingravescit. anhelitus molestus. Urina tamen non deficit. Mens prostrata.

8. ⟨3⟩ ∧4∧ ⋯ ⟨4⟩ ∧5∧ ⋯ ⟨5⟩ ∧6∧ ⋯ ⟨6⟩ ∧7∧

---

gain in strength. His asthma was troublesome, but not extremely so. He took diacodium or opium rather often, which no doubt brought costiveness on the fourth, for which he took castor oil for the first time, on Brocklesby's recommendation.

On 5 October he took a purge again, since he was not quite sure of the castor oil.

On Wednesday his asthma was troublesome and he was very drowsy. He dined liberally on veal, with plenty to drink. Four drams of diacodium.

On Thursday, after a sleepless night his breathing was freer. His breakfast was bread and milk; fish and fruit for dinner. Squills. His stomach was more constricted.

On Friday, 8 October, after a sleepless and troubled night he

10. DOM. Nox molesta.⁹ sacris peractis, diac. 34. prandium mediocre. Spiritus aegre tractus, magna artuum debilitas.¹ Op. gr. 1. Anhelitus laxatus. Ol. Castor. ʒı.

11. LUN. Somnus ferme nullus. jent ʒ18. Somnus longus et placidus in pulvinari. X. Prandij affatim. Ol Cast. bene cessit. Op. gr. 1. N. Hactenus Stoam pedibus petenti declivis licet sit via, crebro fuit interquiescendum, nec non a templo redeunti spiritus impeditus. Artus debiles: nihil virium per aestatem redijt. aliquantulum profeci, sed retro lapsus sum.

12. MART. Nox insomnis, mane squil. gr. 2. cum gr. 3 heri sumptis. nescio tamen an Urina copiosior. Mul[t]um per diem

9. ⟨a prandi⟩   1. ₄Spiritus . . . debilitas₄

---

took a purge, but his bowels were normal. He dined sparingly and slept calmly afterwards. His asthma was severe.

Next day, he found his disease growing worse, the asthma troublesome, and his spirits low.

The night was troubled. Sunday, after church, he took four drams of diacodium, then had a moderate dinner. He breathed with difficulty and found his limbs very weak. One grain of opium relieved the asthma, and he took castor oil again. On the same day Johnson wrote his lawyer friend Scott that although his asthma was more troublesome than it had recently been, it was better than when he came to Ashbourne in July. And his description of his condition is almost wryly humorous: "my legs would not carry me far, if my breath would last, and my breath would not last if my legs would carry me" (*Letters* 1021.1).

On Monday he had had almost no sleep, but after breakfast slept long and peacefully on a sofa. He dined amply and the castor oil had good results. One grain of opium. He observes, "Up to now, in walking to Stowe, though the road is downhill, I have had to rest frequently, and coming back from church my breath is short." His limbs were weak and he found no return of strength

somni. X2. post squillas ventriculus multum laborabat, inde somnus matutinus. Dies tarda.

13. MERC. Nox turbata. X. mens prostrata. diacod 32 parum profeci. Op. gr 1.¼ melius habui.

14. JOV. Noctem ad² 5ᵗᵃᵐ egi in cathedra fere semper insomnis, quinta decubui, nec dormivi. jent. ʒ18. paulum dormivi. Urina parcius fluit sed non tumeo. Appetitio cibi minus acris, fortasse nimis frequenter saturata. Noctes nuper insomnes.

15. V. 16. SAT. Anhelitu molestae opio graves.

17.³ DOM. A templo reverso, spiritus impeditur, artus languent. Op. gr. 1. Somnolentia gravis. Decubiturus sumsi Diac. 32. turbatus sedi ad h. tertiam. decubui; turbatior hora septima sumsi Op. gr. 1. nec quies tamen venire voluit.

2. MS: at   3. ⟨16⟩

from the summer. He had gained a little ground but had fallen back.

On Tuesday, the twelfth, after a sleepless night, he took squills and remembered that he had taken them also on Monday. His stomach was much distressed by them. He had much sleep in the morning and during the tedious day.

On Wednesday, after a disturbed night, two drams of diacodium were of little help to his dejection, but he felt better after a grain and a quarter of opium. In a letter to Heberden (1022), Johnson commented more lightly on his eating: "My appetite is, I think, less keen than it was, but not so abated as that its decline can be observed by any one but myself."

He spent the night in a chair till five, Thursday morning, when he lay down but did not sleep. After breakfast he slept a little. Rather scant urine, but he was not swelling. "Appetite less keen; perhaps too often sated."

Friday and Saturday were troubled with panting, heavy with opium.

18. L. De prima parte diei dictum est. Jnt. ℥18. Prandium copiosum cum fructibus. X benigne, sine Καθ.

19. MART. Nox misera. Lecto relicto, sedens somni aliquantulum cepi. Jentavi. Tumor hydropicus paulatim ingruit, quod ego sensi, et hodie monuit Franciscus. X bis sine Καθ. Pransus modice meliuscule habui. at motus quam minimus anhelitum ciet. vires prostratae. Miserere, Deus. Squl. gr 4. Somnolentia gravis cum anhelitu. X3°. Ante decubi[tum] lassus sumsi Op. gr 1.ss.

20. MERC. Tota nocte mente turbatissima vigilavi. alvum 36 Ol. Cast. levare volui. Prandium modicum, ventriculus laborabat, vino ex uvis crispis flatulento sedatus est. cubui paulum,

---

On Sunday, returning from church, his breathing was hindered, his limbs feeble. A grain of opium, heavy drowsiness. On going to bed he took two drams of diacodium. Disturbed, he sat up till three, then lay down; more disturbed, at seven he took a grain of opium, but sleep would not come.

On Monday he breakfasted, had a liberal dinner with fruit, and found his bowels normal.

On Tuesday, the nineteenth, after a wretched night, he rose, had a little sleep sitting, and then breakfasted. "The dropsy encroaches by degrees; I felt this and today Frank told me of it." He dined sparingly and was a little better, but the slightest movement caused panting. His strength was prostrated: "God have mercy." He took squills and was troubled with heavy drowsiness and panting. Weary, he took one and a half grains of opium at bedtime.

He lay awake all night with a sorely troubled mind. On Wednesday he took castor oil, had a light dinner. Finding his stomach disturbed, he settled it with gooseberry wine. He lay down for a little but did not sleep. His stomach was relieved, and urine seemed to flow. On going to bed he took two drams of diacodium, and castor oil. His urine was copious, almost colourless. He tried

non dormivi. alvus levata est, X molle copiosum. Urina fluere videtur. Decubiturus sumsi Diac 32 ol. Cast. f. 33. Legere volui, nec sustinui. urina copiosa, decubituro erat pene coloris expers.

21. JOV. Prima parte noctis dormivi; deinde convulso pectore diu vigilavi. tandem me levavi et sumptis squil. Pil. 4 cum gr. ss. opij. lecto redditus, somnum cepi. jent. ℥18. prandium liberalius. X durum. vesperi, sub decubitum 34 diac. p. m. Squil pil. 3=7. Urina non parca. 32 diac.

22. VEN. Nox insomnis. vigilijs lassus sumsi scil. pil. 4 op gr. 1 aliquantulum, nec placide dormivi. Prandium e piscibus parcum. multum fructuum, corpus grave. X nihil. Oleum ricini frustra sumptum.

23. SAT. Καθ. X4 primo et secundo affatim; tert. et quart. liquidum. nihil prandij praeter offam farinaceam. turgeo

---

to read but could not keep it up. In spite of this gloomy record, Johnson was able to write at least six letters this day, in one of which, to Hamilton (1024), he wrote that he hoped still "to find new topicks of merriment, or new incitements to curiosity" when he returned to London.

He slept the first part of the night, then, his breast convulsed, he lay long awake. At last he rose, took squills and half a grain of opium, went back to bed and slept. Thursday he breakfasted, and had a rather liberal dinner. In the evening just before bedtime, he took four drams of diacodium and enough squills to make up seven pills during the day, which had effect. Two more drams of diacodium.

On Friday, 22 October, after a sleepless night, weary of lying awake, he took squills and one grain of opium, and had a little unquiet sleep. A sparing dinner of fish, with much fruit. His body was heavy and he took castor oil in vain.

The next day he took a purge, with effect. No dinner except

tamen. prima nocte, corpore quippe exonerato, dormivi placide. experrectus vero, sensi ventriculum durissime constrictum, meque vigil per horas aliquot volutavi. Surrexi tandem et me sacris actionibus paravi, sed talem sensi artuum debilitatem, ut laborem eundi ad templum defugerem. in cathedra igitur desedi, et altum duabus horis dormivi. X2. Prandium modicum. A prandio templum adij. ante cubitum diac. 52.

25. L. Media nocte turbatissimus sumsi opij gr 1 cum tertia parte. Sedatior factus, nihil aut certe parum somni cepi. Constipatus sumsi ol Cast. 51. tristis decubui.

26. Nox insomnis et longa. Mane X ex hesterna catharsi. Stoam adij, pransus sum modice cum multis pyris. X 2° sub noctem tristissimus. Diac 52 Opij granum imminutum sumsi.

---

porridge. "Yet I swell. In the early part of the night I slept peacefully, no doubt because my body was lightened. But on waking, my stomach seemed severely constricted, and for several hours I lay tossing."

At length, Sunday morning, he rose and prepared for worship, but felt so weak that he shrank from the labour of going to church. So he settled down in a chair and slept soundly for two hours. After a moderate dinner he went to church. Before bedtime, two drams of diacodium.

On Monday the twenty-fifth, having been much disturbed in the middle of the night, he had taken a grain of opium, which quieted him somewhat, but he got little or no sleep. Costive, he took castor oil, and lay down sad. But in spite of this dismal day, Johnson could write Brocklesby (1029) that he was not afraid of the journey to London or residence there: "The town is my element, there are my friends, there are my books to which I have not yet bidden farewell, and there are my amusements."

On Tuesday after a tedious, sleepless night, the purge of the previous day took effect. He went to Stowe and dined moderately,

2 7. Post noctem taedij plenam sx. Lactis multum sumsi. deinde sena et sale K. Pharmaco vix hausto, ad prandium accersitus cibo modice usus sum. Purgatio optime cessit. alvo quater mota, post primum nixum, ter vehementissime. Faeces multo cum flatu eruperunt. Unde ventri tanta esset saburra, vix comperio. Decubiturus sumpsi Op. gr. 2.

2 8. jov. Nox placida, sed sine somno. Καθ. medicamini sumendo vix tempus fuit inter jentaculum largum et prandium non parcum. Optime tamen purgatum. Alvus quater mota. vice tertia abeuntem revocavit, et faeces, multo cum flatu, multas ejecit. per somnolentiam diem egi.

2 9. ven. Post brevem in lecto somnum, Pectus convulsum Op. gr. 1 sedare volui. Frustra. hora 9na surrexi, et somnum cepi in sedile. Jentavi. Prandij quod cito secutum est, appetitio nulla. Animus tristis, vires prostratae. Diacod. ℥ss. non nihil recre[a]tus, meliuscule habui. forsan nimis purgatum est. Op. g. 1. X durum.

———————————

with many pears. At night, in very low spirits, he took two drams of diacodium and a grain of opium.

On Wednesday after a night full of tedium, he got up, took much milk, then senna as a purge, and salt. He was called almost at once to dinner, and ate moderately. The purges were effective. "I hardly know why my stomach carries so much ballast." On going to bed, two grains of opium.

Thursday, after a quiet but sleepless night, he took a purge. There was hardly time for medicine between a hearty breakfast and a fairly big dinner. The purges were effective, with flatulence. He was sleepy all day.

That night, after a short sleep in bed, his breast was convulsed; he took a grain of opium, which did not quiet it. Friday he rose at nine and slept in a chair. Spirits low, strength also. Half an ounce of diacodium somewhat restored him. Perhaps, he thinks,

30. SAT. Nox tota somno caruit. Mane sx. sedens dormivi. jent. ℥18. ante cub. Scil. gr 4. media nocte scil gr 4 = gr 8. nullo hactenus eventu. A prandio lassus aliquantulum ἀπόβρι- ξα,²ᵃ at tumeo. decubiturus sumpsi Ol. Cast. ℥i.

31. D. Καθ. jentaculi nihil prandij minimum. X4 ut puto. Ante cubitum sumpsi Op. gr 2.

2a. So MS.

REPERTORIUM.

Moral Demonstration. Ductor dubitantium. 93.
Account of Johnson's Sophocles. Bowyer's Life.

---

he has purged too much. His stool was hard, no doubt from the opium.

He had no sleep that night. He had taken squills before retiring and again at midnight but without effect. On Saturday he rose in the morning and slept sitting. Tired after dinner, he dozed a little. The dropsy was increasing. Castor oil before going to bed.

On Sunday he took a purge but had no breakfast, little dinner. His bowels were free. Two grains of opium before bedtime.

Johnson's "Repertorium," a miscellaneous storehouse of notes on reading, as the title suggests, was apparently all written on or near 31 October, the date on page 11 of the manuscript, since Johnson refers to the same book on both page 1 and page 11, and only two very short notes follow the date.

Moral demonstration is defined by Jeremy Taylor as "a con-jugation of probabilities," as compared with natural or scientific demonstration—the reasonableness of one side of a proposition dispassionately compared with the unreasonableness of the other (*Ductor Dubitantium*, 1660, pp. 123–24). Johnson's page refer-ence is to a later edition.

There is a brief account of the 1758 edition of Thomas John-son's *Sophocles* in Nichols's *Anecdotes of William Bowyer*: "*Four only of these Plays were printed by Mr. Bowyer; but in those the*

Miscellanea Aulica.   Cowley's Letters.
Howe's Living Temple.   Bowyer's Life.
Pope's Letter to Savage, Ruffhead.
Roscommon's Life.   Bakers papers.
Salianus. voluminous Jesuit, Montagu.

---

publick are indebted to him for more than barely the manual
operation" (1782, p. 282). Johnson had four sets of Johnson's
Sophocles, in Greek and Latin, with notes, in his library.

Tom Brown's *Miscellanea Aulica: or, A Collection of State-
treatises, Never Before Publish'd*, 1702, included "Letters by the
famous Mr. Abraham Cowley . . . during King Charles the Second's Exile; written from Paris to Mr. Henry Bennet, afterwards
Earl of Arlington."

Nichols remarks in his *Bowyer* (p. 257 n.) that Dr. Samuel
Clarke, whose sermons Johnson admired, took his a priori argument for Divine Existence from John Howe's *Living Temple,
or That a Good Man Is the Temple of God*, 1675.

Owen Ruffhead printed two letters from Pope to Savage in his
Life of Pope, 1769, pp. 504, 506. Both of them refer to Pope's efforts
in raising an annuity of forty pounds for Savage, of which Pope
paid half, and the second, in 1742, marks Pope's final break with
that strange man. Johnson had not seen the letters when he wrote
his *Savage*, and treated Pope a bit harshly. Although he had used
Ruffhead when writing his *Pope*, he had not quoted from these
letters. The second begins: "Sir, I must be sincere with you, as
our correspondence is now likely to be closed. Your language is
really too high, and what I am not used to from my superiors;
much too extraordinary for me, at least sufficiently so, to make me
obey your commands, and never more presume to advise or meddle
in your affairs, but leave your own conduct entirely to your own
judgment."

There is a manuscript life of Roscommon, not referred to by
Johnson in his *Roscommon*, written by Dr. Knightly Chetwood
and preserved in the British Museum in Thomas Baker's manuscripts, XXXVI.27.

See Patres
1 *Clemens Rom:* Hermas Pastor.
   Linus v. Cav. Barnabas.
2 *Ignatius.* Polycarpus. *Justinus Martyr.* Literae Smyrnae-
   orum de Polycarpo. Theophilus. Tatianus. *Athenagoras.*
   Irenaeus. Clemens Alex. Tertullianus.

James Salian wrote *Annals of the Old Testament* in six folio
volumes, 1618–24. Bishop Richard Montagu, a zealous defender
of the historical position of the English Church, called him "that
voluminous Jesuit" in his *Acts and Monuments of the Church*,
1642, p. 227. It is a pleasant tribute and probably amused Johnson,
who quotes from Montagu again a few pages further on.

The Church Fathers in the long list beginning here are grouped
by Johnson according to centuries. He was evidently reading William Cave's *Apostolici, or . . . Lives . . . of the Primitive Fathers*,
1677, perhaps in the later version *Scriptorum Ecclesiasticorum
Historia Literaria* (2 vols. Basel, 1741–45), in which a short biography is followed by a discussion of the genuine works of the
writer in some detail, closing with a comment on the doubtful
works. Johnson followed Cave's order rather closely, perhaps
noting down as he was reading authors into whose works he wished
to dip later. Page numbers in this comment refer to that work.
Clement I, St. Clement of Rome (fl. ca. A.D. 96), one of the Apos-
tolic Fathers, third or fourth Bishop of Rome, wrote a long epistle
to Corinth on the Christian ministry (1.28). His life is followed
by the *Shepherd of Hermas* (p. 30), an anonymous work mentioning him, and preceded by the life of St. Linus (fl. A.D. 67), second
Bishop of Rome, said to have suffered martyrdom, and buried in
the Vatican (p. 27). Cave's article on St. Barnabas the Apostle
(pp. 18–21) includes considerable discussion of Polycarp and
Ignatius.

The second century begins with St. Ignatius, Bishop of Antioch,
author of many important letters on Church doctrine, and follows
with St. Polycarp (69?–155?), Bishop of Smyrna and martyr, author
of the *Smyrna Letters*. Justin the Martyr (100?–165?) follows,

3 *Acta Felicitatis et Perpetuae.*
Minutius Felix.
Origenes
Cyprianus
Novatianus cum Tertul.
Methodius

----

whose *Apology* furnishes important information about the early Church. Theophilus (fl. 170), Bishop of Antioch, wrote *Ad autolycum*, an apology for Christianity. Because of the association with the other second-century authors, it is not likely that the later and better known Theophilus, Bishop of Alexandria 385–410, is meant. Tatianus, second-century Christian apologist, was an Assyrian convert and author of a harmony of the Gospels. Athenagoras (fl. ca. 177) wrote an *Apology* defending the Christians against accusations of "atheism, eating human flesh, and licentiousness." Irenaeus (b. ca. 130), Bishop of Lyons, was the author of the "first systematic exposition of Catholic belief," and of the oldest existing catechism. Clement of Alexandria (150–220?) was a Greek theologian, and Tertullian (160?–230?) a Latin Church Father.

The third century begins with the anonymous (ca. A.D. 202) *Acts of SS Felicitas and Perpetua* (Cave, 1.99), described by James Bridge in the *Catholic Encyclopedia* as "perhaps of all extant Acta the most beautiful and famous," and is followed by Minucius (ca. 220), author of *Octavius*, a dialogue between a pagan and a Christian (1.101). Origen (185?–254?), Greek writer and Church Father, is next, and then St. Cyprian, martyr and Bishop of Carthage 248–58. Novatianus, a Roman presbyter (fl. 250), one of the earliest anti-popes, opposed Christian toleration of those who, after baptism, sacrificed to idols. He is said to have been martyred under Valerian. Johnson has connected him with Tertullian. St. Methodius of Olympus (fl. ca. 290), was a martyr and an opponent of Origen (Cave, 1.150).

In the fourth century Arnobius Afer, the Elder, teacher of rhetoric during the reign of Diocletian, was the author of *Adver-*

4. Arnobius

Lactantius	*Basilius M.*
Eusebius	Gregorius Naz.
Athanasius	Dionysius. Areop. dictus
Commodianus	Proba Faltonia
Juvencus	Macarius
Firmicus adv. Gentiles	*Ambrosius*
Pachomius	Gregorius. Nyss.
Cyrillus. Hieros:	Hieronymus.
Hilarius	Nemesius.
Apollinarius. Ps. par.	Rufinus.
Epiphanius	Paulinus.
Optatus	*Augustinus.*
Ephraem Syrus	*Chrysostomus.*

sus gentes, a defence of Christianity against the charge that it was responsible for the calamities of the times. Lactantius Firmianus (ca. 260–ca. 340), the "Christian Cicero," a pupil of Arnobius, attacked Epicureanism. Next are Eusebius of Caesarea (260?–340?), theologian and Church historian, and St. Athanasius (293?–373), Greek Church Father. Commodianus, Christian Latin poet (fl. ca. 250), wrote *Instructiones*, ridiculing classic myths, and *Carmen apologeticum*, exhorting man to repent before Judgement Day. Juvencus (Cave, I.200), a priest, wrote a poem on the life of Christ. Julius Firmicus Maternus (Cave, I.204), wrote *De errore profanarum religionum*, which might be described as "against the Gentiles," attacking and exposing the mysteries of Eleusis, Isis, and Mithra. Pachomius (d. ca. 346) founded several monasteries (I.208). St. Cyril of Jerusalem (ca. 315–86) was the author of *Catachesis*, an important series of pre- and post-baptismal lectures on the Christian faith. St. Hilarius (ca. 300–67), Bishop of Poitiers, attacked the Arians; Augustine called him "the illustrious father of the churches." "Apollinarius" is probably Apollinaris, Bishop of Laodicea in Syria (d. 390), who paraphrased the Old and New Testaments. St. Epiphanius (ca. 315–402),

PRECES.

Against the incursion of wicked thoughts.
Repentance and Pardon. *Laud.*
In disease.

Bishop of Constantia, devoted himself to the spread of monasticism and the refutation of Origen. Optatus of Miletus was an opponent of the Donatist schism and a predecessor of Augustine. St. Ephraem Syrus (d. 373) wrote many hymns which still survive (Cave, 1.235). St. Basil the Great (330?–79), Bishop of Caesarea, author of the liturgy still used by the Eastern Church, was a fellow-student of St. Gregory of Nazianus (ca. 329–ca. 389), one of the four great Fathers of the Eastern Church, known for his discourses on the Trinity. Next is Dionysius, called the Areopagite, the Pseudo-Dionysius, whose fifth-century theological works, translated into Latin by Erigena, were of great influence in the Middle Ages. Faltonia Proba (Cave, 1.255), a Roman poetess, wrote a poetic paraphrase of Biblical history "in terms borrowed exclusively from Virgil" (*Catholic Encyclopedia*). Macarius, Bishop of Jerusalem (fl. 330), was a theologian, author of an epistle to Verthanes. Next is St. Ambrose, Bishop of Milan, statesman of the Church and author of the Christmas hymn *Veni Redemptor.* St. Gregory of Nyssa (ca. 331–ca. 396) was one of the four great Fathers of the Eastern Church, younger brother of Basil, a defender of the Nicene creed against Arianism. St. Jerome (340?–420) is most famous for his translation of the Bible, the Vulgate. Nemesius, Christian philosopher (fl. ca. 390), wrote a treatise *On Human Nature*, a system of anthropology, thought by some to have anticipated Harvey's discovery of the circulation of the blood. Rufinus, presbyter and theologian (ca. 340–410), defended the writings of Origen in a dispute with Jerome. St. Paul of Nola (353–431) wrote epistles to Augustine, Jerome, and others. St. Augustine (354–430), Bishop of Hippo, author of *The City of God*, and St. John Chrysostom (345?–407), Patriarch of Constantinople, were familiar to Johnson. He had their works in his library and refers twice to Chrysostom in his diaries.

On the loss of Friends by death; by his own fault; or friend's.
On unexpected notice of the death of other.
Prayer generally recommendatory.
To understand their prayers.
Under dread of Death.

———————

One may guess that the names which Johnson has underlined
in this long list were those of which he had some prior knowledge.
Of this group, besides Augustine and Chrysostom, nine were in
his library: Ambrose, Origen, Athanasius, Eusebius, Ephraem
Syrus, Basil, Justin Martyr, Clement of Alexandria, and Tertullian, whereas he owned only four of those not underlined: Cyril,
Epiphanius, Dionysius the Areopagite, and Jerome. Others were
probably represented in his set of *Bibliotheca veterum patrum*,
Paris, 1624, or present but not listed by title in the sale catalogue
of his library.

The notes on prayers and on scepticism which follow were no
doubt intended for an introductory essay for the book of devotions
which he had long contemplated and which Dr. Adams had urged
on him on 11 June of the current year, when Johnson said: "I
have thought of getting together all the books of prayers which
I could, selecting those which should appear to me the best, putting out some, inserting others, adding some prayers of my own,
and prefixing a discourse on prayer" (*Life*, IV.293). A fortnight
after making these notes, Johnson told Adams that he was now
"in a right frame of mind" for writing the book and "would in
earnest set about it" (*Life*, IV.376).

Under the general heading "Prayers," he lists several types, some
rather unusual, but perhaps to be understood in the light of the
many recent deaths of his old friends, Levet and Miss Williams
among others. Archbishop William Laud's *Private Devotions*
seems to be referred to; for example, "O Almighty God, have
respect unto my prayers, and deliver my heart from the temptations of ill thoughts, that by Thy mercy I may become a fit habitation for Thy Holy Spirit, through Jesus Christ, our Lord. Amen"
(ed. 1855, p. 178). Laud gives eighteen penitentials, some of them

Prayer commonly considered as a stated and temporary duty—performed and forgotten—without any effect on the following day. Prayer a vow. *Taylor.*

SKEPTICISM CAUSED BY

1 Indifference about opinions.
2 Supposition that things disputed are disputable.
3 Denial of unsuitable evidence.
4 False judgement of Evidence.
5 Complaint of the obscurity of Scripture.
6 Contempt of Fathers and of authority.
7 Absurd method of learning objection first.
8 Study not for truth but vanity.

Ep to Gal written against the Hebionites Desposyni q. Montagu. 232.

———

9 Sensuality and a vicious life.
10 False honour, false shame.
11 Omission of prayer and religious Exercises.

OCT. 31—84

Against Despair

———

slightly modified from the *Book of Common Prayer*, and it may be that Johnson was interested in the whole group.

Jeremy Taylor's *Holy Living*, 1650, may have been recalled from memory. Taylor says, "A vow to God is an act of prayer" (C. 4, S. 7, par. 17). Johnson's well-known horror of frivolous vows can be readily understood in this connexion. The heads on scepticism appear to be in preparation for an essay on the subject, perhaps to be included in the book of devotions. "Contempt of Fathers" refers to the Church Fathers, not to parents.

The note on the Epistle to the Galatians interrupts the eleven causes of scepticism, which then continue. Johnson refers to Mon-

MISC:

Sponge—Suet. Vesp. 16

cubic foot of water 6 gall. ½. 26 quarts

Clark Vol 1. 146, 254, 256

NOVEMB. 1. L. Somnolentus fui post noctem insomnem. Vesperi X. Prandium modicum.

---

tagu's *Acts and Monuments*: "As for those Desposyni . . . they were a sort of mungrell Jews, or Christians." Montagu then quotes Jerome: "Called they are Hebionites, from Hebion, The Founder of that Heresie," and continues: "Against which Heresie it is that S. Paul addresseth the Epistle to the Galatians" (pp. 231–32). The sect advocated a return to the Mosaic Law.

"Against Despair," on a page by itself, belongs logically among the types of prayer under "Preces."

As to sponges, in paragraph 16 of Suetonius's *Life of Vespasian* we read: "It is believed, that he advanced all the most rapacious amongst the procurators to higher offices, with the view of squeezing them after they had acquired great wealth. He was commonly said, 'to have used them as sponges,' because it was his practice, as we may say, to wet them when dry, and squeeze them when wet" (Bohn ed., trans. A. Thomson).

The reference to "Clark" is probably to the folio edition of Samuel Clarke's *Works*, 1738–42. Johnson has frequently noted reading his sermons. The first page is in the sermon "Of the Fear of God," and on that page Clarke discusses the differences between superstition and religion. The two later pages, in the sermon "The Nature of Religious Truths," concern Clarke's argument that essential religious truth, whether natural or revealed, is comprehensible even to a person of "mean Capacity." Perhaps Johnson intended to introduce these ideas into the essay he planned for the book of devotions. In the octavo edition of Clarke there is nothing remarkable on the pages noted.

2. MART. Nox insomnis. Mane dormitum pene ad merid. Prandium mediocre. corpus tumet, cingulum erat laxandum Kαθ. X2. ante decubitum aeger animi pectore vexatus, sumpsi Op. gr. 1. nondum compositus, addidi Diac. 34 cum 2 cyathis sacc. sp. paulum recreatus decubui.

3. MERC. Nox sine somno, somnus in sedili placidus. Sumsi scill. pil. 12. decem f. gr. scil nullo hactenus eventu. Jentaculi nihil. Prandij satis. X sponte. Ante cubitum Diacod 34 cum 2 cyathis Sp. Sacch.

4. JOV. N. Praeterita in cathedra dormivi, mane⁴ Acet. Scil. vim magnam sumpsi. Ventriculus vehementer commotus. dolor magnus. Vomitum bis. jent. nullum. Acetum Sq. iteratum, nova aegritudo, non vomitus. Prandij minimum. urina parca. Diacodij 32.

4. MS: many

_____

On Monday, 1 November, we return to the "Sick Man's Journal." Johnson was sleepy after a sleepless night; he dined moderately.

Tuesday, after a sleepless night, he slept in the morning almost till noon. He dined moderately. The dropsy was causing swelling, and he had to let out his belt. Before bedtime, feeling low, and troubled with his breast, he took a grain of opium. Still not composed, he added four drams of diacodium and two cups of rum. Somewhat refreshed, he went to bed.

On Wednesday, after a sleepless night, he slept peacefully in a chair. He took squills, about ten grains, so far without effect. No breakfast; a fair dinner. Before bed, he took four drams of diacodium with two cups of rum.

He slept in a chair during the night. Thursday morning he took a great quantity of squills, and his stomach was violently disturbed, with great pain. He vomited twice. No breakfast. He repeated the squills, was sick again, but did not vomit. Very little dinner. His urine scanty. Two drams of diacodium.

5. VEN. nihil somniferum

6. SAT. nihil somniferum

7. DOM. Diacod 32

8. LUN. Nox praeterita pene tote in cathedra acta, cum somno tamen. horae meridianae occupatae sine taedio. Καθ. bene. Urina paulo, ut spero, uberior. anhelitus non levis, nec solito gravior. X3. Diacod 32.

DEC. 5. 1784. Almighty and most merciful Father, I am now, as to human eyes it seems, about to commemorate[5] for the last time, the death of thy son Jesus Christ, our Saviour and Redeemer. Grant, O Lord, that my whole hope and confidence may be in his merits and in thy mercy: forgive and accept my

5. ⟨I⟩ I . . . ⟨comme⟩ commemorate

On Friday and Saturday he took no narcotics, though he wrote Brocklesby (1033.1), "I have supported myself with opiates till they have made me comatous."

The next day, two drams of diacodium. He wrote Hawkins (1034), "I am relapsing into the dropsy very fast."

He spent almost all of the night in a chair, but he had slept. On Monday, the eighth, the midday hours passed without tedium. "Urine, I hope, rather more abundant." His panting was not slight, but was no worse than usual. Two drams of diacodium.

The "Sick Man's Journal" ends here. Johnson left Lichfield in a day or two, spent a few days with Hector in Birmingham, went to Oxford on the twelfth, and was home on the sixteenth. His last weeks he spent preparing to die: he sent epitaphs for his father, mother, and brother to be put in the church at Lichfield, had a collection of his works sent to Pembroke, burned a large mass of his private papers, gave George Strahan his prayers for publication, and made his will.

His last prayer was printed in full by Hawkins, copied by Strahan, who then deleted the clause "forgive and accept my late

late conversion, enforce[6] and accept my imperfect repentance; make this commemoration [of] him available to the confirmation of my Faith, the establishment of my hope, and the enlargement of my Charity, and make the Death of thy son Jesus effectual to my redemption. Have mercy upon me and pardon the multitude of my offences. Bless my Friends, have mercy upon all men. Support me by the Grace of thy Holy Spirit in the[7] days of weakness, and at the hour of death, and[8] receive me, at my death, to everlasting happiness, for the Sake of Jesus Christ. Amen.

6. ⟨inforce⟩ enforce   7. ⟨com⟩   8. ∧at the hour of death, and∧

---

conversion," no doubt fearing that "late conversion" might be misinterpreted, as indeed it has been, forgetting that one of the definitions in Johnson's *Dictionary* is, "Change from reprobation to grace, from a bad to a holy life." This last prayer shows Johnson calm, no longer troubled by scruples, and ready to meet death, which came on 13 December.

CHRONOLOGICAL LIST OF MANUSCRIPTS
AND PRINTED SOURCES OF THE TEXT

Where the manuscript is not known, the printed source is given.

"Annals," 1709–19	Wright
"Annales," 1725–28	MS Hyde
Diary, Oct–21 Nov 1729	MS Hyde
"Annales," Dec 1729–July 1732	MS Hyde
Diary, June, July 1732	MS Hyde
"Annales," June 1733–5 Aug 1734	MS Hyde
Diary, 1734	MS Hyde
Diary, 27 Aug–7 Sept 1736	Hawkins, p. 163
Prayer, 7 Sept 1738	MS Pembroke
Diary, 1743?	MS Yale
Prayers, 1 Jan 1745–Mar 1750	MS Pembroke
Prayer, 1 Jan 1751	MS Hyde
Prayers, 24, 25 Apr 1752	Strahan, 2d ed., pp. 10–13
Prayer, 26 Apr 1752	Strahan, 3d ed., p. 15
Prayer, 6 May 1752	Strahan, 2d ed., p. 13
Prayers, Nov 1752	Strahan, pp. 10–12
Prayers and Meditations, 1 Jan–3 Apr 1753, Boswell's transcript	MS Hyde
Prayer, 22 Apr 1753	MS Pembroke
Meditations, 22, 23, 29 Apr 1753, Boswell's transcript	MS Hyde
Meditation, 1753?	*Life*, II.143
Prayers and Meditations, 28 Mar 1754	MS Pembroke
Diary, 1755	*Life*, I.285
Meditation, 13 July 1755, Boswell's transcript	MS Hyde
Prayer, July 1755	Strahan, p. 18
Prayer, 1755?	Strahan, p. 74
Prayer, Jan 1756	MS Pembroke
Prayers, Jan–Feb 1756	Strahan, pp. 20–21
Prayers, Mar 1756	MS Pembroke
Prayer, 1756?	MS Pembroke

Prayers and Meditations, 1 Jan 1757– 15 Mar 1759	MS Pembroke
Prayer, 15 Apr 1759	MS Hyde
Prayer, Apr 1759?	Croker, v.444
Prayers and Meditations, 1760–64	MS Pembroke
Diary, 1 Jan–6 Apr 1765	MS Hyde
Prayers and Meditations, 7 Apr 1765	MS Pembroke
Diary, 7 Apr–1 Sept 1765	MS Hyde
Prayer, 26 Sept 1765	MS Pembroke
Meditations, Oct 1765, Boswell's transcript	MS Hyde
Prayer, Nov 1765	MS Pembroke
Diary, 8 Dec–30 Dec 1765	MS Hyde
Prayer, 1 Jan 1766	MS Pembroke
Diary, 1 Jan–3 Mar 1766	MS Hyde
Prayer, 7 Mar 1766	MS Pembroke
Diary, 28 Mar–4 May 1766	MSS Bodleian and Hyde
Prayers and Meditations, 18 Sept– 3 Oct 1766	MS Pembroke
Diary, 8 Nov 1766	MS Hyde
Prayer, 1 Jan 1767	MS Pembroke
Diary, 1 Jan–9 Apr 1767	MS Hyde
Undated notes, May? 1767	MS Pembroke
Prayers and Meditations, 2 Aug– 18 Oct 1767	MS Pembroke
Prayers and Meditations, Lent, 1768	Strahan, pp. 73, 227
Diary, 26 July 1768	*Life*, III.398
Prayer and Meditations, 18 Sept 1768	MS Pembroke
Diary, 14 Nov 1768	Hill, Letter 210 n., from auction cata- logue
Diary, Dec 1768	MS Hyde
Prayer and Meditations, 1 Jan 1769	MS Pembroke
Diary, 1 Jan–7 May 1769	MS Hyde
Prayers and Meditations, 18 Sept 1769– 1 Jan 1770	MS Pembroke
Diary, 1 Jan–5 Feb 1770	MS Hyde
Prayers and Meditations, 28 Mar– 1 June 1770	MS Pembroke

Diary, 24 Mar 1771	MS Hyde
Prayers and Meditations, 1771?	MS Pembroke
Prayer, 31 Mar 1771	MS Pembroke
Diary, ca. 21 Apr–25 Aug 1771	MS Hyde
Prayer and Meditations, 18–23 Sept 1771	MS Pembroke
Diary, 22 Dec 1771	MS Hyde
Prayers and Meditations, 1 Jan 1772–22 July 1773	MS Pembroke
Diary, 1773	*Life*, 11.263
Prayers and Meditations, 24 Sept 1773–1 Jan 1774	MS Pembroke
Welsh Diary, 5 July–24 Sept 1774	MS British Museum
Diary, 27 Nov 1774, 2 Jan 1775	*Life*, 11.288–89
Prayers and Meditations, 13 Apr–18 Sept 1775	MS Pembroke
French Diary, 10 Oct–5 Nov 1775	MS British Museum
Prayers and Meditations, 1 Jan–25 July 1776	MS Pembroke
Diary, Sep–Oct 1776?	MS Tildesley
Prayers and Meditations, 1 Jan–6 Apr 1777	MS Pembroke
Diary, 5–9 Aug 1777 (Welsh Diary, p. 33)	MS British Museum
Diary, 11 Aug–17 Sept 1777	MS Hyde
Prayer, 18 Sept 1777	MS Pembroke
Diary, 18 Sept 1777–1 Jan 1778	MS Hyde
Prayers and Meditations, 17 Apr 1778–4 Apr 1779	MS Pembroke
Diary, 7 Aug 1779	*Life*, 111.398 n.
Prayers and Meditations, 18 Sept 1779–22 June 1781	MS Pembroke
Diary, 9–11 Aug 1781	MS Huntington
Prayer and Meditations, 2 Sept–14 Oct 1781	MS Pembroke
Diary, 1 Jan 1782	MS Bodleian
Meditations, 20 Jan 1782	Hawkins, p. 554
Meditations, 18–31 Mar 1782	MS Pembroke
Diary, 18 May–6 Oct 1782	MS Bodleian
Meditations, 6 Oct 1782	Croker, v.444
Prayer and Meditations, 6–7 Oct 1782	MS Pembroke

Diary, 7 Oct–31 Dec 1782	MS Bodleian
Prayers, "end of 1782"	MS Pennant; 1784 transcription Pembroke
Meditations, 5 Apr 1783	Hawkins, p. 552 n.
Diary, 16–25 June 1783	Hawkins, p. 557 n.
Diary, 10–15 July 1783	MS Huntington
Prayer, 30 July 1783	MS Pembroke
Diary, 15 Aug 1783	MS Hyde
Prayer, Aug 1783	Hawkins, p. 558
Diary, 28–30 Aug 1783	MS Huntington
Prayer and Meditation, 6 Sept 1783	Strahan, p. 210
Diary, 8–16 Sept 1783	Broadley, *Chats on Autographs*, p. 207, and Rogers
Diary, 18 Sept 1783	MS Huntington
Prayer, 1 Jan 1784	MS Morgan
Prayer, 11 Apr 1784	MS Pembroke
Diary, May 1784	*Life*, IV.278
Diary, 8–10 June 1784	MS Hyde
"Aegri Ephemeris," 6–31 July 1784	MS Hyde
Prayer and Meditations, 1 Aug 1784	*Miscellanies*, I.117
"Aegri Ephemeris," 1–12 Aug 1784	MS Hyde
Prayer, 12 Aug 1784	MS Pembroke
"Aegri Ephemeris," 13–28 Aug 1784	MS Hyde
Prayer, 28 Aug 1784	MS Pembroke
"Aegri Ephemeris," 29 Aug–5 Sept 1784	MS Hyde
Prayer, 5 Sept 1784	MS Sexton
"Aegri Ephemeris," 6–17 Sept 1784	MS Hyde
Prayer, 18 Sept 1784	MS Gough Square
"Aegri Ephemeris," 18 Sept–31 Oct 1784	MS Hyde
"Repertorium," 31 Oct 1784	MS Yale
"Aegri Ephemeris," 1–8 Nov 1784	MS Hyde
Prayer, 5 Dec 1784	MS Yale

INDEX

Abate, Niccolo (*1512–70*), painter of frescoes at Fontainebleau, 240
Abels, unidentified, 272
Abergele, North Wales, SJ calls "a mean town," 198
Acta Felicitatis et Perpetuae, 410
"Acts of forgiveness," 259
Adair, James, sergeant-at-law, M.P., 333
Adam, Robert (*1728–92*), builder of Kedleston House for Baron Scarsdale, 170
Adams, George (d. *1773*), mathematical instrument-maker, his *Treatise on the Globes*, 112
Adams, Sarah (*1746–1804*), daughter of Dr. Adams, 370
Adams, Dr. William (*1706–89*), Master of Pembroke College, Oxford: SJ and Thrales breakfast with, 215; SJ visits (*1784*), 370; urges SJ to compile book of prayers, 413
Adanson, Michael (*1727–1808*), SJ reads his *Histoire naturelle du Sénégal*, 95
Aeneas, 273
Aesop, 11, 14–18, 22; edited by Charles Hoole, 11
Aheren, Mrs., unidentified, 87
Alexander the Great, 240; SJ describes bust of, at Meudon, 248
Allen, Edmund (*1726–84*), printer, SJ's neighbour: dines with SJ, 306, 309, 325, 334; SJ repays loan from, 89; SJ visits or is visited by, 90 f., 96, 101, 317, 357
Ambrose, St., 411–13
American, an unidentified, SJ sees, 331
Amiens, SJ, Thrales, and Baretti at, 228
Amiens Cathedral, 230
Andover, Hampshire, SJ passes through, 367
Angel, George, SJ gives guinea to, 357
Anglesey, Island of, 205; SJ and Thrales visit, 202 f.; said to be the Mona of Tacitus, 206

Anne, Queen (*1665–1714*); SJ touched by, 8 f.
Anselme, Père, his *Histoire . . . de la maison royale de France, des pairs,* etc., SJ sees at Sorbonne, 247
Ap Rhees. *See* Rhys
Apollinaris, 411
Apollinarius. *See* Apollinaris
Apollonius, SJ reads his *Argonautica*, 159
Appleby, SJ attempts to procure headmastership of school at, 38
Aquinas, St. Thomas, story of the speaking crucifix, 364 f.
Arabian Nights, SJ reads, 348
Arar. *See* Saône River
Arblay, Madame d'. *See* Burney
Argenson, Antoine René de Voyer, Marquis de Paulmy d' (*1722–87*), statesman and bibliophile: SJ, Thrales, and Baretti visit house of, 233
Argyle Street, London, Mrs. Thrale's house in, 352
Ariosto, Ludovico, 281; compared with Pope, 270 f.; epitaph of, 270–72
Arnauld, Antoine (*1612–94*), French philosopher, 333
Arnobius Afer, the Elder, 410 f.
Arras, SJ, Thrales, and Baretti at, 228
Arundel, Sussex, 348
Ashbourne, Derbyshire, 292
SJ visits (*1739*), 39; (*1770*), 134; (*1771*), 142; (*1772*), 152; with the Thrales (*1774*), 165–71; (*1775*), 227; with Boswell (*1776*), 257; (*1777*), 275–77; (*1779*), 297; (*1781*), 310; (*1784*), 374–99
SJ suggests Boswell meet him there or in London, 326
Ashbourne Grammar School, SJ applies for position at, 31
Ashburton. *See* Dunning
Astle, Rev. Daniel (ca. *1743–1826*): SJ's farewell visit to, 171; SJ prepares list of reading for, 92, 171
Aston, Elizabeth (*1708–85*), 283, 327

426

INDEX

Choisy, royal palace near Paris, SJ,
Thrales, and Baretti visit, 235
Chops, dog at Nicholson's, 9
Christ's Hospital, 357
Chrysostom, St. John, 411 ff.; *Letter
to Caesarius* formerly attributed to,
198; SJ uses part of his prayer, 140;
"differs from Erasmus," 365
Church Fathers, 409–14
Churchill, Charles (*1731–64*), satirist,
author of *The Ghost*, 75
Cicero: *De divinatione*, 254; *De Offi-
ciis*, 252; *Epistles*, SJ reads on road,
163 f.; *Letters*, 26
Clarke, Samuel, D.D. (*1675–1729*)
indebted to Howe's *Living Temple*,
408
Sermons, SJ reads, 105, 122, 159, 305
SJ reads his sermon on death of
Christ, 129
SJ reads his sermon of the humilia-
tion of our Saviour, 132
SJ reads his sermon on Faith, 155
SJ reads his last dissertation on the
Pentateuch, 159
SJ would not admit his name to
Dictionary, because of unortho-
doxy as to the Trinity, 105
Works, 415
Clay, Henry, SJ and Thrales visit his
japanning factory at Birmingham,
220
Clement, St., of Rome, 409
Clement of Alexandria, 409 f., 413
Clough, Sir Richard (d. *1570*), builder
of Bach-y-Graig, 179
Club, the, 87 ff., 355 f.; founded, 77;
SJ dines with, 360; SJ drinks wine
at, 101; SJ goes to, 126; SJ's last
dinner with, 370
Club, Essex Head, 267, 317, 329, 363;
founded, 367
Club, Ivy Lane, founded, 42
Clwyd River, Denbighshire: SJ de-
scribes, 183; SJ calls a brook, 188
Clynnog, Carnarvonshire, 209; SJ and
Thrales see church at, 206
Cobb, Elizabeth, married William
Walton at Lichfield, 281
Cobb, Francis (*1724–1807*), banker of
Lichfield, 270
Cobb, Mrs. Thomas (*1718–93*), SJ and
Thrales have tea with, 164

Coddington, Mr. (unidentified), 324,
354
Colebrooke, Sir George (*1729–1809*),
bankrupt speculator: SJ dines with,
Paris, 250
Colisée, place of amusement, Paris,
238
Collet, SJ's barber, 354; SJ gives
money to, 284 f.; SJ lends money to,
326, 355
Collier, Mary (b. *1754*), and Sophia
(b. *1760*), 354, 358
Collyer, Joseph, translator of Klopstock's *Messiah*: visits SJ, 226; his
death, 226 f.
Combe, Charles, cataloguer of
Hunter's collection of coins, 314
Combermere, 184
Combermere Hall, seat of Sir Lynch
Salusbury Cotton: SJ and Thrales
entertained there, 172–76
Comedy, SJ's scruples about, 363
Commodianus, 411
Common Prayer, Book of, 414; used
or quoted, 47 f., 52, 59 f., 81, 83,
93 f., 104 f., 107, 109 f., 116, 121 f.,
124, 131, 144, 153, 156, 184, 260 ff.,
287, 290 f., 293 f., 296, 306; paraphrased, 37 f., 59 f., 138 f., 161 f.,
299, 302; SJ thinks of writing ele-
mentary book on, 103; SJ's copy of,
passes from Barber to Wright, 266
Compiègne, France, SJ, Thrales, and
Baretti visit, 255
Compton, Rev. James, one-time Benedictine, 332–36, 344, 346, 348, 352,
354, 357, 359; calls on SJ for help
after renouncing Catholicism,
329 ff.; takes letters of ordination
to Dr. Vyse, 335
Conciergerie, Paris, 234
Condé, Prince de (*1736–1818*): SJ,
Thrales, and Baretti visit his Palais
Bourbon, 237 f.; SJ, Thrales, and
Baretti visit seat of, at Chantilly,
254 f.
Congleton, Cheshire, silk centre: SJ
and Thrales pass through, 172
Conversion, misunderstanding of SJ's
"late conversion," 418
Conway, Carnarvonshire, 209 f.; SJ
and Thrales find no room at inn,
199

Johnson, Michael (*cont.*)
Chester, 176
bookselling trips to Birmingham
and Uttoxeter, 176
parchment factory, 13
dies, 28
Johnson, Nathaniel (*1712–37*), SJ's
younger brother: named after
uncle Nathaniel Ford, 5; SJ dreams
of, 67, died, 67
JOHNSON, SAMUEL
I. GENERAL
"Annals," 3–23
birthday, celebrates his, 309
burns his private papers, 417
childhood: birth, 3; put to Marklew to nurse, 4; at school, 11–23
churchgoing, on Feast of the
Transfiguration, 380
death, 418
definitions: "bunn," 263; "palmistry," 40; "snatch," 114
dream of his brother Nathaniel,
67
epitaphs for his father, mother,
brother, 417
engages in Lauder controversy
about alleged plagiarism in
Milton, 43
"estraped," a coinage for "strappado," 232
experiments: drying grape leaves,
362; shaves arm and breast to
see how long it will take hair to
grow again, 297 f.; shaves arms
to see how much time will
restore hairs, 278; use of casting
weights, 283; weighs laurel
leaves, fresh and dry, 285
financial distress of his parents, 7
founds Essex Head Club (*1783*),
329
founds Ivy Lane Club (*1749*), 42
grief for Tetty's death, 127
home in Bolt Court, Fleet Street,
London, 49
home in Gough Square, Staple
Inn, Gray's Inn, Inner Temple
Lane, 81
illnesses: asthma, 272, 367–370;
childhood, 3 ff., 176; dropsy,
368 ff.; gout, 367; hydrocele,
361, 365, 367; scrofula, taken

Johnson, Samuel
I. General (*cont.*)
to be touched by Queen Anne
for, 8; stroke, 359
interest in manufacture: salt,
manufacture of, at Nantwich,
172; Thrale's brewery and Santerre's, 119; visits Boulton's
factory in Birmingham, 220;
visits brass, copper, and iron
works at Holywell, 186 f.;
visits Clay's japanning factory
in Birmingham, 220; visits
mirror factory, Paris, 243 f.;
visits porcelain factory, Sèvres,
248; visits silk mill and china
works, Derby, 170 f., 277
interest in science: balloon
ascents, 119, 387, 397; computation, 82, 277, 362; mensura-
tion, 366, 415; production of
hydrogen, 366
law: SJ proposes to study, 96 f.
legacy from father, 29 f.
letters: to Dr. Adams, 374; to
Burney, 379; to Bowles, 373,
380; to Brocklesby, 377, 380,
384–87, 390, 392, 394 ff.; to Lord
Chesterfield, 55; to Davies, 384;
to Heely, 383; to Hoole, 380; to
Lucy Porter, 372, 384; to Reynolds, 372, 397; to Ryland, 392;
to Sastres, 387; to Mrs. Thrale,
372; to Queeney Thrale, 383;
to Mrs. Thrale, in form of
medical journal, 371
makes a bet, 345
marries Mrs. Elizabeth Jervis
Porter, 33, 36
meditation on his mother's death,
66 f.
meets Boswell, 76
meets Thrales, 84
nocturnal habits of, 42
receives M.A. from Oxford, 55
receives LL.D. from Trinity College, Dublin, 98
receives pension, 76
religious instruction from his
mother, 10
said to have written Hamilton's
only speech in Parliament, 98
schoolbooks, SJ looks over, in

Johnson, Samuel
I. General *(cont.)*
   middle age, 15
   seeks a second wife, 51 f.
   studies: resolves to learn Italian,
     308; proposes a study of
     religion, 105
   subeditor of *Gentleman's Maga-
     zine*, 37
   visits Dr. Percy at Easton Maudit,
     Northamptonshire, 81
   vows, SJ's horror of, 70 f., 79
   wig, new, 102
   works, projected: resolves to write
     a history of memory, 100
II. CHARITIES
   asks Reynolds for donation, 369
   asks Mrs. Thrale for donation,
     89, 369
   resolves to appropriate something
     to charity, 148 f.
   to unnamed persons: boys, 281;
     girl, 274, 350; labourer, 360;
     pew keepers, 95 f., 157; poor
     man, 341; sailor, 345; soldier,
     334; theatre attendant, 86;
     widow, 89; woman, 95, 280 f.,
     334, 355; workmen at Holywell,
     187
   to Mrs. Aheren, 87
   to Angel, 357
   to Elizabeth Barber, 335
   to "Betty," 90, 101
   to Broadhurst, 269 f., 274, 280-83,
     295
   to Poll Carmichael, 284
   to Coddington, 324, 354
   to Collet, 280, 284 f.
   to Coxeter, 85 f.
   to Crow, 323 ff.
   to De Groot, 283, 285
   to Mrs. Desmoulins, 284 ff., 294 f.,
     318, 321, 323
   to Fairy, 327
   to Godwin, 274, 280 f.
   to Phoebe and Elizabeth Herne,
     283-87, 295
   to "Jenny," 321
   to Fisher Johnson's son, 334 f.
   to Thomas Johnson, 286, 295
   to Ladies Charity School, 285 f.
   to Mrs. Le Clerc, 115
   to Levet, 284 f., 295

Johnson, Samuel
II. Charities *(cont.)*
   to Mrs. Levet, 331 f.
   to Mrs. Lowe, 281
   to "Lucy," 85 f.
   to Macbean, 283, 287
   to Mrs. Palfry, 313, 317, 328
   to Mrs. Pellé, 314 f., 321, 323 f.,
     326, 331, 354 ff.
   to Reed, 87 f.
   to Sedgwick, 280
   to Walton, 280 f.
   to Wright, 360
III. PRAYERS AND MEDITATIONS, TOPICS
OF
   against inquisitive and perplex-
     ing thoughts, 383
   at departure, 358
   Hill Boothby's death, 59 f.
   calculation of time needed to ac-
     complish reading, 27, 82, 102,
     132-35
   commending the dead, 51 ff., 60,
     67 f., 78 f., 89, 93, 105, 108,
     131, 150, 156, 263, 265, 296, 306
     ff., 338
   Communion, 358
   contrition, 319
   death of wife, 44 ff.
   Dictionary, 50
   doubtful lawfulness of prayers
     for dead, 50, 79
   engaging in politics with Hamil-
     ton, 98
   health, restoration of, 59 f.
   illnesses, 52, 122 f., 125, 127 ff.
   imaginations, vain or tumultu-
     ous, 46 f., 63, 71, 73 f., 76, 79,
     119, 138
   lust, 64, 70, 76 ff., 92
   melancholy, 55, 119, 257, 264
   mother's death, 69
   Rambler, 43
   resolutions: to attend church, 57,
     71, 73 f., 79, 106, 267 f., 309 f.;
     "breakfast law," 35; to drink
     less, 71 f., 99; to instruct his
     household, 57; to keep ac-
     counts, 82; to keep a journal,
     71, 73, 82, 110, 147, 155, 160,
     268, 303; to read books of
     divinity, 57, 71, 82, 105 f., 155,
     266, 289, 305; to read the Bible,